D1507621

THE
NORMAN WILLIAMS
PUBLIC LIBRARY
WOODSTOCK · VERMONT

DISCARD

Date Sept. 2008

Norman Williams Public Library
Woodstock, Vermont

The Constitution and 9/11

By the Same Author

American Constitutional Law (with David Gray Adler, 7th ed., 2007)

Constitutional Conflicts Between Congress and the President (5th ed., 2007)

In the Name of National Security: Unchecked Presidential Power and the Reynolds Case (2006)

Political Dynamics of Constitutional Law (with Neal Devins, 4th ed. 2006)

Military Tribunals and Presidential Power: American Revolution to the War on Terrorism (2005)

Nazi Saboteurs on Trial: A Military Tribunal & American Law (2d ed. Revised, 2005)

Presidential War Power (2d ed., 2004)

The Politics of Executive Privilege (2004)

The Democratic Constitution (with Neal Devins, 2004)

Religious Liberty in America: Political Safeguards (2002)

Congressional Abdication on War and Spending (2000)

The Politics of Shared Power: Congress and the Executive (4th ed., 1997)

Encyclopedia of the American Presidency (with Leonard W. Levy, 1994)

Constitutional Dialogues: Interpretation as Political Process (1988)

The Constitution Between Friends: Congress, the President, and the Law (1978)

Presidential Spending Power (1975)

President and Congress (1972)

The Constitution and 9/11

Recurring Threats to America's Freedoms

Louis Fisher

University Press of Kansas

© 2008 by the University Press of Kansas

All rights reserved
Published by the University Press of Kansas (Lawrence, Kansas 66045), which was organized by the Kansas Board of Regents and is operated and funded by Emporia State University, Fort Hays State University, Kansas State University, Pittsburg State University, the University of Kansas, and Wichita State University

Library of Congress Cataloging-in-Publication Data

Fisher, Louis.
  The Constitution and 9/11 : recurring threats to America's freedoms / Louis Fisher.
    p. cm.
  Includes bibliographical references and index.
  ISBN 978-0-7006-1600-8 (cloth : alk. paper) — ISBN 978-0-7006-1601-5 (pbk. : alk. paper) 1. War on Terrorism, 2001—Law and legislation—United States. 2. Civil rights—United States. 3. War and emergency powers—United States. 4. Official secrets—United States. I. Title.
  KF7225.F57 2008
  342.7308′5—dc22   2008020145

British Library Cataloguing-in-Publication Data is available.

Printed in the United States of America

10 9 8 7 6 5 4 3 2 1

The paper used in this publication is recycled and contains 50 percent postconsumer waste. It is acid free and meets the minimum requirements of the American National Standard for Permanence of Paper for Printed Library Materials Z39.48-1992.

To my grandfather, Ludwig Fischer, for what he brought with him from abroad and left here for his grandchildren

To bereave a man of life, or by violence to confiscate his estate, without accusation or trial, would be so gross and notorious an act of despotism, as must at once convey the alarm of tyranny throughout the whole kingdom. But confinement of the person, by secretly hurrying him to gaol, where his sufferings are unknown and forgotten; is a less public, a less striking, and therefore a more dangerous engine of arbitrary government. And yet sometimes, when the state is in real danger, even this may be a necessary measure. But the happiness of our constitution is, that it is not left to the executive power to determine when the danger of the state is so great, as to render this measure expedient. For the parliament only, or legislative power, whenever it sees proper, can authorize the crown, by suspending the *habeas corpus* act for a short and limited time, to imprison suspected persons without giving any reason for so doing. . . . To make imprisonment lawful, is must either be, by process from the courts of judicature, or by warrant from some legal officer, having authority to commit to prison; which warrant must be in writing, under the hand and seal of the magistrate, and express the causes of the commitment, in order to be examined into (if necessary) upon a *habeas corpus*. . . . [I]t is unreasonable to send a prisoner, and not to signify withal the crimes alleged against him.

—1 William Blackstone, Commentaries on the Laws of England 131–33 (1765)

Contents

Preface

Following the terrorist attacks of September 11, 2001, the United States abandoned many of its rights and privileges for the accused, both citizens and noncitizens. With political power concentrated in the President, executive-branch officials met in secret to draft policies that supported the arrest and detention of suspected terrorists. They saw no need to make specific charges, provide counsel, or allow the accused an opportunity to examine evidence. Military commissions became a substitute for civil courts and courts-martial. Suspects were flown to foreign prisons for interrogation and torture. Some of the administration initiatives violated existing statutes and treaties. Once again in America, emergency powers were invoked to disregard individual rights and weaken national security.

In *Darkness at Noon*, Arthur Koestler described the experience of N. S. Rubashov, who was interrogated relentlessly by Soviet officials for committing some type of crime against the government. The specific charges were never important. Rubashov understood that an individual, questioned in isolation over a period of time, will eventually confess to something (or anything) to bring the process to an end. There was never hope of mounting an effective defense, analyzing the government's evidence, or confronting accusers. Guilt was established at the beginning—upon his arrest—not at the end. The procedure required the individual to submit himself to the Communist Party and to the state. "The individual was nothing, the Party was all."

The United States supposedly offers a different model. Prosecutors have the burden of making a specific charge and proving it. For criminal cases the bar is placed high: beyond a reasonable doubt. The accused may rely on various tools of self-defense: freedom against self-incrimination, access to counsel, analyzing evidence submitted in open court, and the opportunity to confront witnesses and informers. Judges and jurors have a duty to independently monitor the process and curb executive abuse. Those standards of justice have inspired other nations to adopt procedures of fairness and respect for the dignity of the individual.

At various periods over more than two centuries, America has betrayed its legal and moral principles. That pattern began with the treatment of aliens, enemy aliens, and "seditious" citizens during the John Adams administration. In subsequent years, injustices and persecutions included the exclusion of Chinese and Japanese, forced deportations of "radicals" during and after

World War I, detention of Japanese-Americans in the early 1940s, punitive actions against socialists and Communists, and steps taken after 9/11 against suspected terrorists and "enemy combatants." Once again the United States felt at liberty to hold individuals (citizens or aliens) indefinitely, with no obligation to provide customary procedural safeguards. Powers normally kept separate were merged and concentrated in the executive branch. During these periods of emergencies, American constitutional values lose ground to the forces of fear, expediency, and partisan calculations. The struggle to regain those values comes at great cost, both to individuals and to America's character and reputation.

This book reviews these periods to see what has been forgotten and what has been learned. In the worst of times, individuals have had the courage and understanding to stand against the abuse of government power and defend the accused, not just for their sake but for the national interest. In selecting examples from the past, sometimes ugly and repulsive, the purpose of this book is not to denigrate the United States. I have flourished here and so have family members, coming from different ethnic pasts. I try to highlight the ideals that animate America and the times we honor those principles and are ennobled by them. By reviewing the periods where America falls short of its standards, my hope is to rededicate the commitment to values that enrich us and benefit the world community.

Several of my books, articles, and appearances before congressional committees prepared the way for this study. I wrote two books for the University Press of Kansas on military tribunals: *Nazi Saboteurs on Trial: A Military Tribunal & American Law* (2003) and *Military Tribunals and Presidential Power: American Revolution to the War on Terrorism* (2005). The latter won the Richard Neustadt Book Award, given by the American Political Science Association. With the same press I published a book on the state secrets privilege: *In the Name of National Security: Unchecked Presidential Power and the Reynolds Case* (2006). Articles contributing to this book include "Lost Constitutional Moorings: Recovering the War Power," 81 Ind. L. Rev. 1199 (2006); "Military Commissions: Problems of Authority and Practice," 24 Boston U. Int'l L. J. 15 (2006); "Invoking Inherent Powers: A Primer," 37 Pres. Stud. Q. 1 (2007); "Democratic Checks on Presidential Wars," 29 Nat'l Sec. L. Rept. 1 (2007); "Detention and Military Trial of Suspected Terrorists," 2 J. Nat'l Sec. L. & Pol. 1 (2007); "The State Secrets Privilege: Relying on *Reynolds*," 122 Pol. Sci. Q. 385 (2007); "People v. State: Security Interests Must be Weighed Against America's Broader Interests," Legal Times, October 1, 2007, pp. 66–67; "Congressional Access to National Security Information," 45 Harv. J. Leg. 219 (2008); "NSA

Eavesdropping: Unchecked or Limited Presidential Power?" in *Contemporary Cases in U.S. Foreign Policy*, ed. Ralph G. Carter (Washington, DC: CQ Press, 2008); "Domestic Commander in Chief: Early Checks by Other Branches," 29 Cardozo L. Rev. 961 (2008); and "Extraordinary Rendition: The Price of Secrecy," 57 Am. U. L. Rev. 1403 (2008). In 2007 I testified before the Senate Judiciary Committee on congressional authority over the war power and before the House Judiciary Committee on NSA surveillance. In 2008 I testified before the Senate Judiciary Committee on the state secrets privilege and before the House Committee on Foreign Affairs on revisions to the War Powers Resolution. I wrote five amicus briefs in the military tribunal cases of Hamdan and Padilla and in the NSA surveillance case brought by the Center for Constitutional Rights in New York City.

Two main themes guide this book: the damage done to constitutional values in times of stress, and how abuses are directed at disfavored, isolated groups. I make no effort to be comprehensive, identifying every discriminatory action against every group. I would have to devote extensive sections and chapters to what government and society have done to blacks, Native Americans, Jews, the Irish, Italians, Puerto Ricans, Hispanics, and many other communities that have been persecuted. My book is necessarily selective. For parts of the story I missed, I invite others to fill in the picture.

In the post-9/11 period it has been my good fortune to meet, work with, and learn from many talented scholars, attorneys, reporters, private citizens, and public officials. They are fully engaged in the struggle to preserve constitutional values and confront government abuse. High on my list: Steve Aftergood, Jim Bamford, Rich Barlow, Tom Blanton, Cathy Brauner, Susan Brauner, Danielle Brian, Wilson Brown, Bobby Chesney, David Cole, Ron Collins, Tom Devine, Sibel Edmonds, Mickey Edwards, Bruce Fein, Herb Fenster, Gene Fidell, Sharon Franklin, Meredith Fuchs, Mike German, Melissa Goodman, Jon Hafetz, Pat Herring, Aziz Huq, Jameel Jaffer, Dan Jarcho, Shane Kadidal, Neal Katyal, David Keene, Lew Koch, Judy Loether, Paul McMasters, Joe Margulies, Kate Martin, Greg Nojeim, Rob Pallitto, Andy Patel, Coleen Rowley, Joanne Royce, Charlie Savage, Scott Silliman, David Skaggs, Ginny Sloan, Gary Solis, Jim Tyre, Steve Vladeck, Pat Wald, Bill Weaver, Ben Wizner, and Mark Zaid.

I was delighted to have two extremely able individuals review my manuscript: Steve Aftergood and Aziz Huq. Steve has been a leader in the struggle against government secrecy that harms the nation. Aziz has been active in both litigation and scholarship in defining and defending democratic values. Once again I have the pleasure of working with Mike Briggs of the University Press of Kansas. It is a joy to be part of a very distinguished list of books on the presidency and constitutional law. Ann Robertson provided a very expert and professional review as copyeditor.

In selecting my grandfather (from my father's side) for the dedication, I salute someone who came from the Old World to the New, with all the hope and energy that an immigrant brings, and with all the fears of belonging indelibly to a country and culture that can be easily targeted for arbitrary and irrational punishment. For me, patriotism and loyalty are the steps we take to assure that errors committed in the past are not made again.

CHAPTER 1

America's Values

In the face of the terrorist attacks of 9/11, the Bush administration responded unilaterally with a series of initiatives: creating military tribunals to try suspected terrorists, holding individuals indefinitely without charges or trial, and sending suspects to other countries for interrogation and torture. Secret trials and the use of secret evidence became part of the war against terrorism. In times of heightened stress and calls for national security, the United States was once again violating basic principles of constitutional government and losing its leadership in the world community. What are those overarching values? What steps can be taken to rekindle interest in and respect for constitutional government, lessen the chance of future violations, and restore America's place among democratic nations?

ENGLISH LIBERTIES

America drew from British history to create procedural protections against capricious, abusive government. From the Enlightenment, the framers embraced values of liberty and a belief in the capacity of individuals to participate in self-government. Citizens were not to be "subjects" of a monarch. The dignity and worth of individuals entitled them to participate in public life and be subject to fair procedures if brought to court. Defendants had a right to be tried in open court, upon specific charges, with full access to evidence presented by prosecutors. Writing in 1788, Alexander Hamilton expressed the American fear of arbitrary imprisonment, with individuals denied the opportunity to prove their innocence. He quoted from the eighteenth-century legal scholar William Blackstone: "To bereave a man of life, or by violence to confiscate his estate, without accusation or trial, would be so gross and notorious an act of despotism, as must at once convey the alarm of tyranny throughout the whole nation."[1]

1. The Federalist 533 (Benjamin F. Wright, ed. 2002 ed.) (Federalist No. 84).

How terrifying to be held incommunicado with no chance of self-defense. The Supreme Court has explained that the "traditional Anglo-American distrust for secret trials" is deeply felt. Institutions that depend on secret trials and secret evidence "obviously symbolized a menace to liberty."[2] The framers understood the ever-present danger of arbitrary government. The writ of habeas corpus represented one method of protecting persons unlawfully detained by executive officers. Juries offered another check. The framers added the Bill of Rights to supply additional safeguards, including the rights to a public trial, to confront accusers, and to have access to legal counsel. At various moments in American history those elementary procedures are swept aside. Shortcuts are devised, such as designating certain individuals an "alien enemy," "anarchist," "Communist," or "enemy combatant." The damage falls heavily on disfavored, isolated groups.

Magna Carta

Secret trials and secret evidence have long violated human rights and fundamental notions of fairness in the courtroom. Relief from arbitrary executive power can be traced in part to the Magna Carta of 1215, when the English king promised not to capture or imprison a freeman "except by the lawful judgment of his peers or by the law of the land."[3] The superior law or higher law was not royal or executive will. It was fair process and public trial. The government needed to bring specific charges in open court and persuade independent judges and jurors. No longer were citizens satisfied with whatever the king might allow by divine right or by grace.

Petition of Right

The rights promised by the Magna Carta were undermined in later years by monarchical efforts to place the Crown above the law. Kings claimed to rule by powers drawn from the heavens and therefore not subject to checks from secular institutions or the people. In 1628, Sir Edward Coke played an active role in urging Parliament to pass the Petition of Right, posing a direct challenge to the sovereign power of the King. Claims of executive or royal prerogative, especially over foreign affairs and finances, encountered a legislative branch determined to place legal limits on executive power. Members of the House of Commons

2. In re Oliver, 333 U.S. 257, 268–69 (1948).
3. 1 The Roots of the Bill of Rights 12 (Bernard Schwartz, ed. 1980).

drafted the Petition to cover such disputes as arbitrary arrest, imprisonment without cause, forced loans by royal power, and martial law.[4] American history contains similar patterns of Congress and the federal courts deciding to place legal constraints on Presidents who pressed the limits of executive power. It has been well said that today "we merely defend our civil liberties; three hundred years ago they had to be won."[5] Rights won are easily lost.

In 1628, Charles I was struggling financially after engaging in war against both France and Spain. Needing funds to pursue those military commitments, he resorted to forced loans and imprisoned those who opposed his rule. Coke, invoking the Magna Carta, argued that it was against "the law of the land" for a man to "lie in prison forever and never be called to answer."[6] It was "an unreasonable thing that man had a remedy for his horse or cattle, if detained, and none for his body thus indefinitely imprisoned."[7] Working with other lawmakers on the Petition, he understood the political and constitutional need to insist on *right* rather than on what the King might allow by *grace*. Coke insisted that when "a thing is done graciously, it is not of right." He asked pointedly: "Will you have Magna Carta as a grace?"[8]

The House of Lords proposed that the Petition acknowledge that Parliament had acted "with due regard to leave entire that sovereign power, wherewith your majesty is trusted, for the protection, safety, and happiness of the people." Coke protested that this weak language would undermine the legal rights recognized in the Petition.[9] The Lords, he said, threatened to place sovereign power "above all these laws."[10] He and his colleagues in the Commons successfully blocked all efforts by the Lords to dilute the Petition. The United States has witnessed the same kind of conflicts. Congress and the courts have insisted on legal boundaries on executive power, and the President has been determined to exercise what might be derived from "inherent" powers.

The U.S. Constitution is designed to check capricious and unaccountable executive power. The Fifth Amendment provides that no person shall be "deprived of life, liberty, or property, without due process of law." At a minimum,

4. Stephen D. White, *Sir Edward Coke and "The Grievances of the Commonwealth,"* 1621–1628 (1979), at 17–21, 222–74.

5. Harold W. Wolfram, "John Lilburne: Democracy's Pillar of Fire," 3 Syr. L. Rev. 213, 213 (1952).

6. White, *Sir Edward Coke*, at 227.

7. Id. at 240.

8. Id. at 253.

9. Id. at 266–67.

10. Id. at 267.

due process means that an accused must be given notice of a charge and adequate opportunity to appear and be heard. Other amendments, from the Fourth through the Eighth, supply additional protections to due process.

The seventy-year history of the Soviet Union demonstrates that written constitutional safeguards mean little. Textual provisions are empty unless honored in practice and regularly enforced. Citizens must be willing to challenge arbitrary and abusive action by public officials. Key institutions include an alert citizenry, jury trials, a free press, and an independent legislature and judiciary. Due process also depends on values of fairness and justice. Although the Constitution does not specify the standards required to convict, the requirement that guilt of a criminal charge be proved "beyond a reasonable doubt" is part of custom dating back to early years in America.[11]

As explained by the Supreme Court in 1970, the reasonable-doubt standard "is indispensable to command the respect and confidence of the community in applications of the criminal law. It is critical that the moral force of the criminal law not be diluted by a standard of proof that leaves people in doubt whether innocent men are being condemned."[12] The need for proof beyond a reasonable doubt in a criminal case is "bottomed on a fundamental value determination of our society that it is far worse to convict an innocent man than to let a guilty man go free."[13] Civil litigation permits a lesser standard: proof by preponderance of the evidence.[14] Fundamental to constitutional values is the presumption of innocence for the accused. The burden of establishing guilt rests on the prosecution "from the beginning to the end of the trial."[15] Those constitutional protections can be undermined by prosecutors who threaten the accused with harsh punishment unless they plea bargain to lesser charges.

In the years following 9/11, elementary safeguards were regularly given short shrift. The Bush administration decided not to bring charges against hundreds of detainees (aliens as well as U.S. citizens); they were held indefinitely without charges, trial, or counsel. It would be inaccurate to say that the burden of proving innocence fell to the detainee; in many cases the detainee was never brought to court to mount a defense. In England, in similar situations in the 1600s, certain courageous individuals were willing to step forward and challenge abusive government action in criminal proceedings.

11. In re Winship, 397 U.S. 358, 361 (1970).
12. Id. at 364.
13. Id. at 372 (Harlan, J., concurring).
14. Id. at 371.
15. Agnew v. United States, 165 U.S. 36, 49–50 (1897).

John Lilburne

In 1637, John Lilburne was brought before the Star Chamber in London and charged with printing and publishing seditious books. He was one of the last to come before this judicial body, named *Camera Stellata* for its azure ceilings decorated with stars of gold leaf.[16] It had functioned as the King's Council "sitting judicially."[17] Over the years, it became notorious for its record of corporal punishments.[18] Parliament abolished it in 1641.[19]

Over the course of years, Lilburne was found by the Star Chamber guilty of contempt, publicly lashed, placed in the pillory, and returned to Star Chamber and other courts for additional proceedings, until he was finally vindicated by Parliament. What he succeeded in doing was establishing the right of an accused to remain silent in the face of charges, providing the intellectual support for the Fifth Amendment right not to incriminate oneself. A single, intrepid individual created a right that spread worldwide.

Lilburne's persecution began in December 1637 when he was arrested, taken to Fleet prison, and charged with sending seditious and scandalous books from Holland into England. After several weeks in prison he was brought to the Attorney-General's chamber and questioned by a clerk. He answered a number of questions about his name, place of residence, trade, and trip to Holland. Asked whether in Holland he had seen certain books and who had printed them, Lilburne denied printing the books and having them shipped to England. As the interrogation continued, he responded: "why do you ask me all these questions? these are beside the matter of my imprisonment; I pray come to the thing for which I am accused, and imprisoned."[20] At a certain point he insisted on his right to remain silent to questions that were not relevant to the charges brought against him. The questions, he said,

> are nothing pertinent to my imprisonment, for I am not imprisoned for knowing and talking with such and such men, but for sending over Books; and therefore I am not willing to answer you to any more of these questions, because I see you go about by this Examination to ensnare me: for seeing the things for which I am imprisoned cannot be proved against me, you will get other matter out of

16. J. A. Guy, The Court of Star Chamber and Its Records to the Reign of Elizabeth I, 1 (1985).

17. Id. at 2.

18. Id. at 46.

19. Id. at 65.

20. 3 Howell's St. Tr. 1317 (1809).

my examination: and therefore if you will not ask me about the thing laid to my charge, I shall answer no more: . . . my accusers ought to be brought face to face, to justify what they accuse me of. And this is the answer that for the present I am willing to make: and if you ask me of any more things, I shall answer you with silence. . . . I am unwilling to answer any impertinent questions, for fear that with my answer I may do myself hurt.[21]

After confronting the clerk, Lilburne was taken to the Star Chamber office and asked to take an oath. To that procedure he refused:

He bid me pull off my glove, and lay my hand upon the book. What to do, sir? said I. You must swear, said he. To what? "That you shall make true answer to all things that are asked you." Must I so, sir? but before I swear, I will know to what I must swear. As soon as you have sworn, you shall, but not before.—To that I answered, sir, I am but a young man, and do not well know what belongs to the nature of an oath, and therefore before I swear, I will be better advised.[22]

Presented with an affidavit that claimed he had shipped the books to England, he told the Star Chamber that the affidavit "is a most false lye and untrue."[23] The judges decided that the charges against him had been "verified by affidavit." Lilburne rejected the accuracy of the affidavit and argued that the individual who signed it had done so to purchase "his own liberty."[24] Further, the individual was "known to be a notorious lying fellow."[25] After refusing to take the oath, Lilburne was censured by the court, fined £500, whipped, and placed in the pillory.[26] He was "whipt through the streets, from the prison of the Fleet unto the pillory."[27] The whip was a three-fold knotted cord, applied against his back at least two hundred times.[28] He put his neck into the hole of the pillory, "which being a great deal too low for me, it was very painful to me, in regard of continuance of the time that I stood on the pillory, which was about two hours."[29]

During his time in the pillory, Lilburne discoursed at length with the crowd and took from his pocket several of the supposedly seditious books and

21. Id. at 1318.
22. Id. at 1320.
23. Id. at 1321.
24. Id. at 1323, 1324.
25. Id. at 1325.
26. Id. at 1326.
27. Id. at 1327.
28. Id. at 1345.
29. Id. at 1329.

"threw them among the people," asking them to read the material and see if they discover "any thing in them against the law of God, the law of the land, the glory of God, the honour of the king or state."[30] Warned to shut up by authorities, he continued until he was gagged and left in the pillory before being returned to Fleet.[31]

Standing again before the Star Chamber, Lilburne refused to take the oath, which he regarded as "against the law of the land," against the Petition of Right, and "absolutely against the law of God; for that law requires no man to accuse himself." He told the judges that the oath was "against the very law of nature; for nature is always a preserver of itself, and not a destroyer."[32] The Star Chamber concluded that Lilburne, while in the pillory, "did not only utter sundry scandalous speeches, but likewise scattered divers copies of seditious Books among the people." He was ordered "to be laid alone, with irons on his hands and legs, in the Wards of the Fleet."[33] The Star Chamber ordered the Attorney General and the Solicitor General to investigate whether Lilburne's performance in the pillory resulted in "any speeches tending to Sedition, or to the dishonour of the said Court of Star-Chamber, or any member of the said Court."[34]

When Parliament returned in November 1640, one of its first actions addressed a Lilburne petition and complaint directed to them. Upon reading the petition, Parliament "immediately ordered me my liberty," which Lilburne recalled as being the first prisoner in England ever set free by the legislature.[35] On May 4, 1641, the House of Commons adopted these resolutions: "That the Sentence of the Star-Chamber given against John Lilburn is illegal, and against the Liberty of the subject; and also bloody, cruel, wicked, barbarous, and tyrannical. Resolved upon the question, That reparation ought to be given to Mr. Lilburn for his imprisonment, sufferings, and losses sustained by that illegal sentence."[36] Four years later the House of Lords reached a similar decision, ordering that his sentence "and all proceedings thereupon, shall forthwith be for ever totally vacated, obliterated, and taken off the file in all courts where they are yet remaining, as illegal, and most unjust, against the liberty of the subject, and law of the land, and Magna Charta, and unfit to continue upon

30. Id. at 1338.
31. Id. at 1340.
32. Id. at 1332.
33. Id. at 1341.
34. Id. at 1342.
35. Id.
36. Id.

record."[37] The Lords, however, provided few funds to compensate him.[38]

John Lilburne returned to court several more times: in 1649 for high treason[39] and in 1653 for returning to England after being banished by act of Parliament.[40] In both cases he was acquitted by the jury. When the jurors were separately asked by the government to explain their votes, they refused to give "any other answer."[41] Their response mirrors Lilburne's position that when government asks questions it is not always entitled to an answer. Released from jail in October 1655, he died at home, just over forty years of age. Freedom to Lilburne "must have seemed a forlorn and forsaken thing in 1657, yet the seed bed of liberty had been planted deep and planted well."[42]

William Penn

Lilburne insisted on the right to remain silent. Years later, William Penn established the right of a defendant to know precisely the nature of the charges brought by the government. The charges must be statutorily based and intelligible to the accused. Indefinite laws inherently violate due process. "Men of common intelligence cannot be required to guess at the meaning of the enactment."[43] Vague laws encourage arbitrary and erratic arrests and place almost unfettered discretion in the hands of police and prosecutors.[44] After 9/11, U.S. citizens and aliens were picked up and held in custody not on the basis of statutory crimes, enacted by Congress, but on shifting executive definitions of "suspected terrorist" and "enemy combatant."

The trial of William Penn in 1670 highlights the damage done to individuals faced with indefinite charges. After speaking to a crowd at Gracechurch Street in London, he was indicted for "unlawfully and tumultuously" assembling and congregating to the disturbance of the peace and to the "contempt of the said lord the king, and of his law."[45] Penn asked the court: "I desire you would let me know by what law it is you prosecute me, and upon what law you ground my indictment." There followed this exchange between Penn and the recorder:

37. Id. at 1358.
38. Id. at 1358–60, 1364–68.
39. 4 Howell's St. Tr. 1269–1479 (1816).
40. 5 Howell's St. Tr. 407–60 (1810).
41. Id. at 445–50.
42. Wolfram, "John Lilburne: Democracy's Pillar of Fire," 3 Syr. L. Rev. at 258.
43. Winters v. New York, 333 U.S. 507, 515 (1948).
44. Papachristou v. City of Jacksonville, 405 U.S. 156, 162, 168 (1972).
45. 6 Howell's St. Tr. 951, 955 (1810).

Rec. Upon the common-law.

Penn. Where is that common-law?

Rec. You must not think that I am able to run up so many years, and over so many adjudged cases, which we call common-law, to answer your curiosity.

Penn. This answer I am sure is very short of my question, for if it be common, it should not be hard to produce.

Rec. Sir, will you plead to your indictment?

Penn. Shall I plead to an Indictment that hath no foundation in law? If it contain that law you say I have broken, why should you decline to produce that law, since it will be impossible for the jury to determine, or agree to bring in their verdict, who have not the law produced, by which they should measure the truth of this indictment, and the guilt, or contrary of my fact?

Rec. You are a saucy fellow, speak to the Indictment.

Penn. I say, it is my place to speak to matter of law; I am arraigned a prisoner; my liberty, which is next to life itself, is now concerned: you are many mouths and ears against me, and if I must not be allowed to make the best of my case, it is hard, I say again, unless you shew me, and the people, the law you ground your indictment upon, I shall take it for granted your proceedings are merely arbitrary.[46]

The court insisted that the sole question was whether Penn was guilty of the indictment. His response: "The question is not, whether I am Guilty of this Indictment, but whether this Indictment be legal. It is too general and imperfect an answer, to say it is the common-law, unless we knew both where and what it is. For where there is no law, there is no transgression; and that law which is not in being, is so far from being common, that it is no law at all."[47] The court, calling Penn an "impertinent fellow," described the common law as the law not written: "*Lex non scripta.*" Unsatisfied by that explanation, Penn told the court that "if the common law be so hard to be understood, it is far from being very common." Penn wanted his question answered because "the rights and privileges of every Englishman be concerned in it."[48] His challenge went further: concerning the rights and privileges of every person in every country.

The jury returned to find Penn "guilty," but only "of speaking or preaching to an assembly."[49] That verdict outraged the court, which wanted Penn guilty of creating tumult and disturbing the peace. The court advised the jurors that

46. Id. at 958.
47. Id. at 958–59.
48. Id. at 959.
49. Id. at 963.

they "shall not be dismissed till we have a verdict that the court will accept; and you shall be locked up, without meat, drink, fire, and tobacco; you shall not think thus to abuse the court; we will have a verdict, by the help of God, or you shall starve for it."[50] Twice more the jury returned with verdicts of Penn being guilty only of speaking in Gracechurch Street.[51] The court told the jury that it could not find Penn guilty and his colleague, William Mead, not guilty, because the two were indicted for a conspiracy. Penn took advantage of that opening by arguing that if Mead was not guilty then so must he also be, because "I could not possibly conspire alone."[52]

Forced to return a fourth time, the jury put its verdict in writing, this time finding Penn not guilty.[53] As punishment for thinking independently, the court fined each of the jurors 40 marks and ordered them imprisoned until the amounts were paid.[54] Those fantastic judicial actions were eventually checked through a habeas petition that found this treatment of jurors to be illegal.[55] The Penn trial established not only the requirement for specific charges against an individual but the need for checks against arbitrary and vindictive government action. Independent jurors and a reviewing court found the initial punitive actions to be illegal.

TRIAL SAFEGUARDS

In the U.S. Supreme Court, in 1943, Justice Felix Frankfurter remarked that "the history of liberty has largely been the history of observance of procedural safeguards."[56] Justice Robert Jackson underscored the central value of procedure. He said he would rather live under Soviet law enforced by American procedures than under American law enforced by Soviet procedures.[57] Too often, in a zeal to retaliate and punish, American public officials adopt procedures that resemble the Soviet Union and other authoritarian societies. That

---

50. Id.

51. Id. at 964–65.

52. Id. at 965.

53. Id. at 966.

54. Id. at 967–78.

55. Id. at 969. See Case of the Imprisonment of Edward Bushell for Alleged Misconduct as a Juryman, 6 Howell's St. Tr. 999–1026 (1810).

56. McNabb v. United States, 318 U.S. 332, 347 (1943).

57. Leonard W. Levy, The Origins of the Fifth Amendment ix (1986 ed.).

pattern is sadly evident in the years following the terrorist attacks of September 11, 2001.

Grand Jury

Procedural safeguards include indictment by a grand jury and trial by regular (*petit*) jury. The Fifth Amendment provides that "no person shall be held for a capital, or otherwise infamous crime, unless on a presentment or indictment of a grand jury, except in cases arising in the land or naval forces, or in the militia, when in actual service in time of war or public danger."

Grand juries are one instrument for checking government, particularly executive power. In England, they acquired an independence "free from control by the Crown or judges."[58] Before initiating a criminal trial in America, a federal prosecutor must convince a body of lay persons (usually twenty-three members) that sufficient evidence exists to try a suspect. If satisfied by the evidence, twelve or more jurors may indict, which is a formal charge recommending that the person be brought to trial. After 9/11, the Bush administration decided to hold a number of individuals, both U.S. citizens and noncitizens, without ever bringing them to trial or before a grand jury. Procedural safeguards disappeared.

Grand juries are supposed to be independent checks on government allegations. At times they have been pawns in the hands of zealous and politically motivated prosecutors.[59] Indiscriminate use of grand juries can smear the reputation of an individual targeted for abuse by an administration. The grand jury may be unleashed against radical, nonconformist, and unpopular groups and exploited to harass and intimidate political opposition. But the burden remains on federal prosecutors to develop sufficient evidence to attract the support of grand jurors. Service on a grand jury allows citizens to participate in government decisions, understand them, and check abusive, politically driven prosecutors. Service on a regular jury remains an important opportunity for citizens to prevent the government's use of arbitrary power. Alexis de Tocqueville praised the jury for its ability to educate people in civic affairs: "By obliging men to turn their attention to other affairs than their own, it rubs off that private selfishness which is the rust of society."[60]

---

58. Costello v. United States, 350 U.S. 359, 362 (1956).
59. United States v. Mara, 410 U.S. 19, 23 (1973) (Douglas, J., dissenting).
60. 1 Alexis de Tocqueville, Democracy in America 295 (Bradley ed. 1951).

Self-Incrimination and Coerced Testimony

John Lilburne's struggle for justice influenced the American colonies to include the privilege against self-incrimination in their charters and constitutions. The North Carolina constitution of 1776 provided that in all criminal prosecutions an individual "shall not be compelled to give evidence against himself."[61] Similar language appeared in the Maryland, Virginia, and Pennsylvania constitutions of 1776, the Vermont constitution of 1777, the Massachusetts constitution of 1780, and the New Hampshire constitution of 1784.[62]

The Fifth Amendment provides that "[n]o person . . . shall be compelled in any criminal case to be a witness against himself." The purpose of the privilege is to prevent repressive and arbitrary methods of prosecution, such as "the horror of Star Chamber proceedings" in England.[63] The Star Chamber exercised broad civil and criminal jurisdiction, at the king's discretion. It gained a reputation for secretive, arbitrary, and oppressive procedures, including compulsory self-incrimination, inquisitorial investigation, and the absence of juries. England abolished the Star Chamber in 1641.

American law prohibits the government from prying incriminating evidence from the lips of the accused. Prosecutors are "forced to search for independent evidence instead of relying upon proof extracted from individuals by force of law."[64] After 9/11, government officers and private contractors used coercion and torture when interrogating suspected terrorists. Guantánamo detainees are "persons" under the language of the Fifth Amendment, but executive officials argue that coercive methods of interrogation are permissible because there is, under the Fifth Amendment, no "criminal case." That argument, strained as it is, would not satisfy the restrictions imposed by international law, including the Geneva Conventions. The Military Commissions Act

61. 7 Sources and Documents of United States Constitutions 402 (William F. Swindler ed. 1978) (hereafter "Swindler") (Ch. VII).

62. Maryland: 4 Swindler 373 (Ch. XX); Virginia: 10 Swindler 49 (Sec. 8); Pennsylvania: 8 Swindler 279 (Ch. IX); Vermont: 9 Swindler 490 (Ch. X); Massachusetts: 5 Swindler 94 (Art. XII); New Hampshire: 6 Swindler 346 (Ch. XV).

63. Quinn v. United States, 349 U.S. 155, 161 (1955).

64. United States v. White, 322 U.S. 694, 698 (1944). In 1998, the Supreme Court held that a resident alien cannot invoke the Self-Incrimination Clause to withhold information from the U.S. government out of fear that disclosure might lead to prosecution by a foreign nation. Although an alien is a "person" under the Fifth Amendment, the Court ruled that the Clause applies to prosecution of criminal cases in the United States, not in foreign countries. United States v. Balsys, 524 U.S. 666 (1998).

of 2006, followed by Defense Department regulations issued in 2007, opened the door to the use of coerced testimony.

Prior to 9/11, it had been a hallmark of American justice that due process is denied when witnesses are whipped and tortured until they testify against the accused.[65] In the past, law officers extorted confessions through violence and brutality. In one case, a black suspect was repeatedly hanged by a rope from a limb of a tree and then tied to the tree and whipped until he confessed. Other defendants were stripped and beaten to obtain confessions. Those convictions were reversed on the ground that coerced confessions are inherently suspect as evidence.[66] Even if a confession can be corroborated by independent evidence, the government violates due process if it uses methods that are inquisitorial and threatening.[67] Techniques of persecution are generally inflicted upon "the poor, the ignorant, the numerically weak, the friendless, and the powerless."[68] Coercion includes psychological compulsion, not merely physical beatings.[69]

These practices appeared to be drawn from a dark chapter of American history, safely consigned to the past. Nevertheless, beatings, torture, cruelty, and coerced testimony were used widely after the 9/11 attacks with few institutional checks or even public knowledge. During oral argument before the Supreme Court on April 28, 2004, in the case of Yaser Esam Hamdi, several Justices asked Deputy Solicitor General Paul Clement whether detainees held by the United States were subjected to torture. He assured the Court that the United States was "signatory to conventions that prohibit torture and that sort of thing. And the United States is going to honor its treaty obligations." He explained that using coercion to get information leaves one wondering "about the reliability of the information you were getting," and that the experience of interrogators is that the way to "get the best information from individuals is that you interrogate them, you try a relationship of trust."[70] Clement offered the same assurances during oral argument on the Jose Padilla case.[71]

The Hamdi and Padilla oral arguments began at 10:19 A.M. on April 28, 2004, and ended at 12:20 P.M. Later that day, the public began to see photos of

65. Moore v. Dempsey, 261 U.S. 86, 89 (1923).

66. Brown v. Mississippi, 297 U.S. 278 (1936).

67. Rogers v. Richmond, 365 U.S. 534 (1961).

68. Chambers v. Florida, 309 U.S. 227, 237–38 (1940).

69. Miller v. Fenton, 474 U.S. 104 (1985).

70. U.S. Supreme Court, Yaser Esam Hamdi v. Rumsfeld, oral argument, April 28, 2004, at 48–49, 50.

71. U.S. Supreme Court, Rumsfeld v. Padilla, oral argument, April 28, 2004, at 22.

U.S. abuse toward prisoners at the Abu Ghraib detention center in Iraq. Some of the photos were broadcast that evening by the CBS News program "60 Minutes." Viewers from around the world saw prisoners forced to conduct simulated sex acts and assume positions of sexual humiliation. One photo showed a prisoner standing on a box, his head covered, with wires attached to his fingers, toes, and penis. He was told that if he fell off the box he would be electrocuted. Female U.S. soldiers, grinning and with cigarettes in their mouths, stood next to naked Iraqi prisoners, pointing at their genitals.[72]

The Bush administration explained that those abuses were isolated actions of soldiers poorly supervised. Subsequent investigations showed otherwise. Maj. Gen. Antonio M. Taguba described "numerous incidents of sadistic, blatant, and wanton criminal abuses" inflicted on detainees and referred to the abuse as "systemic and illegal."[73] His report included such actions as keeping detainees naked for several days at a time, a male military police guard having sex with a female detainee, using unmuzzled dogs to intimidate and frighten detainees, and sodomizing a detainee with a chemical light and perhaps a broomstick.[74]

Habeas Petition

Under Article I, Section 9, of the Constitution, the privilege of the writ of habeas corpus "shall not be suspended, unless when in Cases of Rebellion or Invasion the public Safety may require it." Through use of this "Great Writ," judges may decide whether the executive branch is imprisoning someone illegally. Authorities who receive the writ (*habeas corpus* means "you have the body," produce it) must justify the legality of detention. It stands as an independent judicial check on arbitrary executive actions. The Petition of Right of 1628 protested the denial of habeas corpus and the extension of martial law to civilians.[75] The purpose of the Petition and the reliance on habeas corpus was to assure that individuals were being imprisoned for cause. If a writ was returned without cause, a prisoner committed by the King or Privy Council should be released. Some members of the House of Commons argued that the

72. "Photos Show U.S. Troops Abusing Iraqi Prisoners," Los Angeles Times, April 29, 2004, at A4; James Risen, "G.I.'s Are Accused of Abusing Iraqi Captives," New York Times, April 29, 2004, at A13; "Photographs Reveal Atrocities by U.S. Soldiers," Washington Times, April 29, 2004, at A5.

73. Article 15–6 Investigation of the 800th Military Police Brigade, at 16.

74. Id. at 16–17.

75. John H. Langbein, Torture and the Law of Proof 135 (2006 ed.).

writ of habeas corpus flowed naturally from the Magna Carta.[76] The Habeas Corpus Act of 1641 abolished the Court of the Star Chamber.[77]

The writ of habeas corpus is not limited to U.S. citizens. It applies generally "to a prisoner."[78] A habeas petition "shall allege the facts concerning the applicant's commitment or detention."[79] The writ is directed to the person having custody "of the person detained."[80] In a December 28, 2001, legal analysis prepared by two high-ranking attorneys in the Justice Department, they concluded that the "great weight" of legal authority indicated that a federal district court "could not probably exercise habeas jurisdiction" over an alien detained at the U.S. naval base at Guantánamo Bay, Cuba.[81] That position provoked litigation in the federal courts and legislation adopted by Congress (see chapter 7).

Over time, the purpose of the writ has been expanded from protecting rights before conviction to giving relief after conviction. The Warren Court used the writ to enforce Bill of Rights protections in state courts, both broadening federal power over the states and adding substantially to the Court's workload.[82] The Burger Court attempted to cut back on the scope of the writ.[83] Congress has passed legislation to limit the availability of habeas corpus relief for state and federal prisons, and the Court has also been active in limiting the opportunity for prisoners to obtain habeas corpus relief. Restrictions have been placed on death row inmates who want their claims heard in federal court after unsuccessful appeals in state court.[84]

These restrictions on the habeas petition apply to prisoners already found guilty and sentenced. Of much greater concern is the denial of the writ to individuals *yet to be charged* or tried. In the 2004 *Hamdi* decision, Justice Antonin Scalia spoke eloquently about the Great Writ: "The very core of liberty secured by our Anglo-Saxon system of separated powers has been freedom

76. William F. Duker, A Constitutional History of Habeas Corpus 45 (1980).

77. Id. at 47.

78. 28 U.S.C. § 2241(c) (2000).

79. Id. at § 2242.

80. Id. at § 2243.

81. Memorandum for William J. Haynes II, General Counsel, Department of Defense, from Patrick F. Philbin, Deputy Assistant Attorney General, and John C. Yoo, Deputy Assistant Attorney General, December 28, 2001, at 1.

82. Fay v. Noia, 372 U.S. 391 (1963).

83. Wainwright v. Sykes, 433 U.S. 72 (1977); Francis v. Henderson, 425 U.S. 536 (1976).

84. Louis Fisher and David Gray Adler, American Constitutional Law 692–93 (7th ed. 2007).

from indefinite imprisonment at the will of the Executive." He drew from the eighteenth-century English legal scholar William Blackstone this language: "to bereave a man of life, or by violence to confiscate his estate, without accusation or trial, would be so gross and notorious an act of despotism, as must at once convey the alarm of tyranny throughout the whole kingdom."[85] Hamdi was a U.S. citizen, as was Padilla. The availability of the writ for noncitizens has been more controversial, leading Congress in 2006 to reduce access to habeas petitions by individuals designated as "enemy combatants."

A Public Trial

British tradition, dating back to the Norman Conquest, opened trials "to all who cared to observe."[86] American colonies followed that practice, as did the Continental Congress and the young American states. In the 1677 Concessions and Agreement of West New Jersey, in all civil or criminal courts "any persons or persons, inhabitants of the said Province may freely come into, and attend the said courts, and hear and be present, at all or any such tryals as shall be there had or passed, that justice may not be in a corner nor in any covert manner. . . ."[87] In 1683, the Pennsylvania Charter of Liberty specified that "all courts shall be open."[88]

On October 26, 1774, the Continental Congress adopted language pointing to the "great right" of trial by jury, including the opportunity for a defendant to be tried "in open Court, before as many of the people as chuse to attend."[89] In 1776, the North Carolina Declaration of Rights provided that "no freeman shall be convicted of any crime, but by the unanimous verdict of a jury of good and lawful men, in open court, as heretofore used."[90] The Pennsylvania Constitution of 1776 stated that in all criminal prosecutions "a man hath a right to be heard by himself and his council [*sic*], to demand the cause and nature of his accusation, to be confronted with the witnesses, to call for evidence in his favour, and a speedy public trial. . . ."[91] The Vermont Constitution of 1777 required a "speedy public trial."[92]

---

85. Hamdi v. Rumsfeld, 542 U.S. 507, 555 (2004) (Scalia, J., dissenting, joined by Justice Stevens).

86. Richmond Newspapers, Inc. v. Virginia, 448 U.S. 555, 564 (1980).

87. 6 Swindler 408 (Ch. XXIII).

88. 8 Swindler 259 (Ch. V).

89. 1 Journals of the Continental Congress, 1774–1789, at 107 (1904).

90. 7 Swindler 402 (Art. IX).

91. 8 Swindler 278–79 (Art. IX).

92. 9 Swindler 490 (Art. X).

Those values appear in the Bill of Rights. The Sixth Amendment provides that in all criminal prosecutions "the accused shall enjoy the right to a speedy and public trial . . . and to be informed of the nature and cause of the accusation; to be confronted with the witnesses against him; to have compulsory process for obtaining witnesses in his favor, and to have the Assistance of Counsel for his defence." Although those privileges apply to all *persons*, not just U.S. citizens, the Bush administration held two U.S. citizens (Hamdi and Padilla) indefinitely without ever bringing them to trial, specifying charges in court, or providing assistance of counsel. Detainees at Guantánamo were held incommunicado without counsel or charges. When they were brought before a judicial panel it was a military commission, not a federal court. Their rights to confront witnesses against them, obtain witnesses in their favor, have legal counsel, and gain access to evidence against them were severely restricted.

The constitutional right to a public trial protects an individual from secret proceedings where there is no opportunity to hear specific charges brought by government officials, secure counsel, prepare a defense, cross-examine witnesses, or summon witnesses on one's behalf. The American rejection of secret trials has been traced to the Spanish Inquisition, the English Star Chamber, and the French *lettre de cachet*.[93] The *lettre de cachet*—a sealed, royal warrant issued to imprison someone without trial—was often issued in blank to local police to prosecute crimes of opinion.[94] That instrument ceased to exist with the French Revolution but was revived by Napoleon.[95]

America has its own record of secret trials and use of secret evidence. In 1948, the Supreme Court reviewed a Michigan law that authorized a "one-man grand jury" to investigate crime. Under this procedure, a circuit judge met in secret to pursue the investigation. In this case, William Oliver was summoned before a circuit judge to respond to questions about gambling and official corruption. Two other circuit judges were present in an advisory capacity. A stenographer was also present, but the public was excluded. In secret session, the judge told Oliver that neither he nor his advisors believed his responses. Their judgment relied in part on testimony offered earlier by another witness, who had given evidence in secret. Oliver was not present to hear that testimony and was apparently unaware that the testimony had been given. The circuit judge charged Oliver with contempt and sentenced him to sixty days in jail. Oliver had no opportunity to "enjoy the benefits of counsel, no chance to prepare his

93. In re Oliver, 333 U.S. 257, 268–69 (1948).
94. Id. at 269, n.23.
95. Eric A. Arnold, ed., A Documentary Survey of Napoleonic France 305–10 (1994).

defense, and no opportunity either to cross-examine the other grand jury witness or to summon witnesses to refute the charge against him."[96] His sentence was upheld by the State Supreme Court, which saw only portions of Oliver's testimony.[97]

In reversing the conviction, the U.S. Supreme Court noted that grand juries have the power to investigate but not the power to try or convict. Even when witnesses before grand juries provide inadequate or misleading answers, grand juries "do not adjudge the witnesses guilty of contempt of court in secret or in public or at all." Witnesses can be tried on contempt charges only "before judges sitting in open court."[98] The Court denied that a witness could be tried and convicted for contempt of court by a grand jury sitting in secret. It could not find "a single instance of a criminal trial conducted in camera in any federal, state, or municipal court during the history of this country."[99] Given "this nation's historic distrust of secret proceedings, their inherent dangers to freedom, and the universal requirement of our federal and state governments that criminal trials be public, the Fourteenth Amendment's guarantee that no one shall be deprived of his liberty without due process of laws means at least that an accused cannot be thus sentenced to prison."[100] Courts may summarily punish certain conduct but that power is exercised in open court.[101]

Right of Confrontation

In all criminal prosecutions, the Sixth Amendment gives the accused the right to "be confronted with the witnesses against him [and] to have compulsory process for obtaining witnesses in his favor." In 1965, the Supreme Court held that the right of confrontation and cross-examination is a fundamental right made obligatory on the states by the Fourteenth Amendment.[102] Two years later the Court applied against the states the right of an accused to have compulsory process for obtaining witnesses.[103] The Confrontation and Compulsory Process Clauses allow an accused a fair opportunity to present a defense.[104]

96. In re Oliver, 333 U.S.
97. Id. at 264.
98. Id. at 265.
99. Id. at 266 (footnote omitted).
100. Id. at 273.
101. Id. at 274.
102. Pointer v. Texas, 380 U.S. 400 (1965); Douglas v. Alabama, 380 U.S. 415 (1965).
103. Washington v. Texas, 388 U.S. 14 (1967).
104. Pennsylvania v. Ritchie, 480 U.S. 39 (1987); Crane v. Kentucky, 476 U.S. 683 (1986); Lee v. Illinois, 476 U.S. 530 (1986).

They assure that the defendant has a right to be present in the courtroom at every stage of the trial. As the Supreme Court noted in 1892: "A leading principle that pervades the entire law of criminal procedure is that, after indictment found, nothing shall be done in the absence of the prisoner."[105] Actions by the Bush administration after 9/11 consistently violated that principle by keeping the accused out of criminal court.

Defendants can lose this privilege if they are warned by the trial judge that they will be removed if they persist with speech and conduct disruptive to the courtroom.[106] As one remedy, a judge can order the binding and gagging of an obstreperous defendant, but that procedure prevents him from communicating with his counsel, very likely offends the jurors, and does damage to the decorum of a trial.[107] In non-capital cases, when the defendant is free on bail and not in custody, if the accused voluntarily absents himself the trial will continue. Through that conduct the accused waives the right to be present and confront witnesses.[108] The Federal Rules of Criminal Procedure lists the circumstances that do not require the presence of a defendant.[109]

The Confrontation and Compulsory Process Clauses were not available to detainees brought before military panels in Guantánamo. Zacarias Moussaoui, a French citizen, was tried in federal district court for being part of the al Qaeda conspiracy to kill and maim persons and destroy structures in the United States. The Justice Department denied that the Sixth Amendment could be extended overseas to potential witnesses who are "enemy combatants." Any effort to interrogate them, according to the government, would "change the course of a military operation."[110] The two U.S. citizens designated as "enemy combatants"—Hamdi and Padilla—had no right of confrontation because they were never charged and tried in court. Only after being held in military detention for years was Padilla released and prosecuted in a civil court in Florida.

Access by the Press

Judges occasionally issue gag orders to prohibit public comment about a pending case. In 1976, a unanimous Court reversed the decision of a Nebraska

105. Lewis v. United States, 146 U.S. 370, 372 (1892).

106. Illinois v. Allen, 397 U.S. 337 (1970).

107. Id. at 344.

108. Diaz v. United States, 223 U.S. 442, 455 (1912).

109. 18 U.S.C. app. Rule 43(c) (2000). In a case where defendant was absent from certain pretrial actions, it was held that his absence did not deprive him of due process. United States v. Veatch, 674 F.2d 1217, 1225–26 (9th Cir. 1981).

110. Louis Fisher, Military Tribunals and Presidential Power 214–16 (2005).

state court judge who, in anticipation of a trial for a multiple murder, had prohibited newspapers, broadcasters, journalists, news media associations, and
national newswire services from publishing or broadcasting statements by the
accused to law enforcement officers. The Court held that the heavy burden
imposed as a condition of prior restraint had not been met.[111] In 1979, the
Court split 5 to 4 in supporting a trial judge's ruling to close a *pretrial* hearing
to the public and the press. The Court said that the constitutional guarantee
of a public trial is for the benefit of the defendant, not the public: "[W]e hold
that members of the public have no constitutional right under the Sixth and
Fourteenth Amendments to attend criminal trials."[112] Although it found no
constitutional basis, it recognized "a strong societal interest in public trials.
Openness in court proceedings may improve the quality of testimony, induce
unknown witnesses to come forward with relevant testimony, cause all trial
participants to perform their duties more conscientiously, and generally give
the public an opportunity to observe the judicial system."[113]

Because this decision was accompanied by three separate concurrences and
a dissenting opinion, courts around the country were unclear about the underlying principle. Some judges began to close their courtrooms to the public,
not only for pretrial proceedings but for the entire trial and sentencing. At
times they let the public in but kept the press out. Several members of the
Supreme Court, including Warren Burger, Lewis Powell, Harry A. Blackmun,
and John Paul Stevens, took the unusual step of telling audiences around the
country that the 1979 case had been "misread" to permit unacceptable re-
straints on the press.[114]

Within a year, the Supreme Court issued a ruling to emphasize the public's
need to attend trials. Divided 7 to 1, it held that the public's right of access to
criminal trials is implicit in the First (not the Sixth) Amendment. Open trials
promote many interests: the yearning to see justice done, the public education that comes from attending a trial, the maintenance of public trust in the
judicial system, and the opportunity to check the fairness and accuracy of judicial proceedings.[115] A public trial gives assurance "that the proceedings were
conducted fairly to all concerned, and it discouraged perjury, the misconduct
of participants, and decisions based on secret bias or partiality."[116] Citizens in a

111. Nebraska Press Assn. v. Stuart, 427 U.S. 539 (1976).

112. Gannett Co. v. DePasquale, 443 U.S. 368, 391 (1979).

113. Id. at 383.

114. Fisher and Adler, American Constitutional Law 525.

115. Richmond Newspapers, Inc. v. Virginia, 448 U.S. 555 (1980).

116. Id. at 569.

democratic society "do not demand infallibility from their institutions, but it is difficult for them to accept what they are prohibited from observing."[117]

The decision did not rule on whether the public has a right to attend trials of civil cases, and yet the Court noted that "historically both civil and criminal trials have been presumptively open."[118] Unless an overriding interest is articulated in findings, "the trial of a criminal case must be open to the public."[119] A concurrence by Justice William J. Brennan observed: "Secrecy is profoundly inimical to this demonstrated purpose of the trial process." Open trials, he said, "assure the public that procedural rights are respected, and that justice is afforded equally." Closed trials "breed suspicion of prejudice and arbitrariness, which in turn spawns disrespect for law."[120]

Three decisions after 1980 underscored the value of public hearings. In 1982, the Court held that a Massachusetts law, which excluded the general public from trials of specified sexual offenses involving a victim under age 18, was unconstitutional under the First Amendment.[121] Two years later the Court struck down the effort of a state judge to close *voir dire* proceedings in a trial for the rape and murder of a teenage girl.[122] Three days of questioning potential jurors were open to the public, but six weeks were closed.[123] In 1986, the Court reviewed a California case where a nurse was charged with murdering twelve patients by injecting lethal amounts of the heart drug lidocaine. A magistrate excluded the public from the forty-one-day preliminary hearing.[124] The Court held that the closed preliminary hearing was invalid.

Assistance of Counsel

The Sixth Amendment entitles a person "to have the Assistance of Counsel for his defense." Without counsel in a criminal trial, an accused is unable to exercise effectively the rights available in the Constitution: the privilege to remain silent, to cross-examine witnesses, to challenge biased jurors, and a variety of subtle questions of law that tax the resourcefulness of even seasoned lawyers. "A layman is usually no match for the skilled prosecutor whom he confronts in

117. Id. at 572.
118. Id. at 580 n.17.
119. Id. at 581.
120. Id. at 595.
121. Globe Newspaper Co. v. Superior Court, 457 U.S. 596 (1982).
122. Press-Enterprise Co. v. Superior Court of Cal., 464 U.S. 501 (1984).
123. Id. at 510.
124. Press-Enterprise Co. v. Superior Court, 478 U.S. 1 (1986).

the court room. He needs the aid of counsel lest he be the victim of overzealous prosecutors, of the law's complexity, or his own ignorance or bewilderment."[125]

Long before the U.S. Supreme Court recognized the need for counsel to the accused, states had begun to insist that government has a constitutional duty to provide counsel for indigents prosecuted by the state. The Supreme Court of Indiana in 1854 held that a "civilized community" could not put a citizen in jeopardy and withhold counsel from the poor.[126] In 1859, the Wisconsin Supreme Court called it a "mockery" to promise a pauper a fair trial and then tell him he must employ his own counsel.[127] Congress passed legislation in 1892 to provide counsel to represent poor persons and extended that provision in 1910.[128]

The question of providing an attorney for indigent defendants in a criminal case was decided partly by the Supreme Court in 1932 when it held that the Due Process Clause of the Fourteenth Amendment requires the appointment of counsel for someone accused of a capital offense. If a defendant is incapable of making his own defense because of "ignorance, feeblemindedness, illiteracy, or the like, it is the duty of the court, whether requested or not, to assign counsel for him as a necessary requisite of due process of law."[129] Six years later, the Court held that indigents charged with a crime in federal court are entitled by the Sixth Amendment to have the assistance of counsel unless that right is intelligently and competently waived.[130]

The question of exactly how to provide counsel in state prosecutions preoccupied the Supreme Court for more than two decades. In 1942 it ruled that a state's refusal to appoint counsel for an indigent in a criminal proceeding did not deny due process.[131] The Court divided 6 to 3 in that case, and dozens of subsequent decisions whittled away at the majority's position. The denial of counsel in a state case provoked four dissents in 1946.[132] The Court agreed unanimously in 1954 that due process was violated when a state judge denied a defendant the opportunity to obtain counsel on a separate accusation regard-

125. Williams v. Kaiser, 323 U.S. 471, 476 (1945).

126. Webb v. Baird, 6 Ind. 13 (1854).

127. Carpenter v. Dane, 9 Wis. 249 (1859).

128. 27 Stat. 252 (1892); 36 Stat. 866 (1910).

129. Powell v. Alabama, 287 U.S. 45, 71 (1932).

130. Johnson v. Zerbst, 304 U.S. 458 (1938).

131. Betts v. Brady, 316 U.S. 455 (1942).

132. Carter v. Illinois, 329 U.S. 173 (1946).

ing his habitual criminal record.[133] The Court split 5 to 4 in two cases in the late 1950s in which counsel had been denied in a state proceeding.[134]

In 1960, the Court held that lack of counsel for an indigent in a state case deprived the accused of due process. As the two dissenters noted, the Court did not even mention the 1942 precedent, although the decision "cuts serious inroads into that holding."[135] A year later a unanimous Court ruled that due process had been violated by denying counsel to an indigent, ignorant, and mentally ill black man. This was a non-capital felony case. Again, the opinion of the Court ignored the 1942 case.[136] In two other non-capital felony cases, a unanimous Court held that the denial of counsel violated due process.[137]

Finally, in 1963, the Court decided in the celebrated Clarence Gideon case that the Sixth Amendment right of assistance of counsel is incorporated in the Due Process Clause of the Fourteenth Amendment and applied against the states.[138] Gideon had been tried in a state court for a non-capital felony. Subsequent decisions of the Supreme Court assured the right of counsel for a first appeal, post-indictment lineups, preliminary hearings, post-trial proceedings (such as sentencing), and other steps of litigation. Counsel has not been required for additional appeals, a petition for certiorari to the U.S. Supreme Court, and post-conviction relief for death-row inmates.[139] Several decisions have attempted to identify the criteria needed for "effective" assistance of counsel.[140]

These cases apply to criminal trials. For other court actions, defendants have to rely on free legal services or pay for an attorney. In removal proceedings before an immigration judge and in any appeals to the Attorney General, a person threatened with deportation has the privilege of being represented by counsel but "at no expense to the Government."[141] Immigrants represent themselves in more than half of the cases in immigration courts.[142] As

133. Chandler v. Fretag, 348 U.S. 3 (1954).

134. In re Groban, 352 U.S. 330 (1957); Anonymous v. Baker, 360 U.S. 287 (1959).

135. Hudson v. North Carolina, 363 U.S. 697, 704 (1960).

136. McNeal v. Culver, 365 U.S. 109, 117 (1962).

137. Chewning v. Cunningham, 368 U.S. 443 (1962); Carnley v. Cochran, 369 U.S. 506 (1962).

138. Gideon v. Wainwright, 372 U.S. 335 (1963).

139. Fisher and Adler, American Constitutional Law 671.

140. Id. at 670–71.

141. 8 U.S.C. § 1362 (2000).

142. Karin Brulliard, "Battling Deportation Often a Solitary Journey," Washington Post, January 8, 2007, at A1.

explained in subsequent chapters, once Hamdi and Padilla were designated "enemy combatants," they had nonexistent or highly restricted contacts with their attorneys. Detainees in Guantánamo were assigned a "personal representative" who lacked legal training. Later they had attorneys but without assured access to evidence held against them.

EXCEPTIONS TO OPENNESS

The principle of a public trial is waived at times to protect other interests. A judge may decide that a matter must be discussed in his or her chamber (*in camera*), and it may be necessary to allow only one of the parties—the government—in the room (*ex parte*). Other procedures limit public access, including the sealing of papers and records, and holding oral argument in a closed court. Those are important exceptions and merit close scrutiny, but they do not dispense with the fundamental right to confront witnesses, to be free of coerced interrogation, and to have the assistance of counsel.

In Camera *Proceedings*

In a 1976 case, a defendant convicted of violating the Federal Firearms Act accused the government of impermissible misconduct and argued that certain government documents, including those from an FBI operation, would substantiate his allegations. The government asserted that the requested files contained no information relevant to his prosecution, but the court declined to rely on the judgment of one of the parties to the lawsuit. It ordered that the files be examined in the judge's chamber, explaining that in some cases *in camera* inspection is a proper means of resolving the conflict between a defendant's need for evidence and the government's interest in protecting the security of its files.[143] In other cases the use of *in camera* proceedings can violate constitutional rights, such as an individual's right to the counsel of his choice.[144] *In camera* procedures "are extraordinary events in the constitutional framework because they deprive the parties against whom they are directed of the root requirements of due process, *i.e.,* notice setting forth the alleged misconduct with particularity and an opportunity for a hearing."[145] Whenever

143. United States v. Brown, 539 F.2d 467, 470 (5th Cir. 1976).
144. In re Taylor, 567 F.2d 1183 (2d Cir. 1977).
145. Id. at 1188.

a court adjudicates the legal rights of individuals, "the presumption is against the use of secret proceedings."[146]

In 1980, Congress passed the Classified Information Procedures Act (CIPA) to provide procedures for criminal cases involving classified information. The statute responded to the growing use of classified information in cases covering espionage, murder, perjury, narcotics distribution, and other criminal actions.[147] Defendants threatened to reveal classified information during the trial, an initiative at times considered an unscrupulous or questionable defense tactic ("graymail"). In many instances, however, the defendant "will simply be exercising his legal rights" in seeking to use information relevant to his defense.[148] To handle this type of case, the statute authorized the Attorney General to request that a hearing be held *in camera* to protect the disclosure of classified information. In some cases the defendant has the classified information.

In other CIPA cases, when the government has not provided the information to the defendant, the government may describe the material by generic category instead of providing specifics. Upon the defendant's request, the court may order the government to provide the defendant, prior to trial, such details as are needed to give the defendant fair notice to prepare for the hearing. As an alternative, the government may provide a "substitution" of the classified information. The court, in determining whether the substitute gives the defendant substantially the same ability to mount a defense, conducts the hearing *in camera* at the request of the Attorney General. The government may also submit an affidavit explaining why disclosure of classified information may damage national security and ask the court to examine the affidavit *in camera* and *ex parte*.[149] A refusal by the government to disclose classified information needed by the defendant may result in dismissal of an indictment (or one or more of its counts), a finding against the government, and prohibiting the testimony of a government witness.[150] In passing CIPA, Congress "did not intend to allow exclusion of evidence relevant to the defense simply because that evidence was classified."[151]

---

146. Id. For other in camera proceedings, see Waller v. Georgia, 467 U.S. 39, 42 (1984); United States v. De Los Santos, 810 F.2d 1326, 1330–33 (5th Cir. 1987); United States v. Scarpelli, 713 F.Supp. 1144, 1145–46 n.2 (N.D. Ill. 1989); and Woods v. Kulhmann, 977 F.2d 74 (2d Cir. 1992).

147. H. Rept. No. 96–831 (Part 1), 96th Cong., 2d Sess. 6–7 (1980).

148. Id. at 7.

149. 94 Stat. 2026–27, sec. 6 (1980); 18 U.S.C. app. § 6 (2000).

150. United States v. Collins, 720 F.2d 1195, 1197 (11th Cir. 1983).

151. United States v. Smith, 780 F.2d 1102, 1104–05 (4th Cir. 1985).

Ex Parte *Sessions*

Federal judges at times meet in the company of one party to the case: the government attorney.[152] Courts recognize that *ex parte* meetings "are made in derogation of basic constitutional rights and without the benefit of the enlightenment which accompanies an adversary proceeding."[153] If the information is neutral as to the defendant's guilt, the process may not damage the elements of a fair trial. However, if the document clears the individual of an alleged crime, non-disclosure during *in camera, ex parte* proceedings would prejudice the defendant.[154] By having only the government attorney in the judge's chambers, the judge necessarily listens to one side.

The risk of unfairness and bias increases when the judge looks not at a disputed document but at a classified affidavit prepared by the government. Here the judge is at arm's-length from the document and wholly dependent on the integrity of the government's affidavit.[155] A judge may conclude that the affidavit "describes the disputed material in sufficient detail," and that the affidavit "indicates clearly that the disputed records were properly classified," but the judge is in no position to make such determinations with full confidence without examining the document in its unredacted form.[156]

In 1978, in response to presidential claims that they could conduct national security eavesdropping without a warrant, Congress passed the Foreign Intelligence Surveillance Act (FISA). It requires the President, through the Attorney General, to seek a warrant from a special court created by the statute (the FISA court). It meets *in camera* and *ex parte* to review the government's application for a warrant. Documents are not disclosed to the party being monitored.[157] If private parties were not only monitored but later prosecuted, at that point they could gain access to documents. As a court explained in 1985, Congress "did not intend to allow exclusion of evidence relevant to the defense simply because that evidence was classified."[158] The secret FISA court is only a stage of collecting information. It does not try a case.

---

152. United States v. Klimavicius-Viloria, 144 F.3d 1249, 1260–62 (9th Cir. 1998).
153. In re Taylor, 567 F.2d. at 1189.
154. United States v. Kampiles, 609 F.2d 1233, 1248 (7th Cir. 1979).
155. Salisbury v. United States, 690 F.2d 966, 969–70 (D.C. Cir. 1982).
156. Id. at 971, 972.
157. United States v. Squillacote, 221 F.3d 542, 553 (4th Cir. 2000).
158. United States v. Smith, 780 F.2d at 1104–05.

Sealing of Records

Judges may decide to seal a record to prevent access by unauthorized parties. In some cases a trial judge examines an unredacted document *in camera* and determines that portions of the document are not material or relevant to the defendant. The sealed document remains available to an appellate court for possible review.[159] Plea agreements are generally open to the public but they have been sealed and later opened to qualified access.[160] In CIPA cases, after an *in camera* hearing, the court may determine that classified information may not be disclosed and seal the record of an *in camera* hearing.[161] To balance the government's interest in protecting national security information with "the public's right of access to a public trial," a court may release to the public a redacted version of the trial transcripts that had been closed.[162]

Closed Oral Argument

In 1971, in district and appellate courts, the government and private parties handled oral argument on the Pentagon Papers Case *in camera*. The government wanted to prevent newspapers from publishing the "top secret" study prepared by the Defense Department on the Vietnam War. The *New York Times* and other newspapers argued against prior restraint. When the case reached the Supreme Court, Chief Justice Burger told Solicitor General Erwin Griswold that the government's motion to conduct part of the oral argument involving security matters had been denied by the Court. He and Justices John Marshall Harlan and Blackmun would have granted a limited *in camera* argument. Burger advised Griswold that counsel had the option of submitting argument "in writing under seal in lieu of the *in camera* oral argument."[163] Griswold explained to the Court that all three parties had filed both open

159. United States v. Wolfson, 55 F.3d 58, 59 (2d Cir. 1995).

160. Oregonian Pub. v. U.S. Dist. Court for Dist. of Or., 920 F.2d 1462 (9th Cir. 1990). For sealing of a hearing transcript, see Phoenix Newspapers v. U.S. Dist. Court, 156 F.3d 940 (9th Cir. 1998).

161. 94 Stat. 2027, sec. 6(d) (1980); 18 U.S.C. app. § 6(d) (2000).

162. United States v. Pelton, 696 F.Supp. 156, 159 (D. Md. 1986). For other disputes over sealed documents, see United States v. Ressam, 221 F.Supp. 1252 (W.D. Wash. 2002); United States v. Doe, 63 F.3d 121 (2d Cir. 1995); Seattle Times v. U.S. Dist. Ct. for W.D. of Wash., 845 F.2d 1513 (9th Cir. 1988); CBS, Inc. v. United States Dist. Court, 765 F.2d 823 (9th Cir. 1985).

163. New York Times v. United States, 403 U.S. 713 (1971), in 71 Landmark Briefs and Arguments of the Supreme Court of the United States: Constitutional Law 214 (1975).

briefs and closed briefs. For the latter, involving security matters, the government's brief was marked "Top Secret" and the briefs filed by the *New York Times* and the *Washington Post* were marked "*In Camera.*"[164]

Courts resist the argument that CIPA justifies the closure of hearings. Although the First Amendment "does not entitle the press and public to access in every case,"[165] courts recognize the risk that disclosure of classified information may endanger the lives of Americans and foreign informants. Federal judges are concerned that the judiciary "should abdicate its decisionmaking responsibility to the executive branch whenever national security concerns are present."[166] Examples from history demonstrate "how easily the spectre of a threat to 'national security' may be used to justify a wide variety of repressive government actions."[167] Although the government has authority to withhold a classified document, the court, not the government, "decides the consequences of any failure to offer such evidence."[168] In document disputes, courts can decide to dismiss the case.

Secrecy infects a judicial proceeding by preventing the accused from mounting an effective defense and removing the public scrutiny that helps assure that justice is done. Secrecy has a legitimate function in government, as it does in private circles. The next chapter examines the assertion by executive officials that information and documents must be withheld for national security reasons. At times secrecy contributes to the effectiveness of government. On other occasions it invites corruption, abuse, and unconstitutional violations.

164. Id. at 214–15.
165. In re Washington Post, 807 F.2d 383, 390 (4th Cir. 1986).
166. Id. at 391.
167. Id.
168. United States v. Zettl, 835 F.2d 1059, 1063 n.14 (4th Cir. 1987).

Secrets: Real and Contrived

Secrecy became a mainstay for the Bush administration after 9/11. Antiterrorist programs withheld from Congress and the public include National Security Agency surveillance, extraordinary renditions, and Central Intelligence Agency interrogation techniques. Over the past two centuries, national security and foreign policy have relied on secrecy to concentrate power in the presidency and weaken congressional, judicial, and public controls.

Secrecy is a legitimate way to protect many public programs, ranging from undercover operations to atomic weapons and military plans. Yet secrecy can also weaken national security. Many documents are classified "secret" or "top secret" on tenuous or nonexistent grounds. Federal courts, Congress, and the general public need not automatically defer to these executive assertions and judgments. There are too many examples of false, misleading, and damaging claims of secrecy in domestic and foreign affairs to routinely accept and believe government statements.

The word "secret" covers far too much territory. Assigning something that status has no intrinsic worth or virtue. It is a claim, an assertion, and nothing more. The word comes from the Latin *secretus*, from *secernere* "to separate, distinguish."[1] A secret is merely a piece of information that falls into a special category, set apart from other information. Some documents are withheld for legitimate reasons. Others are withheld to conceal blunders, corruption, and illegalities. Unless and until someone looks behind the secrecy label, no one knows what is being hidden—or why.

By statute, Congress has identified a number of government documents and activities that merit confidentiality. Sensitive areas of government range from espionage to protected activities on military bases to the design and capability of nuclear weapons. Whoever exposes those activities to the public or to foreign governments can be fined, imprisoned, or face the death penalty. Examining particular statutes helps cut through the abstract and overbroad notion of secrecy.

---

1. Webster's Third New International Dictionary 2052 (1965).

CONSTITUTIONAL SECRETS

When delegates met in secret at the Philadelphia Convention in 1787 to draft the Constitution, it was decided that deliberations from day to day should be withheld from the public until the draft was agreed to. The debates and votes were deposited with the State Department in 1796 and published in 1819.[2] What became public in 1787 was the draft constitution followed by many published articles, including eighty-five essays by Alexander Hamilton, John Jay, and James Madison later released under the title *The Federalist.*

The Constitution provides one explicit sanction for secrecy. Under Article I, Section 5, each house of Congress "shall keep a Journal of its Proceedings, and from time to time publish the same, excepting such Parts as may in their Judgment require Secrecy. " Occasionally the House and the Senate have met in secret session. In 1811, Congress passed a secret statute that gave President Madison $100,000 to take temporary possession of territory south of Georgia. The law was not published until 1818.[3] During these early decades, Presidents began to assert the need for secrecy in various matters, including the negotiation of treaties.[4]

Article I, Section 9, directs Congress to publish "a regular Statement and Account of the Receipts and Expenditures of all public Money . . . from time to time." The only annual exception to the Statement and Account Clause throughout the nineteenth century was the President's contingency account in foreign intercourse, which allowed the President to decide the extent to which expenditures should be made public. It was a modest amount, beginning with $40,000 in 1790 and increasing gradually to $63,000 by 1899. Other confidential accounts were created during the twentieth century. The most dramatic departures from the Statement and Account Clause are the secret appropriations and expenditures of the U.S. intelligence community, consisting of the CIA, the NSA, the Defense Intelligence Agency, and other parts of the community. The estimated budget for the intelligence community exceeds $40 billion a year.[5]

2. 1 The Records of the Federal Convention of 1787, at xi–xx (M. Farrand ed. 1937) (hereafter "Farrand").

3. 3 Stat. 471–72 (1811).

4. Robert M. Pallitto and William G. Weaver, Presidential Secrecy and the Law 61–63 (2007).

5. Louis Fisher, Constitutional Conflicts between Congress and the President 206–14 (5th ed. 2007).

CLASSIFIED INFORMATION

Disclosure of classified information is subject to fines, imprisonment, and loss of personal property. Classified information is specifically designated by a U.S. government agency for limited or restricted dissemination or distribution. The crime applies to any person who knowingly and willingly communicates, furnishes, transmits, or otherwise makes available classified information to an unauthorized person. It applies to anyone who publishes or uses classified information in any manner prejudicial to the safety or interest of the United States, or for the benefit of any foreign government to the detriment of the United States.

Criminal law applies to four main categories of classified information. First: the nature, preparation, or use of any code, cipher, or cryptographic system of the United States or any foreign government. Second: the design, construction, use, maintenance, or repair of any device, apparatus, or appliance used or prepared or planned for use by the United States or any foreign government for cryptographic or communication purposes. Third: communication intelligence activities of the United States or any foreign government. Fourth: classified information obtained by the process of communication intelligence from any foreign government. Imprisonment shall not exceed ten years. Persons convicted of violating this section of the law shall forfeit to the United States property derived from the illegal transaction.[6]

The system of classification is spelled out in a number of executive orders issued by Presidents. In 1940, President Franklin D. Roosevelt provided guidelines on the categories of "Secret," "Confidential," and "Restricted."[7] President Harry Truman continued those classifications but added "Top Secret."[8] He provided further details a year later.[9] As explained in an executive order issued in 1982 by President Ronald Reagan, classification and declassification are performed not merely to safeguard national security information, but also to recognize that "it is essential that the public be informed concerning the activities of its Government."[10] This policy recognizes that secrecy cannot be pushed to the point of making self-government impossible. Reagan also said: "[i]n no case shall information be classified in order to conceal violations of

---

6. 18 U.S.C. § 798 (2000).

7. Executive Order 8381, 5 Fed. Reg. 1147 (1940).

8. Executive Order 10104, 15 Fed. Reg. 597, 598 (1950).

9. Executive Order 10290, 16 Fed. Reg. 9795 (1951).

10. Executive Order 12356, Public Papers of the Presidents, 1982, I, at 412.

law, inefficiency, or administrative error; to prevent embarrassment to a person, organization, or agency; to restrain competition; or to prevent or delay the release of information that does not require protection in the interest of national security."[11]

The current executive order that governs classified national security information is Executive Order 13292, issued by President George W. Bush on March 25, 2003. Three classification levels are defined: Top Secret, Secret, and Confidential.[12] The Bush executive order retains prohibitions and limitations spelled out by Reagan, stating that in no case shall information be classified in order to "conceal violations of law, inefficiency, or administrative error" or to "prevent embarrassment to a person, organization, or agency."[13]

Decisions on classification and declassification often have nothing to do with national security or protecting the national interest. Documents already in the public sector can be classified, and documents initially classified can be declassified for purely political reasons to give the administration extra leverage in court, with Congress, or the public. Agencies frequently declassify a document and leak sensitive information to discredit a litigant or advance an agency interest.[14] As noted later in this chapter, in a dispute involving a Justice Department subpoena to the ACLU, the government can threaten organizations with possession of a classified document but reverse course when its position becomes untenable. If the government decides to declassify the document, then people will wonder why it was classified in the first place.

ESPIONAGE

All nations spy on others and pass laws to punish those who spy on them. The Continental Congress adopted a resolution on August 21, 1776, stating that all persons not owing allegiance to America, "found lurking as spies in or about the fortifications or encampments of the armies of the United States," shall suffer death or punishment by sentence of a court-martial.[15] The Congress ordered the resolution to "be printed at the end of the rules and articles of

11. Id. at 414, § 1.6(a).

12. 68 Fed. Reg. 15315, Sec. 1.2 (2003).

13. Id. at 15318, Sec. 1.7.

14. For litigation involving Sibel Edmonds, see Louis Fisher, *In the Name of National Security* 249–52 (2006).

15. 5 Journals of the Continental Congress 693.

war."[16] The previous year, Congress had made it punishable by court-martial for members of the continental army to "hold correspondence with, or . . . giv[e] intelligence to, the enemy."[17] Those provisions were carried forth with the new Congress that assembled in 1789.[18]

In 1911, Congress passed legislation to prevent the disclosure of national defense secrets. The statute included fines and imprisonment for whoever entered military facilities or buildings connected with national security in an unauthorized manner, for the purpose of communicating information to a foreign government or to persons not authorized to receive it.[19] The House Judiciary Committee described recent incidents of foreign spies picking up military blueprints, making sketches of fortifications, posing as military officers, and offering money to American soldiers to obtain national defense information. Existing law did not authorize punishment of those offenses.[20] The bill moved through Congress with little debate.[21]

After America entered World War I, Congress passed legislation in 1917 to punish any interference with foreign relations, neutrality, and foreign commerce and to punish espionage.[22] The Espionage Act contains specific sections on gathering and transmitting defense information, gathering or delivering defense information to aid a foreign government, and photographing or sketching defense installations.

Fines and Imprisonment

Section 793 of the Espionage Act contains eight subsections, (a) through (h). They protect against information about military activities being stolen, lost, or placed in the hands of those unclassified to receive it. Section 793(a) applies to whoever obtains information respecting the national defense and has "intent or reason to believe" that the information is to be used to injure the United States or advantage a foreign nation. They are subject to fines or imprisonment for not more than ten years. This section applies to a broad range of military

16. Id.

17. 2 Journals of the Continental Congress 116 (Art. XXVIII).

18. 1 Stat. 96, sec. 4 (1789); 2 Stat. 359 (1806).

19. H. Rept. No. 1942, 61st Cong., 3d Sess. 2 (1911).

20. Id. at 2–5.

21. 46 Cong. Rec. 2029–30 (1911); S. Rept. No. 1250, 61st Cong., 3d Sess. (1911); 46 Cong. Rec. 3516 (1911); 36 Stat. 1084 (1911).

22. 40 Stat. 217 (1917), amended at 40 Stat. 553 (1917) and codified in 1948, 62 Stat. 736–38.

installations and facilities, including any vessel, aircraft, navy yard, fort, canal, railroad, telegraph, or building connected with the national defense. Section 793(b) covers any effort to copy or take "any sketch, photograph, photographic negative, blueprint, plan, map," etc., of anything connected with the national defense.[23] Other subsections of Section 793 prohibit attempts to communicate or deliver those documents to any person not entitled to receive it.

Samuel Loring Morison, who worked at the Naval Intelligence Support Center (NISC) from 1974 until October 1984, was prosecuted under Section 793. His security clearance gave him access to "Top Secret" information and "Sensitive Compartmented Information" (SCI). SCI covers classified information so sensitive that even clearance for Top Secret is not sufficient. Morison had signed a "Non-Disclosure Agreement," obliging him not to disclose any classified information in an unauthorized fashion. He understood, as part of that agreement, that any such disclosure could subject him to prosecution under the Espionage Act and other criminal statutes.[24]

In addition to his official assignment he did off-duty work for *Jane's Fighting Ships*, an annual British publication that covered naval operations internationally. The company also began publishing another periodical, *Jane's Defence Weekly*. Morison received payment for the work he did for *Jane's*. The Navy approved this arrangement with the understanding that he would not forward any classified information to *Jane's*. After some disagreements with the Navy, Morison began to consider full-time employment with *Jane's* and met with its editor-in-chief to discuss possible job opportunities.

The action that led to Morison's prosecution began on July 24, 1984. He saw, on the desk of a colleague who worked in a "vaulted area" closed to all employees without a Top Secret clearance, some glossy photographs of a Soviet aircraft carrier under construction at a Black Sea naval shipyard. He cut off the borders that contained the words "Top Secret," and a warning notice that intelligence sources or methods were involved, and mailed them to *Jane's*, which published the photographs a few days later and made the pictures available to other news agencies. After Navy officers saw the photographs in the August 8, 1984, edition of the *Washington Post*, they searched for the photos and found they were missing. When questioned, Morison denied ever seeing the photos. *Jane's* returned them to the Navy, at which point investigators discovered his fingerprint. The Navy obtained a search warrant and found in

23. 18 U.S.C. § 793(a)–(b) (2000).
24. United States v. Morison, 844 F.2d 1057, 1060 (4th Cir. 1988), cert. denied, 488 U.S. 908 (1988).

Morison's home two "secret" NISC intelligence reports in an envelope to be sent to the editor-in-chief at *Jane's*. He later admitted to taking the photographs, cutting off the margins, and mailing them to *Jane's*. A jury found him guilty on all counts, and the Fourth Circuit confirmed his conviction.[25]

Even when there is no intention to harm the United States, Section 793 prohibits passing secret information to individuals not authorized to receive it. In January 2006, Lawrence Franklin was sentenced to 151 months in prison after pleading guilty to three counts: conspiracy to communicate national defense information, conspiracy to communicate classified information to an agent of a foreign government, and unlawful retention of national defense information. In announcing the sentence, the district judge accepted Franklin's explanation that it was not his intention to hurt the United States, but he nonetheless had violated Section 793.[26]

Death Penalty

Some violations of Section 794 are punished by the death penalty. The section applies to individuals who release information to a foreign government with reason to believe it will be used to injure the United States or benefit the foreign nation. Prohibited actions include efforts to communicate any "document, writing, code book, signal book, sketch, photograph," etc., relating to the national defense. Also covered are efforts to reveal information about nuclear weaponry, military spacecraft or satellites, early warning systems, "or other means of defense or retaliation against large-scale attack." Included are war plans and cryptographic information.[27] The government must show that the individual had "intent or reason to believe" there would be injury to the United States or a benefit to a foreign nation.

Criminal penalties under Section 794(b) apply to whoever, *in time of war*, intends to communicate to the enemy any information with respect to the movement of U.S. armed forces or plans for the conduct of military operations. Prosecutions cover information about fortifications and public defense. Offenses may be punished by death or imprisonment for any terms of years

25. Id. at 1061–62.

26. Jerry Markon, "Pentagon Analyst Given 12 1/2 Years in Secrets Case," Washington Post, January 21, 2006, at A1; David Johnston, "Former Military Analyst Gets Prison Term for Passing Information," New York Times, January 21, 2006, at A30.

27. 18 U.S.C. § 794(a).

or for life.[28] Ronald Pelton, who worked for the National Security Agency, was convicted under Section 794. After leaving the NSA in 1979, the following year he decided to sell classified information about NSA programs to the Soviet Union. In conversations with FBI agents in 1985, Pelton acknowledged that he had sold information to the Soviets and that his actions had harmed the United States.[29] He was sentenced to life in prison.

Free Press Concerns

In the course of the Morison litigation, questions were raised about the First Amendment rights of newspapers and private citizens to gain access to information but those issues were not directly involved.[30] Judge Wilkinson noted in a concurrence: "This prosecution was not an attempt to apply the espionage statute to the press for either the receipt or publication of classified materials."[31] He discussed the risks of limiting the ability of the press to report on government activity: "There exists the tendency, even in a constitutional democracy, for government to withhold reports of disquieting developments and to manage news in a fashion most favorable to itself."[32]

On December 16, 2005, the *New York Times* published a detailed account of President George W. Bush authorizing the NSA to eavesdrop on Americans and others inside the United States without a court-approved warrant. Questions were raised as to whether the newspaper violated the Espionage Act by publishing an account of a secret agency operation.[33] Defenders of the *Times* pointed to the important role performed by the press in uncovering not only secrets but illegal and unconstitutional government programs.[34]

After the sentencing of Lawrence Franklin in January 2006, the Bush administration said that journalists could be prosecuted under espionage laws for receiving and publishing classified information. Justice Department lawyers disclosed this position in papers filed in the case of two former lobbyists

28. Id. at § 794(b).

29. United States v. Pelton, 835 F.2d 1067, 1071 (4th Cir. 1987).

30. United States v. Morison, 844 F.2d. at 1077 (Russell, J.), 1080–81 (Wilkinson, J., concurring), 1085 (Phillips, J., concurring).

31. Id. at 1085.

32. Id. at 1081.

33. Gabriel Schoenfelt, "Has the 'New York Times' Violated the Espionage Act?" Commentary, March 2006, at 23–31.

34. Letters to the Editor in the June 2006 issue of Commentary.

of the American Israel Public Affairs Committee (AIPAC), Steven J. Rosen and Keith Weissman, who allegedly received classified information from Franklin. The department concluded that the two men "have no First Amendment right to willfully disclose national defense information." It recognized "that a prosecution under the espionage laws of an *actual* member of the press for publishing classified information leaked to it by a government source, would raise legitimate and serious issues and would not be undertaken lightly."[35]

On May 21, 2006, Attorney General Alberto Gonzales announced that the Justice Department could prosecute the *New York Times* for publishing classified information about NSA eavesdropping. Citing the 1917 Espionage Act, he said: "I understand very much the role that the press plays in our society, the protection under the First Amendment we want to promote and respect ... but it can't be the case that that right trumps over the right that Americans would like to see, the ability of the federal government to go after criminal activity."[36] That reasoning would allow the government to act illegally and unconstitutionally and punish whoever revealed the activities.

MILITARY INSTALLATIONS

Under Section 795 of the Espionage Act, whenever in the interests of national security the President defines certain "vital" military and naval installations or equipment as requiring protection against the dissemination of information, it shall be unlawful to make any photograph, sketch, picture, etc. of the installation or equipment without first obtaining the permission of the commanding officer of the military or naval post. Whoever violates this section is subject to a fine or imprisonment for not more than one year, or both. Similarly, whoever uses or permits the use of an aircraft or "any contrivance" to make a photograph or sketch of "vital" military installations, in violation of Section 795, shall be fined or imprisoned not more than one year, or both.[37]

35. Walter Pincus, "Press Can Be Prosecuted for Having Secret Files, U.S. Says," Washington Post, February 22, 2006, at A3 (emphasis in original).

36. Walter Pincus, "Prosecution of Journalists Is Possible in NSA Leaks," Washington Post, May 22, 2006, at A4.

37. 18 U.S.C. § 796.

ATOMIC SECRETS

Federal laws impose fines and imprisonment to protect atomic energy information, including documents, sketches, and photographs. Congress passed the Atomic Energy Act of 1946 "to control the dissemination of restricted data in such a manner as to assure the common defense and security."[38] Penalties apply to whoever communicates, transmits, or discloses atomic energy information to any individual with intent to injure the United States or with intent to secure an advantage to any foreign nation.[39] Fines and imprisonment cover those who, without permission, make sketches, pictures, or graphical representation of atomic energy installations owned by the government, after the President has designated the installations or equipment as requiring protection against the dissemination of information.[40]

A prominent trial of individuals charged with transmitting atomic bomb information to another country involved Julius and Ethel Rosenberg. In 1950, they were indicted for communicating to the Soviet Union classified information taken from the atomic bomb project in Los Alamos. Beginning in 1944, David Greenglass, brother of Ethel Rosenberg, had begun obtaining information about the location, personnel, physical description, security measures, camouflage, and experiments at Los Alamos, where he was stationed as a soldier.[41] After the war, he and others continued to gain access to atomic bomb secrets and transfer them to Russia. The indictments charged violation of Section 32 of Title 50, later recodified as Section 794 of the Espionage Act. The jury found the Rosenbergs guilty, and the trial judge sentenced them to death.[42] On appeal, the Second Circuit ruled that the communication to a foreign government of secret material connected with the national defense "can by no far-fetched reasoning be included within the area of First Amendment protected free speech."[43]

On November 17, 1952, the Supreme Court denied a petition for a rehearing.[44] A month later, a district court and the Second Circuit found no

---

38. 60 Stat. 755, 766, sec. 10(a) (1946); James R. Newman, "Control of Information Relating to Atomic Energy," 56 Yale L. J. 769 (1947).

39. 42 U.S.C. § 2274 (2000).

40. Id. at § 2278b.

41. United States v. Rosenberg, 195 F.2d 583, 588 (2d Cir. 1952).

42. Id. at 590.

43. Id. at 591. See also United States v. Rosenberg, 10 F.R.D. 521 (1950).

44. Rosenberg v. United States, 344 U.S. 889 (1952).

grounds for granting the Rosenbergs relief.[45] The Supreme Court vacated a stay of execution that the Second Circuit had granted on February 17, 1953.[46] The Court denied a habeas petition on June 15.[47] In addition to other issues, defense counsel argued that the Atomic Energy Act of 1946 superseded the Espionage Act of 1917.[48] The Atomic Energy Act permitted a death penalty if recommended *by a jury*. In the Rosenberg case, the trial judge imposed the death penalty.[49]

The Court met in special session on June 18 to hear this argument for three hours, deliberated in conference for another three hours, and the next morning vacated a motion for a stay of the execution.[50] It held that the Atomic Energy Act "did not repeal or limit the provisions of the Espionage Act."[51] Six Justices noted that the crimes, covering the period from June 6, 1944, to June 16, 1950, began more than two years before the Atomic Energy Act was passed.[52] Each statute, they argued, "is complete in itself and each has its own reason for existence and field of operation."[53] If the Atomic Energy Act had been used, it would have raised serious questions of an unconstitutional *ex post facto* prosecution.[54] Justices Black, Frankfurter, and Douglas issued separate dissents, objecting that the abbreviated treatment in special session left insufficient time to explore and resolve the legal issues.[55] After President Eisenhower denied clemency,[56] the Rosenbergs were electrocuted that evening, on June 18, shortly after eight o'clock.[57]

In more recent litigation, in 1999 the government charged Dr. Wen Ho Lee with violating the Atomic Energy Act and the Espionage Act by transferring

45. United States v. Rosenberg, 108 F.Supp. 798 (S.D. N.Y. 1952); United States v. Rosenberg, 200 F.2d 666 (2d Cir. 1952).

46. Rosenberg v. United States, 345 U.S. 965 (1953). See also Rosenberg v. United States, 345 U.S. 1003 (1953).

47. Rosenberg v. Denno, 346 U.S. 271 (1953).

48. Rosenberg v. United States, 346 U.S. 273, 283 (1953).

49. Id. at 294; 60 Stat. 755, Sec. 10(b)(2)(3) (1946).

50. Rosenberg v. United States, 346 U.S. at 283, 322; Luther A. Huston, "Court Hears Spy Debate; Rules Today," New York Times, June 19, 1953, at 1.

51. Rosenberg v. United States, 346 U.S. at 289.

52. Id. at 290, 298, 304.

53. Id. at 290.

54. Id. at 295–96.

55. Id. at 296, 301, 310.

56. Public Papers of the Presidents, 1953, at 446–47.

57. "Rosenbergs Executed as Atom Spies after Supreme Court Vacates Stay; Last-Minute Plea to President Fails," New York Times, June 20, 1953, at 1.

secret "legacy codes" related to U.S. nuclear weapons programs, moving them from a secure to a nonsecure computer in order to copy those codes on tape.[58] He was held in solitary confinement for 278 days, without trial, before being released on September 13, 2000.[59] The government withdrew the charge of espionage, but in a plea bargain he pled guilty to mishandling computer files. As he stood before District Judge James Parker, who reviewed the plea agreement, he heard extraordinary language from a federal judge: "I have been misled by our government,"[60] referring to Attorney General Janet Reno, Secretary of Energy Bill Richardson, U.S. Attorney John Kelly, and other top officials.[61] Judge Parker expressed his sadness for Dr. Lee and his family "because of the way in which you were kept in custody while you were presumed under the law to be innocent of the charges the executive branch brought against you." Judge Parker explained that the "real reasons" the executive branch had placed Wen Ho Lee in detention would not be known "because the plea agreement shields the executive branch from disclosing a lot of information that it was under order to produce that might have supplied the answer."[62]

After his release, Dr. Lee sued the government for improperly releasing sensitive information about him to the news media for the purpose of damaging his reputation.[63] He sought to have certain journalists held in civil contempt when they failed to comply with a court order to reveal to him their "confidential sources" within the government.[64] He also charged that executive agencies had leaked information to the press as a means of covering up security failures by the government at a weapons research facility.[65] This is a familiar story. Private citizens or members of Congress will seek information from the executive branch, only to be told that the information is sensitive, classified, or pertains to an investigation or prosecution. And yet when it is politically convenient or advantageous, the government will leak the identical information to destroy someone's reputation.

---

58. United States v. Lee, 79 F.Supp.2d 1280 (D. N.M. 1999). He was charged with violating 42 U.S.C. §§ 2275–76 and 18 U.S.C. § 793.

59. Wen Ho Lee, My Country Versus Me 1 (2001).

60. Id. at 2.

61. Id. at 2–4.

62. Id. at 7.

63. Lee v. U.S. Department of Justice, 287 F.Supp.2d 15 (D.D.C. 2003).

64. Lee v. U.S. Department of Justice, 327 F.Supp.2d 26 (D.D.C. 2004).

65. Lee v. Department of Justice, 401 F.Supp.2d 123 (D.D.C. 2005).

With the courts supporting his effort to have the journalists held in contempt,[66] the government and the news media reached an agreement to pay Dr. Lee $1.6 million to settle his claim that the release of government information violated his privacy. The government provided $895,000 to have him drop his lawsuit, and five media organizations agreed to pay $750,000 so that reporters would not have to give him the names of their government sources.[67] The case began over his misuse of classified information. It ended with the government and the news media compensating Dr. Lee for the release of private information about him.

CIA COVERT AGENTS

The Intelligence Identities Protection Act of 1982 drew public attention in late 2003 after the Bush administration leaked the name of a CIA employee (Valerie Plame). The statute makes it a criminal offense for those authorized to have access to classified information to intentionally identify a covert agent to an individual not authorized to have that information. Those convicted of that offense are subject to fine or imprisonment for not more than ten years, or both.[68] Congress passed this legislation after the 1975 murder of Richard Welch, the CIA Station Chief in Athens, Greece, and threats and attacks on other CIA agents, including those posted in Kingston, Jamaica, in 1980.

The legislation gained support when the Supreme Court in 1981 decided a case involving the revocation of Philip Agee's passport. Agee, an American citizen and former CIA employee, announced at a press conference in London in 1974 his intention "to expose CIA officers and agents and to take the measures necessary to drive them out of the countries where they are operating."[69] His

---

66. Lee v. Department of Justice, 413 F.3d 53 (D.C. Cir. 2005); Lee v. Department of Justice, 428 F.3d 299 (D.C. Cir. 2005). See R. Jeffrey Smith, "Judge Orders Reporters to Reveal Sources," Washington Post, October 15, 2003, at A2; Carol D. Leonnig, "Court Orders 4 Reporters to Reveal Sources in Lee Case," Washington Post, June 29, 2005, at A2; Adam Liptak, "Judges Affirm Decision That Found 4 Reporters in Contempt," New York Times, June 29, 2005, at A14; Jonathan D. Glater, "Full Court Declines to Hear Reporters' Appeal," New York Times, November 4, 2005, at A17.

67. Paul Farhi, "U.S., Media Settle With Wen Ho Lee," Washington Post, June 3, 2006, at A1.

68. 96 Stat. 122, § 601(a) (1982); 50 U.S.C. §§ 421(a) (2000).

69. Haig v. Agee, 453 U.S. 280, 283 (1981).

travel to other countries to expose the "cover" of CIA employees and sources led to the disclosure of classified information and violated his contract not to make any public statements about the CIA without its prior clearance.[70] Welch was murdered in December 1975 after an English-language newspaper in Athens published an article naming him as CIA Station Chief. In July 1980, two days after a Jamaica press conference at which one of Agee's collaborators identified Richard Kinsman as the CIA Station Chief in Jamaica, Kinsman's house was strafed with automatic gunfire. Other acts of violence were committed against CIA employees living abroad, including the assassination of two American officials associated with the CIA.[71]

Among other arguments, Agee invoked a First Amendment right to criticize the government. He conceded that his activities "were causing or were likely to cause serious damage to the national security or foreign policy of the United States."[72] The Court concluded that beliefs and speech "are only part of Agee's 'campaign to fight the United States CIA.'"[73] His disclosures, said the Court, "have the declared purpose of obstructing intelligence operations and the recruiting of intelligence personnel. They are clearly not protected by the Constitution. The mere fact that Agee is also engaged in criticism of the Government does not render his conduct beyond the reach of the law."[74] To the extent that the revocation of his passport inhibited him, it was an inhibition of action, not speech.[75]

During legislative debate in 1980, Senator John Chafee (R-R.I.) said that Congress "has a responsibility to place criminal penalties on those who are in the business [of] exposing our agents without, at the same time, threatening the critic of intelligence policy or the journalist who might reveal the name of an agent in the course of a news report."[76] To protect First Amendment rights, the bill was drafted to place upon government the burden of showing that "there was an intentional disclosure of information which did in fact identify a 'covert agent.'" Moreover, the disclosure would have to be to an individual not authorized to receive classified information, and made in the course of a pattern of intending to identify and expose covert agents. The individual who disclosed the information would need to have reason to believe that his

70. Id. at 284.
71. Id. at 285 n.7.
72. Id. at 287.
73. Id. at 305.
74. Id. at 309.
75. Id.
76. 126 Cong. Rec. 28062 (1980).

activities would impair or impede the foreign intelligence activities of the United States.[77]

The bill passed the House 354 to 56, with amendments,[78] and was debated by the Senate over the course of six days.[79] After adopting other amendments, the Senate passed the bill 90 to 6.[80] The two Houses reconciled their differences and the bill became law. In signing the bill, President Reagan said that it had been drafted "so that it focuses only on those who would transgress the bounds of decency; not those who would exercise their legitimate right of dissent. This carefully drawn act recognizes that the revelation of the names of secret agents adds nothing to legitimate public debate over intelligence policy."[81]

GRAND JURY SECRECY

The Fifth Amendment provides that no person shall be charged with "a capital, or otherwise infamous crime, unless on a presentment or indictment of a Grand Jury, except in cases arising in the land or naval forces, or in the Militia, when in actual service in time of War or public danger." The grand jury draws from Anglo-American practice. In England, it served "as a body of accusers sworn to discover and present for trial persons suspected of criminal wrongdoing." In addition, it served "as a protector of citizens against arbitrary and oppressive governmental action."[82] Over time, the grand jury "acquired an independence in England free from control by the Crown or judges."[83]

When the grand jury "deliberates in secret," part of its purpose is to protect citizens "against unfounded criminal prosecutions."[84] Several justifications are offered to support Rule 6(e) for grand jury secrecy, including the need to (1) prevent the escape of those who might be indicted, (2) promote "the utmost freedom" to the grand jury in its deliberations, (3) encourage witnesses to disclose information about the commission of crimes, and (4) "protect [an] innocent accused who is exonerated from disclosure of the fact that he has

---

77. Id. See 50 U.S.C. §421(a)–(c).
78. 127 Cong. Rec. 21760–61 (1981).
79. 128 Cong. Rec. 2467–87, 2575–95, 4110–26, 4279–99, 4490–4505, 4673–82 (1982).
80. Id. at 4682.
81. Public Papers of the Presidents, 1982, I, 807.
82. United States v. Calandra, 414 U.S. 338, 343 (1973).
83. Costello v. United States, 350 U.S. 359, 362 (1956).
84. United States v. Calandra, 424 U.S. at 343.

been under investigation, and from the expense of standing trial where there was no probability of guilt."[85] Through this system of grand jury secrecy, persons accused but exonerated "will not be held up to public ridicule."[86]

In a grand jury, not less than sixteen nor more than twenty-three citizens meet in closed sessions to decide whether to indict someone of a federal crime. In the room are attorneys for the government, the witness being questioned, interpreters when needed, a stenographer or operator of a recording device, and the jurors. Rule 6(e) provides that a grand juror, an interpreter, a stenographer, an operator of a recording device, a typist who transcribes recorded testimony, an attorney for the government, or any person to whom disclosure is made "shall not disclose matters occurring before the grand jury," except as provided by the rules. No obligation of secrecy may be imposed on any person except in accordance with this rule. A knowing violation of Rule 6(e) may be punished as a contempt of court.[87]

There are several exceptions to the rule of secrecy. Other than its deliberations and the vote of any grand juror, disclosure may be made to a government attorney for use in the performance of that attorney's duty, and also to government personnel deemed necessary by a government attorney to assist in the enforcement of federal criminal law. The rule on grand jury secrecy does not apply to witnesses. They may leave the courtroom and talk to the press about the questions asked and the responses they gave.

Part of the purpose of grand jury secrecy is to protect the names of innocent individuals discussed during the proceedings. The broad scope offered to grand jury investigations can be abused by the government to undermine the independence of private organizations actively engaged in challenging federal power. A recent example is described next.

On November 20, 2006, a U.S. Attorney for the Southern District of New York issued a grand jury subpoena to the American Civil Liberties Union, commanding it to bring to the government a document marked "Secret," dated December 20, 2005, and with the heading "Information Paper." It had been given to the ACLU on or about October 23, 2006. The subpoena requested "[a]ny and all copies" of the document.[88]

---

85. United States v. Rose, 215 F.2d 617, 628–29 (3d Cir. 1954). See also United States v. Sells Engineering, 463 U.S. 418, 424 (1983).

86. Douglas Oil Co. v. Petrol Stops Northwest, 441 U.S. 211, 219 (1979).

87. 18 U.S.C. app. Rule 6(e) (2000). See Richard M. Calkins, "Grand Jury Secrecy," 63 Mich. L. Rev. 455 (1965).

88. Grand Jury Subpoena 0108, subpoena to the American Civil Liberties Union, signed by U.S. Attorney Michael J. Garcia and Assistant U.S. Attorney Jennifer G. Rodgers, Southern District of New York, November 20, 2006.

The ACLU objected that it is beyond the power of a grand jury to subpoena "any and all copies" of a document and that the subpoena was unreasonable and oppressive and violated the organization's First Amendment rights. Neither the ACLU nor any of its employees were targets of a grand jury investigation.[89] Three days later the ACLU issued a more detailed legal analysis, pointing out that the subpoena had no evidentiary or investigatory function but was used "for the purpose of suppressing information."[90] When the ACLU asked the government for its authority to request the document, the Assistant U.S. Attorney identified 18 U.S.C. §§ 793 and 798, relating to espionage.[91] ACLU noted that when parties respond to grand jury subpoenas for documents, they "have the right to make and retain copies, and for various compelling reasons, it is standard to do so."[92] Moreover, the government already had a copy of the document and knew how and when it was transmitted to the ACLU.[93] The ACLU described the subpoena as "solely an improper confiscatory, information-suppressive" effort.[94]

On December 11, 2006, District Judge Jed S. Rakoff met with the parties in a closed courtroom. Assistant U.S. Attorney Jennifer Rodgers expressed concern that any public disclosure of the dispute "would violate the secrecy rules of the grand jury" and any public discussion "would potentially be detrimental to that [grand jury] investigation."[95] Judge Rakoff asked her on what authority a grand jury subpoena would be used for this purpose. She replied that "[o]bviously there is evidentiary value in getting from the ACLU at least one copy of this document."[96]

Her statement conflicted with the language of the subpoena, which commanded "any and all copies." Moreover, the government already had a copy of the document. Rodgers continued: "there is a legitimate purpose in the grand jury seeking all copies from the ACLU. For example, we can't know at

---

89. Declaration of Joshua Dratel in Support of American Civil Liberties Union's Order to Show Cause. In re Grand Jury Subpoena Served on the American Civil Liberties Union, December 8, 2006.

90. Memorandum of Law in Support of the ACLU's Motion to Quash. In re Grand Jury Subpoena Served on the American Civil Liberties Union, December 11, 2006, at 2.

91. Id. at 5.

92. Id. at 10.

93. Id. at 11.

94. Id. at 13.

95. In re Grand Jury Subpoena Served on ACLU, sealed testimony, December 11, 2006, unsealed December 18, 2006 (U.S. District Court, Southern District of New York), at 6–7. The transcript has unnumbered pages.

96. Id. at 10.

this time exactly where the grand jury investigation is . . . to go." If the ACLU complied with the subpoena by giving the government "a thousand photocopies of this classified document that they had in their possession, then it's possible that that would change the focus of the grand jury investigation to look at what they were planning to do with these documents" [i.e., distribute them].[97] ACLU told the court it had one paper copy plus an electronic copy that had been secured.[98] At the close of the hearing, Judge Rakoff ordered that the papers filed in the case remained sealed but said the ACLU was "free to say anything they want."[99]

On December 12, 2006, the government sent a seven-page letter to Judge Rakoff, stating that "there is nothing improper about the subpoena, and nothing imaginary about the grand jury investigation to which it relates."[100] The government explained that the grand jury was investigating "the leaking, to at least the ACLU, of a document classified by the Government," and that the ACLU believed the document "to be of interest to it and to the public."[101] As to the sealed court proceedings, the government insisted that they "'must' be kept secret pursuant to Rule 6 (e) (5) and (6)."[102]

On the following day, Paul McMasters, in an e-mail from the Freedom Forum, reported that the ACLU had asked Judge Rakoff to quash a grand jury subpoena demanding that it turn over "any and all copies" of a December 2005 government document that it possessed. The ACLU regarded the designation of the document as "Secret" to be a "striking, yet typical, example of overclassification."[103] Newspapers picked up the story on December 14, and the *New York Times* and the *Washington Post* published critical editorials the next day.[104]

97. Id. at 11.

98. Id. at 12.

99. Id. at 23.

100. Letter from Assistant U.S. Attorney Jennifer Rodgers to Judge Jed S. Rakoff, U.S. District Court, Southern District of New York, December 12, 2006, at 3 (sealed letter that was unsealed by court order on December 18, 2006).

101. Id. at 5.

102. Id. at 7.

103. E-mail from Paul McMasters, Freedom Forum, to the author, December 13, 2006, 5:54:39 PM.

104. Adam Liptak, "U.S. Subpoena Is Seen as Bid to Stop Leaks," New York Times, December 14, 2006, at A1; Dan Eggen, "U.S. Gets Subpoena to Force ACLU to Return Leaked Memo," December 14, 2006, at A8; "A Gag on Free Speech" (editorial), New York Times, December 15, 2006, at A32; "Pentagon Papers Revisited; The Bush Administration's Ever-expanding War on the First Amendment" (editorial), Washington Post, December 15, 2006, at A34.

On December 18, U.S. Attorney Michael J. Garcia wrote to Judge Rakoff, stating that the government would "withdraw the subpoena in light of changed circumstances, and because we believe that the grand jury can obtain the evidence necessary to its investigation from other independent sources."[105] What were the "changed circumstances"? Concern about agency embarrassment? He said that the government did not object to the court unsealing the December 11, 2006, transcript and the December 12, 2006, letter briefs by the two parties. Furthermore, he reported that the document marked "Secret" had been declassified.[106]

By order of December 18, Judge Rakoff noted that the government had withdrawn its objection to the public disclosure of the letter briefs and the transcript of the oral argument and directed the clerk of the court to make those documents available to the public. He pointed out that the government had declassified the "Secret" document and had withdrawn the subpoena.[107] Newspapers reported the settlement.[108]

The dispute offers a glowing example of a document that should never have been classified at any level, much less "Secret." This is the subject of the 3 1/2-page document: "The Permissibility of Photographing Enemy Prisoners of War and Detainees." The first half describes guidelines for the media when photographing enemy prisoners of war (EPW) and detainees: do not show the face of an EPW or detainee, etc. Obviously that kind of information must be made public to have any effect. The second part of the document provides guidance for U.S. soldiers. They "are prohibited from such photography unless done in an official capacity." For example, detainees "will not be photographed, humiliated or placed in positions with sexual overtones."[109] Why should that be classified? The evident purpose in drafting and disseminating

105. Letter from U.S. Attorney Michael J. Garcia to Judge Jed S. Rakoff, U.S. District Court, Southern District of New York, December 18, 2006, at 1.

106. Id. at 4.

107. Order, In re Grand Jury Subpoena Served on the American Civil Liberties Union, M11–188 (JSR), Judge Jed S. Rakoff, U.S. District Court, Southern District of New York, December 18, 2006.

108. Adam Liptak, "Prosecutors Drop A.C.L.U. Subpoena in Document Fight," New York Times, December 19, 2006, at A22; Robert Barnes, "For ACLU, A Victory in Standoff With U.S.," Washington Post, December 19, 2006, at A9; "Secrecy and Common Sense; For This the Grand Jury Process Was Abused?" (editorial), Washington Post, December 19, 2006, at A28.

109. INFORMATION PAPER, AZFB-JA, SUBJECT: The Permissibility of Photographing Enemy Prisoners of War and Detainees, December 20, 2005, at 3 (classified "SECRET" but declassified by the government on December 15, 2006).

the document was to avoid the type of embarrassing publicity associated with photos of Abu Ghraib prisoners in Iraq. There were no grounds for classifying it originally and none at the time of the confrontation with ACLU.

Several lessons flow from this courtroom drama. First, the executive order issued by President Bush in 2003 directs that "[i]n no case shall information be classified in order to . . . prevent embarrassment to a person, organization, or agency . . . or prevent or delay the release of information that does not require protection in the interest of national security."[110] Either the agency employee responsible for classifying the document was not instructed about presidential policy or that policy was deliberately violated by supervisors. Second, Bush's executive order states that information may be classified "Secret" when "the unauthorized disclosure . . . reasonably could be expected to cause serious damage to the national security that the original classification authority is able to identify or describe."[111] No reasonable argument can be made that the three-page document could do serious damage if made public. Third, the Bush order states that information "shall not be considered for classification unless it concerns" the following eight categories:

(a) military plans, weapons systems, or operations;

(b) foreign government information;

(c) intelligence activities (including special activities), intelligence sources or methods, or cryptology;

(d) foreign relations or foreign activities of the United States, including confidential sources;

(e) scientific, technological, or economic matters relating to the national security, which includes defense against transactional terrorism;

(f) United States Government programs for safeguarding nuclear materials or facilities;

(g) vulnerabilities or capabilities of systems, installations, infrastructures, projects, plans, or protection services relating to the national security, which includes defense against transnational terrorism; or

(h) weapons of mass destruction.[112]

None of those categories apply to the policy of taking photos of detainees or enemy prisoners of war. How could an agency employee mark this document "Secret"? Where was the supervisor? The accountability? Because of the

---

110. 68 Fed. Reg. 15318, Sec. 1.7.
111. Id. at 15315, Sec. 1.2(2).
112. Id. at 15317, Sec. 1.4.

dispute with the ACLU, the miscalculation in this case came to light. How many other errors of classification remain undetected?

WHEN SECRECY BRINGS HARM

Unjustified secrecy can weaken national security. The effort to invade Cuba in 1961, in the Bay of Pigs operation, failed because it was "too secretive, too compartmentalized, no accountability or review, no notes."[113] Extreme CIA secrecy and fragmented records prevented the Joint Chiefs of Staff "from fully auditing the soundness of plans as many changes were made."[114] In analyzing why the Reagan presidency became embroiled in the 1987 Iran-Contra scandal, the Tower Commission Report attributed failures to "the obsession with secrecy." The "concern for preserving the secrecy of the initiative provided an excuse for abandoning sound process. . . . The effect of this informality was that the initiative lacked a formal institutional record."[115] Other examples explored here include the attack on Pearl Harbor, litigation over the Pentagon Papers, the Watergate break-in, and secret presidential documents concerning the terrorist attacks of 9/11.

Pearl Harbor

The U.S. naval base at Pearl Harbor, Hawaii, was caught unprepared on December 7, 1941, suffering heavy losses at the hands of Japanese aircraft. There was, in fact, sufficient warning of the attack and every reason for the base to be on high alert. Because of excessive and dysfunctional secrecy, military and naval leaders failed to warn both the base and the local community. The Roosevelt administration had broken the Japanese diplomatic code and could closely monitor political developments. The system for intercepting and decoding Japanese diplomatic traffic was known as MAGIC. As pointed out by Roberta Wohlstetter in her study on Pearl Harbor: "Never before have we had so complete an intelligence picture of the enemy."[116] Yet few people had access to the information. Those who saw it "had it in hand only momentarily"

113. David M. Abshire, Saving the Reagan Presidency: Trust Is the Coin of the Realm 66 (2005).

114. Id. at 45. See also Richard M. Bissell, Jr., Reflections of a Cold Warrior 152–204 (1996).

115. The Tower Commission Report 68, 69–70 (1987).

116. Roberta Wohlstetter, Pearl Harbor: Warning and Decision 382 (1962).

and therefore had limited time to analyze the material and profit from it.[117] In terms of promotional opportunities, military officers regarded an intelligence assignment as low priority. Any officer "who stayed on the job long enough to become sensitive to signals was an exception, for he would automatically be regarded within the service as being of not very high caliber."[118]

On November 27, 1941, the administration sent this message to military and naval commanders, including those at Pearl Harbor:

> Negotiations with Japan appear to be terminated to all practical purposes with only the barest possibilities that the Japanese Government might come back and offer to continue. Japanese future action unpredictable but hostile action possible at any moment. If hostilities cannot, repeat cannot be avoided the United States desires that Japan commit the first overt act. This policy not, repeat not, be construed as restricting you to a course of action that might jeopardize your defense. Prior to hostile Japanese action you are directed to undertake such reconnaissance and other measures as you deem necessary but these measures should be carried out so as not, repeat not, to alarm civil population or disclose intent. Report measures taken. Should hostilities occur you will carry out the tasks assigned in Rainbow Five [the Army's basic war plan] so far as they pertain to Japan. Limit dissemination of this highly secret information to minimum essential officers.[119]

Part of the message was unambiguous. Diplomatic efforts to avoid war had collapsed and were unlikely to resume. Hostile military action by Japan was possible if not assured. The ambiguous part was how to prepare for an attack. Commanders were instructed to take actions that would not "jeopardize your defense" without "alarm[ing] civil population or disclose intent." Effective preparation required at least informing the naval base so that it would be on high alert. General Walter C. Short in Pearl Harbor assumed the message was intended for General Douglas MacArthur in the Philippines.[120] Short had a choice of three alerts. The first was "defense against sabotage, espionage and subversive activities without any threat from the outside."[121] Clearly that did not apply. Alert Number 2 included everything in Number 1 plus defense against air, surface, and submarine attack. Number 3 was "a defense against an

117. Id. at 186.

118. Id. at 70.

119. Gordon W. Prange, At Dawn We Slept: The Untold Story of Pearl Harbor 402 (1981).

120. Id. at 402–03.

121. Id. at 403.

all-out attack, where everybody moved to their battle stations and carried out their duties as if there was a possible attempt at landing in sight."[122]

To adequately defend the base, Short needed either the second or the third alert. Instead, he picked the first, in part because there had been many anti-sabotage exercises and a continuation of those efforts would not alarm the community. Similarly, if Short chose the second or the third he would run against the directive to confine knowledge to the "minimum essential officers."[123] Yet it was the duty of a military commander "to prepare for the worst and be ready for it at a moment's notice."[124] With the emphasis on secrecy and not alarming the community, Pearl Harbor was at its lowest alert when Japanese planes arrived early on that Sunday morning.

Pentagon Papers

In 1971, the Supreme Court had to decide whether newspapers were constitutionally entitled to publish a Defense Department secret study that revealed a pattern of deceptive administration statements about the war in Vietnam. Daniel Ellsberg, one of several analysts who wrote the study, copied forty-three of the forty-seven volumes and gave them to Senator J. William Fulbright. Ellsberg also shared parts of the study with analysts at the Institute for Policy Studies and turned over most of the material to reporter Neil Sheehan of the *New York Times*.[125] The *Washington Post* gained access to some of the documents.[126] More than a dozen other newspapers began publishing parts of what became known as the Pentagon Papers.[127]

The government asked the courts to block publication of the study and initiated separate lawsuits to prosecute Ellsberg and others for leaking the study. Protecting secrets was not the initial reason within the Nixon administration for taking these legal actions. Nixon and his aides understood that releasing the Pentagon study would have political benefits by damaging the reputations of two Democratic Presidents, John F. Kennedy and Lyndon Johnson.[128] Moreover, Nixon was prepared to release secret documents about the

122. Id. For some reason, Prange put "[*sic*]" after each "their." I removed them.

123. Id. at 404.

124. Id. at 709.

125. John Prados and Margaret Pratt Porter, eds., Inside the Pentagon Papers 7–8 (2004).

126. Id. at 57.

127. Id. at 191.

128. Id. at 91, 92, 96, 103, 114.

alleged involvement of the Kennedy administration in the assassination of the President of South Vietnam, Ngo Dinh Diem.[129]

The government prosecuted Ellsberg and Anthony Russo (who copied the papers with him) with conspiracy to commit an offense or defraud the government, unlawful conversion of public property to personal use, and violation of the Espionage Act.[130] The case floundered when it was learned that the White House had ordered two men to burglarize the office of Ellsberg's psychiatrist to obtain information damaging to Ellsberg.[131] When the district judge handling the case learned of the burglary and the administration's involvement, he dismissed the charges against Ellsberg because of government misconduct.[132]

Regarding publication of the Pentagon Papers, Solicitor General Erwin N. Griswold prepared a brief that advised the Supreme Court that making the study available to the public would pose a "grave and immediate danger to the security of the United States."[133] He understood "immediate" to mean "irreparable" and told the Court that a 1953 case, *United States* v. *Reynolds*, recognized that the President "is uniquely qualified to determine whether the disclosure of 'military and state secrets' would result in danger to the national security."[134]

During oral argument, Griswold identified several items that he said were properly classified as Top Secret.[135] He read language from an executive order that defined Top Secret as information "which requires the highest degree of protection." The Top Secret classification "shall be applied only to that information or material that the defense aspect of which is paramount and the unauthorized disclosure of which could result in exceptionally grave damage to the Nation, such as, leading to a definite break in diplomatic relations affecting the defense of the United States; an armed attack against the United States or its allies; a war or the compromise of military or defense plans, or

129. Id. at 59, 85, 88.

130. Peter Schrag, Test of Loyalty: Daniel Ellsberg and the Rituals of Secret Government 379–81 (1974).

131. Id. at 107–16.

132. Id. at 329–57. See also Daniel Ellsberg, Secrets: A Memoir of Vietnam and the Pentagon Papers (2002); Geoffrey R. Stone, Perilous Times: Free Speech in Wartime 514–15 (2004).

133. 71 Landmark Briefs and Arguments of the Supreme Court of the United States: Constitutional Law 127 (1975).

134. Id. at 129, 139.

135. Id. at 221.

intelligence operations; or scientific or technological developments vital to the national defense."[136] Releasing the study to the public, Griswold warned, "would be of extraordinary seriousness to the security of the United States."[137] Publication "will affect lives. It will affect the process of the termination of the war. It will affect the process of recovering prisoners of war."[138] Divided 6 to 3, the Court decided that the government had failed to meet the heavy burden needed to place prior restraint on publication.[139]

In a speech in 1984, Griswold described how he had tried to identify items in the Pentagon study that, if disclosed, would be a "real threat" to U.S. security. The study contained seven million words. He estimated that if one read the volumes "at a pretty rapid rate of speed, it would take seven weeks—and I had a few hours."[140] To prepare for the case, he asked three people from the Defense Department, the State Department, and the National Security Agency to tell him "what are the things in this which are really bad." They picked forty-two items. Griswold reviewed their selections, "scanning—I couldn't read everything—and I picked out eleven of the forty-two and I waived everything else."[141]

Years later, in an op-ed piece for the *Washington Post*, after the volumes had been made public, Griswold said that he had "never seen any trace of a threat to the national security from the publication. Indeed, I have never seen it even suggested that there was such an actual threat."[142] He said that anyone with experience with classified documents in the federal government becomes aware "that there is massive overclassification and that the principal concern of the classifiers is not with national security, but rather with governmental embarrassment of one sort or another."[143]

Nixon aide H. R. Haldeman believed that publication of the Pentagon Papers would be damaging, but his assessment had nothing to do with national

---

136. Id. at 229.

137. Id. at 221.

138. Id. at 228.

139. New York Times Co. v. United States, 403 U.S. 713 (1971).

140. Erwin N. Griswold, "The Pentagon Papers Case: A Personal Footnote," Yearbook 1984, Supreme Court Historical Society, at 115.

141. Id. at 116.

142. Erwin N. Griswold, "Secrets Not Worth Keeping," Washington Post, February 15, 1989, at A25.

143. Id. For the text of this op-ed, see Louis Fisher and David Gray Adler, American Constitutional Law 278–79 (7th ed. 2007). See also Eleanor Randolph, "Ex-Solicitor General Shifts View of 'Pentagon Papers,'" Washington Post, February 16, 1989, at A52.

security. He worried that the study would undermine the credibility of the government and the President. The public would conclude: "You can't trust the government; you can't believe what they say; and you can't rely on their judgment; and the implicit infallibility of presidents, which has been an accepted thing in America, is badly hurt by this, because it shows that people do things the President wants to do even though it's wrong, and the President can be wrong."[144] Part of the motivation for elevating the Pentagon study to national security status and classifying it as Top Secret was to conceal the fact that White House aides act wrongly and illegally and that Presidents make mistakes.

Some studies conclude that the Pentagon Papers did contain "real secrets" harmful to the nation if published. To Whitney North Seymour, Jr., lead counsel for the government in the Pentagon Papers case in New York, a "large number of the documents posed immediate threats to United States military operations and diplomatic relations."[145] His judgment relied on David Rudenstine's book, *The Day the Presses Stopped*, published in 1996. Rudenstine, however, did not identify particular documents and demonstrate how their publication harmed the United States. His views were tentative and speculative. One document "alleged" injury, another "potentially threatened important national security interests," some "would likely" close up diplomatic channels, while others "might" reduce the rate of American troop withdrawals from Vietnam.[146] Rudenstine stated, quite cautiously: "it now appears that the Pentagon Papers did contain some information that could have inflicted some injury—at least to a degree that makes the concerns of national security officials understandable—if disclosed, which it was not."[147] That is, some of the documents relating to diplomatic matters might have been damaging to national security, but Ellsberg chose not to release them. At the end of the book, Rudenstine appears to find no harm done: "There is no evidence that the newspapers' publication of the Pentagon Papers, followed by the three books during the summer and fall of 1971, harmed U.S. military, defense, intelligence, or international affairs interests."[148]

144. H. R. Haldeman to President Nixon, June 14, 1971, 3:09 P.M. meeting; http:www .gwu.edu/~nsarchiv/NSAEBB/NSAEBB48/.

145. Whitney North Seymour, Jr., "At Last, the Truth Is Out," 19 Cardozo L. Rev. 1359, 1359 (1998).

146. David Rudenstine, The Day the Presses Stopped: A History of the Pentagon Papers Case 8–9 (1996).

147. Id. at 9. See also 84–87, 195–201, 218–24, 267–72, 326–29.

148. Id. at 327.

The Watergate Tapes

The experience with the Pentagon Papers led directly to a disaster for the Nixon administration. To prevent the kind of leaks that occurred with the Pentagon study, President Nixon created a "Plumbers Unit." In June 1972, five people were arrested while trying to burglarize the headquarters of the National Democratic Committee at the Watergate complex in Washington, D.C. Investigation disclosed that others were involved and they were connected with the Republican Committee to Re-elect the President (CRP, or CREEP). In August, President Nixon offered advice that he and others should have taken: "What really hurts in matters of this sort is not the fact that they occur, because overzealous people in campaigns do things that are wrong. What really hurts is if you try to cover it up."[149]

Special Prosecutor Archibald Cox was appointed to conduct an independent investigation into what became known as the Watergate affair. Simultaneously, House and Senate committees began their own inquiries. A Senate hearing disclosed to the public that listening and recording devices had been placed in the Oval Office and other locations occupied by the President.[150] Congress and the judiciary sought access to those tapes to determine whether there had been perjury or obstruction of justice by executive officials. Nixon argued that the constitutional doctrine of executive privilege enabled him to withhold information from judicial and legislative probes. He insisted that he would personally decide what documents could be released and how much they had to be edited.[151]

On July 23, 1973, Nixon received a subpoena directing him to turn over to a federal grand jury the tape recordings of eight specifically identified meetings and one specifically identified phone conversation that had taken place in his office regarding the Watergate break-in. The government's brief opposed the subpoena, arguing that in the exercise of his discretion to claim executive privilege the President "is answerable to the nation but not to the courts."[152] The doctrine of separation of powers, said the brief, prevented the judiciary from compelling the President "to produce information that he has determined it is

---

149. Public Papers of the Presidents, 1972, at 828.

150. Presidential Campaign Activities of 1972: Senate Resolution 60, hearings before the Select Committee on Presidential Campaign Activities, United States Senate, 93d Cong., 1st Sess. 2073 (1973).

151. John R. Labovitz, Presidential Impeachment 201–06 (1978).

152. "Separation of Powers and Executive Privilege: The Watergate Briefs," 88 Pol. Sci. Q. 582, 586–87 (1973).

not in the public interest to disclose."[153] When the tape recordings were finally released, their content had nothing to do with the public interest. They had been withheld to conceal criminal activity. The tapes revealed unmistakable evidence of obstruction of justice, such as Nixon's remarks at a March 22, 1973, meeting: "And, uh, for that reason, I am perfectly willing to—I don't give a shit what happens. I want you to stonewall it, let them plead the Fifth Amendment, cover-up or anything else, if it'll save the plan."[154] The plan was to allow Nixon to remain in office.

President Nixon lost his case in the Supreme Court, which held that in matters of criminal prosecution the decision to release documents is one for the courts, not the President.[155] In unnecessary and unfortunate dicta, Chief Justice Warren Burger, writing for the Court, remarked: "Absent a claim of need to protect military, diplomatic, or sensitive national security secrets," the assertion of executive privilege had to give way to the need for information of defendants in court. There was no need for the Court to mention anything about military or national security secrets. Nixon had not made that claim. But suppose he had, using that ground to withhold materials from the courts and Congress. How could that assertion deny defendants information they needed in a criminal trial? As it turned out, the only secrets at issue related to criminal acts by the administration. The tapes that were finally released disclosed that Nixon had agreed to use the CIA to put a halt to FBI investigations.[156] Nixon recognized that a House vote for impeachment "is, as a practical matter, virtually a foregone conclusion"[157] and announced his resignation.

PDB of August 6, 2001

Secrecy and erroneous classifications can damage national security. This recurrent problem cast a shadow over the preparedness of the United States for the 9/11 terrorist attacks. On August 6, 2001, President Bush received a Presidential Daily Briefing (PDB) entitled "Bin Laden Determined to Strike in US." PDBs are so secret that only a select group of executive officials are authorized to see them. They are not shared with members of Congress, even those who

153. Id. at 587.
154. John J. Sirica, To Set the Record Straight 162 (1979).
155. United States v. Nixon, 418 U.S. 683 (1974).
156. H. Rept. No. 93–1305, 93d Cong., 2d Sess. 53 (1974).
157. Public Papers of the Presidents, 1974, at 622.

serve on the Intelligence Committees. This particular PDB was declassified on April 10, 2004, and released to the 9/11 Commission.

The text begins: "Clandestine, foreign government, and media reports indicate bin Ladin since 1997 has wanted to conduct terrorist attacks in the US. Bin Ladin implied in US television interviews in 1997 and 1998 that his followers would follow the example of World Trade Center bomber Ramzi Yousef and 'bring the fighting to America.'" The text reported that Bin Ladin "wanted to hijack a US aircraft" to gain the release of "Blind Shaykh" 'Umar 'Abd al-Rahman "and other US-held extremists." FBI information "indicates patterns of suspicious activity in this country consistent with preparations for hijackings or other types of attacks, including recent surveillance of federal buildings in New York."[158]

After public release of this document, the White House prepared a "Fact Sheet" stating that the PDB "did not warn of the 9/11 attacks. Although the PDB referred to the possibility of hijackings, it did not discuss the possible use of planes as weapons."[159] Even if the PDB did not predict that planes would be flown into the World Trade Center and the Pentagon, the knowledge that al Qaeda was planning attacks in the United States by using aircraft was of public importance. Had U.S. airlines and airports been alerted, it might have done some good. It appeared to have had little value kept secret.

The 9/11 Commission asked National Security Adviser Condoleezza Rice to testify. White House Counsel Alberto Gonzales, in a letter dated March 25, 2004, explained that she could not testify in public because "the principles underlying the Constitutional separation of powers [are] at stake here." In order for Presidents to receive "the best and most candid advice from their White House staff on counterterrorism and other national security issues, it is important that their advisers not be compelled to testify publicly before congressional bodies such as the Commission." He did not explain why Rice and previous National Security Advisers could regularly appear on national television, be asked questions and answer them, and not have those public events undermine presidential prerogatives. Moreover, Cabinet heads testify before congressional committees and can always respond to a question by saying that the matter involved a confidential discussion with the President.[160]

---

158. The 9/11 Investigations: Staff Reports of the 9/11 Commission (2004), Appendix D.

159. Office of the Press Secretary, White House, "Fact Sheet: The August 6, 2001 PDB," April 10, 2004, at 1; http://www.fas.org/irp/news/2004/04/who41004.html.

160. Louis Fisher, "Talking About Secrets," Legal Times, April 19, 2004, at 67.

When Rice appeared on "60 Minutes" on March 28, 2004, she told Ed Bradley that "I'm not going to say anything in private that I wouldn't say in public. I'm legally bound to tell the truth, I'm morally bound to tell the truth." Her statement seemed to remove any principled objection to public testimony before congressional committees or the 9/11 Commission.[161] If she was bound to tell the truth on national television, she could have done the same before congressional committees and the 9/11 Commission. Five days after Gonzales blocked her appearance, the administration folded. On March 30, Gonzales wrote to the commission to say that President Bush had agreed to allow Rice to testify in public and under oath. A few conditions were attached. This agreement reflected not lofty and abstract principles of separation of powers but, as Gonzales put it, "a matter of comity."[162]

Rice's testimony on April 8 before the commission sparked intense interest in the August 6, 2001, PDB. Initially the administration refused to release the document to the commission. Over a period of time, it gave access to four commissioners. At the hearing, Rice discussed the briefing paper, recalled its title, and dismissed its importance: "It did not warn of attacks inside the United States. It was historical information based on old reporting. There was no new threat information. And it did not, in fact, warn of any coming attacks inside the United States."[163] Further: "there was nothing in this memo that suggested that an attack was coming on New York or Washington, D.C. There was nothing in this memo as to time, place, how or where.... there was nothing actionable in this."[164]

Under pressure from the commission and the public, the administration agreed on April 10 to release the PDB, redacting only the names of foreign intelligence services that supplied some of the information. Although the text of the document provides none of the details that Rice mentioned, regarding time, place, how, or where, the briefing paper warned that (1) Bin Laden was determined to strike in the United States, (2) he wanted to follow the example of the 1993 World Trade Center bombing, (3) al Qaeda members resided in the United States and maintained a support structure that could aid in these attacks, (4) Bin Laden wanted to hijack a U.S. aircraft to gain the release of U.S.-held terrorists, and (5) there was suspicious activity in the United States suggesting a preparation for hijackings "or other types of attacks, including

161. Id.
162. Id.
163. The 9/11 Investigations: Staff Reports of the 9/11 Commission 225 (2004).
164. Id. at 227.

recent surveillance of federal buildings in New York."[165] That information was specific enough to put airports on alert. Why was it merely "historical information" to Rice and the administration? If the administration had decided that the PDB was of little value, why was it classified and kept from Congress, airlines, and airports, where it might have done some good?

Subsequent chapters turn to patterns in U.S. history where external and internal threats single out "undesirable" groups for persecution and prosecution. Tension builds between public officials intent on maintaining control and private citizens determined to participate in their own government. In these times of crisis, or perceived crisis, the constitutional system of checks and balances gives way to centralized authority and arbitrary actions, injurious not only to the individuals receiving the abuse but to the nation and its constitutional values.

165. Id.

CHAPTER 3

Democratic Growing Pains, 1789–1865

After 9/11, traditional rights and procedural safeguards were withheld from individuals who seemed to fit certain classifications: Muslim, Arab, Arab-American, Middle Eastern, alien, suspected terrorist, or "enemy combatant." In times of national crisis, fear, anger, and bias swell in power to inflict personal, institutional, and constitutional damage. The customary acceptance or tolerance of a single individual disappears once the person slides into an abstract, ill-defined, and poorly understood category. Group hate seems easier and more venomous than disliking a single individual. It is more passionate, more irrational, less in need of informed personal judgment. Ignorance helps rationalize injustice and inhuman treatment.

The punishments meted out after 9/11 by federal officials against innocent individuals were not America's first experience with group prejudice. It has happened before. The President, through his exercise of what he considers to be his Commander in Chief powers, coupled with the formidable powers of the law-enforcement community, is positioned to act quickly and decisively against targeted, disfavored groups. What checks exist? Lawmakers need to think and act independently in exercising checks and balances. Judges must insist on fair procedures and an opportunity for self-defense. The first few decades of national government tested the country's commitment to democracy. Repeatedly, executive power was used arbitrarily to punish persons who found themselves in an unpopular and isolated camp. Individual guilt meant nothing; group blame was everything.

GROUP INTOLERANCE

When government authority is challenged, public officials typically turn against groups that seem out of step with the majority. The foreign born are easy prey. So are individuals who think and act independently, who do not "fit in." Why not simply suppress or remove them? Eliminating one group may bring greater harmony to the social order. In his Federalist No. 10 essay, James Madison prepared an exceedingly careful and thoughtful analysis to promote tolerance and acceptance. He concluded that in a democratic society "factions" are entitled to the full range of constitutional liberties and can be held in check not by suppression or extinction but by the regular political process.

Madison's Theories

By faction, Madison meant a number of citizens "united and actuated by some common impulse of passion, or of interest, adverse to the rights of other citizens, or to the permanent and aggregate interests of the community."[1] He first reviewed the tendency of popular governments "to break and control the violence of faction."[2] What remedies were available? He identified two methods: "the one, by removing its causes; the other, by controlling its effects." How does one remove the causes? One way is to destroy "the liberty which is essential to its existence." The other: give "to every citizen the same opinions, the same passions, and the same interests."[3]

For Madison, the idea of eliminating factions by destroying liberty "was worse than the disease." Liberty is to faction as "air is to fire, an ailment without which it instantly expires." A democratic community is designed to encourage liberty. Abolishing liberty to eliminate factions is like abolishing air to eliminate the threat of fire. It eliminates both fire and life. Turning to the second method, Madison said it was "as impracticable as the first would be unwise." As long as individuals are free to exercise their minds, "different opinions will be formed." The first object of government is to protect what he called "the faculties of men, from which the rights of property originate." By protecting different and unequal faculties, individuals will have different opinions and produce different interests and political parties. Madison explained the enduring quality of factions:

> The latent causes of faction are thus sown in the nature of man; and we see them everywhere brought into different degrees of activity, according to the different circumstances of civil society. A zeal for different opinions concerning religion, concerning government, and many other points, as well of speculation as of practice; an attachment to different leaders ambitiously contending for preeminence and power; or to persons of other descriptions whose fortunes have been interesting to the human passions, have, in turn, divided mankind into parties, inflamed them with mutual animosity, and rendered them much more

1. The Federalist 130 (Benjamin F. Wright ed., 2002 ed.).
2. Id. at 129.
3. Id. at 130.

disposed to vex and oppress each other than to co-operate for their common good. So strong is this propensity of mankind to fall into mutual animosities, that where no substantial occasion presents itself, the most frivolous and fanciful distinctions have been sufficient to kindle their unfriendly passions and excite their most violent conflicts.[4]

Should political leaders try to control passions and animosities? Madison saw few grounds for optimism. "It is in vain to say that enlightened statesmen will be able to adjust these clashing interests, and render them all subservient to the public good. Enlightened statesmen will not always be at the helm. Nor, in many cases, can such an adjustment be made at all without taking into view indirect and remote considerations, which will rarely prevail over the immediate interest which one party may find in disregarding the rights of another or the good of the whole."[5] A democratic republic could not, and should not, hope to eliminate the causes of faction. Whatever relief might be available depended on controlling the effects of factions.

If a faction was less than a majority, Madison said it could be controlled by "the republican principle, which enables the majority to defeat its sinister views by regular vote." What if the faction was a majority? In a pure democracy with a small number of citizens, there appeared to be no cure for majority abuse. Madison looked to two safeguards. One was the form of government; the other its size. Instead of functioning under a pure democracy, a republic offered some hope because popular passions would be filtered through the elected representatives of a legislative branch. In a republic, the views of the citizens are passed through elected officials, "whose wisdom may best discern the true interest of their country, and whose patriotism and love of justice will be least likely to sacrifice it to temporary or partial considerations."

The other remedy for factions was to increase the size of a republic. Extend the territory of a republic "and you take in a greater variety of parties and interests; you make it less probable that a majority of the whole will have a common motive to invade the rights of other citizens; or if such a common motive exists, it will be more difficult for all who feel it to discover their own strength, and to act in unison with each other." Dividing a large republic into separate states adds further protection. "The influence of factious leaders may kindle a flame within their particular States, but will be unable to spread a general conflagration through the other States."[6] A religious sect,

4. Id. at 131.
5. Id. at 132.
6. Id. at 136.

having gained overwhelming influence in one region, is likely to be checked by religious denominations in other areas. The greater the number of sects, the greater the chance that harmful designs by one faction will be blocked and neutralized by others.

Madison anticipated a system of self-correction to minimize the risk of one group seriously damaging the national interest. His theory would be tested almost immediately in the young republic. Individuals of different persuasions gained political power and pressed their agendas on others. These conflicts regularly pitted individual liberties against government authority, eventually culminating in the repressive Alien and Sedition Acts of 1798. Factions critical of government were subjected to punishment, suppression, and expulsion. Those issues surfaced even earlier when Congress passed legislation for a militia in 1792, President George Washington released his Neutrality Proclamation in 1793, and the Whiskey Rebellion took shape a year later.

Militias and Individual Freedom

In 1792, Congress debated a bill to establish a uniform militia drawn from the various states.[7] Some members of the House expressed concern about the power of a militia. It would have the capacity to suppress insurrections and repel invasions but also to turn itself against elements of the community. William Vans Murray warned: "Of all the offices of politics, the most irksome and delicate is that by which a Legislature directs the military forces of the community to its own conservation, as it presupposes situations in which resistance to the Government itself is contemplated. Hence, we see a jealousy even in England of the use of the sword, when drawn against any part of the community."[8] Similarly, John Page expressed apprehension about a too ready use of the militia. He thought citizens would not resist "mild and equitable" laws, but that "if Congress should be so infatuated as to enact those of a contrary nature, I hope they will be repealed, and not enforced by martial law."[9]

To curb unwarranted and unjustified use of the militia, Abraham Baldwin offered an amendment to provide that information of any insurrection shall be communicated to the President by either a Justice of the Supreme Court or by a district judge. A judicial check would operate on executive power. His

7. Annals of Cong., 2d Cong., 1st–2d Sess. 418–23, 430, 431, 433, 435, 552–55, 574–80, 701–02, 798–811.

8. Id. at 554.

9. Id. at 574.

motion was agreed to.[10] As enacted, the militia bill provided that whenever the United States shall be invaded, or be "in imminent danger of invasion from any foreign nation or Indian tribe," the President was authorized to call forth such number of the militia as he may judge necessary to repel the invasion. In case of an insurrection in any state against the government, the President was authorized, on application of the state legislature or of the governor when the legislature was unable to sit, to call forth the militia to suppress the insurrection.[11] Whenever the laws of the United States were opposed or the execution of the laws obstructed, "by combinations too powerful to be suppressed by the ordinary course of judicial proceedings," a Supreme Court Justice or district judge must notify the President. Only after the exercise of independent judicial determination could the President order the militia. Moreover, the statute specified that these emergency powers were available to the President only "if the legislature of the United States be not in session."[12]

Neutrality Proclamation

President Washington learned a lesson about the limit of executive power when he issued what has come to be known as the Neutrality Proclamation of 1793, warning Americans to avoid any involvement in the war between France and England. He instructed law officers to prosecute all persons who violated the proclamation. Jurors balked at this presidential initiative to punish people. Insisting that criminal law required congressional action through the regular legislative process, jurors were determined to acquit individuals charged with acting contrary to a presidential proclamation. In England, legally binding proclamations issued by the King were nailed on trees, but America was committed to self-government and consciously rejected monarchical powers.[13] Unable to cite statutory support to justify its actions in court, the government dropped other prosecutions.[14] Washington presented the matter to lawmakers, stating

10. Id. at 577.

11. 1 Stat. 264, sec. 1 (1792).

12. Id., sec. 2. For further legislation on the militia, see 1 Stat. 271 (1792). The judicial check was removed three years later: 1 Stat. 424 (1795). For a good analysis of these early militia statutes, see Stephen I. Vladeck, "Emergency Power and the Militia Acts," 114 Yale L. J. 149 (2004).

13. Francis Wharton, State Trials of the United States during the Administrations of Washington and Adams 84–85, 88 (1849); Henfield's Case, 11 F. Cas. 1099 (C.C. Pa. 1793) (No. 6,360).

14. 2 John Marshall, The Life of George Washington 273 (1832).

that it rested with "the wisdom of Congress to correct, improve, or enforce" the policy his proclamation had established.[15] Congress passed the Neutrality Act of 1794, providing the administration the legal authority it needed to prosecute and punish individuals who violated national policy. The independent spirit of free citizens would frustrate President Washington on other occasions.

Whiskey Rebellion

The Militia Act of 1792 was invoked two years later in response to the Whiskey Rebellion. On March 3, 1791, Congress enacted a federal excise tax on spirits distilled within the United States. Excise laws had a long history of inflaming the public and provoking protests.[16] To American farmers, converting grain into alcohol "was considered to be as clear a national right as to convert grain into flour."[17] Beginning in September 1791, excisemen who attempted to collect revenue were seized, tarred and feathered, and stripped of horse and money.[18] President Washington recognized the checkered history of excise taxes. An excise law was "of odious character with the people; partial in its operation; unproductive unless enforced by arbitrary and vexatious means; and committing the authority of the Government in parts where resistance is most probable, and coercion least practicable."[19]

In September 1792, Washington learned of citizens in western Pennsylvania who had jeered at federal officers "appointed to collect the duties on distilled spirits agreeably thereto."[20] Insults escalated to violence, the exchange of rifle shots between government agents and local militia, several deaths, the capture of a federal marshal, and the destruction of property by fire.[21]

Washington understood that the resistance affected money needed for the country, which was "much to be regretted."[22] He stood ready to "exert all the legal powers with which the Executive is invested, to check so daring and

15. Annals of Cong., 3d Cong., 1–2 Sess. 11 (1793).

16. Townsend Ward, "The Insurrection of the Year 1794, in the Western Counties of Pennsylvania," 6 Pa. Hist. Soc. Memoirs 119, 119–27 (1858).

17. Id. at 126.

18. Id. at 130–31.

19. 32 The Writings of George Washington 96 (John C. Fitzpatrick, ed. 1939). Letter to Secretary of the Treasury Alexander Hamilton.

20. Id. at 143. Letter to Secretary of the Treasury Hamilton.

21. Thomas P. Slaughter, The Whiskey Rebellion 179–81 (1986); Ward, "The Insurrection of the Year 1794," at 138–39, 166–71.

22. 32 The Writings of George Washington 143.

unwarrantable a spirit."[23] Concerned that the rebellion might spread to other states, he issued a proclamation on September 15, 1792, warning those who resisted the law that it was his duty "to take care that the laws be faithfully executed." He directed all courts, magistrates, and officers to see that the laws were obeyed and the public peace preserved.[24]

On August 7, 1794, Washington issued another proclamation, itemizing a long list of abuses against federal agents and stating that he had put into effect the procedures of the Militia Act. He referred to "said combinations" proceeding in a manner "subversive equally of the just authority of the government and of the rights of individuals," and holding "certain irregular meetings" for the purpose of opposing the tax.[25] He gave Justice James Wilson the evidence needed to verify the rebellion and received from Wilson a certification that ordinary legal means were insufficient to execute national law.[26] Washington called upon the militias of four states to put down the rebellion.[27] District Judge Richard Peters joined Treasury Secretary Alexander Hamilton and District Attorney William Rawle in accompanying the troops. Hamilton and Rawle conducted hearings before Judge Peters to identify the instigators, who were later tried in Philadelphia.[28]

"Democratic Societies"

In his response to the Whiskey Rebellion, President Washington had already gone on record by objecting to citizens holding "certain irregular meetings" to express their disagreement with government policies. Political clubs had indeed emerged, supported by opposition newspapers that helped sharpen rhetoric and crystallize grievances.[29] In a letter of September 25, 1794, Washington concluded that the Whiskey Rebellion "may be considered as the first *ripe fruit* of the Democratic Societies."[30] He directed his ire at those who joined these groups and participated in their discussions: "can any thing be more absurd,

---

23. Id. at 144.

24. 1 A Compilation of the Messages and Papers of the Presidents 116–17 (James D. Richardson ed.) (hereafter "Richardson").

25. Id. at 150.

26. Id. at 152.

27. Id. at 153.

28. Homer Cummings and Carl McFarland, Federal Justice 43–45 (1937).

29. Slaughter, The Whiskey Rebellion, at 163–65, 194–95.

30. 33 The Writings of George Washington 506 (emphasis in original). Letter to Burges Hall.

more arrogant, or more pernicious to the peace of Society, than for self created bodies, forming themselves into *permanent* Censors, and under the shade
of Night in a conclave," offering judgments that statutes passed by Congress
were mischievous or unconstitutional.[31]

He emphasized "permanent" to distinguish the activities of these Democratic Societies from "the right of the people to meet occasionally, to petition
for, or to remonstrate against, any Act of the Legislature &ca."[32] Washington
deplored the activities of Democratic Societies "endeavouring to destroy all
confidence in the Administration, by arraigning all its acts, without knowing on what ground, or with what information it proceeds and this without
regard to decency or truth."[33] He sought to "delegitimize them as participants
in the political process."[34]

Writing again on October 8, Washington voiced his contempt for citizens
who met in private organizations to oppose government policy. The "daring
and factious spirit which has arisen (to overturn the laws, and to subvert the
Constitution) ought to be subdued. If this is not done, there is, an end of
and we may bid adieu to all government in this Country, except Mob and
Club Govt. from whence nothing but anarchy and confusion can ensure."[35]
He worried that Edmond Genet, the French diplomat he called a "diabolical
leader," intended "to sow sedition, to poison the minds of the people of this
Country."[36]

On October 16, Washington underscored the threat of Democratic Societies. People would soon understand the ill designs of the leaders of these
self-created societies: "I should be extremely sorry therefore if Mr. [Madison]
from any cause whatsoever should get entangled with them, or their politics."[37]
He believed that these political clubs "will destroy the government of this
Country."[38] Some members of his Cabinet urged prompt and decisive action
to suppress these organizations. Secretary of State Edmund Randolph, on October 11, told Washington that he "never did see an opportunity of destroying

31. Id. (emphasis in original).

32. Id.

33. Id. at 507.

34. Robert M. Chesney, "Democratic-Republican Societies, Subversion, and the Limits
of Legitimate Dissent in the Early Republic," 82 N.C. L. Rev. 1525, 1528 (2004).

35. 33 The Writings of George Washington 523. Letter to Maj. Gen. Daniel Morgan.

36. Id. at 524.

37. 34 The Writings of George Washington 3 (emphasis in original). Letter to Secretary
of State Edmund Randolph.

38. Id.

these self-constituted bodies, until the fruit of their operations was discharged in the insurrection." Randolph counseled: "They may now, I believe, be crushed. The prospect ought not to be lost."[39]

Washington's private correspondence provided the basis for his Sixth Annual Address to Congress, issued on November 19, 1794. He reviewed what he had done to suppress the rebellion in four western counties of Pennsylvania, explaining that the "very forbearance to press prosecutions was misinterpreted into a fear of urging the execution of the laws; and associations of men began to denounce threats against the officers employed." Based on a belief that the government's operation "might be defeated, certain self-created societies assumed the tone of condemnation."[40] In the concluding paragraph of his address, Washington took another slap at the Democratic Societies, urging Congress to unite "to turn the machinations of the wicked to the confirming of our constitution: to enable us at all times to root out internal sedition, and put invasion to flight."[41]

Lawmakers Respond

Washington's sharp rebuke of Democratic Societies provoked impassioned debate in Congress. Thomas Fitzsimons offered a supportive amendment to the House's prepared response to the Sixth Annual Address: "As part of this subject, we cannot withhold our reprobation of the self-created societies, which have risen up in some parts of the Union, misrepresenting the conduct of the Government, and disturbing the operation of the laws, and which, by deceiving and inflaming the ignorant and the weak, may naturally be supposed to have stimulated and urged the insurrection."[42] William Smith warned that if members of the House failed to endorse Washington's views about Democratic Societies, "their silence would be an avowed desertion of the Executive."[43] An extraordinary statement! Any effort by a lawmaker to think independently about a presidential position would amount to desertion. Describing himself as a friend of a free press, Smith asked: "would any one compare a regular town meeting where deliberations were cool and unruffled, to these societies, to the nocturnal meetings of individuals, after they have dined, where they

39. Letter of Edmund Randolph to George Washington, October 11, 1794, George Washington Papers, Series 4, Reel 106, Library of Congress, Manuscript Division.
40. 34 The Writings of George Washington 29.
41. Id. at 37.
42. Annals of Cong., 3d Cong., 1–2 Sess. 899 (1794).
43. Id. at 901.

shut their doors, pass votes in secret, and admit no members into their societies, but those of their own choosing?" Smith reminded his colleagues "that this House has never done much business after dinner."[44]

Several members insisted they had a constitutional right and a personal need to speak their own minds. Was it expected, asked John Nicholas, "that I am to abandon my independence for the sake of the PRESIDENT? He never intended that we should take any such notice of his reference to these societies; but if the popularity of the PRESIDENT has, in the present case, been committed, let those who have hatched this thing, and who brought it forward, answer for the consequences."[45] Josiah Parker spoke in similar fashion. He suspected that Washington, "for whose character and services he felt as much respect and gratitude as any man in America, had been misinformed on this point." For all his admiration for the President, "he was not to give up his opinions for the sake of any man."[46] Parker thought his constituents in Virginia would be repelled by any form of censorship: "They love your Government much, but they love their independence more."[47]

Objecting to the Fitzsimons language, William Giles said that when he saw "the House of Representatives about to erect itself into an office of censorship, he could not sit silent." He trusted that "the fiat of no person in America should ever be taken for truth, implicitly, and without evidence." Noting his respect for President Washington, Giles asked what mischief could come from rebuking such abstractions as "self-created societies." There was not an individual in the country, he said, "who might not come under the charge of being a member of some one or other self-created society. Associations of this kind, religious, political, and philosophical, were to be found in every quarter of the Continent."[48] The Baptists, the Methodists, and the Friends might be called self-created societies. Giles pounded home his message:

> It is out of the way of the Legislature to attempt checking or restraining public opinion. If the self-created societies act contrary to law, they are unprotected, and let the law pursue them. That a man is a member of one of these societies will not protect him from an accusation of treason, if the charge is well founded. If the charge is not well founded, if the societies, in their proceedings, keep within the verge of the law, ... what was to be the sequel? If the House undertake to censure

44. Id. at 902.
45. Id. at 910.
46. Id. at 913.
47. Id. at 914.
48. Id. at 899–900.

particular classes of men, who can tell where they will stop? Perhaps it may be advisable to commence moral philosophers, and compose a new system of ethics for the citizens of America. In that case, there would be many other subjects for censure, as well as the self-created societies.[49]

Giles insisted that members were elected to the House "not for the purpose of passing indiscriminate votes of censure, but to legislate only." If the House adopted Fitzsimons's amendment, it "would only produce recrimination on the part of the societies, and raise them into much more importance than they possibly could have acquired if they had not been distinguished by a vote of censure from that House." Did lawmakers believe that a censure vote, "like the wand of a magician, would lay a spell on these people?"[50] Giles repudiated "all aiming at a restraint on the opinions of private persons."[51] The public "have a right to censure us," he said, and "we have *not* a right to censure them."[52] Toward the end of this lengthy debate, James Madison pulled together a number of themes:

> He conceived it to be a sound principle, that an action innocent in the eye of the law could not be the object of censure to a Legislative body. When the people have formed a Constitution, they retain those rights which they have not expressly delegated. It is a question whether what is thus retained can be legislated upon. Opinions are not the objects of legislation. You animadvert on the abuse of reserved rights: how far will this go? It may extend to the liberty of speech, and of the press. It is in vain to say that this indiscriminate censure is no punishment. If it falls on classes, or individuals, it will be a severe punishment. . . . If we advert to the nature of Republican Government, we shall find that the censorial power is in the people over the Government, and not in the Government over the people.[53]

Nicholas hoped to prevent the damage that would be inflicted by a recorded House vote. President Washington, he said, "knew the business of the House better than to call for any such votes of censure." Nicholas could not agree "to persecution for the sake of opinions." As to what to do about the Democratic Societies, "it was much better to let them alone. They must stand or fall by the general sentiments of the people of America."[54] Gabriel Christie objected to

49. Id. at 900.
50. Id.
51. Id. at 901.
52. Id. at 917 (emphasis in original).
53. Id. at 934.
54. Id. at 904–05.

any sweeping condemnation of Democratic Societies. The one that existed in Baltimore "consists of men whose characters are superior to any censure that might be thrown against them, by the mover of the amendment."[55] Lawmakers who supported the Fitzsimons amendment agreed that the Democratic Society in Baltimore deserved "the greatest respect."[56] Should government, asked Abraham Bedford Venable, "show their imbecility by censuring what we cannot punish? The people have a right to think and a right to speak."[57]

Instead of rebuking "self-created societies," as Fitzsimons originally proposed, the House voted 47 to 45 to delete "self-created."[58] It also rejected an amendment by Giles, who wanted the House language to focus on "combinations of men in the four Western counties of Pennsylvania."[59] Later, the House agreed to a Christie amendment to specify the four western counties of Pennsylvania (initially a tie vote of 46 to 46, after which the Speaker added his vote to the ayes).[60] It then rejected language that "certain self-created societies and combinations of men" in the four western counties, "careless of consequences," helped foment "this daring outrage against social order and the authority of the laws." That motion failed, supported by only nineteen members.[61]

The House finally adopted language about the Whiskey Rebellion, but omitted any reference to "self-created societies" or to societies. One member wanted "societies" inserted, but Nicholas opposed and his amendment "carried by a large majority."[62] The House expressed its concern about "misrepresentations" by individuals "or combinations of men" that might have fomented the rebellion and lamented that the public order had "suffered so flagrant a violation."[63] Thus ended a misguided effort by President Washington and certain lawmakers to single out political societies for censure and upbraid them for expressing opinions about public policy.

The Senate was more supportive of Washington's objection to private clubs that met to discuss political issues. Senators said that the resistance to laws

---

55. Id. at 908.

56. Id. at 909 (see also William Vans Murray, who expressed support for the Fitzsimons amendment at 906–07).

57. Id. at 910.

58. Id. at 914.

59. Id.

60. Id. at 943–44. A William Smith amendment, to insert "countenanced by self-created societies elsewhere," was rejected 42 to 50.

61. Id. at 945.

62. Id.

63. Id.

in the western counties of Pennsylvania "has been increased by the proceed-ings of certain self-created societies relative to the laws and administration of the Government; proceedings, in our apprehension, founded in political er-ror, calculated, if not intended, to disorganize our Government, and which, by inspiring delusive hopes of support, have been influential in misleading our fellow-citizens in the scene of insurrection."[64]

MOVING TOWARD THE ALIEN AND SEDITION ACTS

President Washington continued to harbor distrust about private organiza-tions that met to discuss government matters and attempted to influence public policy. He saw them as unhealthy competitors with the elected and le-gitimate branches of government. His Farewell Address of September 17, 1796, offered this advice: "All obstructions to the execution of the laws, all combina-tions and associations, under whatever plausible character, with the real design to direct, control, counteract, or awe the regular deliberation and action of the constituted authorities, are destructive of this fundamental principle and of fatal tendency."[65] Unlike Madison's acceptance of factions and a belief in self-correcting mechanisms, Washington had no tolerance. These combinations and associations "serve to organize faction; to give it an artificial and extraor-dinary force; to put in the place of the delegated will of the nation the will of a party, often a small but artful and enterprising minority of the community." Public administration became "the mirror of the ill-concerted and incongru-ous projects of faction rather than the organ of consistent and wholesome plans, digested by common counsels and modified by mutual interests."[66] Combinations and associations threatened "to usurp for themselves the reins of government."[67] It would take time to recognize the legitimate and beneficial effects of public participation. Fewer years were needed to understand that government is not the best guardian of liberty.

The congressional debate in 1794 split lawmakers between those who wanted public policy centered in the government and those who extended to citizens every right to meet and discuss the issues of the day. Some members

64. 1 Richardson 160. For a fine analysis of the political clubs forming in the 1790s, see Eugene Perry Link, Democratic-Republican Societies, 1790–1800 (1942).

65. 1 Richardson 209.

66. Id. at 210.

67. Id.

of the House preferred British law and tradition; others admired the principles of the French Revolution. To William Vans Murray, the Democratic Societies endangered America because they were modeled on despotic forms of government in France.[68] All that was missing from these critiques was to name the political society most infamous in France—the Jacobins—and its role in fomenting bloodshed. Giles dismissed this parallel. He worried that if the House denounced Democratic Societies, it would later denounce anti-Democratic Societies.[69] Fisher Ames targeted the Jacobins for rekindling "the fire-brands of sedition" and unchaining "the demon of anarchy."[70] In condemning the Jacobins for "pulling down the old Government," he inconsistently praised the American committees in 1774 and 1775 for being "efficient instruments to pull down the British Government."[71] Passionate rhetoric, in fine display throughout the 1794 debates, found its mark with the Alien and Sedition Acts.

In 1798, tensions mounted for war against France. Public opinion became inflamed after the release of papers about what became known as the XYZ Affair, revealing the disrespect that France had shown to American negotiators.[72] The Federalist Party drafted a series of bills to lengthen the time needed to become a citizen, to deport aliens, and to punish individuals who spoke or wrote what the government interpreted to be seditious statements. The year 1798 shares much in common with the post-9/11 period. On September 20, 2001, in an address to a joint session of Congress, President Bush said: "Every nation, in every region, now has a decision to make: Either you are with us, or you are with the terrorists."[73] Political choices in 1798 seemed similarly stark. The nation's leading newspaper for the Federalist Party, Philadelphia's *Gazette of the United States*, offered this advice: "He that is not for us, is against us."[74] Having watched the horrors of the French Revolution, many in the United States summed up the choices as "anarchy versus order, licentiousness versus authority, the masses versus the classes, and atheism versus religion."[75] Those who bore the brunt of repression in 1798 were the foreign born, both "enemy aliens" and "alien friends." Acting quickly, Congress

68. Annals of Cong., 3d Cong., 1–2 Sess. 906–07.

69. Id. at 917.

70. Id. at 922.

71. Id. at 927.

72. James Morton Smith, Freedom's Fetters: The Alien and Sedition Laws and American Civil Liberties 7–9 (1956).

73. Public Papers of the Presidents, 2001, II, at 1142.

74. Smith, Freedom's Fetters, at 15.

75. Id. at 11.

passed legislation vesting extensive powers and discretionary authority in the President.

Naturalization Bill

Congress acted first by lengthening the time needed for aliens to become a U.S. citizen. Legislation in 1790 had set the period of residence at two years. That waiting period was increased to five years in 1795.[76] Now, in 1798, the time was stretched to fourteen years. The individual would have to declare an intention to become an American citizen at least five years before admission.[77] The 1798 statute further specified: "no alien, who shall be a native, citizen, denizen or subject of any nation or state with whom the United States shall be at war, at the time of his application, shall be then admitted to become a citizen of the United States."[78] Loyalty and good standing did not matter.

House debate began on May 1, 1798. The committee created to consider changes in the naturalization law reported that a longer residence was "essential" and recommended the removal from the country of "all aliens, being males, of the age of fourteen years and upwards," who lived in the United States and were natives or citizens of a country that declared war on the United States, "or shall threaten, attempt, or perpetuate any invasion or predatory incursions upon their territory, as soon as may be after the President of the United States shall make proclamation of such event."[79] The committee recommended lengthening the period of residence from five years to at least ten years, and possibly leaving the bill blank on that issue and filling it in later.[80]

Robert Harper objected that easy citizenship in the past had produced "very great evils" and proposed that "nothing but birth should entitle a man to citizenship in this country."[81] His amendment was ruled out of order. Harrison Gray Otis offered language to prevent an alien, not yet a U.S. citizen, from holding "any office of honor, trust, or profit, under the United States." Harper wanted to add these words to the Otis amendment: "or of voting at the election of any member of the Legislature of the United States, or of any State."[82] Told that his proposal might unconstitutionally interfere with the authority

---

76. 1 Stat. 103 (1790); 1 Stat. 414 (1795).

77. 1 Stat. 566 (1798).

78. Id. at 567, sec. 1.

79. Annals of Cong., 5th Cong., 2–3rd Sess. 1566–67 (1798).

80. Id. at 1567.

81. Id.

82. Id. at 1568.

of states to admit citizens, Harper withdrew the amendment.[83] The Otis proposal, regarding public office, was also withdrawn.[84]

Otis next offered language to permit the removal of aliens who were citizens of a country that had authorized hostilities against the United States.[85] After considerable debate, it was rejected 55 to 27.[86] However, the House adopted language to authorize the removal of aliens who were citizens of a country in a state of declared war against the United States.[87] In the part of the bill left blank, regarding the years of residence required to be a citizen, the House narrowly supported (41 to 40) a motion to insert the number 14.[88]

In addition to the forces of nationalism and xenophobia, the naturalization bill included partisan calculations. It was generally believed that immigrants were more likely to vote for the Republican-Jeffersonian Party.[89] Legislation became "a political maneuver by the Federalists to cut off an increasingly important source of Republican strength."[90] Federalist lawmakers spoke out openly against allowing into the country "hordes of wild Irishmen,"[91] especially because of their "anti-British attitude and their contempt for the party of conservatism and privilege."[92]

Alien Friends

After action on the naturalization bill, Congress turned to two separate bills on aliens, the first known as the Alien Friends Act. The opening section transferred extraordinary powers to the President, making it lawful for him "at any time during the continuance of this act, to *order* all such *aliens* as he shall judge dangerous to the peace and safety of the United States, or shall have reasonable grounds to suspect are concerned in any treasonable or secret machinations against the government thereof, to depart out of the territory of

83. Id. at 1569.

84. Id. at 1571, 1573.

85. Id. at 1573.

86. Id. at 1580.

87. Id. at 1631.

88. Id. at 1776.

89. David P. Currie, The Constitution in Congress: The Federalist Period, 1789–1801, at 254 n. 135 (1997).

90. Smith, Freedom's Fetters, at 23.

91. Id. at 24.

92. Id. at 23.

the United States. . . ."[93] What vague standards: whoever the President decided was dangerous; merely reasonable grounds to suspect; "secret machinations." The statute is referred to as "alien friends" to distinguish it from a bill enacted weeks later that focused on aliens from an enemy state.

Albert Gallatin challenged the need for the legislation. Existing laws, he said, "will reach alien friends if guilty of seditious or treasonable practices, as well as citizens." If those laws were not sufficient, they could be amended. Crimes and punishments, he said, needed to be accurately defined rather than delegated wholesale and carelessly to the President. Persons charged with offenses should "not be left without trial, subject to the arbitrary control of one man only."[94] And why, asked Gallatin, the distinction between aliens and U.S. citizens? Seditious "and turbulent citizens might be as dangerous to the peace of the country, as aliens of a similar description." He conceded that aliens had fewer rights than citizens, but the right of trial by jury under the Fifth and Sixth Amendments extended to *persons*, not solely to citizens.[95]

Those who supported the bill pointed out that the constitutional right to trial applied only to criminal proceedings. Further, the protection of one's borders concerned the sovereign power of any nation to protect itself. To Robert Harper, the President was the only one "possessed of all information which has reference to our foreign relations."[96] Edward Livingston rejected the arguments of Federalists who would allow the President to deport aliens on vague grounds, "individual suspicions, our private fears, our over-heated imaginations."[97] He opposed the decision to concentrate powers—previously left in separate branches—in a single person. The President "alone is empowered to make the law, to fix in his mind what acts, what words, what thoughts or looks, shall constitute the crime contemplated by the bill." The President was "not only authorized to make this law for his own conduct, but to vary it at pleasure, as every gust of passion, every cloud of suspicion, shall agitate or darken his mind."[98] Packing these powers in the President "comes completely within the definition of despotism—an union of Legislative, Executive, and Judicial powers."[99] The previous safeguard of public trial was now "changed into a secret and worse than inquisitorial tribunal. . . . No indictment; no jury;

93. 1 Stat. 570–71 (1798) (emphasis in original).
94. Annals of Cong., 5th Cong., 2–3rd Sess. 1980 (1798).
95. Id. at 1981.
96. Id. at 1998.
97. Id. at 2007.
98. Id. at 2008.
99. Id.

no trial; no public procedure; no statement of the accusation; no examination of the witnesses in its support; no counsel for defense; all is darkness, silence, mystery, and suspicion."[100]

Livingston challenged the argument that aliens could be sent out of the country without trial because the treatment fell short of a criminal offense: "it is said, the bill does not contemplate the punishment of any crime; and therefore the provisions in the Constitution relative to criminal proceedings and Judiciary powers do not apply." The bill referred to actions "dangerous to the peace and safety of the United States" and to "treasonable or secret machinations against the Government thereof." How could such conduct, Livingston asked, not be called a crime?[101] An alien could wait patiently for the expiration of the period that will allow him to become a U.S. citizen, but if someone raised a suspicion about him he could be ordered back to the country that he chose to leave, "whose Government, irritated by his renunciation of its authority, will receive only to punish him."[102]

The Federalists returned fire. John Wilkes Kittera urged passage of the alien friends bill and a strong sedition statute, trusting that the combination would "preserve us from the dangers with which we're threatened from internal enemies." The danger "did not arise from Government having too much power, but from its want of power." France itself, he reminded his colleagues, "removes both alien friends and alien enemies." Deportation "is a right which every man exercises in his own house, by turning out of it, without ceremony, any person whom he thinks dangerous to the peace and welfare of his family." If the alien and sedition bills passed by Congress "be unconstitutional, the Judges will refuse to execute it."[103] For those who believed that the President would not abuse the power granted him, Livingston objected: "Away with that liberty which hangs upon chance! He would disdain to enjoy the liberty which depended upon the will of *one man*, and he should be ashamed of any man who would consent thus to hold it."[104] The bill passed 46 to 40.[105]

In addition to the first section of the Alien Friends Act, transferring unchecked power to the President to deport suspicious aliens, the statute added procedures for notifying the alien about his deportation. If the alien remained within the United States he could be convicted, imprisoned for up to three

100. Id. at 2010–11.
101. Id. at 2011.
102. Id. at 2012.
103. Id. at 2016.
104. Id. at 2021 (emphasis in original).
105. Id. at 2028.

years, and forever barred as a U.S. citizen.[106] An alien could seek from the President a license allowing him to avoid deportation, but the burden of making the case fell entirely on the alien; granting the license was discretionary on the part of the President, and the President could revoke the license "whenever he shall think proper."[107] The statute authorized the President, "whenever he may deem it necessary for the public safety," to remove from the country any alien imprisoned under the provisions of the act. If the alien chose to return without the President's permission, he could be imprisoned upon conviction "so long as, in the opinion of the President, the public safety may require." Presidential action depended on conviction in a court of law.

The final section required every ship commander arriving at an American port to prepare a list of the aliens on board, specifying their names, ages, place of birth, the country from which they came, the nation they belonged to and owed allegiance, their occupation, and a description of the individuals. Failure to do so invited fines, seizure of the ship, and detention of the officers. Circuit and district courts had jurisdiction over the crimes and offenses set forth in the statute. Aliens ordered to be removed could take their goods with them. The statute, enacted on June 25, 1798, took effect for a period of two years.

Alien Enemies

The second alien act had a more limited purpose. It provided that "whenever there shall be a declared war" between the United States and a foreign nation, or "any invasion or predatory incursion shall be perpetrated, attempted, or threatened" against the United States by a foreign nation, the President may make a "public proclamation of the event." At that point "all natives, citizens, denizens, or subjects of the hostile nation," being males age 14 years and up, who resided within the United States and were not naturalized, were subject to removal as alien enemies.[108] There was no need to suspect improper activity. Mere identification with an enemy nation sufficed. The alien would appear before a federal court for a full hearing. If the court found "sufficient cause," it "shall and may" order the alien deported.

Key elements of the Alien Enemies Act survived. In 1918, Congress changed the 1798 language by deleting the provision restricting the section to males.[109]

---

106. 1 Stat. 571, sec. 1 (1798).
107. Id.
108. 1 Stat. 577, sec. 1 (1798).
109. 40 Stat. 531 (1918).

The law today authorizes the President, whenever there is a declared war between the United States and another nation, or a time of "any invasion or
predatory incursion is perpetrated," to issue a proclamation that all "natives,
citizens, denizens, or subjects" of the hostile nation, being 14 years or older,
may be removed as enemy aliens.[110] Federal courts have jurisdiction to hear
the complaint and, with "sufficient cause," order the alien removed.[111]

Sedition Act

The third shift of power to the President came with the Sedition Act. Unlike the two alien bills, the penalties of seditious activity applied to everyone:
aliens and citizens. Fines and sentences awaited whoever wrote or said anything about Congress or the President (1) deemed to be "false, scandalous and
malicious," (2) had the intent to "defame" those political institutions or bring
them into "contempt or disrepute," (3) "excite" any hatred against them, or (4)
"stir up" sedition or act in combination to oppose or resist federal laws or any
presidential act to implement those laws.[112]

The first part of the statute seemed confined to matters "false, scandalous and malicious," but it broadened out to reach utterances intended to "defame" the government, to bring it into "contempt or disrepute," and to excite
the "hatred of the good people." That covers everything. Any criticism of the
government, any misgiving, any question, distrust, or skepticism, could be
grounds for bringing someone into court. Self-government became government against the sovereign people. What was turned aside several years earlier,
during debate on "self-created societies," was now law. People did not censure
government; government censured people.

Persons convicted under this statute were subject to fines not exceeding
$2,000 and imprisonment not exceeding two years. Those prosecuted were
allowed to offer, as part of their defense, "the truth of the matter contained in
the publication charged as a libel."[113] English law had rejected truth as a defense. However, as Albert Gallatin asked: "how could the truth of opinions be
proved by evidence?"[114] Besides, the government could decide for itself what
was true and what was false. The statute continued in force until March 3,

---

110. 50 U.S.C. § 21 (2000).

111. Id., § 23.

112. 1 Stat. 596–97, sec. 2.

113. Id. at 597, sec. 3.

114. Annals of Cong., 5th Cong., 2–3rd Sess. 2162 (1798).

1801, when it was scheduled to expire unless renewed by Congress. The call for renewal never came.

Supporters of the legislation planned to use it to prosecute newspapers critical of Federalist Party policies. John Allen defended the bill: "Let gentlemen look at certain papers printed in this city and elsewhere, and ask themselves whether an unwarrantable and dangerous combination does not exist to overturn and ruin the Government by publishing the most shameless falsehoods against the Representatives of the people of all denominations, that they are hostile to free Governments and genuine liberty, and of course to the welfare of the country; that they ought, therefore, to be displaced, and that the people ought to raise an *insurrection* against the Government."[115] He quoted a passage from the *Aurora*, an opposition newspaper, concluding that its intention "is to persuade the people that peace with France is in our power; nay, that she is sincerely desirous of it, on proper terms, but that we reject her offers, and proceed to plunge our country into a destructive war."[116] From *The Time-Piece*, a paper printed in New York, he read language describing President John Adams as a person "without patriotism, without philosophy" and a "mock monarch."[117]

John Macon warned that passage of the bill would drive opponents of the government underground, forcing them to meet covertly instead of in full view. Legislation on sedition had the effect of creating sedition, both legally and politically: "by passing a law like the present you will force [critics] to combine together; they will establish corresponding societies throughout the Union, and communications will be made in secret, instead of publicly, as has been the case in other countries."[118] Government would be seen not as a protector but as the enemy. Albert Gallatin responded to Allen's reading from newspapers: "His idea was to punish men for stating facts which he happened to disbelieve, or for enacting and avowing opinions, not criminal, but perhaps erroneous."[119] As to the risk of newspapers commenting on public matters, Gallatin estimated that "out of ten presses in the country nine were employed on the side of Administration."[120]

115. Id. at 2094 (emphasis in original).
116. Id.
117. Id. at 2097.
118. Id. at 2105.
119. Id. at 2108.
120. Id. at 2109.

One of the first to be prosecuted under the Sedition Act was Matthew Lyon, a member of the House of Representatives from Vermont. He invited prosecution by claiming that under President Adams "every consideration of the public welfare was swallowed up in a continual grasp for power, in an unfounded thirst for ridiculous pomp, foolish adulation, and selfish avarice."[121] He was found guilty, imprisoned for four months, and fined $1,000. Campaigning from jail, he won reelection to Congress. The Federalists tried to expel Lyon from the House but could not attract the necessary two-thirds majority.[122] Lyon and others prosecuted and convicted under the Sedition Act were pardoned by President Thomas Jefferson.[123] Congress later determined that the Sedition Act was "unconstitutional, null, and void," and appropriated funds to reimburse those who had been fined under the statute.[124] As the Supreme Court noted in 1964, the Sedition Act was rejected not by a court of law but by the "court of history."[125] It was a bitter period. Instead of the country mobilized against an enemy abroad, the enmity was largely between one American and another.

In condemning the sedition bill, Gallatin said it "must be considered only as a weapon used by a party in power, in order to perpetuate their authority and preserve their present places."[126] The bill helped cripple the Federalist Party, remembered for its hostility to popular government, public debate, free press, dissent, civil liberties, and immigrants. After the Sedition Act expired in 1801, many of the values that spurred its enactment (and passage of the alien bills) reappeared soon under two new political parties that emerged after the 1820s: the Anti-Masonic movement and the Know-Nothing Party. The platforms of those parties included planks directed against immigrants, Catholics, members of clubs who met in secret, and organizations that seemed to have too much political power. The Anti-Masonic and Know-Nothing parties ran their course and soon disappeared, but not before persecuting and oppressing individuals who had committed no offense other than belonging to groups, nationalities, or religions that differed from the more settled and established communities.

121. John C. Miller, Crisis in Freedom: The Alien and Sedition Acts 106–07 (1951).

122. Geoffrey R. Stone, Perilous Times: Free Speech in Wartime 54 (2004).

123. 11 Writings of Thomas Jefferson 43 (Bergh ed., 1904) (letter to Mrs. John Adams, July 22, 1804).

124. H. Rept. No. 86, 26th Cong., 1st Sess. 2 (1840); 6 Stat. 802, ch. 45 (1840).

125. New York Times Co. v. Sullivan, 376 U.S. 254, 276 (1964).

126. Annals of Cong., 5th Cong., 2–3rd Sess. 2110 (1798).

ANTI-MASONIC MOVEMENT

Although Benjamin Franklin, George Washington, Andrew Jackson, and other distinguished Americans had been attracted to Freemasonry and found its tenets attractive, the organization provoked distrust because its meetings were in private, members received instructions in passwords and secret rituals, and they took an oath to support one another. A society that meets behind closed doors may generate hostility, as witnessed with the Democratic Societies in western Pennsylvania and their links to the Whiskey Rebellion. Critics could also view the universal principles embraced by Masons as a halfhearted commitment owed to one's nation. Those factors and others raised questions about the loyalty and patriotism of individuals who met at Masonic lodges.

The beliefs of Masonry are drawn from Egyptian and Hebrew sources, eventually combining elements of Judaism, Christianity, and Islam. The movement became "a synthesis, a concordat, for men of every race, of every creed, of every sect."[127] An expert in Freemasonry described the purpose as not social and charitable, "to which so much attention is paid, but the expediting of the spiritual evolution of those who aspire to perfect their own nature and transform it into a more god-like quality."[128] Freemasons looked to architecture not in the sense of physical structures but "to the architecture of the soul's life."[129]

The philosophical and intellectual roots of Freemasons did not protect them from the community's distrust. By the early 1820s, political power was shifting from small-town, agrarian life to large-city industrial society. Masonic lodges, located primarily in cities, became identified with an urban aristocracy pitted against village lower classes. By drawing ideals from the Enlightenment, Freemasonry seemed to pose a threat to religion in general and Christianity in particular. Masons were easily stereotyped as nonsectarian, deistic, and secular.[130] Evangelical Anti-Masons attacked Masonry as "an infidel society at war with true Christianity" because of its oaths and rituals.[131] For some,

---

127. W. L. Wilmshurst, The Meaning of Masonry 29 (1980 ed.). See also pp. 17–18, 23–24. Wilmshurst wrote as a Mason and historian of its development.

128. Id. at 47.

129. Id. at 48–49.

130. Paul Goodman, Towards a Christian Republic: Antimasonry and the Great Transition in New England, 1826–1836 (1988), at vii–ix, 12–13, 21–28, 234–45.

131. Michael F. Holt, "The Antimasonic and Know Knowing Parties," in 1 History of U.S. Political Parties 587 (Arthur M. Schlesinger, Jr., ed., 1973) (hereafter "Schlesinger").

it was a short step to associate Freemasonry with "immorality" and "blank Atheism."[132]

The Anti-Masonic Party traces its origin to the disappearance of William Morgan of Batavia, New York, in September 1826. After separating from the Freemasons, he threatened to publish details about rituals, oaths, and other confidential matters. When he could not be found, rumors spread that he had been murdered by Masons for divulging secrets. Six Masons were convicted of kidnapping. One was sentenced to a year in prison, the others from one to twenty-eight months.[133] Opponents of Masonry were convinced that Morgan was "deliberately murdered at Fort Niagara, and cast into Lake Ontario."[134] Because a number of New York public officials were Masons, it was believed that they had obstructed the state's investigation and would protect their own, even in cases of murder. Anti-Masons believed that they faced "not just the crime of a few zealous individuals but a gigantic conspiracy to subvert the rule of law through Masonic control of newspapers, the legislature and the judiciary."[135] A New York party convention in 1829 let loose these charges: "Free-Masonry is a distinct, peculiar, independent government. It acknowledges no allegiance to civil government, nor alliance with it. It has departments of its own, titles of its own, penalties of its own, laws of its own, revenues of its own, oaths of its own. . . . It has no jurisdictional limits, but the habitable globe."[136] An address to the people of Massachusetts gave this account of the oath taken by the Royal Arch Mason:

> Furthermore, do I promise and swear, that I will aid and assist a companion Royal Arch Mason, when engaged in any difficulty; and espouse his cause, so far as to extricate him from the same, if in my power, whether he be right or wrong. Furthermore do I promise and swear, that a Companion Royal Arch Mason's secrets, given me in charge as such, and I knowing them to be such, shall remain as secure and inviolable in my breast as in his own, murder and treason *not excepted.*[137]

132. Address to the People of Massachusetts, 1828, in Schlesinger, at 648.

133. S. Brent Morris, The Complete Idiot's Guide to Freemasonry 44 (2006). Morris is an editor of a Masonic magazine and a Thirty-Third Degree Mason.

134. Report on the Progress of the Antimasonic Cause, Rochester, N.Y., February 15, 1829, in Schlesinger, at 636.

135. Holt, "The Antimasonic and Know Nothing Parties," Schlesinger, at 577.

136. Schlesinger, at 640.

137. Id. at 649 (emphasis in original).

By 1830, a political party known as the Anti-Masons formed in western New York and grew in strength by attracting those who feared secrecy, conspiracies, and organizations that found their operating principles on values located outside national borders. It was the first third party in American history and the first party to hold a national nominating convention. The platform of 1832, written in Baltimore on September 28, 1831, began with this resolution: "That the existence of secret and affiliated societies is hostile to one of the principal defenses of liberty,—free discussion,—and can subserve no purpose of utility in a free government." Other resolve clauses claimed:

> ... the masonic institution is dangerous to the liberties, and subversive of the laws of the country;
>
> ... the direct object of freemasonry is to benefit the *few*, at the expense of the *many*, by creating a *privileged* class, in the midst of a community entitled to enjoy equal rights and privileges;
>
> ... the *oaths* and *obligations* imposed upon persons when admitted into masonic lodges and chapters, deserve the unqualified reprobation and abhorrence of every Christian, and every friend of morality and justice;
>
> ... these oaths, being illegally administered, and designed to subserve fraudulent purposes, ought not to be regarded as binding in conscience, morality, or honor; but the higher obligations of religion and civil society require them to be explicitly renounced by every good citizen;
>
> ... the gigantic conspiracy in New York, against the life of William Morgan, was the natural result of the oaths and obligations of masonry, understood and acted upon according to their plain and obvious meaning;
>
> ... there is sufficient proof that the perpetrators of the abduction and murder of William Morgan, have, in several instances, been shielded from the punishment due to their crimes, by the Grand Lodge and Grand Chapter of New York, and by subordinate lodges and chapters, according to their masonic obligations, whereby those lodges and chapters have now countenanced those outrages, and become accomplices in their guilt; ... [138]

The Anti-Masonic movement attracted support in New England and influenced the presidential election of 1832, where it picked up 8 percent of the vote. Anti-Masons campaigned strongly against Andrew Jackson, a Mason. William Wirt ran for President under the Anti-Masonic Party, but he made clear in his acceptance letter of September 28, 1831, that he would not engage in broad and indiscriminate attacks on Masons. Wirt, who had served as Attorney

138. Id. at 662–63, Antimasonic National Platform of 1832 (emphasis in original).

General under the James Monroe and John Quincy Adams administrations, said he would not adhere to the demand of some Anti-Masons that he prohibit Masons from serving in the federal government.[139] He also noted that he had been initiated into the mysteries of Freemasonry in his younger years, although he stopped visiting lodges and had not attended one for more than 30 years.[140]

Wirt spoke about the kidnapping and likely murder of William Morgan. Assuming that those who abducted him were Masons, he cautioned against any generalized condemnation of Masonry. As to Morgan's case, "it was quite as unjust to charge that on masonry, as it would be to charge the private delinquencies of some professing Christians on Christianity itself."[141] If elected, he would not allow the power of the presidency to be "prostituted to the purpose of a blind and unjust proscription, involving innocence and honor with guilt and treason; and no man is worthy of a nomination to this high office, in whose judgment and patriotism confidence cannot be placed to make the proper distinction between the two." Were he to misuse the powers of the presidency in this fashion "he would deservedly become an object of disgust, if he could stoop to commit himself by any pledges, in a case like this, as the price of his nomination."[142]

By 1836, the Anti-Masonic movement had run its course and disappeared as a significant factor in American politics. Freemasonry, battered for almost a decade, started a slow recovery in a climate dominated not by religious bigotry but by the overriding issue of slavery. The energy previously poured into Anti-Masonry flowed now to abolitionism.[143] Suspicions and paranoia toward secret groups and conspiracies survived, of course, and worked their way into political life at both the national and local levels.

KNOW-NOTHING PARTY

Hatred of Catholicism had deep roots in the experience of Puritans and Anglicans in England. Efforts to restore the Pope to political power in British life, the Gunpowder Plot, and other political events were well known to those who

---

139. Id. at 664–65.
140. Id. at 666.
141. Id.
142. Id. at 667–68.
143. Goodman, Towards a Christian Republic, at 239–44.

settled in the American colonies.[144] The decision to prosecute Matthew Lyon of violating the U.S. Sedition Act rested in part on his status as an Irish Catholic. Nativism developed in the United States as a potent political force against all those born abroad: Catholics first, others later.

Out of this curious brew came the Know-Nothing (American) Party, which emerged in the 1840s to oppose immigration—especially by Roman Catholics. When members were asked about their oath-bound secret party, they replied "I know nothing." Those who joined became privy to rituals, grips, and secret passwords.[145] Like the members of Congress who passed the Alien and Sedition Acts, Know-Nothings wanted to lengthen the time required for naturalization and prohibit immigrants from holding public office.[146] In 1854 and 1856, the party ran candidates under the banner of the American Party. Prior to that it was known as the Native American Party.

In 1856, Thomas R. Whitney's justification of Know-Nothing policy directed this blast at Catholicism: "What is the Church of Rome, for example, but a budget of mechanical and ostentatious forms and ceremonies, and a promoter of ignorance and low superstition? I find nothing of religion in the jugglery that first stifles intelligence, and then *compels* its illiterate dupes to believe that the figure of a woman painted on canvas, can, and does exhibit signs of physical life, as the so-called 'Winking Virgin,' or that a dry thorn will emit drops of blood, on the anniversary of the crucifixion."[147]

Consistent with the tenets of nativism, Whitney explained that one of the "surest guarantees of permanent nationality is the perfect homogeneousness of the people."[148] To his mind, immigrants threatened to defile and corrupt the uniformity of the American character. Immigration brought to U.S. shores the "loftiest intelligence and the meanest intellect—the man of wealth, and the starving millions—the statesman, the philosopher, the idiot, the criminal, and the insane. . . . To believe that a mass so crude and incongruous, so remote from the spirit, the ideas, and the customs of America, can be made to harmonize readily with the new element into which it is cast, is, to say the least, *unnatural.*"[149] One might as well hope, he said, "to harmonize the tribes of the

144. Ray Allen Billington, The Protestant Crusade, 1800–1860: A Study of the Origins of American Nativism (1964 ed.).

145. Holt, "The Antimasonic and Know Nothing Parties," Schlesinger, at 593.

146. Id. at 596–97.

147. Thomas R. Whitney, A Defense of the American Policy (1856), cited by Schlesinger, at 680 (emphasis in original).

148. Id. at 682.

149. Id. at 687 (emphasis in original).

forest with the tribes of the commercial mart—the savage of Minnesota with the money-changer of Wall Street."[150]

In addition to blocking access by foreigners with a religion at odds with prevailing Protestant beliefs, he saw in Catholicism a control of government similar to that feared of Masonry. He offered three postulates: "I. That the Church is a political government, claiming temporal authority over every nation and people of the earth; II. That it is now striving directly, to establish its temporal or political power in these United States; and III. That its form of government is diametrically opposed to the genius of American Republicanism."[151]

Finally, Whitney opposed immigrants because of the leftist and destabilizing political beliefs he expected they would bring, particularly after the development of communism and socialism in Europe and the political revolutions of 1848. He expressed alarm at the prospect of "Red Republicans, agrarians, and infidels, a restive, radical, discontented people, at war with government."[152] Those "malcontents" were men who "stood by the side of Robespierre" and "the worst blood of France," men with "white hearts and red hands," made red "with the blood of the innocent! Men who would gladly abolish both law and Gospel at a single swoop!"[153]

The Know-Nothing Party profited from the collapse of the Whig Party in 1852. Two years later, many of the former Whigs voted Know-Nothing and produced victories in Massachusetts, New York, and California. Virginia's Know-Nothing platform of 1854 began: "Determined to preserve our political institutions in their original purity and vigor, and to keep them unadulterated and unimpaired by foreign influence, either civil or religious...."[154] The American (Know-Nothing) Platform of 1855 combined opposition to immigration and Roman Catholics with positions on slavery and the Kansas-Nebraska Act. Section VI urged the repeal of state laws "allowing foreigners not naturalized to vote."[155] Section VIII zeroed in on Catholicism. The goal was to fulfill the maxim "*Americans only shall govern America*" and to exclude from American shores any religion that fostered an allegiance with "any foreign power, potentate or ecclesiastic."[156] Cycles of immigration are ironic. Newcomers, after arriving from distant shores, decide within a short time—even within a

150. Id.
151. Id. at 683.
152. Id. at 688.
153. Id. at 690.
154. Id. at 699.
155. Id. at 702.
156. Id. at 703 (emphasis in original).

generation—to view themselves as "Americans" and join others in opposing the unwelcome influx of any foreigners.

SLAVERY

Section XII of the Know-Nothing platform of 1855 addressed the issue of slavery. It condemned "the systematic agitation of the Slavery question by those parties having elevated sectional hostility into a positive element of political power." Concluding that it was impossible to reconcile the different opinions on slavery, it counseled that it was necessary to maintain "the existing laws upon the subject of slavery, as a final and conclusive settlement of that subject, in spirit and in substance."[157] As a consequence, Congress should not interfere with the establishment of slavery in new territories in the western part of the country if citizens there supported it. Congress should have no power "to establish or prohibit slavery in any territory."[158]

During this period, Abraham Lincoln debated slavery and consistently opposed the Know-Nothing Party. Writing to Joshua F. Speed on August 24, 1855, he remarked on the speed with which America was retreating from fundamental principles set forth in the Declaration of Independence: "I am not a Know-Nothing. That is certain. How could I be? How can any one who abhors the oppression of negroes, be in favor of degrading classes of white people?" He expressed regret for the rapid "progress in degeneracy" in America. As a nation, it began by declaring that "all men are created equal." Lincoln then observed: "We now practically read it 'all men are created equal, *except negroes.*' When the Know-Nothings get control, it will read 'all men are created equal, except negroes, *and foreigners, and catholics.*' When it comes to this I should prefer emigrating to some country where they make no pretense of loving liberty—to Russia, for instance, where despotism can be taken pure, and without the base alloy of hypocracy [*sic*]."[159]

The Know-Nothing movement remained politically active for a short period, from 1854 to 1856. Its anti-slavery members joined the newly created

157. Id. at 704.
158. Id.
159. 2 The Collected Works of Abraham Lincoln 323 (1953) (emphasis in original). For other comments by Lincoln on Know-Nothingism and the spread of slavery, see id. at 228–29, 234–40, 284–85, 286–87, 344–45, 368–73, and 3 id. 333.

Republican Party, particularly after the Supreme Court's *Dred Scott* ruling in 1857. The pro-slavery wing of the American Party remained strong at the local and state levels but was not a national force after 1860. The secrecy followed by Know-Nothingism attracted criticism and suspicion. Rumors circulated about "dread plots hatched against democracy."[160] As the country sped headlong into civil war, the South saw in the Know-Nothing Party a fundamental commitment to nationalism over state's rights.[161]

Lincoln's suspension of habeas corpus is cited today as a precedent to support policies taken by the Bush administration after 9/11. There are several key differences. Lincoln took a number of emergency actions after the firing on Ft. Sumter in April 1861, including suspending the writ of habeas corpus, raising armies, and withdrawing funds from the Treasury without an appropriation. Unlike the Bush administration, however, he never claimed that he possessed full legal or constitutional authority to act as he did. He stated that his actions were not "beyond the constitutional competency of Congress."[162] Thus, Lincoln admitted to exercising a combination of Article I and Article II powers. For that reason, he came to Congress to request retroactive authority, which he obtained. In debating his request, lawmakers acted on the explicit assumption that his actions had been illegal.[163] President Bush exercised many powers not in public but in secret and under the assumption that he possessed "inherent" authorities that required no action by Congress.[164]

Two other points. The Constitution states that the privilege of the writ of habeas corpus "shall not be suspended, unless when in Cases of Rebellion or Invasion the public Safety may require it." There was rebellion in 1861. After passing retroactive legislation to legitimize Lincoln's action, Congress passed a statute in March 1863 outlining the procedures for suspension. There was neither rebellion nor invasion after 9/11. Furthermore, Attorney General Edward Bates advised Lincoln in 1861 that he had limited emergency authority to suspend habeas. Bates qualified his opinion by saying that if the language in the Constitution meant "a repeal of all power to issue the writ, then I freely admit that none but Congress can do it." The President's power in time of emergency

---

160. Billington, The Protestant Crusade 417.

161. Id. at 424.

162. 7 Richardson, Messages and Papers of the Presidents 3225.

163. Fisher, Presidential War Power, at 48.

164. See the March 2007 issue of *Presidential Studies Quarterly*, which is devoted to inherent presidential power as claimed by President George W. Bush for his post-9/11 actions.

was "temporary and exceptional."[165] President Bush claimed he had powers that were permanent and fully lawful.

The first seven decades of republican government in the United States saw deep divisions over basic principles. Some citizens believed in democracy and public discourse; others wanted an aristocratic and elitist government capable of punishing citizens who spoke out too much and too critically of public policy. Mixed with that issue were political movements to expel or suppress "unpatriotic" and "alien" groups. Those impulses continued when millions of immigrants came to the New World after 1865, entering a land flowing with opportunities and animosities.

165. 10 Op. Att'y Gen. 74, 90 (1861); Fisher, Military Tribunals and Presidential Power, at 42–44.

CHAPTER 4

Targeting Undesirables, 1865–1940

In the decades leading to the Civil War, America singled out different groups for punishment: slaves, aliens, seditionists, French, Masons, Native Americans, immigrants, and Catholics. After the war, new targets moved into view: Chinese, Japanese, anarchists, Socialists, Communists, Germans, and the "Unfit." For those arriving as an immigrant, they could expect an extra hardship. Individuals engaging in violence or conspiracy merited indictment and trial through the regular law enforcement system, but most suffered from a climate of fear and ignorance that had strong parallels to the Alien and Sedition Acts. Traditional procedural safeguards lost ground to public pressures for expedited punishment, imprisonment, and banishment, no matter how arbitrary and ill-founded.

CHINESE IMMIGRANTS

The social and political climate after the Civil War gave a green light to the pursuit of private wealth, particularly after the heavy sacrifices exacted by the war. The dominant themes guiding this development included materialism, scientific discovery, and industrial capitalism. The economic engine called for millions of immigrants to work the farms, factories, and mines. States offered economic incentives to attract workers from abroad. When the economy paused or contracted, Congress enacted laws to restrict immigrants and began to adopt racial tests. The doctrine of nativism, vigorous at the time of the Alien and Sedition Acts and the Know-Nothings, reasserted itself with a flourish in the guise of Americanism, patriotism, and loyalty to the nation. Loyalty to the Constitution often ran a distant second.

Treaty Understandings

Chinese immigrants occupy a special niche in America. As with other newcomers, they arrived in large numbers for work and individual advancement. Unlike others who came and assimilated, steps were taken by states and Congress to block their future access. Initially, treaties entered into between the United States and China in 1844 and 1858 recognized and encouraged free trade and travel.[1] Treaty language in 1868 highlighted the benefits: "The United States of America and the Emperor of China cordially recognize the inherent and inalienable right of man to change his home and allegiance, and also the mutual advantage of the free migration and emigration of their citizens and subjects, respectively, from the one country to the other, for purposes of curiosity, of trade, or as permanent residents."[2] Chinese visiting or residing in America were to enjoy "the same privileges, immunities, and exemptions in respect to travel or residence, as may there be enjoyed by the citizens or subjects of the most favored nation."[3]

The 1868 treaty anticipated legislation that would make it a penal offense for U.S. citizens or Chinese subjects to take Chinese to any foreign country, or for a Chinese subject or U.S. citizen to take U.S. citizens to China or any other foreign country, "without their free and voluntary consent respectively."[4] Those liberal sentiments collided with increasing tension between the two countries. After the discovery of gold in California in 1848, laborers came from China in great numbers and competed successfully with American workers as artisans and mechanics. Many other immigrants came to the United States to settle and become citizens; Chinese often arrived planning to make money within a short time and return home to their families. They worked in the mines, on the farms, in factories, and helped build the Transcontinental railroad. Finding it difficult to acquire wealth and return home, many stayed. Federal law on naturalization limited citizenship to those "free" and "white." Unless Congress changed the law, the Chinese had no opportunity to become U.S. citizens.[5]

To stem the flow, residents of the Pacific Coast insisted that states and Congress pass legislation to restrict immigration from China.[6] By 1871, both of the major parties in California adopted anti-Chinese planks in their platforms.[7]

1. 8 Stat. 592 (1844); 12 Stat. 1069 (1858).
2. 16 Stat. 740, Art. V (1868).
3. Id. at 740, Art. VI.
4. Id., Art. V.
5. Gunther Barth, Bitter Strength: A History of the Chinese in the United States, 1850–1870, at 179–80 (1964); 1 Stat. 103, sec. 1 (1790); 1 Stat. 414, sec. 1 (1795).
6. Charles J. McClain, In Search of Equality: The Chinese Struggle Against Discrimination in Nineteenth-Century America 9–30, 43–63 (1994); The Chinese Exclusion Case, 130 U.S. 581, 590–96 (1889).
7. Roger Daniels, The Politics of Prejudice: The Anti-Japanese Movement in California and the Struggle for Japanese Exclusion 17 (1977 ed.).

Congressional legislation in 1875 required U.S. consular officers to determine whether an immigrant from China, Japan, "or any Oriental country" had entered into an agreement for a term of service within the United States "for lewd and immoral purposes." If an agreement existed, the individual would be denied a certificate to enter the country.[8] Whoever attempted to bring these individuals into the country for illegal purposes faced fines and imprisonment.[9]

California passed legislation to block access to "lewd and debauched women" arriving from other countries. In 1876, the Supreme Court struck down the statute, in part because of the power it placed "in the hands of a single man."[10] The Court found the procedures repugnant because the immigration commissioner need only go aboard a vessel "filled with passengers ignorant of our language and our laws, and without trial or hearing of evidence . . . point with his finger to twenty, as in this case, or a hundred if he chooses, and say to the master, 'These are the idiots, these are the paupers, these are convicted criminals, these are lewd women, and these others are debauched women.'"[11] If the owner of the ship disagreed he was forbidden to land the passengers and received a heavy penalty. The commissioner exerted a powerful leverage with this implied message: "I am open to an offer; for you must remember that twenty per cent of all I can get out of you goes into my own pocket, and the remainder into the treasury of California."[12]

The Court remarked that foreigners arriving in the United States, "however distinguished at home their social, their literary, or their political character, are helpless in the presence of this potent commissioner."[13] The accused could offer any amount of surety or cash, but such gestures were of limited hope. A "silly, an obstinate, or a wicked commissioner may bring disgrace upon the whole country, the enmity of a powerful nation, or the loss of an equally powerful friend."[14] The Court pictured this scenario: "The woman whose error has been repaired by a happy marriage and numerous children, and whose loving husband brings her with his wealth to a new home, may be told she must pay a round sum before she can land, because it is alleged that she was debauched by her husband before marriage." Whether her conduct is such to justify the commissioner "in calling her lewd may be made to depend on the sum she

8. 18 Stat. 477 (1875) [Part 3].
9. Id., sec. 2.
10. Chy Lung v. Freeman, 92 U.S. 275, 278 (1876).
11. Id.
12. Id.
13. Id. at 279.
14. Id.

will pay for the privilege of landing in San Francisco."[15] In future rulings, federal courts would be less sympathetic and supportive of Chinese and other immigrants.

Presidential Resistance

Congress, busy drafting bills to restrict the immigration of Chinese, encountered two presidential vetoes before legislation could be enacted in 1882. President Rutherford B. Hayes penned the first veto on March 1, 1879. The bill limited the number of Chinese passengers to fifteen per vessel, regardless of the size or tonnage of the ship "or by any consideration of the safety or accommodation of these passengers." To Hayes, the purpose of the bill was "to repress this immigration to an extent falling but little short of its absolute exclusion."[16] Furthermore, the bill required the partial abrogation of a treaty with China governing trade and immigration. Hayes described the terms of that treaty as consistent with "our fearless liberality of citizenship, our equal and comprehensive justice to all inhabitants, whether they abjured their foreign nationality or not, our civil freedom, and our religious toleration had made all comers welcome, . . ."[17] He understood the treaty to merely bar the introduction of Chinese laborers "by methods which should have the character of a forced and servile importation."[18]

Hayes could find no precedent for Congress abrogating a treaty other than its action in 1798 against French treaties, on the eve of going to war against France. He believed that the power of modifying or abrogating an existing treaty to be part of the treaty-making power reserved not to Congress as a whole but to the President and the Senate.[19] Recognizing that the original treaty with China may require modifications to protect against "a larger and more rapid infusion of this foreign race than our system of industry and society can take up and assimilate with ease and safety," he vetoed the bill.[20]

Three years later, President Chester A. Arthur vetoed a similar measure. He urged Congress not to repudiate treaty obligations but rather discover an-

---

15. Id. at 281.

16. 9 A Compilation of the Messages and Papers of the Presidents 4466 (James D. Richardson ed.) (hereafter "Richardson").

17. Id. at 4467–68.

18. Id.

19. Id. at 4471.

20. Id. at 4469–70.

other path "without coming in conflict with the rights of China."[21] The House sustained the veto.[22] In 1880, the United States proceeded to modify the existing treaty to allow Congress to regulate and limit the immigration of Chinese laborers without affecting the travel rights of teachers, students, merchants, and others who wanted to visit America.[23] When Chinese negotiators asked how the United States might implement the new treaty provisions, they were told that Congress might adopt language to address specific circumstances, such as a demand for Chinese labor in the South and a surplus of workers in California. Chinese commissioners were satisfied with that explanation.[24] The modified treaty recognized that Congress could regulate, limit, or suspend immigration from China but not absolutely prohibit it. Moreover, whatever limitations or suspensions were imposed would cover only Chinese laborers.[25]

The bill that reached President Arthur proposed the exclusion of Chinese laborers for the next 20 years. He could find nothing in the negotiation of the revised treaty to justify a restriction that covered "nearly a generation."[26] Arthur pointed to the contributions of thousands of Chinese laborers who were "largely instrumental in constructing the railways which connect the Atlantic and the Pacific."[27] He feared that the harsh 20-year exclusion would "repel Oriental nations from us and to drive their trade and commerce into more friendly lands."[28] In vetoing the bill, he urged Congress to draft legislation with "a shorter experiment."[29] The House upheld the veto.[30]

Unable to override the veto, Congress enacted legislation in 1882 recognizing that "the coming of Chinese laborers to this country endangers the good order of certain localities within the territory thereof."[31] The bill suspended the immigration of Chinese laborers for ten years and recognized the rights of Chinese "other than a laborer" to visit the United States if in possession of a valid certificate.[32] Congress defined "Chinese laborers" to mean "both

21. 10 Richardson 4699.

22. 8 Cong. Rec. 2275–77 (1879).

23. 10 Richardson 4700–01.

24. Id. at 4702.

25. Id. at 4703.

26. Id.

27. Id. at 4704.

28. Id. at 4705.

29. Id.

30. 13 Cong. Rec. 2617 (1882).

31. 22 Stat. 58 (1882).

32. Id. at 60, sec. 6.

skilled and unskilled laborers and Chinese employed in mining."[33] Legislation enacted later in 1882 excluded "all foreign convicts except those convicted of political offenses."[34] A law passed in 1884 placed further restrictions on China.[35] During this period, mobs forced Chinese from their homes, often with four hours' notice, and torched their communities.[36]

Judicial Supervision

Chew Heong, a Chinese laborer, arrived in the United States on November 17, 1880, and remained in the country until June 1881. He traveled to Honolulu and did not return to the United States until September 1884, after enactment of the Chinese Exclusion Acts. Lacking the certificate required by those statutes, he was prohibited from entering the country. Because of his circumstances, the Supreme Court held in 1884 that he could reenter without a certificate.[37]

Two years later, a case before the Court involved a municipal ordinance in California designed to regulate public laundries. As implemented by the Board of Supervisors, 80 white owners received licenses to operate, but licenses were denied to 200 Chinese-owned laundries. Could law be administered in such a discriminatory manner? For the first time, the Court had to decide the meaning of "persons" in the Fourteenth Amendment: "Nor shall any State deprive any person of life, liberty, or property without due process of law; nor deny to any person within its jurisdiction the equal protection of the laws." Did the word "person" apply to both noncitizens and aliens? Looking to American constitutional principles, the Court said that room could not be left "for the play and action of purely personal and arbitrary power."[38] In striking down the ordinance because of its discriminatory application, the Court held that the Fourteenth Amendment extends to all persons without regard to differences of race, color, or nationality.

In 1888, Congress enacted another statute to prohibit Chinese laborers from entering the United States. Chinese officials, teachers, students, merchants, and travelers "for pleasure or curiosity" were permitted to visit if they first obtained authority from the Chinese government "or other Government to

33. Id. at 61.
34. Id. at 214.
35. 23 Stat. 115 (1884).
36. Jean Pfaelzer, Driven Out: The Forgotten War against Chinese Americans (2007).
37. Chew Heong v. United States, 112 U.S. 536 (1884).
38. Yick Wo v. Hopkins, 118 U.S. 356, 370 (1886); see McClain, In Search of Equality, at 98–125.

which they may at the time be citizens or subjects." Individuals who violated the statute "shall be removed from the United States to the country whence he came."[39]

A year later, the Supreme Court interpreted that statute to abrogate previous treaties in this area. Chae Chan Ping, a subject of the Emperor of China and a laborer, left San Francisco on June 2, 1887, to visit China. He carried a certificate entitling him to return to the United States, pursuant to the 1882 and 1884 statutes. He returned to San Francisco on September 7, 1888. A month later, on October 1, Congress passed legislation providing that "every certificate heretofore issued" in pursuance of previous treaties "is hereby declared void and of no effect, and the chinese [*sic*] laborer claiming admission by virtue thereof shall not be permitted to enter the United States."[40] Chae Chan Ping was denied entrance by the collector of the port, who concluded that legislation by Congress nullified his certificate. The Supreme Court agreed. If a treaty related to a subject within the power of Congress, it could be repealed or modified at the pleasure of Congress and in either case "the last expression of the sovereign will must control."[41]

As to the right of Chae Chan Ping to reenter with his certificate, the Court held that Chinese laborers returning to the United States were aliens subject to U.S. sovereign power over its territories and its borders.[42] There is no doubt about the authority of a sovereign nation to exclude paupers, criminals, and other categories of people who attempt to enter. But what of someone like Chae Chan Ping who had already resided and worked in the United States and wanted to return, and did so with a certificate authorized by statute? Those issues, said the Court, "are not questions for judicial determination."[43] Any relief had to come from the political branches.

Federal courts accepted the authority of Congress to temporarily detain or imprison an alien, pending decisions on exclusion or expulsion, but the Court drew a line in 1896 on statutory provisions that authorized the imprisonment of Chinese aliens "at hard labor for a period of not exceeding one year and thereafter removed from the United States."[44] In meting out such "infamous punishment," the Court insisted that there be judicial trial to establish the

39. 25 Stat. 476, 579, sec. 13 (1888).
40. Id. at 504 (1888).
41. The Chinese Exclusion Case, 130 U.S. 581, 600 (1889).
42. Id. at 603.
43. Id. at 609.
44. 27 Stat. 25, sec. 4 (1892).

guilt of the accused.[45] It violated constitutional values to have Congress define an offense "as an infamous crime, find the fact of guilt and adjudge the punishment by one of its own agents."[46] Aliens as well as U.S. citizens could not be held to answer for an infamous crime "unless on a presentment or indictment of a grand jury, nor be deprived of life, liberty or property without due process of law."[47] In cases not involving punishment, courts continued to treat decisions by administrative officers over exclusion as final and conclusive unless abuse of discretion or authority could be shown.[48]

In 1892, Congress again passed legislation to block Chinese persons coming to the United States, making the statute effective for another ten years.[49] Legislation in 1902 extended the prohibition "until otherwise provided by law."[50] Congress repealed the Chinese Exclusion Acts in 1943 after receiving an urgent message from President Franklin D. Roosevelt. As he explained, political calculations had changed as a result of World War II: "China is our ally. For many years she stood alone in the fight against aggression. Today we fight at her side."[51] He asked Congress "to wipe from the statute books those anachronisms in our law which forbid the immigration of Chinese people into this country and which bar Chinese residents from American citizenship."[52] Two months later the bill to repeal the Chinese Exclusion Acts cleared Congress.[53]

Arbitrary Administration

During operation of the Chinese Exclusion Acts, federal courts occasionally intervened to place some constraints on arbitrary executive action. Chin Yow, claiming to be a U.S. citizen, was ordered deported. The Supreme Court in 1908 ruled that he must have an opportunity to show his citizenship in a deportation proceeding.[54] His attorney stated that he was not allowed to see and read the evidence presented to the immigration officer.[55] The record also indicated that Chin Yow was prevented by the officials of the commissioner "from

45. Wong Wing v. United States, 163 U.S. 228, 237 (1896).
46. Id.
47. Id. at 238.
48. United States v. Ju Toy, 198 U.S. 253 (1905).
49. 27 Stat. 25 (1892).
50. 32 Stat. 176 (1902).
51. The Public Papers and Addresses of Franklin D. Roosevelt 427 (1943 vol., 1950).
52. Id.
53. 57 Stat. 600 (1943).
54. Chin Yow v. United States, 208 U.S. 8 (1908).
55. Id. at 9.

obtaining testimony, including that of named witnesses."[56] Even though the Court accepted the decision of the government as final, "that is on the presupposition that the decision was after a hearing in good faith, however summary in form." In cases of conflict between the substantive rights of citizens to enter the country and prove their citizenship and "the Commissioner's fiat on the other, when one or the other must give way, the latter must yield." The question was then whether the judge would be some type of administrative official or a federal judge.

Detailed studies of the enforcement of the deportation laws revealed serious abuses by executive officials. Immigration inspectors were selected by the Civil Service Commission and given a written examination, but there was no oral interview, character investigation, educational requirements, or preliminary training before being assigned to work.[57] In deciding whether an alien should be deported, it was the practice to make a preliminary examination of the suspect under oath, in a private hearing, without the alien having assistance of counsel or other representation.[58] In many cases the examining inspector merely took notes at the hearing and dictated them later. Even when a stenographer took notes, the transcript was incomplete and episodic.[59] Often the alien did not understand the significance of questions asked.[60] In one study, less than half of the aliens had been advised that anything they said during the preliminary examination could be used against them in subsequent proceedings, even though information obtained at the preliminary stage could lead to criminal prosecution.[61]

After the preliminary examination, the alien was entitled to have counsel, but few could afford one. As a result, "in the great majority of cases throughout the country the alien is unrepresented."[62] Other objectionable features of the exclusion and deportation procedure included illegal searches and seizures to obtain evidence against an alien and the use of hearsay testimony and rumors to support a decision.[63] In theory the examining inspector was a subordinate gathering information for action by a superior office; in practice he

56. Id. at 11.

57. National Commission on Law Observance and Enforcement, Report on the Enforcement of the Deportation Laws of the United States 47 (1931).

58. Id. at 59.

59. Id. at 62–63.

60. Id. at 64.

61. Id. at 66–67.

62. Id. at 85.

63. Id. at 133–37, 144. William C. Van Vleck, The Administrative Control of Aliens: A Study in Administrative Law and Procedure 111–12, 170–74 (1932).

was a prosecutor who presided over a hearing, controlled its direction, built a case that was unlikely to be overturned on appeal or review, and was unlikely to have any legal training.[64]

A unanimous decision by the Supreme Court in 1920 reviewed the exclusion of a Chinese man who claimed to have been born at Monterey, California, and was therefore a U.S. citizen. Anonymous information reached immigration officials, stating he was not who he said he was. Those statements came from witnesses with the promise that their names would not be disclosed. The Chinese individual was denied access to this material.[65] The Court was troubled by this record, but decided the case on other information that had been withheld: the fact that three white witnesses vouched for the identity of the Chinese man not only on the basis of photographs but by seeing him in person.[66] That fact was not made part of the record.[67] The Court held that any report that "suppressed or omitted" such crucial information "was not a fair report and a hearing based upon it was not a fair hearing within the definition of the cases cited."[68] The authority that Congress had given to the Secretary of Labor over Chinese immigrants and persons of Chinese descent was "a power to be administered, not arbitrarily and secretly, but fairly and openly."[69]

Two years later, the Court held that Chinese nationals who had been admitted into the country by immigration authorities and later threatened with deportation were entitled to a judicial hearing to present their case. Determinations by executive officials to deport someone are final and conclusive but not when there has been a denial of a fair hearing, where a finding was not supported by evidence, or there was an application of an erroneous rule of law.[70] To deport someone who claims to be a citizen not only deprives the individual of liberty but "may result also in loss of both property and life; or of all that makes life worth living."[71]

64. Van Vleck, The Administrative Control of Aliens, at 230.
65. Kwock Jan Fat v. White, 253 U.S. 454, 455–56 (1920).
66. Id. at 462.
67. Id. at 463.
68. Id. at 464.
69. Id.
70. Ng Fung Ho v. White, 259 U.S. 276, 284 (1922).
71. Id.

TREATMENT OF JAPANESE

Japanese arriving in America encountered prejudice and discrimination as with other immigrants, but their history is different from Europeans and even from many Chinese. Other newcomers took time to ground themselves in their new country and find their way. The Japanese "rapidly began to challenge whites in many businesses and professions—as a group, Japanese in the United States became very quickly imbued with what, in Europeans, would be called the Protestant ethic."[72] The United States took steps to exclude Japanese, as with Chinese, and deny them the right to be U.S. citizens.

In the period after the Civil War, Japanese immigrants were largely overshadowed by the U.S. response to Chinese entering the country. However, a congressional statute in 1875 included Japan among "any Oriental country" for exclusion from the United States in cases of "lewd and immoral purposes."[73] Other statutes offered additional grounds for excluding aliens, including those who had no means of support, no relatives or friends in the United States, and those liable to become a public charge. Legislation in 1891 authorized the exclusion of aliens who were designated as "idiots, insane persons, paupers or persons likely to become a public charge, persons suffering from a loathsome or a dangerous contagious disease," and other categories of people.[74]

Japanese immigration to the United States often followed a two-step process: first to the Hawaiian Islands, as workers under contract, and then to the Pacific Coast, primarily to California. Over a nine-year period, from 1886 to 1894, more than 30,000 Japanese were brought to the Islands.[75] The Japanese did very well in agriculture, small businesses, and gradually leased and bought their own land. Despite their success, they continued to be "aliens ineligible for citizenship." The statute specifying that policy did not come until 1924, but earlier treaties, statutes, and court cases prepared the legal basis. Naturalization laws still restricted citizenship to those who were free and white.

Court Cases

In 1891, a female subject of the Emperor of Japan arrived at the port of San Francisco, where she was denied entry. Her passport stated that she came in

72. Daniels, The Politics of Prejudice, at 106.
73. 18 Stat. 477 (1875) [Part 3].
74. 26 Stat. 1984, sec. 1 (1891).
75. Daniels, The Politics of Prejudice, at 5.

the company of her husband, which the government concluded was not true. She claimed to have been married for two years and that her husband had been in the United States for one year. Arriving with $22, she was expected to stop at a hotel until her husband called for her.[76] The issue was whether the findings and conclusions of collectors and immigration officials were final and conclusive or could be reviewed and overturned by federal courts. The Supreme Court in 1892 decided that a statute giving federal courts concurrent jurisdiction in certain immigration matters did not give courts authority to decide cases that Congress had "committed to the final determination of executive officers."[77] Federal courts would revisit that ruling in 1899.

A treaty with Japan in 1894 appeared to grant both countries "full liberty to enter, travel, or reside in any part of the territories of the other Contracting Party, and shall enjoy full and perfect protection for their persons and property." Citizens of the United States and Japan were promised "free access to the Courts of Justice in pursuit and defence of their rights." To exercise that right effectively, they were at liberty to "choose and employ lawyers, advocates, and representatives to pursue and defend their rights before such Courts."[78] The treaty assured reciprocal freedom of commerce and navigation, including the liberty to come with ships and cargo and enter all places open to foreign commerce with the same treatment as native citizens or subjects.[79]

In 1899, a district court in the state of Washington limited the right of immigration officers to make final and conclusive determinations on the detention and expulsion of aliens. An immigration inspector in Seattle decided that T. Yamasaka was a pauper and likely to become a public charge. He therefore held him in custody.[80] The court decided that these discretionary actions by executive officers were subject to review by judges to protect the guarantee of personal liberty in the Fifth Amendment. The language in that constitutional safeguard "does not distinguish between citizens and aliens, but lays down the broad principle that no person shall be deprived of life, liberty, or property without due process of law."[81] Those charged with being a pauper had a right to defend themselves in court, with the final right to remain in the country "determined judicially."[82] That decision was reversed by the Ninth Circuit a

76. Nishimura Ekiu v. United States, 142 U.S. 651, 652 (1892).

77. Id. at 664.

78. 29 Stat. 848, Art. I (1894).

79. Id. at 849, Art. II.

80. In re Yamasaka, 95 Fed. 652 (D. Wash. 1899).

81. Id. at 655.

82. Id. at 656.

year later, holding that the district court had incorrectly ruled that the Secretary of the Treasury lacked authority to do what was done to Yamasaka.[83]

A case in 1903 further explored the rights of a Japanese immigrant. The government claimed that Kaoru Yamataya landed at the port of Seattle, Washington, as a pauper. She did not understand English and had no assistance from counsel or friends to show that she was not a pauper or likely to become a public charge. The government ordered her to appear as a witness in a criminal case against another party, without her realizing that the investigation put her in legal jeopardy.[84] Her attorneys charged that this "pretended" investigation gave a government official the "combined capacity of prosecutor, judge and jury."[85]

The Supreme Court held that the final determination of facts about an immigrant "may be entrusted by Congress to executive officers."[86] There were only two dissents (and no opinions issued by them). When a statute grants discretionary power to an officer, "he is made the sole and exclusive judge of the existence of those facts, and no other tribunal, unless expressly authorized by law to do so, is at liberty to reëxamine or controvert the sufficiency of the evidence on which he acted." The judiciary had no independent authority to order the entry of foreigners who had never been naturalized or established residence in the country "in opposition to the constitutional and lawful measures of the legislative and executive branch of the National Government."[87]

What of constitutional due process? The Court offered this reasoning: "As to such persons, the decisions of executive or administrative officials, acting within powers expressly conferred by Congress, are due process of law."[88] What if their decisions were contrary to fact or based on false information? Did it make a difference if the evidence was competent or incompetent? Here the Court supplied exceedingly cloudy guidelines:

> ... this court has never held, nor must we now be understood as holding, that administrative officers, when executing the provisions of a statute involving the liberty of persons, may disregard the fundamental principles that inhere in "due process of law" as understood at the time of the adoption of the Constitution. One of these principles is that no person shall be deprived of his liberty without

83. United States v. Yamasaka, 100 Fed. 404, 407 (9th Cir. 1900).
84. The Japanese Immigrant Case, 189 U.S. 86, 88, 90 (1903).
85. Id. at 91.
86. Id. at 98.
87. Id.
88. Id.

opportunity, at some time, to be heard, before such officers, in respect of the matters upon which that liberty depends—not necessarily an opportunity upon a regular, set occasion, and according to the forms of judicial procedure, but one that will secure the prompt, vigorous action contemplated by Congress, and at the same time be appropriate to the nature of the case upon which such officers are required to act.[89]

The Court conceded that it would not be competent for an executive officer to "arbitrarily" take an alien into custody and deport him without giving "all opportunity to be heard upon the questions involving his right to be and remain in the United States." Yet the Court was satisfied if an alien "had notice, although not a formal one."[90] The Court recognized as true that Yamataya "pleads a want of knowledge of our language; that she did not understand the nature and import of the questions propounded to her; that the investigation made was a 'pretended' one; and that she did not, at the time, know that the investigation had reference to her being deported from the country."[91] Nevertheless, such considerations "cannot justify the intervention of the courts."[92] The Court said that if her lack of knowledge of English put her "at some disadvantage in the investigation conducted by that officer, that was her misfortune, and constitutes no reason, under the acts of Congress, or under any rule of law, for the intervention of the court by *habeas corpus.*"[93]

Exclusion Policy

In 1907, in the face of efforts by California to draft restrictive legislation against the Japanese, President Theodore Roosevelt negotiated a settlement to block Japanese from coming to America. Legislation passed by Congress that year included a provision that did not mention the Japanese but was obviously aimed at them. The language empowered the President, whenever satisfied that passports issued by a foreign government to its citizens "are being used for the purpose of enabling the holders to come to the continental territory of the United States to the detriment of labor conditions therein," to refuse to permit such citizens to enter the country.[94] Roosevelt issued an executive

89. Id. at 100–01.
90. Id. at 101.
91. Id. at 101–02.
92. Id. at 102.
93. Id.
94. 34 Stat. 898, sec. 1 (1907); Daniels, The Politics of Prejudice, at 40–44.

order to implement this provision, writing it in such a way as to be the least offensive to Japan.[95]

The next step was to draft a "Gentleman's Agreement," finalized in 1908, with Japan agreeing not to issue passports to the United States for skilled or unskilled laborers unless they had already lived in the United States. However, many of the unmarried Japanese men returned to the United States with "picture brides" and from those marriages had children who automatically became U.S. citizens.[96]

Not Eligible for U.S. Citizenship

Even with some quid pro quos between the Federal Government and California, prejudice toward the Japanese still ran high. Part of the animosity came from Japan's defeat of Russia in 1905, sending a powerful message around the world. For the first time in the modern period an Asian nation had defeated a Western power. As expressed by one writer, it marked a contemporary first when "a colored nation worsted a white one."[97] The superpatriotism of World War I supplied encouragement to many pseudo-scientific studies about the racial superiority of Anglo-Saxon peoples and the fear of being corrupted by alien races. Writers gloried in speaking about "clean, virile, genius-bearing blood."[98] William Randolph Hearst, functioning through his newspapers and movie empire, warned the public about military threats from Japan and stirred the pot with "yellow peril" propaganda.[99]

Those who favored exclusion of the Japanese were satisfied with a Supreme Court decision in 1922. Takao Ozawa, born in Japan, lived in the United States continuously for 20 years, graduated from Berkeley High School, spent three years as a student at the University of California, and educated his children in American schools. His family attended American churches and used English at home. The Court conceded that "he was well qualified by character and education for citizenship."[100] Yet a federal district court held that Ozawa, born in Japan and of the Japanese race, was not eligible to be a U.S. citizen.

The Supreme Court treated the issue as one of statutory interpretation, turning to language in the first naturalization act of 1790 that allowed "any

95. Daniels, The Politics of Prejudice, at 44.
96. Id. at 44–45.
97. Id. at 70.
98. Id. at 67.
99. Id. at 70, 75–76.
100. Ozawa v. United States, 260 U.S. 178, 189 (1922).

alien, being a free white person," to become a U.S. citizen.[101] The Civil War Amendments made aliens of African nativity and persons of African descent eligible for citizenship. The Court found nothing in subsequent congressional legislation to expand eligibility for U.S. citizenship beyond free white persons and former black slaves.[102] Although white persons differ markedly in color of hair and skin, the Court took "white person" to mean a person of the Caucasian race.[103] Even though "border line cases" existed among Caucasians, the Court found that Ozawa was "clearly of a race which is not Caucasian" and was therefore ineligible to be a U.S. citizen.[104]

This decision encouraged Congress to pass an immigration act that restricted Japanese admission to the United States. An option would have been a quota system, allowing only a fixed number of Japanese and other nationalities to enter the country. Congress chose a race-based policy of exclusion. Without mentioning the Japanese or any other Asian nationality, the statute of 1924 provided: "No alien ineligible to citizenship shall be admitted to the United States" unless such alien is admissible under other sections cited in the statute.[105] The exclusion applied to anyone not a free white person or former black slave. Congressional policy of making Japanese and other "non-white" races ineligible for U.S. citizenship remained until 1952, when Congress adopted this language: "The right of a person to become a naturalized citizen of the United States shall not be denied or abridged because of race or sex or because such person is married."[106]

ANARCHISTS AND OTHER UNWANTED CLASSES

Many of the new workers from Europe recalled the revolutions of 1848, and some brought with them the principles (and practices) of Marxism and radical techniques used to confront abusive political authority. The labor movement divided between those who fought for progressive reforms within capitalism and those who viewed capitalism as fundamentally hostile to individual liberty and workers' rights. Demands for major reforms were delayed by the eco-

101. Id. at 192 (1 Stat. 103, sec. 1 [1790]; 1 Stat. 414, sec. 1 [1795]).
102. Id. at 192–95.
103. Id. at 197.
104. Id. at 198. See also Yamashita v. Hinkle, 260 U.S. 199 (1922).
105. 43 Stat. 162, sec. 13(c) (1924).
106. 66 Stat. 239, sec. 311 (1952).

nomic dislocations following the depressions of 1873–1877 and 1893–1897.[107] Opponents of labor rights viewed the violence of the Haymarket Affair in 1886, in Chicago, as the work of foreign anarchists. The bomb explosion spread fear throughout the country. Newspapers lashed out at "long-haired, wild-eyed, bad-smelling, atheistic, reckless foreign wretches."[108] The 1901 assassination of President William McKinley by Leon Czolgosz, an anarchist born in Detroit of Polish immigrants, added fresh motivation for new and restrictive legislation on immigrants.

Legislation on Anarchists

In his first annual message on December 3, 1901, President Theodore Roosevelt attacked anarchists and recommended prompt passage of legislation to bar such people from the United States. He called Czolgosz "a professed anarchist, inflamed by the teachings of professed anarchists, and probably also by the reckless utterances of those who, on the stump and in the public press, appeal to the dark and evil spirits of malice and greed, envy and sullen hatred."[109] Regarding anarchistic speeches, writings, and meetings as "essentially seditious and treasonable,"[110] he urged Congress to pass legislation forbidding such people from entering the United States and to deport those already here.[111] Warming to the task, he advised Congress to not only exclude anarchists "but also all persons who are of a low moral tendency or of unsavory reputation."[112]

Legislation in 1903 levied a duty of two dollars for each passenger arriving in America who was not a citizen of the United States, Canada, Cuba, or Mexico. The funds would be deposited in the Treasury as an "immigrant fund" to cover the costs of public officials who administered and adjudicated immigration law.[113] The statute identified broad categories of aliens who would not be admitted into the United States under any circumstances:

> All idiots, insane persons, epileptics, and persons who have been insane within five years previous; persons who have had two or more attacks of insanity at any

107. John Higham, Strangers in the Land: Patterns of American Nativism, 1860–1925 35–105 (2004 ed.).

108. Id. at 55.

109. 13 Richardson 6643.

110. Id. at 6644.

111. Id.

112. Id.

113. 32 Stat. 1213 (1903).

time previously; paupers; persons likely to become a public charge; professional beggars; persons afflicted with a loathsome or with a dangerous contagious disease; persons who have been convicted of a felony or other crime or misdemeanor involving moral turpitude; polygamists, anarchists, or persons who believe in or advocate the overthrow by force or violence of the Government of the United states or of all government or of all forms of law, or the assassination of public officials; prostitutes, and persons who procure or attempt to bring in prostitutes or women for the purpose of prostitution; . . .[114]

Other sections treated anarchists in more detail. Anyone who disbelieved in or who was opposed to "all organized government," or who was a member of or affiliated with organizations that entertained and taught disbelief in or opposition to all organized government, or who advocated or taught "the duty, necessity, or propriety of the unlawful assaulting or killing of any officer or officers, either of specific individuals or of officers generally, of the Government of the United States or of any other organized government, because of his or their official character," were barrred from entering the United States or any territory or place subject to U.S. jurisdiction.[115] Anarchists so defined were prohibited from being naturalized or made a U.S. citizen.[116]

Congress did not apply this exclusionary policy to such groups as persons convicted of an offense "purely political, not involving moral turpitude"; skilled labor if labor of like kind could not be found in the country; and "professional actors, artists, lecturers, singers, ministers of any religious denomination, professors for colleges or seminaries, persons belonging to any recognized learned profession, or persons employed strictly as personal or domestic servants."[117]

How was this statute to be implemented? Congress provided few procedures to explain the exclusion of "idiots" and "anarchists." Basically, the surgeon of a vessel would make a physical and oral examination of each alien and from that inquiry decide that "he believes that no one of said aliens is an idiot, or insane person, or a pauper, or is likely to become a public charge, or is suffering from a loathsome or a dangerous contagious disease, or is a person who has been convicted of felony or other crime or misdemeanor involving moral turpitude, or a polygamist, or an anarchist, . . ."[118] If no surgeon sailed with the

114. Id. at 1214, sec. 2.
115. Id. at 1221, sec. 38.
116. Id. at 1222, sec. 39.
117. Id.
118. Id. at 1216, sec. 13.

vessel, the mental and physical examinations and the verifications of the lists were made "by some competent surgeon employed by the owners of the said vessel."[119] Upon arrival, aliens were also examined for defects and diseases by medical officers of the U.S. Marine-Hospital Service or civil surgeons.[120]

From 1903 to 1921, the United States excluded thirty-eight persons charged with anarchistic beliefs and deported fourteen aliens for anarchism from 1911 to 1919.[121] John Turner was one of the individuals excluded. His attorneys, Clarence Darrow and Edgar L. Masters, argued that the statute abridged Turner's freedom of speech.[122] The Supreme Court found no constitutional violations. Turner did not "become one of the people to whom these things are secured by our Constitution by an attempt to enter forbidden by law."[123] Darrow and Masters objected that Congress had provided for the trial of an alien "by a Board of Special Inquiry, secret and apart from the public; without indictment; without confrontation of witnesses; without the privilege to the accused of obtaining witnesses; without the right of counsel."[124] The Court had no difficulty in dismissing that complaint on the ground that the rights available to an accused in a criminal proceeding do not apply to the exclusion or deportation of an alien.[125]

In a concurrence, Justice David Brewer expressed concern about the type of power Congress had placed in executive officials: "I do not believe it within the power of Congress to give to ministerial officers a final adjudication of the right to liberty or to oust the courts from the duty of inquiry respecting both law and facts."[126] Scholars examining the administrative processes used to exclude and deport aliens were also disturbed by the lack of basic procedural rights. Brewer found it unnecessary to consider what rights Turner might have had "if he were only what is called by way of differentiation a philosophical anarchist, one who simply entertains and expresses the opinion that all government is a mistake, and that society would be better off without any."[127]

119. Id. at 1217, sec. 14.

120. Id., sec. 17.

121. William Preston, Jr., *Aliens and Dissenters: Federal Suppression of Radicals, 1903–1933*, at 33 (2d ed. 1994).

122. Turner v. Williams, 194 U.S. 279, 286 (1904).

123. Id. at 292.

124. Id. at 286.

125. Id. at 289–90.

126. Id. at 295.

127. Id. at 296. See United States ex rel. Turner v. Williams, 125 Fed. 253 (Cir. Ct. S.D. N.Y. 1903). Also on the exclusion of anarchists, see Jane Perry Clark, *Deportation of Aliens from*

Espionage and Sedition

With America's entry into the Great War in Europe, Congress passed legislation designed to punish espionage and sedition, categories to be turned against socialists and radicals. Legislation in 1917 made it a felony for anyone, when America was at war, to "willfully make or convey false reports or false statements with intent to interfere with the operation or success of the military or naval forces of the United States or to promote the success of its enemies." It prohibited anyone to "willfully cause or attempt to cause" insubordination in the military or naval forces. Punishments included a fine up to $10,000 or imprisonment for not more than twenty years, or both.[128]

Congress amended the statute the next year to cover seditious utterances. Whoever, when the United States was at war, "shall willfully utter, print, write, or publish any disloyal, profane, scurrilous, or abusive language about the form of government of the United States, or the Constitution of the United States, or the military or naval forces of the United States, or the flag of the United States, or the uniform of the Army or Navy of the United States," or used any language intended to bring the form of government of the United States, the Constitution, or U.S. armed forces "into contempt, scorn, contumely, or disrepute," would be punished by a fine of not more than $10,000 or imprisonment for not more than 20 years, or both. How were such words as "scurrilous" to be applied? The new language penalized anyone who willfully uttered, printed, wrote, or published any language intended to "incite, provoke, or encourage resistance to the United States, or to promote the cause of its enemies, or shall willfully display any flag of any foreign enemy," or attempted to curtail the production of any products necessary for the war effort.[129]

Radicals and antiwar critics paid a heavy price. Rose Pastor Stokes, a Russian socialist, was convicted for saying that "I am for the people and the government is for the profiteer."[130] States passed their own prohibitions on seditious utterances. Joseph Gilbert was prosecuted and sentenced under a Minnesota law for commenting: "We were stampeded into this war by newspaper rot to pull England's chestnuts out of the fire."[131] Some federal judges pushed back against the government. In one case, federal agents and soldiers conducted a warrantless raid on a union to seize pamphlets and other evidence to be used

the United States to Europe 215–31 (1931).
128. 40 Stat. 219, sec. 3 (1917).
129. Id. at 553 (1918).
130. Geoffrey R. Stone, Perilous Times: Free Speech in Wartime 171 (2004).
131. Id. at 211.

against its members. There was no disorder, said the court, "save that of the raiders."[132] The court remarked on the illegalities:

> Assuming petitioner is of the so-called "Reds" and of the evil practice charged against him, he and his kind are less a danger to America than are those who indorse or use the methods that brought him to deportation. These latter are the mob and the spirit of violence and intolerance incarnate, the most alarming manifestation in America today. Far worse than the immediate wrongs to individuals that they do, they undermine the morale of the people, excite the latter's fears, distrust of our institutions, doubts of the sufficiency of law and authority; they incline the people toward arbitrary power, which for protection cowards too often seek, and knaves too readily grant, and subject to which the people cease to be courageous and free, and become timid and enslaved.[133]

After 9/11, some states reflected on their abuses of World War I opponents. In May 2006, Montana Governor Brian Schweitzer issued pardons for seventy-five men and three women who had been convicted under its sedition law. He told relatives of the convicted: "Across this country it was a time in which we had lost our minds."[134]

Initially, the Supreme Court strongly supported the government's effort to punish those who resisted the war. It upheld the conviction of Charles Schenck and other members of the Socialist party for mailing printed circulars intended to obstruct the recruiting and enlistment of U.S. soldiers. In a brief opinion for a unanimous Court, Justice Oliver Wendell Holmes upheld the convictions on the ground that the circulars constituted "a clear and present danger" that Congress had a right to control. He admitted that "in many places and in ordinary times the defendants in saying all that was said in the circular would have been within their constitutional rights."[135] At other places in the opinion Holmes seemed to identify not merely "a clear and present danger" but even a "tendency" to create harm.[136]

Holmes offered this analogy: "The most stringent protection of free speech would not protect a man in falsely shouting fire in a theatre and causing a

---

132. Ex parte Jackson, 263 F. 110, 111 (D. Mont. 1920).

133. Id. at 113.

134. Christopher M. Finan, From the Palmer Raids to the Patriot Act: A History of the Fight for Free Speech in America 303 (2007). See Clemens P. Work, Darkest before Dawn: Sedition and Free Speech in the American West (2005); H. C. Peterson and Gilbert C. Fite, Opponents of War, 1917–1918 (1957).

135. Schenck v. United States, 249 U.S. 47, 52 (1919).

136. Id. at 51, 52.

panic."[137] The fire-in-a-theater argument was more emotional than persuasive reasoning. Falsely shouting fire in a crowded theater to produce panic has
nothing to do with circulating a leaflet that expresses an *opinion* about a war
or military commitment. The first can never be justified. What condemns the
second? Holmes danced past that question. Academic criticism of the "clear
and present danger" standards prompted Holmes within a few years to change
his position.

A week later, Holmes wrote two other unanimous, brief opinions upholding convictions of those who opposed the war. Once again he relied on a non
sequitur: "We venture to believe that neither Hamilton nor Madison, nor any
other competent person then or later, ever supposed that to make criminal
the counseling of a murder within the jurisdiction of Congress would be an
unconstitutional interference with free speech."[138] The individuals were prosecuted for publishing articles in opposition to the draft, not for counseling
murder. One case involved the prosecution of Eugene Debs, leader of the Socialist Party, for speaking against the draft.[139] These decisions by Holmes appeared to drop the clear and present danger test and prefer a "bad tendency"
standard designed to curb speech whenever it poses a threat or a danger to
society. In the Debs trial, Holmes explained that the jury was instructed that
they could not find him guilty "for advocacy of any of his opinions unless the
words used had as their natural tendency and reasonably probable effect to
obstruct the recruiting service, &c., and unless the defendant had the specific
intent to do so in his mind."[140]

In a penetrating critique in the *Harvard Law Review* in June 1919, law professor Zechariah Chafee, Jr., defended the right of citizens to not only criticize
government in time of peace but especially in time of war and emergency conditions. He argued that the First Amendment declared a national policy that
favored broad discussion of all public questions. Such a position should make
Congress reluctant and cautious in enacting restrictions on what citizens said
and wrote.[141] The First Amendment protected not merely an individual's interest in speaking out but society's interest in hearing criticism on the commitment of military force and permitting impassioned debate that directly

---

137. Id. at 52.

138. Frohwerk v. United States, 249 U.S. 204, 206 (1919).

139. Debs v. United States, 249 U.S. 211 (1919).

140. Id. at 216. For background on the "bad tendency test," see David M. Rabban, Free
Speech in Its Forgotten Years 132–46 (1997).

141. Zechariah Chafee, Jr., "Freedom of Speech in War Time," 32 Harv. L. Rev. 932, 934
(1919).

and forcefully challenges the government. Such criticism is not seditious. It is a citizen's duty.

Chafee aimed his critique particularly at the bad tendency test and its survival in all the years since the English scholar William Blackstone offered legal doctrines. The response by Jefferson and Hamilton to the Sedition Act of 1798, Chafee said, "leaves the Blackstonian interpretation of free speech in America without a leg to stand on."[142] The First Amendment "is just as much a part of the Constitution as the war clauses, and that it is equally accurate to say that the war clauses cannot be invoked to break down freedom of speech."[143] For those who believed that the Bill of Rights can be placed on the shelf in time of war by the "uncontrolled will" of the government, he insisted that the first ten amendments to the Constitution "were drafted by men who had just been through a war."[144] In a direct attack on the bad tendency test: "the First Amendment forbids the punishment of words merely for their injurious tendencies."[145]

Chafee regretted that Holmes, in his decisions in *Schenck*, *Frohwerk*, and *Debs*, "did nothing to emphasize the social interest behind free speech, and show the need of balancing even in war time."[146] He thought that the clear and present danger test was a better guide for future free speech cases than the bad tendency test.[147] Even after the government has declared war and committed its weight behind military action, "there is bound to be a confused mixture of good and bad arguments in its support, and a wide difference of opinion as to its objects. Truth can be sifted out from falsehood only if the government is vigorously and constantly cross-examined, so that the fundamental issues of the struggle may be clearly defined, and the war may not be diverted to improper ends, or conducted with an undue sacrifice of life and liberty, or prolonged after its just purposes are accomplished."[148] Chafee believed that legal proceedings "prove that an opponent makes the best cross-examiner." For that reason, "it is a disastrous mistake to limit criticism to those who favor the war."[149]

Chafee's onslaught forced rethinking by some Justices. In a decision issued on November 10, 1919, the Court upheld the convictions of those who

142. Id. at 953.
143. Id. at 955.
144. Id.
145. Id. at 960.
146. Id. at 968.
147. Id. at 969.
148. Id. at 958.
149. Id.

advocated that workers not produce war materials, objected to U.S. involvement in the war, encouraged resistance, and advocated a general strike. All five defendants were born in Russia and had lived in the United States for periods varying from five to ten years, "but none of them had applied for naturalization."[150] For many, their decision not to apply for citizenship was a telltale sign of disloyalty and clear evidence of belonging to an enemy class. They were self-described "rebels," "revolutionalists," "anarchists," and "socialists."[151] This decision featured a dissent by Holmes joined by Brandeis. The string of unanimous opinions had ended.

In reviewing his handiwork in *Schenck, Frohwerk,* and *Debs,* Holmes found no reason to doubt that the questions of law posed in those cases "were rightly decided."[152] While refusing to disown his offspring, his jettisoning of the balancing test was clear. He now underscored his reliance on a variant of the clear and danger test: "I do not doubt for a moment that by the same reasoning that would justify punishing persuasion to murder, the United States constitutionally may punish speech that produces or is intended to produce a clear and imminent danger that it will bring about forthwith certain substantive evils that the United States constitutionally may seek to prevent." That power, Holmes said, "is greater in time of war than in time of peace because war opens dangers that do not exist at other times."[153]

Holmes was not prepared to adopt Chafee's heightened commitment to free speech in time of war. He agreed that government could punish those who advocated "substantive evils." But Congress could not "forbid all effort to change the mind of the country."[154] He found nothing in the leaflets printed and distributed by the defendants of any intent to create an immediate danger to the war aims of the government. He objected to sentencing individuals to twenty years in prison for publishing leaflets "that I believe the defendants had as much right to publish as the Government has to publish the Constitution of the United States now vainly invoked by them."[155] Holmes advanced the theme of social costs that Chafee had developed:

> Persecution for the expression of opinions seems to me perfectly logical. If
> you have no doubt of your premises or your power and want a certain result

150. Abrams v. United States, 250 U.S. 616, 617 (1919).
151. Id. at 617–18.
152. Id. at 627.
153. Id. at 627–28.
154. Id. at 628.
155. Id. at 629

with all your heart you naturally express your wishes in law and sweep away all opposition. . . . But when men have realized that time has upset many fighting faiths, they may come to believe even more than they believe the very foundations of their own conduct that the ultimate good desired is better reached by free trade in ideas—that the best test of truth is the power of the thought to get itself accepted in the competition of the market, and that truth is the only ground upon which their wishes safely can be carried out. That at any rate is the theory of our Constitution. It is an experiment, as all life is an experiment. Every year if not every day we have to wager our salvation upon some prophecy based upon imperfect knowledge.[156]

The Sedition Act of 1918 prohibited "any disloyal, profane, scurrilous, or abusive language" about the form of government, the Constitution, soldiers and sailors, the flag, or uniform of the armed forces. State laws, declaring it a misdemeanor to teach or advocate that citizens should not assist the United States in carrying on a war with its enemies, were upheld.[157] A New York law punished persons for advocating the overthrow of government. The Supreme Court sustained the statute in a 1925 ruling, defining advocacy as "a call to action" rather than the expression of abstract doctrine.[158] Holmes and Brandeis objected to the Court's reasoning, insisting that "[e]very idea is an incitement."[159] They found in the activities of the defendants "no present danger of an attempt to overthrow the government by force."[160]

Two decisions by the Supreme Court in 1927 tackled the issue of syndicalism: the doctrine that workers could use force to seize control of the economy and the government. A unanimous Court upheld California's statute against criminal syndicalism, but a concurrence by Justice Brandeis offered a masterful essay on the principles of free speech, the essential value of liberty in a democratic society, and the risks to political stability when government allows fear to breed repression and hate.[161] "Those who won our independence by revolution," he said, "were not cowards. They did not fear political change. They did not exalt order at the cost of liberty."[162]

156. Id. at 630.
157. Gilbert v. Minnesota, 254 U.S. 325 (1920).
158. Gitlow v. New York, 268 U.S. 652 (1925).
159. Id. at 673.
160. Id.
161. Whitney v. California, 274 U.S. 357, 375–78 (1927).
162. Id. at 377.

The Red Scare

The peace treaty in 1919 might have tempered political repression in America, inviting a return to normalcy and free discourse. Instead, widespread fear and hysteria continued after the war because of the Bolshevik Revolution of 1917, a peace treaty between Russia and Germany in March 1918, and the determination of Communist leaders to spread their doctrines and control into Europe and abroad. In the post-war years, the assumption that the United States "was under serious attack by the Reds found a wide acceptance."[163] The level of threat was heightened for those who believed that the Bolsheviki were "German-spawned" and acting as agents of the Kaiser.[164] Tension increased throughout 1919 with a steady diet of labor strikes, riots, and violence.[165]

The tone of the coming confrontation is reflected in an article published by Attorney General Mitchell A. Palmer in February 1920, entitled "The Case Against the Reds." He faulted Congress for failing to pass legislation that he said was needed to prevent radicals from taking over the government. He presented a frightening picture: "Like a prairie-fire, the blaze of revolution was sweeping over every American institution of law and order a year ago. It was eating its way into the homes of the American workman, its sharp tongues of revolutionary heat were licking into the altars of the churches, leaping into the belfry of the school bell, crawling into the sacred corners of American homes, seeking to replace marriage vows with libertine laws, burning up the foundations of society."[166]

In November 1919, the Justice Department began its first major roundup of radicals and aliens, preparing them for deportation. Out of 650 arrested, 249 were deported on December 21. Two weeks later, on January 2, 1920, what was known as the "Palmer raids" picked up an additional four thousand radicals in thirty-three cities. Some three thousand of those were deported.[167] Palmer's attitude toward immigrants and aliens is evident when he described those captured as having "sly and crafty eyes . . . lopsided faces, sloping brows and misshapen features," reflecting "cupidity, cruelty, insanity and crime."[168] Acting Secretary of Labor Louis F. Post supplied a brake to these actions by having

---

163. Robert K. Murray, Red Scare: A Study in National Hysteria, 1919–1920, at 16 (1964 ed.).

164. Id. at 34.

165. Id. at 57–152.

166. George E. Mowry, The Twenties: Fords, Flappers & Fanatics 122 (1963).

167. Stone, Perilous Times, at 223–24 (2004); Preston, Aliens and Dissenters 208–37.

168. Stone, Perilous Times, at 224.

his department review each of the cases. Through his intervention he canceled a number of deportation orders.[169]

Federal courts turned aside a number of deportations because of procedural violations. On February 12, 1920, a district court in Montana declared a deportation proceeding unfair on several grounds, including the government's refusal to produce a witness for cross-examination. The government, without a warrant, raided the working place of the Butte Union of the Industrial Workers of the World (IWW or Wobblies) in February 1919, destroyed property, beat union members, and seized papers and documents. The court noted: "There was no disorder save that of the raiders."[170] It issued a blunt warning to government misconduct. No emergency "in war or peace" warrants the violation of the individual rights of personal security and safety and orderly and due process of law. In an emergency, "real or assumed, tyrants of all ages have found excuse for their destruction." Without those fundamental rights, "democracy perishes, autocracy reigns, and the innocent suffer with the guilty."[171] What of the threat posed by "Reds" and the practices charged against them? The defendant in the case was "less a danger to America than are those who indorse or use the methods that brought him to deportation." The court expressed its concern about mob violence, creating fear among the public, and the exercise of arbitrary government power, which "cowards too often seek, and knaves too readily grant, and subject to which the people cease to be courageous and free, and become timid and enslaved."[172]

In June 1920, a federal district court in Massachusetts reviewed the pending deportation of twenty aliens charged only with being members of the Communist Party or the Communist Labor Party. The court acknowledged that proceedings for the deportation of aliens are not criminal proceedings, but pointed out that the Fourth, Fifth, Sixth, and Fourteenth Amendments are not limited to citizens but apply to all persons within the United States, including aliens. Aliens may not be deprived of their liberty without due process of law and are exempt from unwarranted searches and seizures. In a deportation proceeding, "an unfair or otherwise misleading record is as much a fraud upon the law and upon the Secretary of Labor as upon the alien."[173]

---

169. Higham, Strangers in the Land 231; Louis F. Post, The Deportations Delirium of Nineteen-Twenty: A Personal Narrative of an Historic Official Experience (1923).

170. Ex parte Jackson, 263 Fed. 110, 111 (D. Mont. 1920).

171. Id. at 113.

172. Id.

173. Colyer v. Skeffington, 265 Fed. 17, 30 (D. Mass. 1920).

The court explained that Congress had entrusted the administration of immigration laws to the Department of Labor, not the Department of Justice.[174] However, the conduct of the January 2 raid marked a wholesale transfer of Labor's statutory duties to Justice, "relegating the Department of Labor to the function, almost purely formal, of making records of cases, in effect predetermined by the Department of Justice."[175] Justice carried out the raid in a manner that violated rules that had been promulgated by Labor.[176] Justice violated the statutory provisions that Congress had adopted for search warrants in the Espionage Act of 1917.[177] Rules were changed in midstream to deny the right of an alien to have assistance from counsel, withholding professional help sorely needed for those unable to understand English.[178] The Justice Department gathered evidence to be used against the aliens, only after which they could consult an attorney.[179]

This process bears similarities to the treatment after 9/11 of U.S. citizens designated as an "enemy combatant" (Hamdi and Padilla) and detainees held at Guantánamo Bay. An alien picked up in the Palmer raids "had no counsel to represent him until the hearing was practically closed."[180] The Justice Department told agents to hold aliens incommunicado until advised otherwise.[181] One alien committed suicide by "throwing himself from the fifth floor and dashing his brains out in the corridor below in the presence of other horrified aliens."[182]

For nine of the aliens, the court decided the deportation orders were invalid because of deficiencies in the trial: unreliable records, unfair hearings, and a lack of due process.[183] The court found no evidence that the Communist Party "is an organization advocating the overthrow of the government of the United States by force or violence."[184] Statements by the court and subsequent decisions by the Department of Labor set other aliens free.[185] Attorney General

174. Id. at 28.
175. Id. at 36.
176. Id. at 44 (Rule 22, Subdivision 10, at 29–30).
177. Id. at 44–45 (40 Stat. 228–30, Title XI).
178. Id. at 46–47.
179. Id.
180. Id. at 49.
181. Id. at 37 (fifth paragraph).
182. Id. at 45.
183. Id. at 71–76.
184. Id. at 79 (see also 58–64).
185. Id. at 79–80.

Palmer, who expected the raids to vault him into the White House, was so discredited by his arbitrary actions and exaggerated threats that the prospects for higher office evaporated.[186]

GERMANS

Germans settled in America before its independence from England and continued coming in great numbers from the 1830s forward, filling every occupation from peddler to small shop owner to the heights of the banking industry. With each decade they prospered, assimilated, and moved from poor communities to better ones. As with other immigrants, they made the always difficult journey from newcomer to neighbor, downtrodden to well-to-do, suspected to accepted, from stranger to American. By the end of the century, Germans had made their way to a comfortable place in American culture and fully integrated, or so it seemed.[187]

Impact of the Great War

The war in Europe, beginning in 1914, directed a spotlight on a new and hated enemy: Germany. The admirable values used earlier to describe Germans—hardworking, devoted to learning, music, philosophy, literature, and the sciences—were pushed aside to make room for frightening and ugly stereotypes: "the will to war, will to power and will to overpower."[188] The new generalization was German militarism and imperialism. Kaiser Wilhelm II was savaged in the American press as an unscrupulous and overbearing autocrat.[189] German-Americans wrote critically of their home country, accusing the spirit of Prussianism of

> throwing overboard everything that civilization and humanitarian progress of centuries had accomplished toward lessening the cruelty, the hatred and the sufferings engendered by war and toward protecting non-combatants from its terrors . . . the violation of innocent Belgium, in defiance of solemn treaties,

186. Murray, Red Scare 250–60.
187. For example, Stephen Birmingham, "Our Crowd": The Great Jewish Families of New York (1967).
188. Id. at 318.
189. Frederick C. Luebke, Bonds of Loyalty: German Americans and World War I, at 70–78 (1974).

and unspeakable treatment inflicted on her people, the bombardment without warning of open places (which Germany was the first to practice), the destruction of great monuments of art which belong to all mankind, the *Lusitania* horror, the strewing of mines; the use of poison gases, causing death by torture or incurable disease; the taking of hostages—these are the facts that the noncombatant nations charge against Germany.[190]

Similar to indiscriminate attacks after 9/11 against Muslims and Arabs, Germans during World War I were labeled as butchers and terrorists. British and American propaganda "relentlessly portrayed the war as an Armageddon in which the forces of freedom were arrayed in a fight to the death against autocracy. In this Manichean conflict, the Allies sought to liberate the human spirit while the Central Powers worked to enslave it."[191] Germans were no longer Germans. They acquired a new name: Huns, a modern type of Vandal bent on primitive and cruel destruction. As with the post-9/11 period, German attacks on Belgian civilians "shocked the civilized world, because armies in modern Europe had generally avoided terrorism."[192]

In 1915, German submarines sank the unarmed British liner *Falaba,* damaged the American oil tanker *Gulflight,* and torpedoed the British liner *Lusitania,* which had left New York City bound for Liverpool. Some 1,200 passengers lost their lives, including 124 Americans. The ship carried thousands of cases of ammunition to assist Great Britain, raising legitimate questions about America violating its announced policy of neutrality. Other acts of German sabotage in the United States were efforts to stop the flow of munitions to Germany's enemies at a time when America was technically neutral. Targets included industrial plants and the spectacular explosion of Black Tom Island in New York harbor on July 30, 1916.[193] German air attacks against England were the first aerial bombings in history, condemned as the wanton targeting of innocent civilians. In addition to documented German outrages, British and American propagandists were all too eager to add fictional but highly

---

190. Birmingham, "Our Crowd," at 318 (March 1915 letter from Otto Kahn to his brother-in-law, Felix Deutsch. Intercepted by a French censor and gradually circulated around the world, including publication in the *New York Times).*

191. William G. Ross, Forging New Freedoms: Nativism, Education, and the Constitution, 1917–1927, at 30 (1994).

192. Id. at 33.

193. Chad Millman, The Detonators: The Secret Plot to Destroy America and an Epic Hunt for Justice (2006); Jules Witcover, Sabotage at Black Tom: Imperial Germany's Secret War in America, 1914–1917 (1989); Henry Landau, The Enemy Within (1937).

potent stories of German atrocities against civilization. Brutalities were committed by both sides, but the eventual victory by Allies allowed them to insist on trials for "war criminals" and to demand heavy reparation payments by Germany.[194]

Vigilante justice turned against German-Americans in the United States. In Illinois, on the night of April 4, 1918, a mob forced Robert Prager to kiss the flag and sing "The Star-Spangled Banner." The crowd dragged him down the street wrapped in "Old Glory," after which he was marched out of town and lynched.[195] Superpatriots committed other acts of violence against German-Americans: beatings, floggings, tar-and-feathering, painting German churches yellow, and burning and dynamiting them.[196]

The need to raise money to finance America's involvement in the war prompted a series of Liberty Loan campaigns. German-Americans who failed to contribute were denounced for lacking patriotism.[197] On their own, German societies and communities subscribed, and oversubscribed, in large numbers. Germans who declined to finance the war were summoned before an extra-legal "slacker court," "loyalty court," or an "Incognito Military Court" where they were threatened with violence, loss of jobs, eviction from homes, confiscation of farm animals, and other punishments.[198]

Teaching German Outlawed

Hostility against German-Americans prompted some states, particularly in the Middle West, to prohibit the use of the German language in schools and in public. On May 23, 1918, Iowa Governor William L. Harding issued a proclamation that designated English as the sole medium of instruction in public, private, and denominational schools. He prescribed English as the exclusive means of communication in public addresses and conversations in public places, including on trains and over the telephone.[199] In justifying his proclamation, Harding explained that "there is no use in anyone wasting his time praying in other languages than English. God is listening only to the English tongue."[200] Other states, including Kansas, Minnesota, Missouri, Nebraska,

---

194. James Morgan Read, Atrocity Propaganda, 1914–1919 (1941).
195. Luebke, Bonds of Loyalty, at 3–10.
196. Id. at 14–15, 280–81.
197. Carl Wittke, German-Americans and the World War 149 (1936).
198. Id. at 157–60.
199. Id. at 44.
200. Id. at 45.

North Dakota, South Dakota, and Montana, restricted the use of German in schools. In a scene that would have fit well in Nazi Germany in the 1930s, a mob in Lewistown, Montana, seized German textbooks from the high school and carried them outside to be burnt.[201]

The armistice that brought the Great War to a close in 1919 did not end attacks on German-Americans or lift restrictions on the use of German in schools. Germans in America learned that the more they could disguise their past, the safer they were. People changed their names from Schmidt to Smith, Schneider to Snider, Mueller to Miller, Schwartz to Black, Weiss to White. Germantown, Nebraska, changed its name to Garland. In Iowa, the town of Berlin became Lincoln. Being German carried greater liabilities than being Jewish. My father and his father did their best to conceal not just their Jewish background but, much more importantly, their ties to German culture. The 1920 census states that my grandfather's mother tongue was French (it was German) and his parents came from France and Switzerland (they came from Hungary and present-day Croatia, all part of the Austro-Hungarian Empire). My grandfather was born in Vienna, Austria. Changing Fischer to Fisher was a modest but well-advised step.

Test cases challenging statutory restrictions on teaching the German language were filed in Iowa, Nebraska, and Ohio. Nebraska prohibited the teaching in any private, denominational, parochial, or public school of any modern language, other than English, to any child who had not attained and successfully passed the eighth grade. The state defended the statute as a legitimate exercise of the police power. The purpose was to prevent the teaching of foreign languages to children "of tender years before such children are grounded in the English tongue."[202] The statute did not forbid the use of foreign languages by persons of maturity, nor did it prevent the study of foreign languages after the eighth grade. The state wanted to "create an enlightened American citizenship in sympathy with the principles and ideals of this country, and to prevent children reared in America from being trained and educated in foreign languages and foreign ideals before they have had an opportunity to learn the English language and observe American ideals."[203]

The state reasoned that if it was within the police power of a state to regulate wages, set standards for housing conditions in crowded cities, prohibit dark rooms in tenement houses, and compel landlords to put windows in

---

201. Id.
202. Meyer v. Nebraska, 262 U.S. 390, 393 (1923).
203. Id. at 393–94.

their tenements to enable tenants to enjoy the sunshine, "it is within the police power of the State to compel every resident of Nebraska so to educate his children that the sunshine of American ideals will permeate the life of the future citizens of this Republic."[204] Twenty-one other states enacted similar foreign language laws.[205]

Enter the Supreme Court

Writing for the Supreme Court in 1923, Justice James McReynolds described the case from Nebraska. On May 25, 1920, while instructing at the Zion Parochial School, Robert T. Meyer was arrested for teaching the reading of German to a student who had not attained and successfully passed the eighth grade. The state statute was passed on the ground that "an emergency exists."[206] The statute was not passed merely as part of the police power. It specifically dealt with a pending emergency without specifying how long that emergency would last and what type of circumstances would bring it to an end. Nebraska did not prohibit the teaching of all foreign languages. The proscription applied only to modern languages. Schools could still instruct students in Latin, Greek, and Hebrew.[207]

The Court looked to the purpose of the Fourteenth Amendment, which prohibits any state from depriving "any person of life, liberty, or property, without due process of law." What did "liberty" consist of? Justice McReynolds concluded that it meant not merely freedom from bodily restraint "but also the right of the individual to contract, to engage in any of the common occupations of life, to acquire useful knowledge, to marry, establish a home and bring up children, to worship God according to the dictates of his own conscience, and generally to enjoy those privileges long recognized at common law as essential to the orderly pursuit of happiness by free men."[208] The breadth of that liberty "may not be interfered with, under the guise of protecting the public interest, by legislative action which is arbitrary or without reasonable relation to some purpose within the competency of the State to effect."[209]

"Mere knowledge of the German language," McReynolds said, "cannot reasonably be regarded as harmful."[210] Learning other languages has been

204. Id.
205. Id. at 395.
206. Id. at 397.
207. Id. at 400–01.
208. Id. at 399.
209. Id. at 399–400.
210. Id. at 400.

regarded as "helpful and desirable." Nebraska's decision to allow the teaching of ancient but not modern languages interfered with the opportunity of students to acquire knowledge and the power of parents to control their children's education. The state's desire to have English as the mother tongue of all children could not override the liberty interests of child and parent. McReynolds drew attention to the dangers of the Ideal Commonwealth imagined by Plato, where the state had authority to take children from their parents and raise them for interests known only to the state. Individual rights were subordinated to the interests of the state. McReynolds did not want that model of government imposed on America.

Turning to the Nebraska law, McReynolds said no emergency "has arisen which renders knowledge by a child of some language other than English so clearly harmful as to justify its inhibition with the consequent infringement of rights long freely enjoyed."[211] The statute was arbitrary and had no reasonable relation to any objective within the competency of the state. Available evidence contradicted the position of Nebraska that learning a modern language before the eighth grade did any damage to the health, morals, or understanding of a child.[212]

In companion cases involving similar statutes from Iowa and Ohio, the Court struck down those laws as well.[213] Justice Holmes dissented in both cases. His reasoning is of special interest because it applies to state laws designed to sterilize the "unfit," discussed in the next section. Holmes found it impossible to conclude that the circumstances present in Nebraska and other states prevented them from passing legislation "regarded as a reasonable or even necessary method of reaching the desired result."[214] If children heard only Polish or French or German spoken at home, why was it unreasonable to provide that the child hear and speak only English at school? Holmes did not explain why modern languages could be prohibited but schools could teach Latin, Greek, and Hebrew. He ended on this note: "I think I appreciate the objection to the law but it appears to me to present a question upon which men reasonably might differ and therefore I am unable to say that the Constitution of the United States prevents the experiment being tried."[215] Within

---

211. Id. at 403.

212. Id.

213. Bartels v. Iowa, 262 U.S. 404 (1923).

214. Id. at 412.

215. Id. For the lower court decision on the Iowa case, see State v. Bartels, 191 Iowa 1060 (1921). Lower court case in Ohio: Pohl v. State, 102 Ohio St. 474 (1921). Lower court decisions in Nebraska: Nebraska Dist. of Evangelical Lutheran Synod v. McKelvie, 104 Neb. 93

a few years Holmes had an opportunity to pass judgment on another political and legal experiment: mandatory sterilization of individuals considered by the state to lack the proper qualities to be parents. Plato's *Republic* would soon be revisited.

THE UNFIT

Just as some states relied on the police power to prohibit the teaching of German in schools, so did public officials and private citizens decide that under the broad banner of "public health and safety" they could use mandatory sterilization to prevent certain individuals from having children. In the 1850s, Herbert Spencer's *Social Statics* and Charles Darwin's *The Origin of Species* analyzed the process of natural selection that led to "survival of the fittest." Gregor Mendel conducted his experiments on genetics and heredity, but it was left to Francis J. Galton in the 1860s to suggest that "bountiful breeding of the best people would evolve mankind into a superlative species of grade and quality."[216]

Theories of eugenics continued to develop after the Civil War. An 1877 study by Richard Louis Dugdale, *The Jukes*, popularized the notion that crime was largely hereditary. Cesare Lombroso's *Criminal Man* (1896–1897) identified anthropological features that marked the born criminal. A study published in 1893 claimed that "it is established beyond controversy that criminals and paupers, both, are degenerate; the imperfect, knotty, knurly, worm-eaten, half-rotten fruit of the race."[217] The eugenics movement supplied the remedy: compulsory sterilization.

In the hands of reformers and progressives at the time of World War I, eugenics became a respected argument for opposing mixed marriages and excluding "lower stock" immigrants from Mediterranean countries, Eastern Europe, and Russia. Sterilization was designed to have wide application. A model eugenics law published in 1922 contemplated sterilization for the feeble-minded, insane, "criminalistic" (including the delinquent and "wayward"), epileptic, inebriates and drug users, diseased (tuberculosis, syphilis, and leprosy), blind

(1919); Meyer v. State, 107 Neb. 657 (1922); Nebraska Dist. of Evangelical Lutheran Synod v. McKelvie, 108 Neb. 448 (1922).

216. Edwin Black, War Against the Weak: Eugenics and America's Campaign to Create a Master Race 15 (2003).

217. Henry M. Boies, Prisoners and Paupers 266 (1893).

and seriously impaired vision, deaf and seriously impaired hearing, deformed (including the crippled), and a definition of dependents that reached to "orphans, ne'er-do-wells, the homeless, tramps, and paupers."[218]

Prisoners

Some early decisions by federal courts rejected state efforts to sterilize prisoners for eugenic reasons. In 1914 a federal district court struck down a law in Iowa that required the vasectomy of criminals convicted twice of a felony. Part of the legal problem lay with the definition of felony, broadened in some cases to cover offenses previously considered misdemeanors, such as breaking an electric globe or unfastening a strap in a harness.[219] The district court regarded vasectomy as a cruel and unusual punishment: "This belongs to the Dark Ages."[220] It found the secrecy surrounding the decision to authorize vasectomies repugnant: "There is no actual hearing. There is no evidence. The proceedings are private. The public does not know what is being done until it is done. Witnesses are not produced, or, if produced, they are not cross-examined. What records are examined is not known. The prisoner is not advised of the proceedings until ordered to submit to the operation."[221] To the court, the statute represented legislative punishment without a jury trial.[222]

In 1918, another federal district court struck down a Nevada law that authorized state trial courts to compel certain criminals to submit to a vasectomy. The law covered those convicted of rape, carnal abuse of a female under the age of ten, and those adjudged to be a habitual criminal. The law was optional in the sense that the trial court "may" order the operation depending on the proclivities of the judge. The federal court found the statute unconstitutional by inflicting a cruel and unusual punishment.[223] Whether vasectomy was actually performed depended on the judge's personal preference. The court described vasectomy as "no more cruel than branding, the amputation of a finger, the slitting of a tongue, or the cutting off of any ear; but, when resorted to as punishment, it is ignominious and degrading, and in that sense is cruel. Certainly it would be unusual in Nevada."[224]

---

218. Harry Hamilton Laughlin, Eugenical Sterilization in the United States 446–47 (1922).
219. Davis v. Berry, 216 Fed. 413, 417–18 (S.D. Iowa 1914).
220. Id. at 416.
221. Id. at 418.
222. Id. at 419.
223. Mickle v. Henrichs, 262 Fed. 687, 688 (D. Nev. 1918).
224. Id. at 690.

After 9/11, some federal officials and private citizens argued that if the government could kill a terrorist on the battlefield it could surely do the lesser, such as torturing the individual during interrogation to obtain information. The federal court in the Nevada case found this kind of logic wholly deficient: "It will not do to argue that, inasmuch as the death penalty may be inflicted for this crime, vasectomy, or any other similar mutilation of the body, cannot be regarded as cruel, because the greater includes the less. The fact that the extreme penalty is not exacted is evidence that the criminal is considered worthy to live, and to attempt reformation. . . . [A] fair opportunity to retrieve his fall is quite as important as the eugenics possibilities of vasectomy."[225]

Carrie Buck's Case

The eugenics lawsuit that reached the Supreme Court originated in Virginia. In 1925, the Virginia Supreme Court of Appeals upheld the state's compulsory sterilization law. Carrie Buck had been committed to the State Colony for Epileptics and Feeble-Minded at the age of 18. Her mother had been committed to the same institution, and Carrie had just given birth to an illegitimate child who the state claimed was of "defective mentality." Under Virginia law, the superintendent of the institution could propose to a board that a mental defective be sterilized—vasectomy for men and salpingectomy (cutting the Fallopian tubes) for women. The statute claimed that "heredity plays an important part in the transmission of insanity, idiocy, imbecility, epilepsy and crime."[226] The Virginia court was satisfied that the right to enact sterilization laws "rests in the police power."[227]

By an 8 to 1 margin, the Supreme Court in 1927 affirmed the decision of the Virginia court. Writing for the majority, Justice Holmes dismissed Buck's appeal by noting that "[w]e have seen more than once" that during times of war and emergency the public welfare

> may call upon the best citizens for their lives. It would be strange if it could not call upon those who already sap the strength of the State for these lesser sacrifices, often not felt to be such by those concerned, in order to prevent our being swamped with incompetence. It is better for all the world, if instead of waiting to execute degenerate offspring for crime, or to let them starve for their imbecility, society can prevent those who are manifestly unfit from continuing their kind.

225. Id. at 691.
226. Buck v. Bell, 143 Va. 310, 312 (Sup. Ct. App. Va. 1925).
227. Id. at 319.

The principle that sustains compulsory vaccination is broad enough to cover cutting the Fallopian tubes. . . . Three generations of imbeciles are enough.[228]

Holmes did more than simply defer to the Virginia legislature. He assumed, without evidence, that certain citizens selected by the state for sterilization would bear incompetent, degenerate, imbecilic children. He spoke of offspring committing crime when crime was never an issue with Carrie Buck or her child. He equated vaccination with vasectomy and salpingectomy. Unlike the federal district court in Nevada, Holmes accepted the logic that the greater sanctions the lesser. With that reasoning, someone found guilty of a capital crime can, in lieu of the death penalty, be tortured, or the policeman who has every right to kill an assailant may torture him instead. The greater does not justify the lesser.

As for Holmes's remark about three generations of imbeciles, Carrie's child was not mentally impaired.[229] Carrie had been considered a good student until she had to withdraw to work at various households.[230] There are no strong grounds for concluding that her mother was imbecilic. After responding to a series of questions put to her by a state commission, a justice of the peace signed an order declaring that she was "suspected of being feebleminded or epileptic."[231] There was never scientific agreement on the meaning of feeblemindedness.[232] After a brief hearing, Carrie's mother was driven to a state institution where she remained for the rest of her life.

Carrie Buck's lawsuit was not a "case or controversy" to be decided by a federal court. It was not a dispute where adversaries on opposing sides squared off to pursue conflicting interests. Instead, her case is what is called a "friendly suit"—a legal dispute wholly contrived by parties who acted in collusion to clarify legal risks. Irving Whitehead, her attorney, was a longtime friend of the state legislature who had drafted the sterilization law and served on the board of the institution where Carrie lived. While on the board, he helped approve the sterilization of more than two dozen women. In that capacity he worked

228. Buck v. Bell, 274 U.S. 200, 207 (1927).

229. J. David Smith and K. Ray Nelson, The Sterilization of Carrie Buck: Was She Feebleminded or Society's Pawn? (1989); Paul A. Lombardo, "Three Generations, No Imbeciles: New Light on *Buck v. Bell*," 60 N.Y.U. L. Rev. 30 (1985). See also Clement E. Vose, Constitutional Change 5–20 (1972); James B. O'Hara and T. Howland Sachs, "Eugenic Sterilization," 45 Geo. L. J. 20 (1956); and Walter Berns, "*Buck v. Bell:* Due Process of Law?" 6 West. Pol. Q. 762 (1953).

230. Black, War Against the Weak, at 108–09.

231. Id.

232. Id. at 55, 76–85.

with the physician at the institution who regularly advocated sterilization, made that recommendation for Carrie, and wanted the law tested to remove any fear of liability or prosecution.[233]

In his private correspondence, both before and after joining the Supreme Court, Holmes spoke approvingly of "putting to death the inadequate" and killing everyone "below standard."[234] He admired the students at Heidelberg "with their sword-slashed faces" and thought that dangerous sports and occupations were necessary "for the breeding of a race fit for headship and command."[235] Holmes generally "sneered" at political and moral causes, except for eugenics.[236] Scholars who examine his personal letters discover "a kind of fascist ideology."[237] Justice Brandeis, supposedly a stickler for facts, joined Holmes's mistaken belief that there had been three generations of imbeciles.

The Supreme Court's decision in *Buck* v. *Bell* preceded by a few years Nazi Germany's biological experiments and extermination of millions of Jews, Poles, gypsies, and other groups, all part of a plan to produce a "master race." Today, instead of sterilization being forced on the "unfit," the operation is submitted to voluntarily each years by thousands of fit adults for a variety of personal reasons. In 2002, Virginia Governor Mark Warner formally apologized for the state's policy of eugenics, under which some 8,000 people had been involuntarily sterilized from 1927 to 1979. He called the eugenics movement "a shameful effort in which state government never should have been involved."[238] Nationwide, the practice affected an estimated 65,000 Americans.[239]

233. Lombardo, "Three Generations, No Imbeciles," at 33–60; Black, War Against the Weak, at 110–17.

234. Albert W. Alschuler, Law Without Values: The Life, Work, and Legacy of Justice Holmes 27 (2000).

235. Id. at 22.

236. Id. at 11.

237. Id. at 16. See Mary L. Dudziak, "Oliver Wendell Holmes as a Eugenic Reformer: Rhetoric in the Writing of Constitutional Law," 71 Iowa L. Rev. 833 (1986); Robert L. Burgdorf, Jr., and Marcia Pearce Burgdorf, "The Wicked Witch Is Almost Dead: *Buck* v. *Bell* and the Sterilization of Handicapped Persons," 50 Temple L. Q. 995 (1977).

238. William Branigin, "Va. Apologizes to the Victims of Sterilizations," Washington Post, May 3, 2002, at B1.

239. Id. See also Craig Timberg, "Va. House Voices Regret for Eugenics," Washington Post, February 3, 2001, at A1; Scott Christianson, "Bad Seed or Bad Science: On Reflection, a Family Long Seen as Congenital Misfits Were Victims of Skewed Data," New York Times, February 8, 2003, at A19.

By 1940, the United States had weathered a century and a half of wars, depressions, and social struggle. It had greatly expanded its territory and population, accepting millions of different cultures, races, and religions. It was now about to embark on the sacrifices of another world war and an anti-Communist drive that followed immediately thereafter. Choices made during that period have many parallels with repressive policies adopted after 9/11.

CHAPTER 5

World War II and the Cold War

In 1940, Congress responded to Nazi aggression in Europe by passing legislation to punish sedition. The statute (the Smith Act) led to several prosecutions, including the Great Sedition Trial of 1944. As war spread to the Pacific,
more than 100,000 Japanese Americans were moved from their homes on the
West Coast to detention camps inland. Arguments by the government to justify this action were later found to be false. Violations of civil liberties that occurred during the war continued after hostilities were over. Employees in the
government and the private sector were brought before loyalty boards to face
accusations by anonymous sources. The campaign against "subversives" during this period of McCarthyism far outstripped the civil liberties violations
committed by Palmer's Red Scare after World War I.

THE SEDITIONISTS

On March 28, 1940, Congress passed legislation to revive and revise the Espionage Act of 1917.[1] Three months later, after France fell quickly to Nazi forces,
Congress passed the Smith Act to prohibit subversive activities and amend
legislation dealing with the admission and deportation of aliens.[2] The stun-
ning swiftness of France's collapse was attributed by some to "fifth column"
activities of Nazi and Communist sympathizers inside the country. The fear
of internal subversion within the United States generated powerful pressures
for congressional action. On May 16, 1940, President Franklin D. Roosevelt
warned the nation about the "treacherous use of the 'fifth column' by which
persons supposed to be peaceful visitors were actually a part of an enemy unit
of occupation."[3]

1. 54 Stat. 79 (1940).
2. Id. at. 670.
3. 9 The Public Papers and Addresses of Franklin D. Roosevelt 198 (1941). See Richard W.
Steele, Free Speech in the Good War 74–81 (1999).

Title I of the Smith Act borrowed some language from the Espionage Act of 1917. It was unlawful for anyone to intentionally "interfere with, impair, or influence the loyalty, morale, or discipline of the military or naval forces of the United States." It was unlawful to advise in any manner (including printed matter) insubordination, disloyalty, mutiny, or refusal of duty by members of the U.S. military.[4] Congress drafted the statute broadly to prohibit individuals from writing or speaking in a manner to suggest that a contemplated or actual war was against the nation's interest and would have damaging consequences economically, politically, socially, and constitutionally.

Section 2 of the Smith Act covered attempts to overthrow government. The language did not use the word sedition, as in 1798, but implementation of the statute resulted in sedition trials. It was unlawful for any person to knowingly or willfully advocate the overthrow of any government in the United States, by force or violence, or the assassination of any public officer. Criminal penalties applied to those who printed or distributed any matter that advocated the overthrow of any government in the United States by force or violence. Speaking critically of government was not by itself a crime. Action by force or violence was needed. Concern was not primarily to the individual, operating alone, but to those who worked through groups.[5] Convictions carried a fine of up to $10,000 and imprisonment for not more than ten years. If convicted, the person could not be employed by the United States or any federal department or agency.

Title II covered deportation. Any alien who, within five years of entering the country, "knowingly and for gain" encouraged any other alien to enter the country in violation of law could be taken into custody and deported. Deportation also applied to aliens who, at any time after entry, had been convicted of possessing or carrying in violation of law any automatic or semi-automatic weapon, including sawed-off shoguns. Title III required the registration and fingerprinting of aliens.

Minneapolis Trial

In 1941, Attorney General Francis Biddle authorized criminal action against the Socialist Workers Party (SWP) in Minneapolis. The SWP followed a Trotsky-ite ideology and gained control over a Teamster local. The Teamster constitution prohibited Communists from membership but a compromise in the late

4. Id.
5. Id. at 671.

1930s continued to bar the Stalinist Communist Party while making an exception for the Trotskyites. Within a few years the International Brotherhood of Teamsters tried to purge the Trotskyites. In 1941, the Teamsters supported a war-preparedness program and the Trotskyites opposed it. The prosecution put the Justice Department in the middle of an inter-union controversy.[6]

The grand jury indicted twenty-nine party members in two counts. The first count relied on the 1861 Sedition Act, which had never been used. The second count invoked the Smith Act: conspiracy to overthrow the government and advocating insubordination in the U.S. armed forces. The trial court found five not guilty; the jury acquitted five others. One defendant died. The remaining eighteen were found not guilty on the first count but guilty on the second. The convictions were affirmed on appeal to the Eighth Circuit.[7] Biddle anticipated that the case would continue to the Supreme Court and it would declare the Smith Act unconstitutional under the First Amendment.[8] He thought that no case could be made that the SWP, with its 3,000 members, constituted a threat to overthrow the government. To his surprise, the Court refused to review the case, and Biddle regretted that he authorized this prosecution.[9]

The government prosecuted the SWP members in part for their antiwar philosophy and for Marxist and Leninist documents that demonstrated—to the government—that the teaching of Communist doctrine was equal to advocating the overthrow of government. To the defendants, their thoughts and doctrines did not amount to a "clear and present danger" as understood by the Supreme Court. Opposition to a war, they said, could not be considered disloyal, unpatriotic, or criminal. One of the defendants, James P. Cannon, told the court that SWP members believed that the allies were "fighting for interests of this small group of financiers and bankers" but that he and other defendants were willing to fight fascist forces in Europe.[10]

The Eighth Circuit rejected the defendants' argument that their conduct was protected by the free speech provision of the First Amendment. The Smith Act did not, said the court, restrict free thought nor did it prohibit

6. Ralph C. James and Estelle James, "The Purge of the Trotskyites from the Teamsters," 19 West. Pol. Q. 5 (1966).

7. Dunne v. United States, 138 F.2d 137 (8th Cir. 1943).

8. Francis Biddle, In Brief Authority 151 (1962).

9. Id. at 152.

10. "Causes of Minneapolis Sedition Trial," materials compiled by Macalester College. See http://www.macalester.edu/courses/poli206207/crisis_times/second_red_scare_Causes%20of%20the%20Trial.htm.

criticism of the government.[11] Congress did not "limit expression of opinion or of criticisms of the Government or of its officials or officers (civil or military) or of their actions so long as such expressions are not made with intent to bring about the unlawful things and situations covered by the section and, in addition, so long as they do not have a natural tendency and a reasonable probability of effecting these forbidden results."[12]

The court relied on the "bad tendency" test rather than the more restrictive "clear and present danger" standard of *Schenck* v. *United States* (1919). While recognizing that *Schenck* had provided important guidance on free speech issues, the court said "it is by no means of universal application" and declined to prefer it over the competing *Gitlow* doctrine of 1925.[13] The court accepted the good faith efforts of the executive branch in conducting these prosecutions. To the extent that the defendants implied "that those officials would not act honestly, it is unique, unpleasant and unsound."[14] The court read the Declaration of Principles of the SWP as intending to "effectuate this overthrow of the existing capitalistic society and the Government which supports it."[15] From the writings and statements of Leon Trotsky, the court concluded that the purpose of the SWP was to create a Red Army capable of using force to overthrow government by the "proletariat."[16]

The Great Sedition Trial

Various groups in the United States, from the left to the right, plotted throughout the 1930s to undermine U.S. domestic and foreign policy. The Communists had difficulty in finding a natural home in the United States. Marxist theory combined with atheism was not a product easily marketed in America. However, the harsh economic conditions of the 1930s had made Communist ideals attractive to many, and World War II found the United States and Soviet Russia allied against Nazi Germany. Other than those favorable periods, Communism remained in a political backwater in the United States.

Right-wing and fascist groups, such as the American Nazi Party, had some advantages. They demonstrated political skills by pretending to adopt

11. Dunne v. United States. 138 F.2d at 140.
12. Id. at 142.
13. Id. at 145 (Gitlow v. New York, 268 U.S. 652 [1925]).
14. Id. at 142–43.
15. Id. at 148.
16. Id. at 149.

nativism and "True Americanism" as guiding principles.[17] A mass demonstration in Madison Square Garden in 1939 featured, as a backdrop, a huge figure of George Washington flanked by large black swastikas.[18] Hitler, Mussolini, and Franco were the objects of devotion, balanced by fulminations against President Franklin D. Roosevelt, Jews, and Communists.[19] For some occasions, swastikas came in red, white, and blue, delicately offset by a Christmas tree.[20] A brochure from the American Nazi Party mixed a number of popular values: "The American National-Socialist Party an American organization dedicated to the restoration and preservation of American aims, ideals and traditions for the Americans of Aryan extraction, and opposed to the invasion of International Autocracy so that this nation under God shall have a new birth of freedom, pledges itself. . ."[21]

Attorney General Biddle held off from prosecuting fascist groups unless they were about to use violence against the country. Still less did he want to bring lawsuits against individuals who made "seditious" statements. Freedom of speech, he concluded, should not be curtailed unless "public safety was directly imperiled."[22] President Roosevelt, however, pursued a different agenda. In Cabinet meetings, as the discussion went round the table, his customary affability stopped when it came to Biddle. Instead of asking him if he had anything to report, Roosevelt repeatedly asked: "When are you going to indict the seditionists?"[23] Biddle finally acquiesced and agreed to bring a case.

On July 23, 1942, the government indicted twenty-eight individuals on sedition charges. The group consisted of major and minor figures. Some of the more prominent names, including William Dudley Pelley, would face separate prosecutions.[24] The sedition trial stretched on year after year. One defendant,

17. John Roy Carlson, Under Cover 23, 27 (1943). Carlson is a pseudonym for Avedis Derounian, an Armenian immigrant who came to the United States at age 12 after seeing fascism firsthand in Greece and Bulgaria. He spent four years undercover to study Nazi and fascist organizations in the United States. For an evaluation of Derounian's book, see Leo P. Ribuffo, The Old Christian Right: The Protestant Far Right from the Great Depression to the Cold War 189–93 (1983).

18. Geoffrey R. Stone, Perilous Times 235 (2004).

19. Carlson, Under Cover, at 27–28, 34.

20. Id. at 33.

21. Id. at 35.

22. Francis Biddle, In Brief Authority 235 (1962).

23. Id. at 238.

24. E.g., United States v. Pelley, 132 F.2d 170 (7th Cir. 1942), cert. denied, 318 U.S. 764 (1943); Pelley v. Matthews, 163 F.2d 700 (D.C. Cir. 1947), cert. denied, 332 U.S. 811 (1947); Pelley v. United States, 214 F.2d 597 (7th Cir. 1954).

Elmer J. Garner, died. Eventually so did the trial judge, Edward C. Eicher. Finally, in 1947, the federal judiciary announced it had enough and dismissed the case for lack of prosecution. After the trial began even Biddle admitted it "had become a dreary farce."[25]

The government accused the defendants of interfering with and impairing "the loyalty, morale and discipline of U.S. armed forces, causing insubordination, mutiny, and refusal of duty."[26] One of the charges claimed they had engaged in a systematic campaign to defame public officials and promote propaganda that the United States was governed not by elected representatives "but by a secret foreign group of persons and organizations opposed to American principles and ideas and seeking to overthrow the Constitution."[27] According to the government, some of the defendants argued that World War II was the brainchild of "international Jewry-organized finance," British-American capitalists, British imperialists, international bankers, international capitalists, "Mongolian Jews," Communists, and other persons who sought to undermine "our republican form of government."[28] New indictments were brought on January 4, 1943, including the original twenty-eight defendants but adding five others.[29] The first count of the indictments was found defective by the trial court because it charged the defendants with actions taken before enactment of the Smith Act.[30]

A third round of indictments appeared on January 3, 1944.[31] The trial began on April 16. The defendants included Gerhard W. Kunze of the German-American Bund and George Sylvester Viereck. They were already serving time in prison for espionage and failing to register as German agents.[32] Even before a jury could be formed, twenty-two attorneys for the defendants staged an open revolt to protest the exclusion of the press from the courtroom. Chief Justice Eicher promised sufficient space for reporters.[33] Chronic delays resulted

25. Biddle, In Brief Authority, at 242.

26. Lewis Wood, "28 Are Indicted on Sedition Charge," New York Times, July 24, 1942, at 1.

27. Id.

28. Id.

29. "33 Are Indicted in Sedition Cases," New York Times, January 5, 1943, at 1.

30. Dillard Stokes, "Defendants Face New Charges in Nazi Network Prosecution," Washington Post, March 6, 1943, at 1.

31. "U.S. Indicts 30, Alleging Nazi Plot to Incite Mutiny and Revolution," New York Times, January 4, 1944, at 1.

32. "30 Charged With Sedition to Go on Trial in D.C. Today," Washington Post, April 17, 1944, at 1.

33. "22 Attorneys for Defense Revolt, Halt Sedition Case," Washington Post, April 20, 1944, at 1.

from contempt actions against defense attorneys and ruling on their motions for a mistrial. Much time was consumed in selecting jurors and considering peremptory challenges from the defendants.[34]

The press objected to the government's attempt to prosecute a group of individuals with widely varying connections to seditious activities. Lawyers for the defendants regularly compared court proceedings to the infamous Moscow purge trials.[35] An editorial in the *Washington Post* said it was "a pity that the Department of Justice did not foresee this elementary objection to mass trials before embarking on such an adventure."[36] The newspaper later accurately predicted that "the trial may run for several years, after the war is over."[37] Justice Eicher's death on November 30, 1944, forced a mistrial and dismissal of the jury.[38]

O. John Rogge, who had been prosecuting the case for the Justice Department, was uncertain whether he had sufficient facts to continue the case successfully, particularly in light of some decisions handed down by the Supreme Court. In the Flag-Salute Case decided June 14, 1943, Justice Robert Jackson wrote for a 6 to 3 majority: "If there is any fixed star in our constitutional constellation, it is that no official, high or petty, can prescribe what shall be orthodox in politics, nationalism, religion, or other matters of opinion or force citizens to confess by word or act their faith therein."[39] Other decisions by the Court, issued just before or during the sedition trial, undermined the government's case by emphasizing the clear and present danger case, the right of U.S. citizens to criticize their government, to belong to the Communist Party, and to praise Hitler.[40] In a case decided June 12, 1944, the Court reversed the conviction of a U.S. citizen who had attacked Jews, President Roosevelt, and mailed pamphlets (including to the military) opposing the war.[41]

34. Note, "The Sedition Trial: A Study in Delay and Obstruction," 15 U. Chi. L. Rev. 691, 701 (1948). See also Steele, Free Speech in the Good War, at 223–33.

35. James E. Chin, "Dennis Calls Sedition Trial 'Corny Farce,'" Washington Post, May 19, 1944, at 1.

36. "Mass Trial" (editorial), Washington Post, July 16, 1944, at 4B.

37. "Courtroom Farce" (editorial), Washington Post, July 28, 1944, at 14.

38. For some of Justice Eicher's rulings in this case, see United States v. McWilliams, 54 F.Supp. 791 (D.D.C. 1944). See also Dilling v. United States, 142 F.2d 473 (D.C. Cir. 1944).

39. Board of Education v. Barnette, 319 U.S. 624, 642 (1943).

40. E.g., Taylor v. Mississippi, 319 U.S. 583, 589 (1943); Schneiderman v. United States, 320 U.S. 118, 157 (1943); Baumgartner v. United States, 322 U.S. 665 (1944).

41. Hartzel v. United States, 322 U.S. 680 (1944). See also Keegan v. United States, 325 U.S. 478 (1945).

On January 25, 1946, with the war over, a district court heard motions to dismiss the case. On March 1 the Justice Department advised the court that it wanted to send Rogge to Germany to search for additional evidence.[42] In trying to set a date for trial, Rogge still had "serious doubts" whether a conviction could be sustained.[43] On November 22, a district court ruled that after four and a half years and with the prospect of another trial lasting more than a year, it would be a "travesty of justice" to permit a retrial.[44] The D.C. Circuit in 1947 agreed to dismiss the case for lack of prosecution.[45]

CRACKPOTS, SUBVERSIVES, AND COMMUNISTS

In 1938, the House created the Un-American Activities Committee (HUAC), chaired by Martin Dies of Texas. Initially the committee focused on the German-American Bund and other fascist organizations on the right, but increasingly turned its attention to Communism. Published hearings identified 640 organizations, 483 newspapers, and 280 labor organizations as "Communistic," including the Boy Scouts, the ACLU, the Catholic Association for International Peace, and the Camp Fire Girls.[46] The committee also released the names of federal employees considered "either communists or affiliates of subversive organizations."[47]

42. United States v. McWilliams, 69 F.Supp. 812, 813 (D.D.C. 1946).

43. Id. at 813–14.

44. Id. at 815.

45. United States v. McWilliams, 163 F.2d 695 (D.C. Cir. 1947). See also Elmhurst v. Pearson, 153 F.2d 467 (D.C. Cir. 1946); Elmhurst v. Shoreham Hotel, 58 F.Supp. 484 (D.D.C. 1945). For other discussion on the Great Sedition Trial, see O. John Rogge, The Official German Report 173–218 (1961); Ribuffo, The Old Christian Right 208, 213–14. One of the defendants, David Baxter, published his reflections about the trial. David Baxter, "The Great Sedition Trial of 1944: A Personal Memoir," Journal of Historical Review, available at http://www/ihr.org/jhr/v06/v06p–23_Baxter.html. He regarded the prosecution as a "warm up" by the government in preparation for going after much more prominent Americans who opposed President Roosevelt and the war. Id. at 7. Those names would have included Henry Ford, Charles Lindbergh, and other top members of the America First Committee, but no prosecutions were ever brought. Max Wallace, The American Axis: Henry Ford, Charles Lindbergh, and the Rise of the Third Reich (2004). Another defendant, Lawrence Dennis, joined with one of the attorneys at the trial, Maximilian J. St. George, to write about the indictments, Rogge's opening statement, jury selection, and other elements of the trial. Lawrence Dennis and Maximilian St. George, A Trial on Trial: The Great Sedition Trial of 1944 (1984; originally published in 1945 by the National Civil Rights Committee).

46. Stone, Perilous Times, at 246.

47. Id. at 247.

During House debate on February 1, 1943, lawmakers took turns singling out the groups they thought menaced America. Dies focused largely on writers, publishers, political activists, and executive officials he linked to the Communist Party.[48] He warned that there had been "for 4 or 5 years a well-organized attempt to build up in this country a united front of radicals—a united front of Communists, crackpots, Socialists, men of different shades of totalitarian beliefs."[49] He began to read the names and positions of individuals in the executive branch who had "wormed their way into this bureaucratic set-up, in order to make crystal clear just what we mean by irresponsible, unrepresentative, crackpot, radical bureaucrats."[50]

One name was Frederick L. Schuman of the Federal Communications Commission, someone Dies said was "of violent political views. His Communist affiliations are a matter of public record."[51] Another official was Goodwin B. Watson, also with the FCC. Dies claimed that Watson had a "long record of Communist views and his numerous affiliations with Communist-front organizations."[52] Dies linked other executive officials to Communist and Socialist causes,[53] identifying thirty-eight who, in his view, held subversive political views.[54]

The Kerr Subcommittee

In an effort to avoid a Star Chamber atmosphere, the House created a special subcommittee to examine claims against federal employees. The subcommittee was authorized to hold hearings, require the attendance of witnesses, subpoena documents, and report its results. The purpose was to determine whether the employees were unfit to remain in office because of their present or past association with organizations "whose aims or purposes are or have been subversive to the Government of the United States."[55] Subcommittee chairman John Kerr later acknowledged: "We discovered after organization the fact that there had never been declared judicially or by any legislative body what constituted subversive activities in respect to this Government."[56] The House passed the resolution creating the special subcommittee.[57]

48. 89 Cong. Rec. 475–78 (1943).
49. Id. at 478.
50. Id. at 479.
51. Id.
52. Id.
53. Id. at 479–81.
54. Id. at 481–84.
55. Id. at 734.
56. Id. at 4582.
57. Id. at 742.

On May 14, the House began debate on the subcommittee's findings. The hearings allowed individuals accused of subversive activities to "have a right and an opportunity to come and present their opinions and their defense to those charges."[58] The subcommittee offered draft language to deny the use of federal appropriations to pay the salaries of three executive officials: Goodwin B. Watson, William E. Dodd, Jr., and Robert Morss Lovett.[59] Emanuel Celler of the Judiciary Committee objected that Congress was attempting "to discharge certain men in the Government service because of their opinions. It is primarily just that."[60] By using the power of the purse to remove administration officials, Congress was "arrogating to ourselves executive powers."[61] He predicted that if Congress in the early years of the Republic had decided it could remove executive officials whose views and opinions seemed too radical, Thomas Jefferson, Benjamin Franklin, and John Quincy Adams "could not have stood the test, and that appropriations for their salaries would have been summarily cut off."[62] To George Outland, the proposal to remove executive officials by an amendment to an appropriations bill was "extremely dangerous" because it "sets up no definite standards as to what is subversive and opens wide the path of intolerance."[63]

Legislative Punishment

Under subcommittee procedures, Congress could charge someone with subversive ideas—for whatever reason—and use the funding power to remove the official from the administration. John Coffee, a member of the House, objected that lawmakers were "sitting here as judge, as jury, and as prosecutor."[64] The impeachment process allows the House to draw up articles of impeachment and engage in fact-finding. However, impeachment is merely a charge; conviction requires two-thirds support in the Senate. An editorial in the *Washington Post* said that the House procedure allowed Congress to dismiss executive employees "on shadowy grounds which have never been enacted into law."[65]

58. Id. at 4554.
59. Id. at 4558.
60. Id. at 4546.
61. Id.
62. Id.
63. Id. at 4546–47.
64. Id. at 4548.
65. Id.

During House debate, George Outland protested that Congress was attempting to punish people for belonging to organizations that lawmakers disliked. The House was replaying the accusations against "Democratic Societies" in 1794. Outland warned that the outcome for the three executive employees "becomes a matter solely of opinion, not of law, and we have prided ourselves that in this democracy of ours we are governed by laws, not by the whims of men. Such action smacks far more of the tactics of the Nazis and the Fascists, against whom we are fighting, than of the spirit of American justice and fair play."[66]

The transcript of testimony taken by the subcommittee was not available to the House until the time for voting,[67] prompting Vito Marcantonio to remark: "We are to vote on an amendment to an appropriation bill, to expel three people from the Federal Government without a single word of the hearings before us."[68] He added: "We inveigh against them the charge of subversiveness. Hitler used the Reichstag trial, he used the Communist bogey, the same pattern that we employ here for the present restriction and subsequent destruction of democratic rights."[69]

Samuel Hobbs called the subcommittee amendment "a bill of pains and penalties within the meaning of the constitutional prohibition: "No bill of attainder * * * shall be passed (art. I, sec. 9.)"[70] He cited court rulings that defined a bill of attainder as a legislative act that inflicts punishment without a judicial trial.[71] Subcommittee member Keefe denied there had been punishment, a bill of attainder, or pains and penalties.[72] He argued that "constitutional officers" in the three branches could not be removed in the manner of the three men under discussion, but the latter were "pure and simple employees of the United States Government" who lacked employment rights.[73] The amendment deleting funds for the three employees easily passed the House, 318 to 62.[74]

In the Senate, Scott Lucas of Illinois objected to discharging government employees "upon secret testimony which was developed by the Kerr committee

---

66. Id. at 4547.
67. Id. at 4592.
68. Id.
69. Id. at 4593.
70. Id. at 4597.
71. Id.
72. Id. at 4598.
73. Id. at 4599.
74. Id. at 4605.

of the House of Representatives, and about which the Senate knows nothing."[75] To remove employees by following these procedures "is tantamount to convicting them as being Communists without a hearing or trial."[76] Bennett Champ Clark of Missouri said the Senate was asked to participate in "an essentially penal proceeding, certainly imposing moral obloquy upon them, without knowing what we are doing."[77] The Senate voted 69 to 0 to delete the House amendment stripping the three men of their salary.[78] The House insisted on its amendment, pressuring the Senate to yield and permit enactment of the urgent appropriations bill.[79] The Senate voted 52 to 17 to reject the conference report with the House amendment.[80]

After further debate and roll-call votes, the language denying salaries for the three men remained in the bill sent to President Roosevelt.[81] He signed the bill "reluctantly" because of the urgent need for agency funds. Had it been possible to veto the House amendment "without delaying essential war appropriations, I should unhesitatingly have done so."[82] He condemned the bill language for removing federal employees for their "political opinions," a position he considered "not only unwise and discriminatory, but unconstitutional" as a bill of attainder.[83] The bill marked "an unwarranted encroachment" upon the executive and the judicial branches.[84] Congress allowed payment to the three officials up to November 15, 1943, unless prior to that date they had been appointed by the President with the advice and consent of the Senate.[85]

Challenges in Court

Dodd, Lovett, and Watson filed suit in federal court. The attorney representing Congress insisted that congressional powers over appropriations were plenary and not subject to judicial review.[86] The Court of Claims, without reaching

75. Id. at 5604.
76. Id.
77. Id. at 5605.
78. Id. at 5606.
79. Id. at 6407.
80. Id. at 6415–16.
81. Id. at 6647, 6691–95, 6729–39.
82. The Public Papers and Addresses of Franklin D. Roosevelt, 1943 Volume, at 385 (1950).
83. Id. at 386.
84. Id.
85. 57 Stat. 450, sec. 304 (1943).
86. United States v. Lovett, 328 U.S. 303, 306–07 (1946).

the constitutional issue, ruled that the three men were entitled to recover the salaries they had lost.[87] The Supreme Court went directly to the constitutional question: "Were this case to be not justiciable, congressional action, aimed at three named individuals, which stigmatized their reputation and seriously impaired their chance to earn a living, could never be challenged in any court. Our Constitution did not contemplate such a result."[88] The Court held that the language in the appropriations bill fell precisely within the category of congressional actions that the Constitution forbids: "No Bill of Attainder or ex post facto Law shall be passed."[89] No one would argue, said the Court, that Congress could have passed a valid law stating that after its investigation the three men were "guilty" of the crime of engaging in "subversive activities," defining that term "for the first time, and sentenc[ing] them to perpetual exclusion from any government employment."[90]

The Court noted that the special House subcommittee "held hearings in secret executive session." Although those charged with subversive associations were invited to testify, their lawyers (including lawyers representing their agencies) were not permitted to be present.[91] The evidence, other than that offered by the accused, "appears to have been largely that of reports made by the Dies Committee, its investigators, and Federal Bureau of Investigation reports, the latter being treated as too confidential to be made public."[92] No record indicated how much of the committee and agency files consisted of untested allegations taken from anonymous and unreliable informants.

Congress continued to test the limits of the Bill of Attainder Clause. A section of a 1959 statute made it a crime for a Communist Party member (or one who had been a member during the preceding five years) to serve as a member of the executive board of a labor organization. The Supreme Court, split 5 to 4, held that the provision constituted a prohibited bill of attainder.[93] Here is the statutory language: "None of the funds appropriated or otherwise made available by this Act may be used, pursuant to the Comprehensive Employment Training Act [CETA], for the participation of individuals who publicly ad-

---

87. Lovett v. United States, 66 F.Supp. 142, 148 (Ct. Cl. 1945). In their concurrences, Judges Whitaker and Madden concluded that the statute constituted a forbidden bill of attainder. Id. at 148, 151.

88. United States v. Lovett, 328 U.S. at 314.

89. Id. at 315.

90. Id. at 316.

91. Id. at 310–11.

92. Id. at 311.

93. United States v. Brown, 381 U.S. 437 (1965).

vocate the violent overthrow of the Federal Government, or who have within the past five years, publicly advocated the violent overthrow of the Federal Government."[94]

No names appear in the statute, but a district court said that the legislative history "left no doubt that it was specifically intended" to exclude Dorothy Blitz from the CETA program "because of her political beliefs and affiliations and because she expressed those beliefs in her community."[95] Blitz was a member of the Communist Workers Party.[96] The court found the statutory language unconstitutional on its face for penalizing mere advocacy of an idea, including violent revolution.[97] The "Blitz Amendment" did not distinguish between "mere advocacy and advocacy which incites and is likely to produce violent action."[98] Deciding the statute violated the First Amendment, the court saw no need to address the Bill of Attainder Clause.[99] After Blitz was reinstated in the CETA program, the Supreme Court vacated the district court judgment and remanded the case with instructions to dismiss the complaint as moot.[100] Following the remand, the district court granted attorney's fees to Blitz.[101]

JAPANESE AMERICANS

Congress passed the Smith Act in 1940 in anticipation of "fifth column" activities in the United States. Two years later, the federal government used that argument to move against more than 100,000 Japanese Americans on the West Coast. Stories in the *New York Times* on February 11, 1942, reported that the FBI had found ammunition and other contraband while raiding Japanese colonies in the Monterey Bay district, 80 miles south of San Francisco. According to the newspaper account, FBI agents discovered an assortment of maps, radio microphones, and mimeographing equipment in a Buddhist temple.[102] Federal and state officials met with military leaders to discuss the prospect

94. Blitz v. Donovan, 538 F.Supp. 1119, 1123 (D.D.C. 1982), citing P.L. 97–92.

95. Id.

96. Id. at 1122.

97. Id. at 1125.

98. Id. at 1126.

99. Id. at 1127 n.16.

100. Donovan v. Blitz, 459 U.S. 1095 (1983).

101. Blitz v. Donovan, 569 F.Supp. 58 (D.D.C. 1983).

102. Lawrence E. Davies, "20 Aliens on Coast Seized With Guns," New York Times, February 11, 1942, at 12.

of moving Japanese Americans from coastal areas to inland concentration camps.[103]

On February 12, Walter Lippman published a column in the *Washington Post* called "The Fifth Column on the Coast," claiming that the Pacific Coast was "in imminent danger of a combined attack from within and from without."[104] He said it was "a fact that communication takes place between the enemy at sea and enemy agents on land," although acknowledging that since the beginning of the war against Japan "there has been no important sabotage from the Pacific Coast." Citing no evidence he warned: "It is a sign that the blow is well-organized and that it is held back until it can be struck with maximum effect." The problem was not just "enemy aliens" but the problem of "native-born American citizens." He referred to the Pacific Coast as a combat zone, part of which "may at any moment be a battlefield," and no one—citizen or alien—has a constitutional right "to reside and do business on a battlefield."[105] After 9/11, officials in the Bush administration would refer to the entire United States as a battlefield.

During congressional hearings on February 21 and 23, California's Attorney General Earl Warren testified on the location of Japanese in his state, county by county. The maps prepared for his use were "disturbing" because along the coast from Marin County to the Mexican border "virtually every important strategic location and installation has one or more Japanese in its immediate vicinity."[106] Without condemning all Japanese as disloyal, he relied on this logic: "I do not mean to suggest that it should be thought that all of these Japanese who are adjacent to strategic points are knowing parties to some vast conspiracy to destroy our state by sudden and mass sabotage. Undoubtedly, the presence of many of these persons in their present locations is mere coincidence, but it would seem equally beyond doubt that the presence of others is not coincidence."[107] Lacking any evidence of subversive activities, he presented a sinister and threatening picture. The Japanese population of California was, "as a whole, ideally situated, with reference to points of strategic importance,

103. Lawrence E. Davies, "West Coast Widens Martial Law Call," New York Times, February 12, 1942, at 10.

104. Walter Lippman, "Today and Tomorrow: The Fifth Column on the Coast," Washington Post, February 12, 1942, at 9.

105. Id.

106. "National Defense Migration" (Part 29), hearings before the Select Committee Investigating National Defense Migration, House of Representatives, 77th Cong., 2d Sess. 10973 (1942).

107. Id. at 10974.

to carry into execution a tremendous program of sabotage on a mass scale should any considerable number of them be inclined to do so."[108]

Asked if he had any way of knowing whether someone from the Japanese community was loyal to the United States or loyal to Japan, Warren offered a racial explanation. When dealing "with the Caucasian race we have methods that will test the loyalty of them, and we believe that we can, in dealing with the Germans and the Italians, arrive at some fairly sound conclusions because of our knowledge of the way they live in the community and have lived for many years." With the Japanese "we are in an entirely different field and we cannot form any opinion that we believe to be sound. . . . Many of them who show you a birth certificate, stating that they were born in this State, perhaps, or born in Honolulu, can hardly speak the English language because, although they were born here, when they were 4 or 5 years of age they were sent over to Japan to be educated and they stayed over there through their adolescent period at least, and then they came back here thoroughly Japanese."[109]

In response to other questions, Warren continued to spin evidence out of nothing. He told the committee he had recently met with forty district attorneys and about forty sheriffs to discuss the problem of aliens. He asked whether any Japanese (California-born or Japan-born) had ever provided any information on subversive or disloyal activities in the United States. They answered unanimously that "no such information had ever been given to them," a response Warren found "almost unbelievable." German or Italian aliens, he said, voluntarily gave information to local, state, and federal authorities. "We get none from the other source."[110] He dismissed the possibility that Japanese were unaware of subversive activities because they had no such knowledge.

The Curfew Order

On February 19, 1942, President Roosevelt issued Executive Order 9066 requiring all persons of Japanese ancestry within a designated military area to "be within their place of residence between the hours of 8 p.m. and 6 a.m." A month later, Congress ratified and confirmed Roosevelt's order and authorized curfew orders promulgated by the military commander of the Western Defense Command, General John L. DeWitt.[111] A unanimous opinion by the

---

108. Id.
109. Id. at 11015.
110. Id.
111. 56 Stat. 173 (1942).

Supreme Court upheld the curfew against Gordon Hirabayashi, a U.S. citizen who had never been to Japan.[112] The Court accepted the government's action as a necessary response to "the danger of sabotage and espionage."[113] In his concurrence, Justice Douglas wrote: "If the military were right in their belief that among citizens of Japanese ancestry there was an actual or incipient fifth column, we were indeed faced with the imminent threat of a dire emergency."[114] What if the military were not right? What if it acted on racial theories? In another concurrence, Justice Murphy remarked that distinctions "based on color and ancestry are utterly inconsistent with our traditions and ideals."[115] He was unaware of another time that the judiciary had "sustained a substantial restriction of the personal liberty of citizens of the United States based upon the accident of race or ancestry."[116] The curfew order, he said, "bears a melancholy resemblance to the treatment accorded to members of the Jewish race in Germany and in other parts of Europe."[117]

Detention Camps

The next step was moving Japanese Americans from their homes on the West Coast to detention camps inland. This time the Court, in a case involving Fred Korematsu, split 6 to 3 in upholding the government's action. Murphy, one of the dissenters, protested that the exclusion order resulted from an "erroneous assumption of racial guilt" found in General DeWitt's report, which referred to all individuals of Japanese descent as "subversives" belonging to "an enemy race" whose "racial strains are undiluted."[118] DeWitt's report paralleled some of the logic present in Earl Warren's testimony: "The very fact that no sabotage has taken place to date is a disturbing and confirming indication that such action will be taken."[119] Murphy condemned the Court's "legalization of racism."[120]

Justice Jackson wrote another stinging dissent. If any fundamental assumption underlay the U.S. legal system "it is that guilt is personal and not

112. Hirabayashi v. United States, 320 U.S. 81, 84 (1943).

113. Id. at 94–95.

114. Id. at 106.

115. Id. at 110.

116. Id. at 111.

117. Id.

118. Korematsu v. United States, 323 U.S. 214, 235–36 (1944).

119. Id. at 241 n.15.

120. Id. at 242.

inheritable."[121] The Constitution expressly provides that "no Attainder of Treason shall work Corruption of Blood, or Forfeiture except during the Life of
the Person attainted."[122] Yet "here is an attempt," Jackson wrote, "to make an
otherwise innocent act a crime merely because this prisoner is the son of parents as to whom he had no choice, and belongs to a race from which there is
no way to resign."[123] He found it revolting for the Court to take at face value a
military report based on evidence withheld from the Court and assertions for
which no evidence could be assembled. He referred to DeWitt's report as an
"unsworn, self-serving statement, untested by any cross-examination."[124]

On the same day that the Court issued *Korematsu* it decided the case of
Mitsuye Endo, who was first placed in a relocation center in California and
then moved to a center in Utah. She was an American citizen of Japanese ancestry. Although General DeWitt's program started with the proposition that
Japanese were inherently and racially "subversive," the War Relocation Authority (WRA) segregated detainees into the categories of loyal and disloyal.[125]
The WRA and the Justice Department conceded that Endo was "a loyal and
law-abiding citizen" and did not argue that she could be held any longer in a
relocation center.[126] A unanimous Court agreed she should be released.[127] A
citizen "who is concededly loyal presents no problem of espionage or sabotage. Loyalty is a matter of the heart and mind, not of race, creed, or color."[128]
That generous rhetoric collided with the Court's rulings in *Hirabayashi* and
Korematsu upholding the government.

An American Apology

On February 20, 1976, President Gerald Ford issued a proclamation publicly
apologizing for what was done to Japanese Americans: the "uprooting of loyal
Americans."[129] The proclamation stated that Roosevelt's order terminated
upon the cessation of the hostilities of World War II on December 31, 1946.
Ford called upon Americans "to affirm with me this American Promise—that

121. Id. at 243.
122. U.S. Const., art. III, sec. 3.
123. Korematsu v. United States, 323 U.S. at 243.
124. Id. at 245.
125. Ex parte Endo, 323 U.S. 282, 291 (1944).
126. Id. at 294–95.
127. Id. at 297.
128. Id. at 302.
129. Proclamation 4417, 41 Fed. Reg. 7741 (1976).

we have learned from the tragedy of that long-ago experience forever to treasure liberty and justice for each individual American, and resolve that this kind of action shall never again be repeated."[130]

In 1980, Congress established a commission to gather facts to determine the wrong done by Roosevelt's order.[131] The commission's report, released December 1982, minced no words. It is titled: *Personal Justice Denied.* Among other findings, the commission stated that Executive Order 9066 "was not justified by military necessity, and the decisions which followed from it—detention, ending detention and ending exclusion—were not driven by analysis of military conditions. The broad historical causes which shaped these decisions were race prejudice, war hysteria and a failure of political leadership." Further: "Widespread ignorance of Japanese Americans contributed to a policy conceived in haste and executed in an atmosphere of fear and anger at Japan." A "grave injustice" was done to U.S. citizens and resident aliens of Japanese ancestry.[132]

In 1988, Congress passed legislation to implement the commission's findings. The statute established a trust fund of $1.25 billion to pay up to $20,000 to eligible individuals.[133] Payments made four decades after the detentions could never compensate for the lost years, the humiliation, and the economic sacrifices of having to sell property at reduced values before being sent to detention camps. The statute had a larger purpose. As President Ronald Reagan said in signing the bill: "what is most important in this bill has less to do with property than with honor. For here we admit a wrong; here we reaffirm our commitment as a nation to equal justice under the law."[134] Amendments in 1992 increased the size of the trust fund.[135] By 1999, the government had completed a $1.6 billion reparations program, making payments of $20,000 each to 82,210 internees or their heirs.[136]

During this period, Gordon Hirabayashi and Fred Korematsu returned to court to have their convictions overturned on the basis of documents that had been uncovered, showing that executive officials had deceived the federal judiciary in the 1940s. Vital evidence had been withheld by the administration.

---

130. Id.

131. 94 Stat. 964 (1980).

132. Commission on Wartime Relocation and Internment of Civilians, Personal Justice Denied (Washington, D.C.: December 1982), 18.

133. 102 Stat. 903, 905–06, sec. 104–05 (1988).

134. Public Papers of the Presidents, 1988, II, 1054.

135. 106 Stat. 1167 (1992); Public Papers of the Presidents, 1992, II, 1681.

136. "Redress for War Internees Ended," New York Times, February 15, 1999, at A15.

At the time of Korematsu's case, Justice Department attorneys learned that a 618-page document called *Final Report*, prepared by the War Department for General DeWitt, contained erroneous claims about alleged espionage efforts by Japanese Americans. Analyses conducted by the FBI and the Federal Communications Commissions rejected War Department assertions that Japanese Americans had sent signals from shore to assist Japanese submarine attacks along the Pacific coast. Justice Department officials knew they had a moral and legal obligation to inform the judiciary about the false information. A footnote, to be included in the Justice Department brief for *Korematsu*, identified the errors and misconceptions that appeared in the *Final Report*. The footnote repudiated the claim of shore-to-ship signaling, but it was so reworked and watered down that the courts could not possibly have understood how the administration had misled them.[137]

A district court, on the basis of documents submitted to it by Korematsu and his attorneys, concluded that the administration during World War II "knowingly withheld information from the courts when they were considering the critical question of military necessity in this case."[138] The court compared the first version of the footnote, which alerted the judiciary to conflicts within the Roosevelt administration, to the final version that made no mention of contradictory reports.[139] The court concluded that "there is substantial support in the record that the government deliberately omitted relevant information and provided misleading information in papers before the court."[140] As a result, it vacated Korematsu's conviction.

The second challenge came from Hirabayashi, who had been convicted of violating the curfew order. The Justice Department argued that the exclusion of everyone of Japanese ancestry from the West Coast was required by military necessity and the lack of time needed to separate loyal Japanese from those who might be subversive. It did not claim it was impossible to separate loyal and disloyal Japanese.[141] However, General DeWitt had taken the position that because of racial ties, filial piety, and strong bonds of common tradition, culture, and customs, it was "impossible to establish the identity of the loyal and the disloyal with any degree of safety."[142] For him, there was no "such a thing

137. Peter Irons, Justice at War 278 (1983).

138. Korematsu v. United States, 584 F.Supp. 1406, 1417 (D. Cal. 1984).

139. Id. at 1417–18.

140. Id. at 1420.

141. Hirabayashi v. United States, 627 F.Supp. 1445, 1453, 1454 (W.D. Wash. 1986).

142. Id. at 1449.

as a loyal Japanese."[143] The initial draft report contained those remarks by De-Witt. The final report, reflecting changes by the War Department, did not. The Justice Department received the final report but not the draft version.

A district court held in 1986 that although the department "did not know-ingly conceal" from Hirabayashi's counsel and the Supreme Court DeWitt's reasons for excluding Japanese, it was necessary to charge the government with concealment because it was information known to the War Department, an arm of the government.[144] The government's failure to disclose to Hirabayashi, his counsel, and the Supreme Court the positions of DeWitt "was an error of the most fundamental character," and Hirabayashi "was in fact seriously prejudiced by that non-disclosure in his appeal from his conviction of failing to report."[145] The district court vacated his conviction for failing to report to civilian control stations, but declined to vacate his conviction for violating the curfew order.[146] On appeal, the Ninth Circuit vacated both convictions.[147]

LOYALTY OF FEDERAL EMPLOYEES

In the midst of World War II, pressures built within the country for some type of loyalty pledge to be signed by citizens and aliens. In 1942, a group called "Bundles for America" drafted the text of "A Pledge for Americans," express-ing pride in being an American, supporting "loyally and in friendship" all the countries in the world joined in the fight against the Axis powers, and ending with "So help me God!" The pledge stated that whoever signed it would not listen to "idle rumors" or repeat "destructive gossip."[148]

The following year, President Roosevelt created an interdepartmental com-mittee to review allegations that federal employees were engaged in "subversive activity."[149] He acted shortly after Congressman Dies claimed that hundreds of federal employees were affiliated with Communist groups or causes. Depart-ments and agencies were directed to refer complaints to the FBI for investiga-tion. Attorney General Biddle had released a report the previous year stating

143. Id. at 1452.
144. Id. at 1454.
145. Id. at 1457.
146. Id. at 1457–58.
147. Hirabayashi v. United States, 828 F.2d 591 (9th Cir. 1987).
148. "Loyalty Pledge to be Circulated," New York Times, May 28, 1942, at 12.
149. Executive Order 9300 (February 5, 1943), reprinted in Eleanor Bontecou, The Fed-eral Loyalty–Security Program 272–73 (1953).

that thirty-six federal employees had been discharged for activities associated with alleged subversive organizations. Of those discharged, only two were on the list of 1,100 names assembled by the Dies committee.[150]

Loyalty Security Boards

On March 25, 1947, President Harry Truman issued procedures to determine the loyalty of federal employees.[151] His executive order stated that the presence within the government "of any disloyal or subversive person constitutes a threat to our democratic processes." As a precaution against abusive and irresponsible charges, he insisted on "protection from unfounded accusations of disloyalty."[152] However, his procedures allowed the government to rely on secret informants whose identity and credibility could be withheld from the accused.

The loyalty program covered individuals seeking federal jobs and those already employed. Anyone applying for a civilian position faced a loyalty investigation conducted by the Civil Service Commission (CSC). Federal employees would be investigated by their department or agency. Investigations of applicants relied on FBI files, CSC files, military and naval intelligence files, the files of any other "appropriate government investigative or intelligence agency," HUAC files, and other sources. Whenever "derogatory information with respect to loyalty of an applicant is revealed a full field investigation shall be conducted."[153] Prejudicial information might come from unreliable or malicious sources, including former spouses, employers, associates, and neighbors. In one loyalty case, Justice Douglas warned that informants "may bear old grudges. Under cross-examination their stories might disappear like bubbles. Their whispered confidences might turn out to be yarns conceived by twisted minds or by people who, though sincere, have poor faculties of observation and memory."[154]

150. "Names Committee on Subversion," New York Times, February 7, 1943, at 20.

151. Executive Order 9835, 12 Fed. Reg. 1935 (1947).

152. Id. For the political context to Truman's order, see Alan D. Harper, The Politics of Loyalty: The White House and the Communist Issue, 1946–1952 (1969); Robert Griffin and Athan Theoharis, eds., The Specter: Original Essays on the Cold War and the Origins of McCarthyism (1974); Peter L. Steinberg, The Great "Red Menace": United States Prosecution of American Communists, 1947–1952 (1984); Richard M. Freeland, The Truman Doctrine and the Origins of McCarthyism (1985 ed.).

153. 12 Fed. Reg. 1935 (Part I.4).

154. Peters v. Hobby, 349 U.S. 331, 351 (1955) (Douglas, J., concurring).

Loyalty boards, composed of not less than three agency employees, heard complaints and wrote regulations. Employees charged with disloyalty had a right to a hearing before the board and could appear personally, bring counsel or a representative of the employee's choosing, present evidence, call witnesses, submit affidavits, and appeal a recommendation for removal.[155] Agency heads retained authority to suspend an employee "at any time pending a determination with respect to loyalty."[156] Employees were entitled to be informed of the nature of the charges in sufficient detail to prepare a defense. Charges would be stated "as specifically and completely as, in the discretion of the employing department or agency, security considerations permit, . . ."[157] The investigative agency "may refuse to disclose the names of confidential informants, provided it furnishes sufficient information about such informants on the basis of which the requesting department or agency can make an adequate evaluation of the information furnished by them, . . ."[158] Some agencies, through their directives, gave access to the names of confidential informants.[159]

The Attorney General's List

The Loyalty Review Board received from the Justice Department the name of each foreign or domestic organization that the Attorney General designated as "totalitarian, fascist, communist or subversive, or as having adopted a policy of advocating or approving the commission of acts of force or violence to deny others their rights under the Constitution of the United States, or as seeking to alter the form of government of the United States by unconstitutional means."[160] How and why organizations appeared on this list was left unexplained. There was no notice or hearing. The general public and federal agencies were expected to trust in secret determinations.[161]

In 1951, the Supreme Court reviewed three "communist" organizations on the AG list and regarded the designations as "patently arbitrary." The Attorney General had not relied on "either disclosed or undisclosed facts supplying a

155. 12 Fed. Reg. 1937 (Part II.1.a).

156. Id. at 1937–38 (Part II.4).

157. Id. at 1937 (Part II.2.b).

158. Id. (Part IV.2).

159. Bontecou, The Federal Loyalty–Security Program, at 60–64.

160. 12 Fed. Reg. 1938 (Part III.3).

161. For further details on the AG list, see Bontecou, The Federal Loyalty–Security Program, at 157–204.

reasonable basis for the determination."[162] Determining that an organization belongs on the list "must be the result of a process of reasoning. It cannot be an arbitrary fiat contrary to the known facts."[163] Baseless and unsubstantiated decisions to add names to the list "cripple the functioning and damage the reputation of those organizations in their respective communities and in the nation."[164] The Court required the government to either substantiate its charges or remove organizations from the list.

Justice Black, concurring, regarded "officially prepared and proclaimed government blacklists" as possessing "almost every quality of bills of attainder." He knew that the classic bill of attainder was a legislative action, as with the *Lovett* case, but he could not believe that the framers "inadvertently endowed the executive with power to engage in the same tyrannical practices that had made the bill such an odious institution."[165] Also concurring, Justice Frankfurter found a deprivation of due process whenever the executive branch felt at liberty to "maim or decapitate" an organization "on the mere say-so of the Attorney General."[166] Justice Jackson, in a third concurrence, agreed with Frankfurter on that point.[167] Critics warned that the AG list discouraged memberships in groups, promoted "conformity and standardization," and constrained the freedoms of thought and association.[168]

Truman's order included some general standards for rejecting an applicant or removing a federal employee. It was to be "on grounds relating to loyalty" and "on all the evidence." "Reasonable grounds" must exist for believing that the person is disloyal to the U.S. government.[169] However, evidence, including assertions from secret informers, could be withheld from the accused. Disloyalty would be determined by actions to commit sabotage, espionage, treason, or sedition. (Those four categories are all covered by criminal laws and subject to prosecution, with full procedural safeguards available to the accused.) Also

---

162. Joint Anti-Fascist Refugee Committee v. McGrath, 341 U.S. 123, 126 (1951).

163. Id. at 136.

164. Id. at 139.

165. Id. at 144.

166. Id. at 161.

167. Id. at 186.

168. John Lord O'Brian, National Security and Individual Freedom 25–26 (1955). For other contemporary critiques of Truman's order and loyalty tests, see John Lord O'Brian, "Loyalty Tests and Guilt by Association," 61 Harv. L. Rev. 592 (1948) and Clifford J. Durr, "The Loyalty Order's Challenge to the Constitution," 16 U. Chi. L. Rev. 298 (1949).

169. 12 Fed. Reg. 1938 (Part V.1).

proscribed in Truman's order: advocacy of revolution or force or violence to alter the constitutional form of the U.S. government.

Three other general standards followed. The first consisted of intentional, unauthorized disclosure to any person, "under circumstances which may indicate disloyalty to the United States," of documents or information of a confidential or non-public character obtained through a federal job. Next: performing or attempting to perform duties to serve the interests of another government "in preference to the interests of the United States." Last: membership in, affiliation with, "or sympathetic association" with any foreign or domestic organization designated by the Attorney General as "totalitarian, fascist, communist, or subversive" or advocating the commission of acts of force or violence "to deny other persons their rights under the Constitution" or seeking to alter the form of government "by unconstitutional means."[170] Truman's order was amended in 1951 and revoked in 1953 by President Dwight D. Eisenhower, who issued his own order on security requirements.[171]

Applying Truman's Order

O. Edmund Clubb spent more than two decades with the U.S. Foreign Service before becoming director of the State Department's Office of Chinese Affairs in 1950. Security concerns reached a pitched level that year. The Korean War began in June, a year after Mao's Communist Party had won the civil war in China. The political beliefs and associations of every U.S. specialist on China received close scrutiny to see who was responsible for "losing" China. In January 1951, Clubb was notified that he was under investigation by the department's Loyalty Security Board, in part because an unnamed informant said he had delivered "a sealed envelope" to the office of the left-wing *New Masses* magazine in 1932. After formal charges were brought, Clubb was suspended from his official duties. He was eventually cleared, but the experience convinced him he had no future in government.

Years later, Clubb explained the procedures followed by the State Department. The Loyalty Security Board functioned as "accuser, prosecutor, judge, and jury in a matter where the accused was not enabled to know what it was all about."[172] The board relied on information supplied by informants never

---

170. Id. (Part V.2).
171. 16 Fed. Reg. 3690 (1951); 18 Fed. Reg. 2489 (1953).
172. O. Edmund Clubb, The Witness and I 147 (1974).

made known to him. He had no right to confront or cross-examine his accusers and was denied access even to the full text of the accusation. He discovered that the board at times substituted wording of its own to significantly change the meaning of an accusation—to his disadvantage.[173]

The charges against Clubb fell into three groups: "political unorthodoxy, dangerous associations, and a visit to a leftist magazine 19 years before."[174] Among the insinuations was the claim by an unknown informant that from 1934 to 1935, Clubb had "distinct pink tendencies."[175] After rounds of hearings before the board, the State Department decided that Clubb must be separated from the Foreign Service as a security risk. He successfully appealed and was restored to active duty.[176] However, "clearance" never removes the shadow over an employee. Found innocent, Clubb "was put on the shelf, damaged goods, to be out of the way."[177] Under those conditions, he retired from federal service on February 12, 1952.

Other federal employees, high and low, were brought before loyalty security boards. One case involved a proofreader at the Government Printing Office, employed for seven years with no access to classified materials. In a previous loyalty investigation he had been cleared. In 1954, he was told again to appear before a screening board of three fellow employees. Because it was a "preliminary" hearing he had no right to bring counsel. Different names, affiliations, and associations were mentioned at that hearing. He was not informed about the charges or what questions might be raised. The transcript of that hearing was not given to him or his counsel. He was advised that his retention in the federal government was not consistent with the interests of national security. The only charge: "you continued sympathetic association with a known Communist, read Communist literature and made pro-Communist statements."[178] He was immediately suspended.

His counsel later learned that the agency did not use the AG list but rather a list provided by HUAC.[179] The employee denied that he had ever had continued sympathetic association with a known Communist and could recall only one person of that description, who he knew from 1933 to 1935. He said he was

---

173. Id. at 147–48.
174. Id. at 149.
175. Id. at 161.
176. Id. at 269.
177. Id. at 270.
178. Albert Fried, McCarthyism: The Great American Scare 34 (1997).
179. Id.

in "strong disagreement" with the views of that individual.[180] He admitted to being active for a time with the People's Party, but it was never cited as a Communist organization by the Attorney General or any legislative committee.[181] The person he knew from 1933 to 1935 had copies of the *Daily Worker*, which he looked at out of curiosity but not sympathy.[182] His agency asked about his subscription to *Consumer Reports*. He said he read it to learn about the best products at the least price and had no reason to believe it was subversive.

At the formal hearing, the agency produced no witnesses and expressed no interest in hearing from four character witnesses brought to testify on his behalf. His counsel nevertheless had the witnesses speak and made a concluding argument. At the hearing, the loyalty board expressed surprise that the counsel had not been permitted to read the transcript of the preliminary hearing. It was made available to him. Among the questions put to the employee were these: (1) "How do your distinguish between the Russian system of government and ours? (2) What was your reaction upon receiving these charges? Didn't you feel remorseful for some of the things you did in your life? (3) Don't you think that any person is a security risk who at one time or another associated with a Communist—even though it was not a sympathetic association and even though he may not have known at the time that the person was a Communist and even though the association terminated many years ago?"[183] The employee learned by letter three weeks later that the agency had reached an adverse decision on his security status. No reasons were offered for the ruling.[184]

The model of federal loyalty security boards spread to state and local governments and to private organizations. Applicants and employees were put through the same drill, often at great cost to their reputations and livelihoods. Writers, actors, singers, musicians, and other professionals were blacklisted and forced from their field of work.[185] To Henry Steele Commager, writing in 1947, the "new loyalty" amounted to conformity, requiring the "uncritical and unquestioning acceptance as it is—the political institutions, the social relationships, the economic practices."[186] Loyalty should mean devotion to the best interests of the country "and may require hostility to the particular

---

180. Id. at 35.
181. Id.
182. Id.
183. Id. at 37.
184. Id.
185. See Fried, McCarthyism, for specific examples.
186. John C. Wahlke, ed. Loyalty in a Democratic State 97 (1952).

policies which the government pursues."[187] Ironically, the governments best known for demanding conformity were totalitarian.[188]

After he left the White House, Truman wrote about the federal loyalty program. He said that "if a man cannot be prosecuted in the courts, then he should not be persecuted by a Senate or House committee."[189] He should not have been persecuted in the executive branch either. Truman disagreed "in taking hearsay charges against any person, especially against anyone who has the background to qualify as a government servant."[190] His executive order allowed precisely that. In blocking access by Congress to confidential files held by the executive branch, he failed to recognize that those same files could be used irresponsibly to wreck federal careers. The records of the CSC, the FBI, and other agencies, he admitted, "contain many unsupported, uninvestigated, and unevaluated charges . . . [and may] contain items based on suspicion, rumor, prejudice, and malice, and therefore, if released, may do great harm to the reputation and careers of many innocent people."[191]

THE COURTS TAKE A LOOK

In gingerly fashion, federal courts began to place some limits on the power of government to charge public employees with disloyalty. As is typical of the federal judiciary, clear-cut and intelligible challenges to loyalty boards came initially from dissenting judges in the lower courts or on the Supreme Court. The Court prefers to avoid constitutional issues until they are first shaped and crystallized by others, usually over a period of time.

Dorothy Bailey

A D.C. Circuit decision in 1950 concerned the removal of Dorothy Bailey from her federal job on the ground of disloyalty. The Civil Service Commission received information "to the effect that you are or have been a member of the Communist Party or the Communist Political Association; that you have attended meetings of the Communist Party, and have associated on numerous

187. Id. at 99.
188. Id. at 101.
189. 2 Memoirs by Harry S. Truman: Years of Trial and Hope 270 (1956).
190. Id.
191. Id. at 281.

occasions with known Communist Party members." The commission said it had information she was a member of the American League for Peace and Democracy (ALPD) and the Washington Committee for Democratic Action, both names appearing on the AG list.[192]

Bailey received a hearing and was entitled to an appeal but had no opportunity to confront and cross-examine her secret accusers. She admitted past membership for a short time in the ALPD but "vigorously asserted her loyalty to the United States."[193] She denied under oath any membership in and any relationship or sympathy with the Communist Party, any activities associated with Communism, or any affiliation with groups that advocated the overthrow of the U.S. government. She recalled attending one Communist meeting in 1932 in connection with a seminar study on the platforms of different political parties when she was a student at Bryn Mawr. She spoke under oath; her informers did not.[194]

Two judges of the three-member panel upheld her dismissal. The court denied that she had any right to trial-type procedures, including the right to confront and cross-examine witnesses against her.[195] If the Government in the exercise of its power "injures an individual, that individual has no redress."[196] They deferred wholly to executive branch judgments in deciding to eliminate disloyal employees.[197] The court's decision was affirmed per curiam by an equally divided, 4 to 4, Supreme Court.[198]

Dissenting in this case, Judge Edgerton showed an appreciation for individual rights and procedural due process that would later take root and find expression in the Supreme Court. A finding of disloyalty, he said, "is closely akin to a finding of treason. The public hardly distinguishes between the two."[199] The informants were not identified to Bailey or even to the loyalty board.[200] Four individuals appeared at the hearing to testify that the suggestion of disloyalty on her part was "inconceivable" and "out of reason."[201] No witness offered evidence against her, even hearsay evidence. No affidavits were

192. Bailey v. Richardson, 182 F.2d 46, 49–50 (D.C. Cir. 1950).

193. Id. at 50.

194. Id. at 66 (Edgerton, J., dissenting).

195. Id. at 55–57 (Prettyman, J.).

196. Id. at 63.

197. Id. at 51, 64.

198. Bailey v. Richardson, 341 U.S. 918 (1951).

199. Bailey v. Richardson, 182 F.2d at 66 (Edgerton, J., dissenting).

200. Id.

201. Id.

introduced against her. The hearing record consisted of evidence entirely in her favor, and yet the board found "on all the evidence" there were reasonable grounds to believe she was disloyal. The board relied on confidential FBI reports not made available to Bailey, including claims by the informants.[202]

As Edgerton noted, the procedures followed by the loyalty board put any American "at the mercy not only of an innocently mistaken informer but also of a malicious or demented one unless his defect is apparent to the agent who interviews him."[203] To Edgerton, Bailey's dismissal violated both the Constitution and Truman's order. The actions by the loyalty board violated the order because it called for a hearing and a determination based on evidence. As interpreted by Edgerton, the order implied an opportunity to cross-examine opposing witnesses.[204] If the government decided to preserve the anonymity of informants, the employee "must be cleared or the proceedings dropped."[205] Dismissal for disloyalty, Edgerton said, was punitive in nature and required the safeguards of a judicial trial. Dismissals for such charges as incompetence are not punitive and are entirely within the authority of the executive. Punishment, however, "is infliction of harm, usually for wrong conduct but in appellant's case for wrong views." Dismissals for disloyalty are punitive, as reflected in the Supreme Court's 1946 *Lovett* case.[206]

Edgerton objected that the term "disloyal" was so indefinite that neither Truman's order nor Bailey's loyalty review board attempted to define it.[207] He said loyalty security boards would ask federal employees: "Do you read a good many books?" "What books do you read?" "What magazines do you read?" "What newspapers do you buy or subscribe to?" "How do you explain the fact that you have an album of Paul Robeson records in your home?" "Do you ever entertain Negroes in your home?"[208] The result was to force government employees to adopt only "the most orthodox opinions on political, economic, and social questions," all of which "abridges not only freedom of speech but freedom of thought."[209] The next constitutional right to fall would be freedom

---

202. Id. at 66–67.
203. Id. at 67.
204. Id. at 68.
205. Id. at 69.
206. Id.
207. Id. at 71.
208. Id. at 72.
209. Id. at 73, 74.

of assembly. Edgerton closed with this admonition: "We cannot preserve our liberties by sacrificing them."[210]

State and Local Programs

In the early 1950s, the Supreme Court began to review loyalty programs at the city and state level. Los Angeles required its employees to sign affidavits disclosing whether they were or ever had been members of the Communist Party or the Communist Political Association. Employees had to take an oath that they did not advocate the overthrow (by force, violence, or other unlawful means) of the U.S. government or the government of California and that they were not a member of any group that supported those goals. In 1951, the Court found no constitutional objection to this oath, provided it did not apply to persons who joined innocent of the purpose of a proscribed organization or those who broke with the organization once its character became apparent.[211]

A year later the Court upheld a New York City law that allowed the removal of any teacher in a public school who belonged to an organization that advocated the overthrow of government by force, violence, or any unlawful means. Three Justices dissented. Douglas and Black objected that the law "proceeds on a principle repugnant to our society—guilt by association. A teacher is disqualified because of her membership in an organization found to be 'subversive.'"[212] Douglas and Black viewed the law as the start of a police state, with teachers under constant surveillance: "their pasts are combed for signs of disloyalty; their utterances are watched for clues to dangerous thoughts. . . . Supineness and dogmatism take the place of inquiry."[213]

Judicial tolerance reached a limit in 1952 when a unanimous Court struck down an Oklahoma law that required each state employee, as a condition of employment, to take a loyalty oath stating that he was not, and had not been for the preceding five years, a member of any organization listed by the U.S. Attorney General as a "communist front" or "subversive." The Court held that the Due Process Clause does not permit a state, in an attempt to use membership in an organization to block public employment, to punish innocent association. A state employee might have joined a proscribed organization

---

210. Id. at 74.
211. Garner v. Los Angeles Board, 341 U.S. 716, 723 (1951).
212. Adler v. Board of Education, 342 U.S. 485, 508 (1952).
213. Id. at 510.

unaware of its activities and purposes. The individual might have severed ties after learning about the character of the group. A group formerly subversive could rid itself of those principles.[214] Excluding someone on grounds of disloyalty, in the view of the community, produces a deep stain and becomes "a badge of infamy."[215] In a concurrence, Justice Black said that governments "have ample power to punish treasonable acts," but they must not have "a further power to punish thought and speech as distinguished from acts."[216]

Other Federal Actions

At the federal level, the Court remained cautious when confronting Congress, the President, or executive power. It looked for ways to protect individuals rejected on loyalty grounds without deciding key constitutional issues. For example, the Civil Service Commission's Loyalty Review Board decided there was a reasonable basis to bar a consultant to a federal agency for three years. He had been twice cleared of charges of disloyalty. On the third round, he was denied any opportunity to confront and cross-examine his secret accusers, but the Court decided not to rule on that ground.[217] Instead, it ruled that the board had acted in violation of an executive order.[218]

The Court adopted the same tactic in 1956 in handling the suspension of a food and drug inspector for the Department of Health, Education, and Welfare who had been charged with close association with alleged Communists and an allegedly subversive organization. In 1950, Congress had passed legislation authorizing the summary suspension of federal employees.[219] The statute was expressly applicable to departments and agencies involved with national security, although it could be extended by the President to other agencies. The Court concluded that the term "national security" in the statute related only to "those activities which are directly concerned with the Nation's safety, as distinguished from the general welfare," and when determinations had been made that the employee's position was affected with the "national security."[220] As a result, the inspector's suspension was not authorized by the statute. Although avoiding constitutional questions, the Court remarked that because

214. Wieman v. Updegraff, 344 U.S. 183, 190 (1952).
215. Id. at 191.
216. Id. at 193.
217. Peters v. Hobby, 349 U.S. 331, 337–38 (1955).
218. Id. at 338.
219. 64 Stat. 476 (1950).
220. Cole v. Young, 351 U.S. 536, 543 (1956).

of the "stigma attached to persons dismissed on loyalty grounds," the need for procedural safeguards was especially great.[221] If ambiguities existed they should be "resolved against the Government."[222]

This same pattern of deciding cases on nonconstitutional grounds appears in a 1956 decision by the Court. The State Department's Loyalty Security Board repeatedly cleared John S. Service, a Foreign Service Officer, of charges of being disloyal and a security risk. Those findings had been approved by the Deputy Under Secretary, whose judgments favorable to an employee were final under departmental regulations. Nevertheless, the Loyalty Security Board of the Civil Service Commission found there was reasonable doubt as to Service's loyalty, advised the Secretary of State to that effect, and the Secretary discharged him the same day. A unanimous Court held that the removal violated State Department regulations that were binding on the Secretary.[223]

A similar case appeared in 1959. Once again the Court decided that the head of a department, in this case Interior, had failed to follow departmental regulations in dismissing an employee. In his appearance before a security hearing board, no evidence was produced in support of the charges against him (sympathetic associations with Communists or Communist sympathizers). No witnesses testified against him. The board subjected him to an extensive cross-examination that exceeded the charges that had been specified. Departmental regulations required that board hearings be orderly and that restrictions be imposed as to relevancy, competency, and materiality of matters considered. The inquiry conducted by the board, however, "developed into a wide-ranging inquisition into this man's educational, social, and political beliefs, encompassing even a question as to whether he was 'a religious man.'"[224]

Private Employees in Defense Industries

After deciding these cases on procedural grounds, the Court in 1959 began to address the basic constitutional right to confront and cross-examine witnesses against an accused. The case arose when the federal government revoked a security clearance granted to William Lewis Greene, an aeronautical engineer employed by a private manufacturer. He was discharged from his job solely because of the revocation. Jobs in that field were thereafter closed to him. A

221. Id. at 546.
222. Id. at 556.
223. Service v. Dulles, 354 U.S. 363 (1957).
224. Vitarelli v. Seaton, 359 U.S. 535, 543 (1959).

joint military Personnel Security Board (PSB) advised his company that it was necessary to revoke his clearance for security reasons. If he remained with the company, its continued access to classified information and federal contracts would be in jeopardy.[225]

In preparing for the hearing he was entitled to, Greene learned that the PSB had information indicating that between 1943 and 1947 he had associated with Communists, visited officials of the Russian Embassy, and attended a dinner given by an allegedly Communist Front organization. At the hearing, he explained that specific "suspect" persons he supposedly associated with were actually friends of his ex-wife, that she held leftist political views he did not agree with, and that those disagreements led to a divorce. He denied categorically that he had ever been a Communist and spoke at length about his opposition to the theory of Communism. His witnesses at the hearing vouched for his loyalty. Top company officials agreed with his statement that he had visited the Russian Embassy only to sell company products to Russia. The government presented no witnesses, and Greene had no opportunity to confront and question the persons whose statements reflected adversely on him. The hearing reversed PSB's action and renewed his authority to work on secret contract work.[226]

A year later, the Navy advised his company that Greene could no longer have access to classified security information. The action came without a hearing. Although the company valued his knowledge and ability and urged the Navy to reconsider, he was discharged. The following year Greene, at a hearing, was told he could not have access to certain information, including the names of confidential informants.[227] After the hearing, the government announced he would be denied a security clearance.

Greene sued in federal court. By the time the case reached the Supreme Court, the issue was crystallized in this fashion: "whether the Department of Defense has been authorized to create an industrial security clearance program under which affected persons may lose their jobs and may be restrained in following their chosen professions on the basis of fact determinations concerning their fitness for clearance made in proceedings in which they are denied the traditional procedural safeguards of confrontation and cross-examination."[228]

---

225. Greene v. McElroy, 360 U.S. 474, 477 (1959).
226. Id. at 478–80.
227. Id. at 486.
228. Id. at 493.

The procedures for granting and denying clearances to employees in the defense industry had developed over a period of years without benefit of congressional statute or executive orders issued by the President. The Court said that certain legal principles "have remained relatively immutable." One vital principle: when governmental action "seriously injures an individual, and the reasonableness of the action depends on fact findings, the evidence used to prove the Government's case must be disclosed to the individual so that he has an opportunity to show that it is untrue."[229] Examining documentary evidence is important, but so is evidence obtained from those who might have faulty memory or might be "perjurers or persons motivated by malice, vindictiveness, intolerance, prejudice, or jealousy."[230] The rights of confrontation and cross-examination are identified in the Sixth Amendment for criminal cases, but they can apply to other governmental actions.

Even the members of the clearance boards involved in Greene's case did not see the informants or know their identities. They relied on an investigator's summary report on what the informants said.[231] The Court found no congressional statute or presidential order to justify or authorize the type of procedure followed by the government in granting and denying clearances to individuals in the private sector on the basis of secret informants.[232] In Greene's case, the Court decided that in the absence of explicit authorization from either the President or Congress, the government was not empowered to deprive him of his job "in a proceeding in which he was not afforded the safeguards of confrontation and cross-examination."[233]

Rachel Brauner

After Greene's case, the Supreme Court reviewed the dismissal—on loyalty grounds—of an employee at a cafeteria operated by a private concessionaire on the premises of the Naval Gun Factory in Washington, D.C. Rachel Brauner, a short-order cook, worked at the Gun Factory for more than six years. Access to the building was restricted, with guards posted at all entry points. The Gun Factory was responsible for designing, producing, and inspecting naval ordnance, including highly classified weapons systems. She needed an identification badge to work in the building.

229. Id. at 496.
230. Id.
231. Id. at 498–99.
232. Id. at 499–508.
233. Id. at 508.

The cafeteria was prohibited from hiring personnel who failed to meet "the security requirements or other requirements under applicable regulations."[234] On November 15, 1956, Brauner was required to turn in her badge because the security officer determined she did not meet security requirements. No charges were made against her. She received no facts to justify or explain the decision. The cafeteria's union requested a meeting to discuss her case, but the Navy said a hearing would serve "no useful purpose."[235] The dispute was referred to a board of arbitrators, which offered her no relief.[236]

When Brauner sought help from the courts, a district court dismissed her complaint. By the time her appeal reached the D.C. Circuit, the Supreme Court had decided Greene's case, and a panel of three judges, with one dissenter, reversed the district court and held that the regulations that deprived her of her badge were unauthorized and invalid.[237] The D.C. Circuit then voted to take the case up en banc, allowing all nine judges to hear and decide her case. In a decision issued on April 14, 1960, the court split 5 to 4 in upholding the government. Chief Judge Prettyman made short work of her case. He emphasized that it was not a case of someone discharged from her job. By losing her badge, she had an opportunity to work with the same company but at a location outside the District of Columbia, in suburban Virginia.[238] Her case was unlike Greene's, whose denial of security clearance meant debarment from his entire profession.[239] Prettyman denied that she had been stigmatized: "Nobody has said that Brauner is disloyal or is suspected of the slightest shadow of international wrongdoing."[240] However, she had lost her badge for reasons of security. The four dissenters believed that the district court had to be reversed because of *Greene* v. *McElroy*. On October 10, 1960, the Supreme Court agreed to take the case to decide whether Brauner's case was analogous to Greene's.[241]

In Greene's situation, the Court found no authorization from Congress or the President for the procedures that denied him access to classified

234. Cafeteria Workers v. McElroy, 367 U.S. 886, 888 (1961).

235. Id.

236. Cafeteria & Restaurant Wkrs. U., Local 473 v. McElroy, 284 F.2d 173, 176 (D.C. Cir. 1960).

237. Id. at 193–95.

238. Id. at 176–77.

239. Id. at 181.

240. Id. at 183.

241. Cafeteria & Restaurant Workers Union, Local 473, AFL-CIO, et al. v. McElroy, 364 U.S. 813 (1960).

information. As for Brauner, the Navy possessed full authority to protect the security of the Gun Factory. The sole remaining question was whether the Navy's decision to withdraw her badge violated the Due Process Clause of the Fifth Amendment. Was she entitled to know the specific grounds for her exclusion and to appear at a hearing to refute the allegations? Five Justices said she had no such right. They concluded that being denied a badge because of security requirements was not the same as being called disloyal.[242] They assumed that Brauner could not be constitutionally excluded from the Gun Factory "if the announced grounds for her exclusion had been patently arbitrary or discriminatory—that she could not have been kept out because she was a Democrat or a Methodist." The reason for her exclusion was "entirely rational" and in accord with the contract with the cafeteria.[243] But since the charges were never specified and no grounds were given, there was no way for the Court to assert entire or even partial rationality.

Four members of the Court—Brennan, Warren, Black, and Douglas—dissented. They said it was inconsistent of the Court to argue that Brauner could not be removed on such grounds as race, religion, or political opinion, and then say her dismissal was permissible for failure to meet "security requirements." Unless a government official "is foolish enough to admit what he is doing—and few will be so foolish after today's decision—he may employ 'security requirements' as a blind behind which to dismiss at will for the most discriminatory of causes."[244] Brauner might be "the victim of the basest calumny, perhaps even the caprice of the government officials in whose power her status rested completely."[245] If she could not be removed for the "arbitrary" reasons of race, religion, or political opinions, why allow removal for "security requirements" if that phrase is a cloak to cover arbitrary actions? Although she was not called disloyal or subversive, being excluded as a security risk is "most odious in our times" and carries "much more sinister meaning."[246] They believed she was entitled to some process other than summary action by the Navy followed by arbitration.

242. Cafeteria Workers v. McElroy, 367 U.S. at 898.
243. Id.
244. Id. at 900.
245. Id. at 900–01.
246. Id. at 901.

THE SPIRIT OF MCCARTHYISM

McCarthyism is a political phenomenon much larger than the Wisconsin Senator's campaign against Communism in the early 1950s. It existed before Joseph McCarthy and may resurface at any time, in the United States and anywhere else. In its fundamentals, it separates people into good and bad and strips the latter of constitutional rights. An elementary principle of American law is that guilt is individual and personal, evidence must establish guilt, and the burden is on the government to prove its case. McCarthyism assigns guilt to a group, relies on unproven allegations rather than evidence, and places the burden on the individual to cleanse his or her name. The dictionary defines McCarthyism as a political attitude "closely allied to know-nothingism" and is used to attack individuals "on the basis of unsubstantiated charges."[247]

Long before Senator McCarthy was in a position to conduct his crusade against Communism, Truman indulged in McCarthyism by issuing his 1947 order creating loyalty boards. Whoever sought federal jobs or were already employed faced accusations never made clear to them, based on allegations by anonymous accusers. Three years later, Truman rebuked Congress for trying to do what he had already done. In vetoing the Internal Security Bill, he said the legislation "would put the Government of the United States in the thought control business."[248] He had already accomplished that with his executive order: punishing individuals not for what they did but for what they thought. The bill, he said, gave "Government officials vast powers to harass all of our citizens in the exercise of their right of free speech."[249] With his executive order as a model, citizens across the country seeking jobs in government at every level and in the private sector found their right of free speech abridged. He objected that the language of the bill "is so broad and vague that it might well result in penalizing the legitimate activities of people who are not communists at all, but loyal citizens."[250] He well described the impact of his own order.

On February 9, 1950, in a speech in Wheeling, West Virginia, Senator McCarthy lifted a piece of paper he claimed held the names of 205 Communists working in the State Department. In fact he had no list, but his dramatic allegation inflamed the public and attracted broad support. Later he called Secretary of Defense George Marshall a traitor, ridiculed Secretary of State Dean

247. Webster's Third New International Dictionary, Unabridged (1993), at 1353.
248. Public Papers of the Presidents, 1950, at 645.
249. Id. at 646.
250. Id. at 647.

Acheson, and argued for the impeachment of President Truman. As committee chairman he used the panel to call public officials and private citizens to testify, ruined many careers without ever uncovering Communists, and eventually destroyed his political and personal life.[251]

One of the first to challenge McCarthy was Margaret Chase Smith, Republican Senator from Maine. In a floor statement on June 1, 1950, she predicted that legitimate feelings of fear and frustration "could result in national suicide and the end of everything that we Americans hold dear." She protested that some lawmakers were using the Senate as "a forum of hate and character assassinations sheltered by the shield of congressional immunity." Senators were free to use defamatory and slanderous language against individual Americans that would be considered out of order if directed against a colleague.[252] Senators who resorted to character assassinations ignored basic principles of Americanism: "The right to criticize. The right to hold unpopular beliefs. The right to protest. The right of independent thought." Without those basic rights "thought control would have set in."[253]

Years of reckless accusations by McCarthy, some of it directed at his own institution, forced the Senate's hand. On December 2, 1954, the Senate voted 67 to 22 to "condemn" him for bringing the Senate into "dishonor and disrepute" and acting to "impair its dignity."[254] Ironically, he was condemned partly for what he said in criticizing the select committee that was created to study the censure charges against him. He complained that the committee in preparing its report "imitated Communist methods—that it distorted, misrepresented, and omitted in its effort to manufacture a plausible rationalization."[255] What he did not understand when giving it out, as subcommittee chairman, he understood when receiving it.

McCarthyism continued after his death in 1957. Congress passed legislation in 1950 to create the Subversive Activities Control Board (SACB) to investigate Communist activities. The board required the public registration of

---

251. David Caute, The Great Fear: The Anti-Communist Purge Under Truman and Eisenhower (1978); Ellen W. Schrecker, No Ivory Tower: McCarthyism and the Universities (1986); Robert Griffith, The Politics of Fear: Joseph R. McCarthy and the Senate (1987 ed.); Victor S. Navasky, Naming Names (2003 ed.); Larry Ceplair and Steven Englund, The Inquisition in Hollywood (2003 ed.); David M. Oshinsky, A Conspiracy So Immense: The World of Joe McCarthy (2005 ed.).

252. 96 Cong. Rec. 7894 (1950).

253. Id.

254. 100 Cong. Rec. 16392 (1950).

255. Id.

"communist-action" and "communist-front" organizations.[256] Once stigmatized in that fashion, members of the organizations were vulnerable to various penalties. Several court decisions held that the registration feature violated the Fifth Amendment prohibition against self-incrimination.[257] Congress put the board back on its feet in 1968 by authorizing it to determine, through hearings, whether individuals and organizations were Communist. The following year an appellate court declared that the new procedure violated the First Amendment freedom of association. With the Supreme Court refusing to review this decision, the board seemed ready to go out of business.[258]

At the moment of apparent extinction, President Nixon issued an executive order in 1971 to expand the board's power and field of inquiry.[259] Senator Sam Ervin introduced a resolution stating that the President had no power "to alter by Executive order the content or effect of legislation enacted by Congress." The Senate adopted his amendment to prohibit the use of appropriated funds to implement the executive order. Representative Don Edwards attempted to instruct conferees to accept Ervin's amendment, but his motion was tabled.[260] An amendment by Senator William Proxmire to delete $450,000 from the SACB—its entire budget—was defeated.[261]

The battle continued the next year when the House passed a bill to provide legislative support for Nixon's executive order. Proxmire again offered his amendment to strip the board of its funds. During debate, Ervin remarked that the board had held hearings on 111 cases the previous year. "That is all they did last year," he added, "except draw their breath and their salaries."[262] The Senate adopted Proxmire's amendment, but House and Senate conferees compromised by giving the board $350,000. Also enacted was an express prohibition

---

256. 64 Stat. 997 (1950).

257. Communist Party of the United States v. SACB, 367 U.S. 1 (1961); Albertson v. SACB, 382 U.S. 70 (1965); United States v. Robel, 389 U.S. 258 (1967).

258. Boorda v. SACB, 421 F.2d 1142 (D.C. Cir. 1969), cert. denied, 397 U.S. 1042 (1970). For the rejuvenating statute, see 81 Stat. 765 (1968).

259. Executive Order 11605, 36 Fed. Reg. 12831 (1971). A federal court, without deciding the issue, said there was no precedent for a President "delegating to an independent, quasi-judicial body far-reaching responsibilities different in form and effect from those specifically given that body when created by the Congress." American Servicemen's Union v. Mitchell, 54 F.R.D. 14, 17 (D.D.C. 1972).

260. Ervin's legislation: S. Res. 163, 92d Cong., 1st sess. (1971); 117 Cong. Rec. 30248 (1971). Adopting Ervin's amendment: 117 Cong. Rec. 25898–902 (1971). Edwards: id. at 27305–12.

261. 117 Cong. Rec. 25888–98 (1971).

262. 118 Cong. Rec. 21063–64 (1972). House passage: 118 Cong. Rec. 19075–103 (1972). Proxmire amendment: id. at 21053–74.

against using any of the funds to carry out Nixon's executive order.[263] Clearly there was no life left in the SACB. Beginning with the fiscal 1974 budget, the administration did not even bother requesting funds for the board.

McCarthyism, supposedly part of the conservative movement, elevates nativism, chauvinism, nationalism, and governmental power over individual rights. Ironically, it borrows from Communism: the State is all, the individual little. Its spirit flourished during the Alien and Sedition Acts of 1798, the Palmer raids after World War I, and many other periods that violated constitutional liberties. It surfaces in times of crisis and emergency when the government argues, in the name of national security, that it must forgo public trials, withdraw procedural safeguards, block access to evidence, and limit free speech and free association. Those forces reappeared after September 11, 2001.

263. 86 Stat. 1134, sec. 706 (1972).

CHAPTER 6

Military Tribunals and Detention

On November 13, 2001, President George W. Bush surprised the nation by authorizing the creation of military tribunals to try individuals who gave assistance to the terrorist attacks on 9/11. Military tribunals had not been used since World War II, but the administration looked to a Supreme Court decision of 1942 (*Ex parte Quirin*) as an "apt precedent" to support Bush's order. The administration also depended heavily on the availability of "inherent" powers for the President. Under that theory, the executive branch could establish tribunals as it liked, without interference from Congress or the courts, including the conduct of secret trials with evidence withheld from detainees and their attorneys. The administration argued that statutory restrictions on detention camps, enacted in 1950 and amended in 1971, did not prevent the President or the military from holding U.S. citizens indefinitely without access to trial, evidence, or counsel.

HISTORICAL PRECEDENTS

The Bush administration advised federal courts that military tribunals "have tried enemy combatants since the earliest days of the Republic under such procedures as the President has deemed fit."[1] Through that statement the administration hoped to shore up its argument for inherent presidential power. However, the history of military tribunals supports an entirely different theory: tribunals were created under such procedures as *Congress* saw fit to spell out by statute. Those tribunals generally followed the procedures established by Congress for courts-martial and were never used to single out a broad class of noncitizens, as was done in the Bush military order.

The framers understood the need to limit executive authority to establish military tribunals unless there was clear congressional approval. On June 30, 1775, the Continental Congress adopted rules and regulations for the military

---

1. Brief for Appellants, Hamdan v. Rumsfeld, No. 04–5393 (D.C. Cir. December 8, 2004), at 53.

in a series of sixty-nine Articles of War.[2] From the very beginning, the punishment of offenses by the military was "wholly statutory, having been . . . enacted by Congress as the legislative power."[3] As Commander in Chief during the Revolutionary War, George Washington adhered faithfully to the Articles of War by reviewing death sentences imposed by courts-martial.[4] He recognized that changes in the military code "can only be defined and fixed by Congress."[5]

The Bush administration claimed that the Founding-era history supported presidential establishment of military tribunals: "It was well recognized when the Constitution was written and ratified that one of the powers inherent in military command was the authority to institute tribunals for punishing enemy violations of the laws of war," and that General Washington had appointed a "Board of General Officers" in 1780 to try British Major John André as a spy.[6] At the same time, the administration insisted, "there was no provision in the American Articles of war providing for the jurisdiction in a court-martial to try an enemy for the offense of spying."[7]

Those arguments are false. The Continental Congress adopted a resolution in 1776 expressly providing that enemy spies "shall suffer death . . . by sentence of a court martial, or such other punishment as such court martial shall direct," and ordered that the resolution "be printed at the end of the rules and articles of war."[8] The previous year, Congress had made it punishable by court-martial for members of the Continental Army to "hold correspondence with" or "give intelligence to" the enemy.[9] According to the Bush administration, "the drafters of the Constitution surely intended to give the President the same authority that General Washington possessed during the Revolutionary War to convene military tribunals to punish offenses against the laws of war."[10] In fact, General Washington received what future Presidents would

---

2. William Winthrop, Military Law and Precedents 953–60 (2d ed. 1920).

3. Id. at 21.

4. 13 The Writings of George Washington 136–40 (John C. Fitzpatrick ed., 1931).

5. 17 The Writings of George Washington 239 (Fitzpatrick ed.).

6. Brief for Appellants, Hamdan v. Rumsfeld, No. 04–5393 (D.C. Cir. December 8, 2004), at 58.

7. Id.

8. 5 Journals of the Continental Congress, 1774–1789, at 693.

9. American Articles of War of 1775, art. 28, reprinted in Winthrop, Military Law and Precedents, at 955.

10. Brief for Appellants, Hamdan v. Rumsfeld, No. 04–5393 (D.C. Cir. Dec. 8, 2004), at 58–59.

receive: statutory authority and specific directions and limits determined by the legislative branch.

It was a conceptual and historical mistake for the Bush administration to search for presidential power at the time of Major André's trial in 1780. There was no President at that time. There was only one branch of government: the Continental Congress. There was no separate executive or judiciary. Those branches would not appear until the drafting of the Constitution in 1787 and the operation of the new government in 1789.

Lessons after 1789

The Bush administration told a court in 2004: "Throughout this country's history, Presidents have exercised their inherent authority as Commanders in Chief to establish military commissions, without any authorization from Congress. In April 1818, for example, military tribunals were convened, without Congressional authorization, to try two British subjects for inciting the Creek Indians to war with the United States."[11] This is poor history (and law). The prosecution of the two British subjects during the Seminole War in Florida highlights the abuses to which executive-created military tribunals have always been prone. After the tribunal changed its sentence for one of the men from death to corporal punishment, General Andrew Jackson directed that the individual be shot and his order was carried out. Far from claiming inherent authority over the creation of military tribunals, President James Monroe sought to distance himself from Jackson's actions by forwarding documents about the episode to Congress for its investigation.[12]

A year later, a House committee issued a report highly critical of Jackson. It found no law that authorized the men's trial before a military court except the charge that one was "acting as a spy," of which he was found not guilty. It concluded there was not even "a shadow of necessity for [their] death."[13] Similarly, a Senate report rejected the theory that the two men were "outlaws and pirates" and further noted that "[h]umanity shudders at the idea of a cold-blooded execution of prisoners, disarmed, and in the power of the conqueror."[14] Military

11. Id. at 59.
12. 2 A Compilation of the Messages and Papers of the Presidents 612 (James D. Richardson ed., 1925); 15 Annals of Cong. 2135–50 (1818).
13. 1 American State Papers: Military Affairs 735 (1819).
14. 15 Annals of Cong. 267 (1819).

jurist William Winthrop later remarked that if an officer ordered an execution, in the manner of Jackson, he "would *now* be indictable for murder."[15]

The Bush administration looked to the military commissions created during the Mexican War for evidence of independent presidential authority.[16] The experience in Mexico provides no support for that claim. In his capacity as commander of U.S. forces in Mexico, General Winfield Scott originally justified military tribunals as an emergency measure to control undisciplined action and misconduct by American troops.[17] He never questioned the constitutional authority of Congress over commissions. He asked for statutory authority in advance and explained that he was merely filling a gap by instilling discipline among his troops in an effort to avoid guerrilla warfare. Scott knew from military history that lawless action by American soldiers in Mexico would invite and incite an insurgency.[18] Rather than assert inherent and unchecked authority, he relied heavily on the existing Articles of War (enacted by Congress) and practices in the States. He further provided that no commission "shall try any case clearly cognizable by any court martial."[19]

Military commissions during the Civil War were grounded in statutes that recognized their existence and operation as early as 1862.[20] Some of the military commissions were glaringly defective. For example, Captain Henry Wirz, the superintendent of the notorious Andersonville prison, was unfairly blamed by a commission for horrendous conditions and was "hurried to his death by vindictive politicians, an unbridled press, and a nation thirsty for revenge."[21] The military commission hastily set up to try alleged conspirators in Lincoln's assassination was, in the words of Lincoln's former Attorney General Edward Bates, "not only unlawful, but . . . a gross blunder in policy:

15. Winthrop, Military Law and Precedents, at 465 (emphasis in original). For more on Jackson's troubles with tribunals in Florida and New Orleans, see Louis Fisher, *Military Tribunals and Presidential Power* 25–31 (2005).

16. Brief for Appellants, *Hamdan v. Rumsfeld*, No. 04–5393 (D.C. Cir. December 8, 2004).

17. 2 Winfield Scott, Memoirs of Lieut.-General Scott, LL.D. 392–93 (1864).

18. Timothy D. Johnson, Winfield Scott: The Quest for Military Glory 166–70 (1998).

19. Id. at 544. For additional details on Scott's actions in Mexico, see Fisher, *Military Tribunals and Presidential Power*, at 32–35.

20. 12 Stat. 598, sec. 5 (1862). See also 12 Stat. 736, sec. 30 (1863) and 13 Stat. 356, sec. 1 (1864).

21. Darrett B. Rutman, "The War Crimes and Trial of Henry Wirz," 6 Civil War Hist. 117, 118 (1960). See Fisher, *Military Tribunals and Presidential Power*, at 62–65.

It denies the great, fundamental principle, that ours is a government of *Law,* and that the law is strong enough, to rule the people wisely and well."[22] Bates objected to military tribunals because the people who serve "are selected by the military commander *from among his own subordinates,* who are bound to obey him, and responsible to him; and therefore, they will, commonly, find the case as required or desired by the commander who selected them."[23] Courts-martial, he pointed out, exist because of a statute enacted by Congress "and the members thereof have *legal* duties and rights," whereas military tribunals "exist only by the will of the commander, and that will is their only known rule of proceeding."[24]

THE *QUIRIN* PRECEDENT

For legal authority to create military tribunals, the Bush administration relied heavily on *Ex parte Quirin* (1942), the decision by the Supreme Court upholding the authority of President Franklin D. Roosevelt to try eight German saboteurs by military tribunal. In many respects, the Bush military order mirrored Roosevelt's proclamation and military order.[25] In an op-ed piece published a week after Bush's order, former Attorney General William P. Barr and former federal prosecutor Andrew G. McBride referred to the Nazi saboteur case as the "most apt precedent."[26] In 2004, a plurality of the Supreme Court referred to *Quirin* as "the most apposite precedent" on the detention of U.S. citizens.[27] In that same decision, a dissent by Justices Scalia and Stevens dismissed *Quirin* as "not this Court's finest hour."[28] What defects were Scalia and Stevens flagging?

22. Howard K. Beale, ed., The Diary of Edward Bates, 1859–1866, at 483 (1933) (emphasis in original).

23. Id. at 502 (emphasis in original).

24. Id. (emphasis in original). See Fisher, Military Tribunals and Presidential Power, at 65–70.

25. For similarities between the Bush and Roosevelt orders, see Louis Fisher, Nazi Saboteurs on Trial: A Military Tribunal and American Law 159–60 (2003).

26. William P. Barr and Andrew G. McBride, "Military Justice for al Qaeda," Washington Post, November 18, 2001, at B7.

27. Hamdi v. Rumsfeld, 542 U.S. 507, 523 (2004) (plurality opinion by Justice O'Connor).

28. Id. at 569 (Justices Scalia and Stevens, dissenting).

German Saboteurs Arrive

In June 1942, eight German saboteurs reached the United States by two submarines. The men were trained and prepared to use explosives against railroads, factories, bridges, and other strategic targets. One of the Germans, George Dasch, turned himself into the FBI and helped the agency quickly locate his colleagues. President Roosevelt issued a proclamation to create a military tribunal to try them, and a month later the tribunal found all eight guilty.

Initially, when FBI agents interrogated Dasch and the other seven, they planned to arraign them before a district judge and try them in civil court. Why were they later tried before a military tribunal? There are several reasons. FBI agents told Dasch that if he agreed to plead guilty in civil court they would begin the paperwork for a presidential pardon. This offer was ill-advised. Confessions from suspects are supposed to be given voluntarily, without a promise or inducement from the government. The government became worried that if Dasch appeared in open court he would say that he had given himself in and helped the government find his colleagues. The public assumed that the executive branch possessed uncanny capacity to detect and apprehend enemy saboteurs. The administration wanted that impression undisturbed.

The likely penalty in civil court would have been two or three years. Roosevelt wanted a sentence of death, a penalty he could get through a military tribunal. Also, trial in civil court or even a court-martial would be governed by established procedures. With a military tribunal, the administration could make up rules and procedures as it liked, which is what it did.[29]

Roosevelt's military tribunal possessed all the attributes of arbitrary government. He created the tribunal, named the generals to serve on it (all subordinate to him), named the prosecutors and defense counsel (subordinates also), and when the tribunal issued its verdict the trial record was transmitted to Roosevelt for final action. A virtually closed circle with no independent checks. Under the Articles of War, any conviction or sentence by a military court was subject to review within the military system, including the Judge Advocate General's office. Roosevelt vested "final reviewing authority" in himself. The tribunal began with few rules. The tribunal created them when it responded to motions made by the government and defense counsel as the trial progressed.[30]

29. Fisher, Nazi Saboteurs on Trial, at 45–49.
30. Id. at 48–49, 52–53; Fisher, Military Tribunals and Presidential Powers, at 111–12.

Secretary of War Henry L. Stimson vigorously opposed the tribunal. He saw no reason for Attorney General Francis Biddle to commit the time and energy in the middle of World War II to prosecute the case instead of leaving that task to another government attorney.[31] Joining Biddle as co-prosecutor was Maj. Gen. Myron C. Cramer, Judge Advocate General of the Army. Stimson objected to that assignment, insisting that it was the role of the Judge Advocate General to serve in an independent capacity after the trial to assure the fairness of its proceedings.

Review by the Supreme Court

With the military tribunal nearing its completion, defense counsel decided to take the dispute to civil court. The Supreme Court labored under several procedural deficiencies. On July 27, 1942, it publicly announced that oral argument would begin on July 29, before there had been any action by lower courts.[32] At 8 P.M., on July 28, a federal district court dismissed a habeas petition by the defense counsel.[33] At noon the following day, the Supreme Court began to hear the case. The briefs filed by the opposing parties are dated the same day that oral argument began.[34] The Justices were therefore unprepared to analyze complex issues of military law and Articles of War that are rarely placed before the Court. The nine hours of oral argument, spread across two days, were as much for the benefit of the Justices as the litigants.

A second deficiency was the absence of review by the appellate court, the D.C. Circuit. The case came directly from the district court to the Supreme Court, an issue that several Justices found objectionable. Defense counsel agreed to take their papers to the appellate court.[35] On July 31, after two days of oral argument, the Court received the case from the D.C. Circuit. At 11:59 A.M. it officially took the case from the appellate court and one minute later issued a one-page per curiam that upheld the jurisdiction of the military commission.[36] The per curiam was empty of legal justifications. Instead, the Court

31. Diary of Henry L. Stimson, July 1, 1942, Roll 7, at 136, Manuscript Room, Library of Congress.

32. Lewis Wood, "Supreme Court Is Called in Unprecedented Session to Hear Plea of Nazi Spies," New York Times, July 28, 1942, at 1.

33. Ex parte Quirin, 47 F.Supp. 431 (D.D.C. 1942).

34. 39 Landmark Briefs 395, 463, 495.

35. Id. at 499–501.

36. Myron C. Cramer, "Military Commissions: Trial of the Eight Saboteurs," 17 Wash. L. Rev. & St. B. J. 247, 253 (1942).

promised to release a full opinion at a later date.[37] As a result, the public knew what the Court did but not why. The full opinion was not released until nearly three months later, on October 29.

The Justices knew that President Roosevelt had violated the Articles of War, as enacted by Congress, but did not know how to handle that issue of illegality. In drafting the full opinion, Chief Justice Harlan Fiske Stone worked with the knowledge that on August 8, after the military commission finished its deliberations and found the eight Germans guilty, six had been electrocuted pursuant to Roosevelt's order. On September 10, Stone wrote to Justice Felix Frankfurter that he found it "very difficult to support the Government's construction of the articles [of war]," adding that it "seems almost brutal to announce this ground of decision for the first time after six of the petitioners have been executed and it is too late for them to raise the question if in fact the articles as they construe them have been violated." Only after the war, Stone said, would the facts be known, with release of the trial transcript and other documents to the public. By that time, the two surviving saboteurs could raise legal questions successfully, which "would not place the present Court in a very happy light."[38] If the survivors prevailed in court, Stone said, "it would leave the present Court in the unenviable position of having stood by and allowed six to go to their death without making it plain to all concerned—including the President—that it had left undecided a question on which counsel strongly relied to secure petitioners' liberty."[39]

While Stone drafted the full opinion, Justice Frankfurter prepared a memorandum that spoke confidently that "there can be no doubt that the President did *not* follow" Articles 46 through 53.[40] Having released the per curiam, the Justices were in no position to look too closely, or at least to do so publicly, at Roosevelt's violation of the Articles of War. As constitutional scholar Alpheus Thomas Mason noted, the Justices' "own involvement in the trial through their decision in the July hearing practically compelled them to cover up or excuse the President's departures from customary procedures."[41] Years later, Justice William O. Douglas wrote that "it was unfortunate the Court took the

---

37. Ex parte Quirin, 317 U.S. 1, 11 (1942).

38. Letter from Chief Justice Stone to Justice Frankfurter, September 10, 1942, Papers of Felix Frankfurter, Part III, Reel 43, Manuscript Room, Library of Congress.

39. Papers of Harlan Fiske Stone, "Memorandum re Saboteur Cases," September 25, 1942, at 2, Manuscript Room, Library of Congress.

40. "Memorandum of Mr. Justice Frankfurter, In re Saboteur Cases," Papers of William O. Douglas, Box 77, at 1 (emphasis in original), Manuscript Room, Library of Congress.

41. Alpheus Thomas Mason, "*Inter Arma Silent Leges,*" 69 Harv. L. Rev. 806, 826 (1956).

case," recalling that while "it was easy to agree on the original per curiam," the Court "almost fell apart when it came time to write out the views."[42]

Academic Critiques

After the Court released the full opinion in late October 1942, Justice Frankfurter asked Frederick Bernays Wiener, his former student but by then an acknowledged expert on military law, to evaluate the decision. Wiener told him that the weaknesses in the decision flowed "in large measure" from the administration's disregard for "almost every precedent in the books" when it established the military tribunal.[43] Wiener emphasized that court-martial procedures had "almost uniformly been applied to military commissions," and that it was "too plain for argument" that the President could not waive or override the required review by the Judge Advocate General's office.[44] The only precedent for using the Judge Advocate General of the Army as a prosecutor— the trial of the Lincoln conspirators—was one that "no self-respecting military lawyer will look straight in the eye." Even in that sorry precedent, he said, "the Attorney General did not assume to assist the prosecution."[45]

Justice Douglas criticized the procedures followed by the Court in 1942. During an interview held in 1962, he said the experience with *Quirin* indicated "to all of us that it is extremely undesirable to announce a decision on the merits without an opinion accompanying it. Because once the search for the grounds, the examination of the grounds that had been advanced is made, sometimes those grounds crumble."[46] Alpheus Thomas Mason concluded that the Court could do little other than uphold the jurisdiction of the military commission, being "somewhat in the position of a private on sentry duty accosting a commanding general without his pass," an outcome that put the judiciary "in danger of becoming part of an executive juggernaut."[47]

Recent evaluations of *Quirin* have been more harsh. Michal Belknap concluded that Stone went to "such lengths to justify Roosevelt's proclama-

42. William O. Douglas, The Court Years, 1939–1975, at 138–39 (1980).

43. "Observations of Ex parte Quirin," signed "F.B.W.," at 1, November 5, 1942, Papers of Felix Frankfurter, Part III, Reel 43, Manuscript Room, Library of Congress.

44. Id. at 8.

45. Id. at 9. For more detailed criticism by Wiener, see Fisher, Nazi Saboteurs on Trial, at 129–34.

46. Conversation between Justice Douglas and Professor Walter Murphy, June 9, 1962, at 204–05, Seeley G. Mudd Manuscript Library, Princeton University.

47. Alpheus Thomas Mason, Harlan Fiske Stone: Pillar of the Law 665, 666 (1956).

tion" that he preserved the "form" of judicial review while "gutt[ing] it of substance."[48] Once Justices decided to march to the beat of war drums, the Court "remained an unreliable guardian of the Bill of Rights."[49] Belknap described a memo by Frankfurter ("F. F.'s Soliloquy"), written while Stone was drafting the full opinion, as the work of a judge "openly hostile to the accused and manifestly unwilling to afford them procedural safeguards."[50] David J. Danelski called the full opinion of *Quirin* "an agonizing effort to justify a *fait accompli*."[51] The opinion represented a "constitutional and propaganda victory" for the executive branch but "an institutional defeat" for the Supreme Court.[52] Danelski cautioned the Court to "be wary of departing from its established rules and practices, even in times of national crisis, for at such times the Court is especially susceptible to co-optation by the executive."[53]

The Roosevelt administration later concluded that its handling of the eight Germans in 1942 was so flawed procedurally that it was not a model worth repeating. On November 29, 1944, two more German agents arrived by submarine, reaching land in Maine and making their way to New York City, where they were apprehended. At first, the Roosevelt administration was going to try them in the same manner as in 1942. However, Secretary Stimson intervened forcefully to take the matter out of Roosevelt's hands and transfer the responsibility to military professionals in New York. Instead of Roosevelt naming the members of the tribunal, the prosecutors, and the defense counsel, those duties went to a commanding general. Instead of the trial record going directly to the President, as in 1942, it was processed through the Judge Advocate General's office, consistent with Article of War 50 1/2. Through these actions the Roosevelt administration reconsidered and rejected what it had done two years earlier.[54]

Many other violations of civil liberties and basic procedural rights occurred during and immediately after World War II, including martial law in Hawaii and the trials of three Japanese military leaders after the war. Like *Quirin*, the trial of General Tomoyuki Yamashita was not a precedent worth honoring or

48. Michal Belknap, "The Supreme Court Goes to War: The Meaning and Implications of the Nazi Saboteur Case," 89 Mil. L. Rev. 59 (1980).

49. Id. at 95.

50. Michael Belknap, "Frankfurter and the Nazi Saboteurs," Yearbook 1982: Sup. Ct. Hist. Soc., at 66. For the language of the Soliloquy, see Fisher, Nazi Saboteurs on Trial, at 117–21.

51. David J. Danelski, "The Saboteurs' Case," 1 J. Sup. Ct. Hist. 61, 61 (1996).

52. Id. at 80.

53. Id.

54. Fisher, Nazi Saboteurs on Trial, at 138–44.

repeating. The trial was flawed from start to finish, with twelve international correspondents voting 12 to 0 that he should have been acquitted. Instead, he was sentenced to death by hanging. As Justice Wiley Rutledge said in a dissenting opinion, it was not in the American tradition "to be charged with crime which is defined after his conduct, alleged to be criminal, has taken place; or in language not sufficient to inform him of the nature of the offense or to enable him to make defense."[55]

DETENTION CAMPS

The Bush administration's reliance on *Quirin* to detain U.S. citizens is further weakened by the legislative history of what is known as the Non-Detention Act. In 1950, Congress passed the Emergency Detention Act, responding to the existence of "a world Communist movement" that intended to establish "a Communist totalitarian dictatorship in all the countries of the world."[56] The statute authorized the detention of persons when "there is reasonable ground to believe" they will probably commit or conspire with others to commit espionage or sabotage. Detention was supposed to respect constitutional rights and privileges, while at the same time permitting Congress and the President to fully protect the nation.[57]

Congress authorized detention in a time of "Internal Security Emergency," covering "any person"—citizen or noncitizen.[58] Within forty-eight hours after being apprehended, individuals were entitled to be taken to a preliminary hearing, charged, given access to counsel, and allowed limited rights to cross-examine witnesses against them. This brand of "preventive detention" depended on truncated trials and secret evidence. The government was not required to disclose the identity or evidence of government agents or officers if "dangerous to national safety and security to divulge."[59] In 1952, Congress passed legislation to authorize the construction of detention camps to house these individuals.[60]

55. In re Yamashita, 327 U.S. 1, 43 (1946) (Rutledge, J., dissenting). For more details on the trials of Japanese military leaders and the different standard applied to U.S. military leaders, see Fisher, Military Tribunals and Presidential Power, at 143–54.

56. 64 Stat. 1019, Title II, sec. 101 (1950).

57. Id. at 1021, sec. 101, paragraphs (14) and (15).

58. Id., sec. 103(b).

59. Id. at 1022, sec. 104 (d).

60. 66 Stat. 138 (1952).

In 1971, Congress repealed the Emergency Detention Act and adopted this language: "No citizen shall be imprisoned or otherwise detained by the United States except pursuant to an Act of Congress."[61] Called the Non-Detention Act, it is also referred to as Section 4001(a). After 9/11, the Bush administration argued in court that this section "does not apply to the military's wartime detention of enemy combatants."[62] According to the administration, the statute restricts the Attorney General but not the President or the military services. This legal argument depends on the location of Section 4001(a) in the U.S Code, which contains all federal laws. It appears in Title 18 (covering crimes and criminal procedure), not in Title 10 (armed forces) or Title 50 (war and national defense).[63] In the administration's words, the existing Title 18 "was directed to the Attorney General's control over federal prisons; its terms, which remain unchanged, stated that the 'control and management of Federal penal and correctional institutions, *except military or naval institutions*, shall be vested in the Attorney General.'"[64]

To accept this reasoning, one would have to believe that when Congress in 1971 decided to repeal the Emergency Detention Act and give new safeguards to U.S. citizens, it at the same time allowed the President and military authorities to imprison and detain those individuals without an Act of Congress. Nothing in the legislative history of the 1971 statute offers any support to this imaginative interpretation.

The Political Climate of 1971

Congress passed the Non-Detention Act in an atmosphere of fear and anxiety about the power and intention of the national government. The purpose of Section 4001(a) is understood by recalling the political pressures that existed after urban riots spread across the nation. In signing the 1971 legislation, President Richard M. Nixon explained that the administration was "wholeheartedly" in support of repealing the Emergency Detention Act. He wanted to underscore the nation's "abiding respect for the liberty of the individual" and regretted "the kind of anxiety" the 1950 statute triggered.[65]

---

61. 85 Stat. 347 (1971).

62. Respondent's Opposition to the Motion for Summary Judgment, Padilla v. Hanft, November 22, 2004 (D. S.C.), at 20.

63. Id. at 29.

64. Id. (emphasis in original).

65. Public Papers of the Presidents, 1971, at 986.

Nixon's statement did not distinguish between two types of detention: by the Attorney General (prohibited) and by the President or the military (permitted). The 1971 statute would not have eased the anxiety of individuals and groups if they thought they were vulnerable to detention by presidential and military action. Nixon's statement referred to "special emergency powers which the Constitution grants to the Chief Executive" without elaborating on the scope of independent constitutional authorities. Did he mean some type of presidential inherent power to order the military to arrest and detain U.S. citizens without statutory authority? Such a claim would contradict his assurance that "every citizen will be afforded due process of law."[66]

Congressional Purpose

Congress in 1971 responded to two pressures. In 1968, the Japanese American Citizens League, with more than 25,000 members and 92 chapters in 32 states, spearheaded a nationwide drive to repeal the Emergency Detention Act.[67] Second, in 1968 the House Committee on Un-American Activities submitted a report that recommended the possible use of detention camps for certain black nationalists and Communists.[68] It was in this climate that Deputy Attorney General Richard G. Kleindienst wrote to the Senate Committee on the Judiciary in 1969, recommending repeal of the Emergency Detention Act. He explained that repeal "will allay the fears and suspicions—unfounded as they may be—of many of our citizens."[69]

In 1969, the Senate passed legislation to repeal the Emergency Detention Act. Senator Daniel Inouye, who introduced the bill, said he became aware of rumors that the federal government "was readying concentration camps to be filled with those who hold unpopular views and beliefs." The rumors were widely circulated and accepted "in many urban ghettoes as well as by those dissidents who are at odds with many of the policies of the United States. Fear of internment, I believe, lurks for many of those who are by birth or choice not 'in tune' or 'in line' with the rest of the country."[70]

66. Id.

67. 117 Cong. Rec. 31535 (1971) (statement by Rep. Evins).

68. H. Rept. 90–1351, 90th Cong., 2d Sess. 59 (1968); S. Rept. No. 632, 91st Cong., 1st Sess. 3 (1969) (letter of Sen. Inouye).

69. S. Rept. No. 632, at 4.

70. 115 Cong. Rec. 40702 (1969).

The bill passed the Senate by voice vote.[71] The House did not act on the bill. Instead, the House Committee on Internal Security reported legislation in 1970 to amend certain provisions of the Emergency Detention Act. The committee expressed concern about misconceptions that the statute would "authorize the establishment of 'concentration camps' for the incarceration of racial groups."[72] As a remedy, it proposed this language: "No citizen of the United States shall be apprehended or detained pursuant to the provisions of this title on account of race, color, or ancestry."[73] A black member of the House, Louis Stokes of Ohio, said the new language would do nothing "to quash the fears and rumors of the black community."[74]

Legislative History

Debate on Section 4001(a) provides convincing evidence that Congress intended to limit *all government power* by the Attorney General, the President, and military authorities. In 1971, the House Committee on Internal Security reported a bill to amend the Emergency Detention Act.[75] The House decided to repeal rather than amend the Act. The House Judiciary Committee adopted this amendment by Rep. Spark Matsunaga: "No person shall be detained except pursuant to title 18."[76] The Justice Department advised Congress that the power of government to detain individuals was not limited to Title 18, but appeared in other titles of the U.S. Code. The committee rewrote the language: "No citizen shall be imprisoned or otherwise detained by the United States except pursuant to an Act of Congress."[77]

Assistant Attorney General Robert Mardian told House Judiciary that the Justice Department was "unequivocally in favor" of repealing the Emergency Detention Act, reminding lawmakers of the letter from Kleindienst noting that the Act was "extremely offensive to many Americans."[78] People's fears and suspicions would not be put to rest if the President or military authorities claimed independent or inherent power to imprison and detain U.S. citizens suspected

71. Id.
72. H. Rept. No. 1599, 91st Cong., 2d Sess. 1 (1970).
73. Id. at 17.
74. Id. at 23.
75. H. Rept. No. 94, 92d Cong., 1st Sess. (1971).
76. 117 Cong. Rec. 31755 (1971) (statement by Rep. Ichord).
77. H. Rept. No. 116, 92d Cong., 1st Sess. 1 (1971).
78. Id. at 3.

of posing a danger to national security. The committee left unchanged the following language in the existing Section 4001: "The control and management of Federal penal and correctional institutions, except military or naval institutions, shall be vested in the Attorney General. . . ."[79] The Bush administration in 2004 interpreted this passage as an invitation for military imprisonment and detention, but the language merely recognized that the Attorney General's jurisdiction does not cover military or naval institutions. Nothing in the language of Section 4001 sanctioned military detentions.

During House debate, several lawmakers acknowledged that Congress was about to place limits not merely on the Attorney General but also on the President and the military. H. Allen Smith expressed concern that the bill would interfere with the kind of emergency actions taken by President Roosevelt immediately after Pearl Harbor, including taking aliens into custody. In 1942, Roosevelt authorized the military to order the curfew and detention of Japanese-Americans without first receiving statutory authority. Smith supported repeal of the Emergency Detention Act but objected to language that would "handicap" the President's ability to act in times of emergency.[80] The Justice Department explained that statutory authority already existed to protect the country from "sabotage and espionage or other similar attacks."[81] The availability of those statutory authorities underscored that Section 4001(a) applied broadly to civilian authorities, the President, and the military.

Further Clarification

Robert Kastenmeier, who managed the House bill, explained why an amendment crafted by Tom Railsback would restrict both civilian and military authorities. The new language "avoids the pitfalls that might be created by repealing the Detention Act by leaving open the possibility that people might nevertheless be detained without the benefit of due process, merely by executive fiat. . . . [T]here must be statutory authority for the detention of a citizen by the United States."[82] Kastenmeier emphasized that "[r]epeal alone might leave citizens subject to arbitrary executive action, with no clear demarcation of the limits of executive authority."[83]

79. Id. at 6.
80. 117 Cong. Rec. 31536 (1971).
81. Id. (statement of Rep. Matsunaga, quoting Assistant Attorney General Yeagley).
82. Id. at 31540–41.
83. Id. at 31541.

Richard Ichord opposed Railsback's amendment, warning that it would deprive the President of his emergency powers to cope with sabotage and espionage agents in war-related crises and would do "patent violence to the constitutional principle of separation of powers."[84] Ichord wanted the President left free to detain U.S. citizens in times of emergency. Lawrence Williams also opposed the Railsback amendment, "not want[ing] to see the President's hands tied."[85] Railsback recognized some room for presidential emergency power. He wanted to eliminate presidential authority to establish detention camps "except in those cases of emergency when martial law may properly be invoked." Congress had no power or authority to "affect executive martial-law powers which arise when the processes of government cannot function in an orderly way. For that is truly a 'nonlaw' situation."[86] Under his interpretation, Presidents could detain U.S. citizens only by declaring an emergency so severe that the normal legislative authorities reserved to Congress would be exercised by the executive branch and military authorities, as was the case in Hawaii immediately following Pearl Harbor.[87]

Ichord offered an amendment, stating that repeal of the Emergency Detention Act "shall not be construed to preempt, disparage, or affect the powers accorded to or the duties imposed upon the President under the Constitution and other laws of the United States: provided, however, that no citizen of the United States shall be apprehended or detained for the prevention of espionage or sabotage solely on account of race, color, or ancestry."[88] He had two objectives: to preserve what he considered to be the President's independent powers under Article II of the Constitution, and to assure blacks they would not be detained for color alone.

The first objective was one that Railsback and the House Judiciary Committee intended to block, other than in a state of martial law. The second objective would do little to ease the concerns of the black community, especially in cities. The executive branch could easily justify their detention not on grounds of race, color, or ancestry but because of political beliefs and associations. Ichord's amendment failed by a large margin, 124 to 272.[89] An earlier Ichord amendment, to revise some of the provisions of the Emergency Deten-

---

84. Id. at 31542.
85. Id. at 31554.
86. Id. at 31755.
87. Fisher, Military Tribunals and Presidential Power, at 130–39.
88. 117 Cong. Rec. 31545 (1971).
89. Id. at 31766.

tion Act, fell by a vote of 22 to 68.[90] After the Judiciary Committee amendment (as modified by Railsback) was agreed to, 290 to 111, the bill cleared the House 356 to 49.[91] The Senate passed the House bill by voice vote.[92]

In signing the bill, President Nixon explained that no President had ever attempted to use the provisions of the Emergency Detention Act. Six detention camps were built but never used.[93] Nonetheless, the continued existence of the 1950 authority "has aroused concern among many Americans that the act might someday be used to apprehend and detain citizens who hold unpopular views" and might re-create "a situation comparable to the detention of Americans of Japanese ancestry during World War II." Nixon emphasized "this Nation's abiding respect for the liberty of the individual. Our democracy is built upon the constitutional guarantee that every citizen will be afforded due process of law. There is no place in American life for the kind of anxiety— however unwarranted—which the Emergency Detention Act has evidently engendered." The country had "no reason to fear that the normal processes of law" would be unable to deal with future situations, "no matter how grave. . . . But we do have a great deal to fear if we begin to lose faith in our constitutional ideals.[94]

The Supreme Court has interpreted the Non-Detention Act broadly to prohibit "detention *of any kind* by the United States, absent a congressional grant of authority to detain."[95] The political climate of 1971 and the detailed legislative history explain the purpose of repealing the Emergency Detention Act. It was to strip from the executive branch—both its civilian and military components—any claim of independent authority to round up, imprison, and detain disfavored individuals or groups, unless it wanted to declare martial law. Nevertheless, after the terrorist attacks of 9/11 the Bush administration argued that it could detain U.S. citizens indefinitely, without trial or counsel.

ENEMY COMBATANTS

In the months following 9/11, a number of suspected terrorists were not taken to civil court to be charged (as with John Walker Lindh, "shoe-bomber"

90. Id. at 31761.
91. Id. at 31768, 31781.
92. Id. at 32145.
93. Public Papers of the Presidents, 1971, at 986.
94. Id. See 85 Stat. 347 (1971).
95. Howe v. Smith, 452 U.S. 473, 479 n.2 (1981) (emphasis in original).

Richard Reid, and Zacarias Moussaoui) or brought before a military tribunal.[96] Instead, they were designated "enemy combatants" and held incommunicado without being charged, tried, or given access to an attorney. In *Ex parte Quirin*, the Supreme Court distinguished between lawful combatants and unlawful combatants. The first are held as prisoners of war and may not be prosecuted for criminal violations for belligerent acts that no not constitute war crimes. They wear uniforms or display a fixed distinctive emblem and conduct their operations in accordance with the laws and customs of war.[97] When the Nazi saboteurs arrived by submarine in 1942 they understood this difference and brought along articles of military clothing in case they were apprehended on shore. They would then be treated as prisoners of war. If arrested in civilian clothing they could be treated as spies and executed.[98]

On November 26, 2002, the General Counsel of the Defense Department defined "enemy combatant" as "an individual who, under the laws and customs of war, may be detained for the duration of an armed conflict." The term included "a member, agent, or associate of Al Qaida or the Taliban." The General Counsel looked to this language from *Quirin* for support: "Citizens who associate themselves with the military arm of the enemy government, and with its aid, guidance and direction enter this country bent on hostile acts are enemy belligerents within the meaning of the Hague Convention and the law of war."[99] That definition covered both U.S. citizens and aliens.

Were U.S. citizens protected by the Non-Detention Act? The Bush administration said "No" for two reasons. The first was constitutional: "Article II alone gives the President the power to detain enemies during wartime, regardless of congressional action."[100] The second argument was statutory, claiming that the Authorization for Use of Military Force (AUMF) Act of 2001, which supported military operations against Afghanistan, represented a sufficiently broad delegation of power by Congress to satisfy the requirement in the Non-Detention Act that there be an "Act of Congress."[101] However, no member of Congress in

96. For details on the Moussaoui trial, see Fisher, Military Tribunals and Presidential Powers, at 211–20.

97. Hague Convention of October 18, 1907, 36 Stat. 2296.

98. Fisher, Nazi Saboteurs on Trial, at 23, 26–27, 35.

99. Letter of November 26, 2002, from William J. Haynes II, General Counsel, Department of Defense, to Senator Carl Levin, at 1–2.

100. Letter of September 23, 2002, from William J. Haynes II, General Counsel, Department of Defense, to Alfred P. Carlton Jr., President, American Bar Association, at 2.

101. Respondent's Answer to the Petition for Writ of Habeas Corpus, Padilla v. Hanft, C/A No. 02:04–2221–26AJ (D. S.C. 2004), at 1–2, 10–12, 18–22.

debating the AUMF ever supported, expressly or by implication, the detention of U.S. citizens and their incarceration without trial for indefinite periods. If Congress wanted to amend or waive the Non-Detention Act, it knew how to do so consciously and deliberately by making reference to it during debate.

In court, the Justice Department insisted that whenever the administration decided to detain a U.S. citizen indefinitely, without trial, federal judges had no right to interfere with executive judgment. Courts "may not second-guess the military's determination that an individual is an enemy combatant and should be detained as such. . . . Going beyond that determination would require the courts to enter an area in which they have no competence, much less institutional expertise, intrude upon the constitutional prerogative of the Commander in Chief (and military authorities acting at his control), and possibly create 'a conflict between judicial and military opinion highly comforting to enemies of the United States.'"[102]

In other briefs, the Justice Department conceded that federal judges may have a review function in determining whether the President had properly designated an individual as an enemy combatant, but the review function "is limited to confirming based on *some evidence* the existence of a factual basis supporting the determination."[103] What was this evidence? As shown below, the administration wanted the judiciary to accept as "some evidence" whatever executive officials submitted to court without any opportunity for an accused enemy combatant, with the support of counsel, to see the evidence and challenge the executive assertion. The courts cannot determine that evidence is legitimate if they are presented with assertions from one side, and particularly when the evidence is based on secret informers who cannot be cross-examined.

YASER ESAM HAMDI

Born in Louisiana and therefore a U.S. citizen, Yaser Esam Hamdi was captured in Afghanistan, held at Guantánamo Bay, moved to a naval brig at the Norfolk Naval Station and from there to a brig in Charleston, South Carolina.

---

102. Brief for Respondents-Appellants, Hamdi v. Rumsfeld, No. 02–6895 (4th Cir. 2002), at 29–30, 31.

103. Respondents' Response to, and Motion to Dismiss, the Amended Petition for a Writ of Habeas Corpus, Padilla v. Bush, 02 CIV. 4445 (MBM) (S.D. N.Y. 2002), at 15 (emphasis added).

Designated an enemy combatant, he was not charged but instead held incommunicado without access to an attorney. After years of litigation and a Supreme Court decision in 2004, the United States agreed to send Hamdi to Saudi Arabia. His detention and designation depended heavily on a document signed by a Pentagon official who had no direct knowledge of Hamdi.

The Mobbs Declaration

A declaration signed by Michael H. Mobbs, a Pentagon official, was filed in federal court to justify Hamdi's detention. Dated July 24, 2002, the declaration drew from intelligence sources and unnamed informants. Mobbs stated that his responsibilities at the Defense Department made him "familiar with the facts and circumstances related to the capture of Yaser Esam Hamdi and his detention by U.S. military forces." According to Mobbs, Hamdi traveled to Afghanistan in 2001 where he "affiliated with a Taliban military unit and received weapons training." He remained with the Taliban unit following the terrorist attacks of September 11 "and after the United States began military operations against the al Qaeda and Taliban on October 7, 2001."[104]

This part of the declaration describes Hamdi as involved in a civil war between the Taliban and the Northern Alliance forces, not a terrorist action directed against the United States. Mobbs further stated that Hamdi's Taliban unit surrendered to Northern Alliance forces, and he was transported to several prisons in Afghanistan under Alliance control. During interrogation by a U.S. team, he identified himself as a Saudi citizen born in the United States. At the time of the interrogation, as stated in the declaration, "Al Qaeda and Taliban were and are hostile forces engaged in armed conflict with the armed forces of the United States and its Coalition partners," making Hamdi an "enemy combatant." The declaration concludes: "A subsequent interview of Hamdi has confirmed the fact that he surrendered and gave his firearm to Northern Alliance forces which supports his classification as an enemy combatant."[105] That information offers support for someone involved in a civil war in Afghanistan, not necessarily a person engaged in terrorist actions against the United States.

104. Declaration of Michael H. Mobbs, Special Adviser to the Under Secretary of Defense for Policy, filed in Hamdi v. Rumsfeld, No. 2:02CV439 (E.D. Va.), at 1–2 (para. 2 and 3), http://www.pbs.org/wgbh/pages/frontline/shows/sleeper/tools/mobbshamdi.html, accessed July 6, 2007.

105. Id. at 2 (para. 9).

In District Court

In trial court, Hamdi's case was heard by Federal District Judge Robert G. Doumar, who regularly challenged arguments made by the Justice Department and regarded the "Mobbs Declaration" as wholly deficient. Doumar's parents came from Syria and Lebanon as Christian Arabs, became U.S. citizens, and quickly assimilated into America with only English spoken at home. Fair play and due process were important values for him.[106] One of Doumar's early orders, on June 13, 2002, allowed Hamdi to meet with his attorney "because of fundamental justice provided under the Constitution of the United States," with the meeting to be "private between Hamdi, the attorney, and the interpreter, without military personnel present, and without any listening or recording devices of any kind being employed in any way." That decision was promptly reversed by the Fourth Circuit.[107]

Judge Doumar described the case as the first time that an American citizen has been held incommunicado and subjected to indefinite detention in the continental United States "without charges, without any findings by a military tribunal, and without access to a lawyer."[108] He said it was uncertain whether Hamdi was "an enemy combatant, . . . an unlawful enemy combatant, or just a bystander."[109] The Fifth Amendment prohibits the government from depriving any person of liberty without due process of law. Doumar ruled that Hamdi was entitled to due process.[110]

Did the Mobbs Declaration provide due process? Judge Doumar concluded it fell short of the minimal criteria needed for judicial review, prompting "more questions than it answers."[111] The declaration did not explain what authority Mobbs possessed in classifying someone as an enemy combatant. A Justice Department official during the court hearing could not explain the government's authority.[112] Although the administration referred to Hamdi as an "illegal" enemy combatant, Mobbs spoke only of "enemy combatant." His declaration did not explain why Hamdi was treated differently than other captured Taliban, or why he was held incommunicado for eight to ten months

106. Richard Leiby, "An American Justice," Washington Post, September 6, 2002, at C1, C4.

107. Hamdi v. Rumsfeld, 294 F.3d 598, 602 (4th Cir. 2002).

108. Hamdi v. Rumsfeld, Civil Action No. 2:02cv439 (E.D. Va. 2002), at 1.

109. Id. at 5.

110. Id. at 8.

111. Id. at 9.

112. Id. at 10.

without the government bringing criminal charges against him. What did it mean, asked Judge Doumar, that Hamdi was "affiliated" with a Taliban military unit? Why did that warrant the designation of enemy combatant? The declaration "never claims that Hamdi was fighting for the Taliban, nor that he was a member of the Taliban."[113] The declaration asserted that Hamdi met the "criteria" for enemy combatants without setting forth the criteria.[114]

Judge Doumar decided that without access to the screening criteria and Hamdi's statement, it would be impossible to evaluate whether he was properly classified as an enemy combatant. The declaration by Mobbs was "little more than the government's 'say-so' regarding the validity of Hamdi's classification as an enemy combatant."[115] Doumar's decision was repeatedly reversed on appeal.[116] The Fourth Circuit juggled two values: the judiciary's duty to protect constitutional rights (especially of U.S. citizens) versus the deference that courts should grant to military decisions reached by the President. Each time the Fourth Circuit came down squarely on the side of presidential power.[117]

What was the "some evidence" that the Fourth Circuit depended on? It was the declaration by Mobbs, who put his name on a document prepared by intelligence analysts. In a dissenting opinion, Judge Diana Gribbon Motz described the Mobbs affidavit as purely a hearsay statement by "an unelected, otherwise unknown, government 'advisor.'"[118] Mobbs did not claim "*any* personal knowledge of the facts surrounding Hamdi's capture and incarceration."[119] He merely reviewed "undisclosed and unenumerated 'relevant records and reports.'"[120] Judge Motz objected that the panel's decision marked the first time that a federal court had eliminated constitutional protections for a citizen "solely on the basis of the Executive's designation of that citizen as an enemy combatant, without testing the accuracy of the designation."[121]

Mobbs remained at arm's length from evidence and the Fourth Circuit even more so. Hamdi, a U.S. citizen, had no right to see the evidence against him

---

113. Id. at 11.

114. Id. at 13.

115. Id. at 14.

116. Hamdi v. Rumsfeld, 294 F.3d 598 (4th Cir. 2002); Hamdi v. Rumsfeld, 296 F.3d 278 (4th Cir. 2002).

117. Hamdi v. Rumsfeld, 316 F.3d 450, 463 (4th Cir. 2003); 337 F.3d 335 (4th Cir. 2003) (en banc).

118. Hamdi v. Rumsfeld, 337 F.3d 335, 368 (4th Cir. 2003) (Motz, J., dissenting).

119. Id. at 373 (emphasis in original).

120. Id.

121. Id. at 369.

or to know the names of the informants who supplied it. How credible was information provided by members of the Northern Alliance? Did they have a financial incentive to identify individuals as Taliban or al Qaeda? According to newspaper reports, Northern Alliance commanders expected to receive $5,000 when they designated someone as Taliban and $20,000 for individuals described as al Qaeda fighters.[122]

Action by the Supreme Court

With Hamdi's case headed for the Supreme Court, the Bush administration on December 2, 2003, decided to give him access to a lawyer. He was allowed to see an attorney "as a matter of discretion and military policy," not as a matter of constitutional right. The administration announced that the exception for Hamdi "should not be treated as a precedent."[123] When Hamdi's attorney visited him several months later, the administration insisted that a military observer must remain in the room to record the session. His attorney, Frank W. Dunham, Jr., at first considered canceling the meeting because it would violate the tradition of attorney-client privilege. Finally agreeing to go, he knew he would be prohibited from talking to him "about anything that's substantive to the case."[124]

On June 28, 2004, eight Justices of the Supreme Court rejected the administration's central proposition that Hamdi's detention was quintessentially a presidential decision and could not be reevaluated or overturned by the courts. Except for Justice Clarence Thomas, all members of the Court decided they had the institutional authority and competence to review and override presidential judgments in the field of national security. The Court's action was fragmented among a plurality of four (Sandra Day O'Connor, William Rehnquist, Anthony Kennedy, Stephen Breyer), joined at times by a concurrence/ dissent from David Souter and Ruth Bader Ginsburg, and at other times a dissent from Antonin Scalia and John Paul Stevens.

The plurality agreed on a core principle: "we necessarily reject the Government's assertion that separation of powers principles mandate a heavily circumscribed role for the courts in such circumstances. . . . Whatever power the

122. Petition for Writ of Certiorari, Hamdi v. Rumsfeld, No. 03–7338, U.S. Supreme Court, at 9 n.8.

123. Jerry Markon and Dan Eggen, "U.S. Allows Lawyer for Citizen Held as 'Enemy Combatant,'" Washington Post, December 3, 2003, at A1.

124. Jerry Markon, "Military to Watch Prisoner Interview," Washington Post, January 31, 2004, at B3.

United States Constitution envisions for the Executive in its exchanges with other nations or with enemy organizations in times of conflict, it most assuredly envisions a role for all three branches when individual liberties are at stake."[125] On that central value the plurality was joined by Souter, Ginsburg, Scalia, and Stevens. The plurality also held that an enemy combatant "must receive notice of the factual basis for his classification, and a fair opportunity to rebut the Government's factual assertions before a neutral decisionmaker."[126] Souter and Ginsburg agreed, but with different reasoning. They found Hamdi's detention forbidden by the Non-Detention Act and unauthorized by the AUMF. Without speculating on the type of procedures that should be available to Hamdi, they concluded that the administration had "failed to justify holding him in the absence of a further Act of Congress, criminal charges, a showing that the detention conforms to the laws of war, or a demonstration that §4001(a) is unconstitutional."[127]

Scalia and Stevens, in their dissent, did not offer details about how to give Hamdi notice of the charges or opportunity to present his case before a neutral decision maker. Similar to Souter and Ginsburg, they focused on more fundamental issues, concluding that he was entitled to a habeas decree requiring his release "unless (1) criminal proceedings are promptly brought, or (2) Congress has suspended the writ of habeas corpus."[128] The plurality held that Hamdi "unquestionably has the right to access to counsel in connection with the proceedings on remand."[129] Souter and Ginsburg did not disagree on that point.[130]

Scalia and Stevens strongly objected to the plurality's effort to prescribe in advance a host of procedural rules to guide a future trial for Hamdi, including putting the burden of proof on him rather than on the government, allowing testimony by hearsay rather than by live witnesses, and allowing the "neutral" decision maker to be a military officer.[131] To Scalia and Stevens, the plurality had no business or competence in offering those procedures and others. Questions of that nature should be left to Congress and its clear Article I authority to enact rules and procedures for the military: "If civil rights are to be curtailed during wartime, it must be done openly and democratically, as the

---

125. Hamdi v. Rumsfeld, 542 U.S. 507, 535–36 (2004).
126. Id. at 533.
127. Id. at 553.
128. Id. at 573.
129. Id. at 539.
130. Id. at 553.
131. Id. at 575.

Constitution requires, rather than by silent erosion through an opinion of this Court."[132]

The plurality agreed with the administration that the AUMF constituted "explicit congressional authorization for the detention of individuals," thus satisfying the Non-Detention Act.[133] The plurality cited nothing in the text or the legislative history of the AUMF that "explicitly" indicated a willingness on the part of Congress to authorize the detention of U.S. citizens. In fact, a few paragraphs later the plurality said "it is of no moment that the AUMF does not use specific language of detention."[134] If no member of Congress made any mention of detaining U.S. citizens, there was neither explicit nor implicit congressional authorization for the detention of individuals. Souter and Ginsburg disagreed sharply with the plurality on its analysis of the AUMF and the Non-Detention Act.[135]

The plurality endorsed Hamdi's right to "a fair opportunity to rebut the Government's factual assertions before a neutral decisionmaker," drawing attention to earlier rulings that due process requires a "neutral and detached judge."[136] The plurality spoke of the need for "an independent tribunal," an "independent review," and an "impartial adjudicator."[137] After identifying those fundamental values, it then seemed satisfied by some kind of review panel within the executive branch, perhaps even "an appropriately authorized and properly constituted military tribunal."[138] The plurality seemed to forget how Hamdi became an enemy combatant. President Bush reached that judgment on the basis of the Mobbs Declaration, prepared by someone who had no actual knowledge about Hamdi. No review panel within the executive branch, much less within the military, could possibly possess the plurality's sought-for qualities of neutrality, detachment, independence, and impartiality in passing judgment on a presidential decision.

After the Court's ruling, the administration decided to release Hamdi rather than try him before some type of executive or military panel. Were the grounds for holding him so feeble they could not survive even that process? As conditions of release, he was required to renounce his U.S. citizenship, move to Saudi Arabia, and agree not to sue the federal government that his civil

132. Id. at 578.
133. Id. at 517.
134. Id. at 519.
135. Id. at 541–51.
136. Id. at 553.
137. Id. at 534–35.
138. Id. at 538.

rights had been violated.[139] Thus ended the first effort by the administration to hold a U.S. citizen incommunicado for years, without trial, on the claim that he was a threat not merely to the United States but to civilized society. Why would a dangerous terrorist, if there was a basis for the charge, be set free? The case of the second U.S. citizen, Jose Padilla, raised additional questions about executive judgments.

JOSE PADILLA

Born in New York, Jose Padilla was held by the military after 9/11 as a suspect in a plot to detonate a radiological dispersal device—or "dirty bomb"—in the United States. That allegation was later replaced by a new charge: an intent to blow up apartment buildings. As with Hamdi, declarations prepared by executive officials without direct knowledge were submitted to courts to justify Padilla's detention. The two cases, however, were different. As explained by Judge Wilkinson of the Fourth Circuit, to compare the battlefield capture of Hamdi to the domestic arrest of Padilla in Chicago is "to compare apples and oranges."[140] But according to the administration, one can be an enemy combatant without fighting on a battlefield: "In a time of war, an enemy combatant is subject to capture and detention wherever found, whether on a battlefield or elsewhere abroad or within the United States."[141]

The FBI arrested Padilla in Chicago on May 8, 2002, as a material witness to secure his testimony before a grand jury in New York City. As a material witness, he was entitled by statute to legal counsel and was represented by Donna Newman. After President Bush designated him an enemy combatant, the material witness warrant was withdrawn and the government moved Padilla to a naval brig in Charleston, South Carolina. Newman received no advance notice of the designation and had no opportunity to challenge it in court. At that point Padilla lost all rights to legal counsel, with the exception of brief, monitored visits after the Supreme Court on February 20, 2004, agreed to hear his case.

139. Jerry Markon, "U.S. to Free Hamdi, Send Him Home," Washington Post, September 23, 2004, at A1; "Hamdi Set to be Flown Home," Washington Post, September 28, 2004, at A28.

140. Hamdi v. Rumsfeld, 337 F.3d at 344.

141. Respondents' Response to, and Motion to Dismiss, the Amended Petition for a Writ of Habeas Corpus, Padilla v. Bush, 02 CIV 4445 (MBM) (S.D. N.Y.), at 23.

Another Mobbs Declaration

On August 27, 2002, Michael H. Mobbs signed a declaration making certain statements about Padilla "to the best of my knowledge, information and belief, and under the penalty of perjury."[142] The administration was relying on someone's *belief?* As with his declaration on Hamdi, Mobbs had no direct knowledge but noted that he had "reviewed government records and reports" on Padilla. Interestingly, his declaration came almost three months after President Bush had determined on June 9, 2002, that Padilla was an enemy combatant. On what ground had Bush made his determination? Mobbs explained that the declaration was based on "multiple intelligence sources, including reports of interviews with several confidential sources."[143]

A footnote in the Mobbs Declaration raised substantial questions about the credibility and reliability of the sources. Based on information developed by U.S. intelligence and law-enforcement agencies, "it is believed that the two detained confidential sources have been involved with the Al Qaeda terrorist network." Once again belief substituted for evidence. The footnote continues: "It is believed that these confidential sources have not been completely candid about their association with Al Qaeda and their terrorist activities. Much of the information from these sources has, however, been corroborated and proven accurate and reliable." Clearly some of the information had not been corroborated. How was the balance supported? "Some information provided by the sources remains uncorroborated and may be part of an effort to mislead or confuse U.S. officials." One of the sources "in a subsequent interview with a U.S. law enforcement official recanted some of the information that he had provided, but most of the information has been independently corroborated by other sources." The footnote cautions: "at the time of being interviewed by U.S. officials, one of the sources was being treated with various types of drugs to treat medical conditions."[144] Padilla's attorneys, Donna Newman and Andrew Patel, observed that Mobbs in his footnote "conceded that the government's 'confidential sources' probably were not 'completely candid,' and that one source recanted and another was being treated with drugs." Patel remarked: "Someone who's a confirmed liar and someone else who's on drugs and one of the two has recanted. You really think

142. Declaration of Michael H. Mobbs, Special Advisor to the Under Secretary of Defense for Policy, August 27, 2002, at 1 (hereafter "Mobbs Declaration on Padilla").
143. Id. at 2.
144. Id. n.1.

someone should be locked up for a year in solitary confinement based on *that?*"[145]

Part of the declaration is unrelated to the status of being an enemy combatant. Padilla was convicted of murder in Chicago "in approximately 1983" and remained in prison until he was eighteen. In Florida, in 1991, he was convicted of a handgun charge and sent to prison. He began to refer to himself as Ibrahim Padilla. In 1998 he moved to Egypt, where the administration says he was known as Abdullah Al Muhajir. "In 1999 or 2000 Padilla traveled to Pakistan. He also traveled to Saudi Arabia and Afghanistan." During this period he "has been closely associated with known members and leaders of the Al Qaeda terrorist network."[146] Fact or belief? "While in Afghanistan in 2001, Padilla met with senior Usama Bin Laden lieutenant Abu Zubaydah. Padilla and an associate approached Zubaydah with their proposal to conduct terrorist operations within the United States. Zubaydah directed Padilla and his associate to travel to Pakistan for training from Al Qaeda operatives in wiring explosives."[147] Fact or belief?

According to the declaration, Padilla and his associate "conducted research in the construction of a 'uranium-enhanced' explosive device." They planned to build and detonate a "dirty bomb" within the United States. The plan of Padilla and his associate "allegedly was still in the initial planning stages, and there was no specific time set for the operation to occur."[148] Allegedly? What confidence did the administration place in this information?

District Court in New York

On December 4, 2002, a district judge in New York City ruled that Padilla had a right to consult with counsel under conditions that would minimize the likelihood that he could use his lawyers as "unwilling intermediaries for the transmission of information to others."[149] Judge Michael B. Mukasey held that Padilla had a right to introduce facts in his defense, and the most convenient way to do that was to present them through counsel.[150] Moreover, Mukasey insisted that the government offer clearer evidence to support the designation

145. Paula Span, "Enemy Combatant Vanishes into a 'Legal Black Hole,'" Washington Post, July 30, 2003, at A8 (emphasis in original).

146. Mobbs Declaration on Padilla, at 3.

147. Id.

148. Id.

149. Padilla ex rel. Newman v. Bush, 233 F.Supp.2d 564, 569 (S.D. N.Y. 2002).

150. Id. at 599.

of Padilla as an enemy combatant. Mukasey did not grant Padilla access to counsel because of the Sixth Amendment, which is limited to "all criminal proceedings." The administration had not filed any charges against Padilla or taken him to court. Instead, Mukasey looked to congressional policy on habeas corpus petitions, entitling an applicant to "deny any of the facts set in the return or allege any other material facts" (28 U.S.C. § 2243).

In a later ruling, Judge Mukasey rejected the administration's position that the "some evidence" standard was sufficient to support the lawfulness of Padilla's detention. He said that no court of which he was aware had applied that standard "to a record that consists solely of the government's evidence, to which the government's adversary has not been permitted to respond."[151] He underscored the differences between Hamdi and Padilla: "Unlike Hamdi, Padilla was detained in this country, and initially by law enforcement officers pursuant to a material witness warrant. He was not captured on a foreign battlefield by soldiers in combat. The prospect of courts second-guessing battlefield decisions, which they have resolutely refused to do . . . does not loom in this case."[152]

After the administration appealed, the Second Circuit on December 18, 2003, held that the President lacked inherent constitutional authority as Commander in Chief to detain American citizens on American soil outside a zone of combat. To justify such detention, he needed specific congressional authority to satisfy the Non-Detention Act. The court decided that the AUMF did not authorize Padilla's detention.[153] The administration argued that the habeas petition directed at Defense Secretary Donald Rumsfeld should be either dismissed or transferred to the district court in South Carolina, where Padilla was being held. However, the Second Circuit concluded that the "legal reality of control" rested with Rumsfeld, not with the commander of the naval brig in South Carolina. Only Rumsfeld "could inform the President that further restraint of Padilla as an enemy combatant is no longer necessary."[154] In rejecting the administration's argument that President Bush had inherent authority to detain Padilla, the court held that the Constitution "entrusts the ability to define and punish offenses against the law of nations to the Congress, not the Executive."[155]

151. Padilla ex rel. Newman v. Rumsfeld, 243 F.Supp.2d 42, 54 (S.D. N.Y. 2003).
152. Id. at 56.
153. Padilla v. Rumsfeld, 352 F.3d 695 (2d Cir. 2003).
154. Id. at 707.
155. Id. at 714.

The administration insisted that the Nazi saboteur case "conclusively establishes the President's authority to exercise military jurisdiction over American citizens."[156] The Second Circuit disagreed, finding that the 1942 decision "rested on express congressional authorization." Moreover, at the time of *Quirin*, the Non-Detention Act did not exist. And finally, the German saboteurs "admitted that they were soldiers in the armed forces of a nation against whom the United States had formally declared war." Padilla had made no such admission and disputed his designation as enemy combatant.[157]

Following the ruling by the Second Circuit and the government's decision to appeal to the Supreme Court, the administration announced it would permit Padilla to consult with Donna Newman. As with Hamdi, access to an attorney was "a matter of discretion and military authority," was not required by domestic or international law, and "should not be treated as a precedent."[158] On March 3, 2004, Newman and Padilla talked through a glass security window while two government officials listened to the conversation and videotaped the meeting. She said that "this was not an attorney-client meeting," she was not allowed to ask "about the conditions of his confinement," and she also wanted to be able to send Padilla documents without having them first reviewed by the government. As it was, she gave him some newspaper articles about his case.[159] The government also consented to a longstanding request from the International Committee of the Red Cross to meet with Padilla.[160]

Supreme Court

The Supreme Court heard oral argument on April 28, 2004. Much of the discussion focused on whether the habeas petition challenging Padilla's confinement was properly filed in New York City rather than against the custodian at the naval brig in South Carolina. Deputy Solicitor General Paul Clement acknowledged that on the question of jurisdiction (hearing the case in New York or South Carolina) "it is true that the immediate custodian rule is not

156. Id. at 715.

157. Id. at 716.

158. Thomas E. Ricks and Michael Powell, "2nd Suspect Can See Lawyer," Washington Post, February 12, 2004, at A16.

159. Michael Powell, "Lawyer Visits 'Dirty Bomb' Suspect," Washington Post, March 4, 2004, at A10.

160. Deborah Sontag, "Terror Suspect's Path from Streets to Brig," New York Times, April 25, 2004, at 1.

a hard and fast rule and it has been—exceptions have been made."[161] Justice O'Connor found considerable uncertainty in this area.[162] Later, trying to navigate the field with some dexterity, Clement offered the curious position that "this Court has relaxed the rules . . . but it has never deviated."[163]

After the Court heard oral argument and began the process of drafting a decision, Deputy Attorney General James Comey issued an extraordinary public statement on June 1. He told reporters that the Justice Department was able "for the first time to tell the full story of Jose Padilla," permitting the American public "to understand the threat he posed and also [to] understand that the president's decision was and continues to be essential to the protection of the American people."[164] The claim of a "full story" was not credible because it came from one side: the administration's. Second, was Comey somehow trying to influence the Justices? If he wanted to inform the public, why not wait a few weeks until after the Court's decision was released? Padilla's attorney, Donna Newman, listened to Comey and thought: "Okay, that's his opening statement. Now when do I get to speak up? Everything my client says to me is classified. I can't offer any defense."[165]

Comey described a plan by Padilla to locate high-rise apartment buildings in the United States that had natural gas supplied to all floors. According to Comey, Padilla and his associates would rent two apartments in each building, "seal those apartments, turn on the gas, and set times to detonate and destroy the buildings simultaneously at a later time."[166] Comey did not explain the source of his information or the credibility and reliability of the informers. The public was left to weigh the significance of secret, one-sided evidence released by the government.

On June 28, the Court divided 5 to 4 in deciding that Padilla's habeas petition had been filed with the wrong court. It should have been filed, said the majority, with a district court in South Carolina, where Padilla was housed in a naval brig. Chief Justice Rehnquist, joined by O'Connor, Scalia, Kennedy,

161. U.S. Supreme Court, Rumsfeld v. Padilla, oral arguments, April 28, 2004, at 56.

162. Id. at 5–6.

163. Id. at 16.

164. U.S. Department of Justice, "Remarks of Deputy Attorney General James Comey Regarding Jose Padilla, June 1, 2004," at 1, available under the Department of Justice Web site, archived documents for the Deputy Attorney General, 2004 (hereafter "Comey's Remarks").

165. Michael Powell, "Padilla Case Puts Lawyers in Limbo, Too," Washington Post, June 5, 2004, at A3.

166. Comey's Remarks, at 4.

and Thomas, regarded the commander of the naval brig as the only proper respondent because she, not Rumsfeld, was Padilla's custodian. Rehnquist reasoned that limiting district courts to "their respective jurisdictions" helps prevent forum shopping by habeas petitioners.[167] Justice Stevens, writing for the dissenters, agreed that habeas petitioners should not be allowed to engage in forum shopping, but pointed out that if the administration had given Donna Newman notice of its intent to ask the district court to vacate the material witness warrant and place Padilla in the custody of the Defense Department, with eventual transfer to South Carolina, she could have filed a timely petition in New York.[168] If anyone was engaging in forum shopping to select a jurisdiction (the Fourth Circuit) more friendly to the government, it was the administration, not Padilla and his counsel.

The Rapp Declaration

With the case now in district court in South Carolina, the Bush administration based its authority to detain Padilla not on the Mobbs Declaration but a successor statement signed by Jeffrey N. Rapp, another Pentagon official. It was executed and signed on August 27, 2004. Like Mobbs, Rapp had no direct knowledge of Padilla. He signed his name to a declaration based on intelligence sources and unnamed informants.

Various claims appear in the Rapp Declaration without any sources, nor was there any attempt (as with Mobbs) to indicate the reliability of informers, drug use, and lack of candor. Here are some examples from Rapp: "In mid-November 2001, an air strike destroyed a safehouse in Afghanistan and killed [Mohammed] Atef. Padilla was staying at a different al Qaeda safehouse that day, and he and other al Qaeda operatives participated in an attempt to rescue survivors and retrieve Atef's body from the rubble."[169] "Padilla discussed with Zubaydah the idea of conducting terrorist operations involving the detonation of explosive devices in the United States."[170]

The most dramatic change from the Mobbs Declaration was omitting any allegation about a dirty bomb and inserting a description about the plan to blow up apartment buildings, as Comey had publicly described in June 2004.

167. Rumsfeld v. Padilla, 542 U.S. 426, 446–47 (2004).

168. Id. at 458–60, 462.

169. Declaration of Mr. Jeffrey N. Rapp, Director, Joint Intelligence Task Force for Combating Terrorism, August 27, 2004, at 4, included as Exhibit B in Respondent's Answer to the Petition for Habeas Corpus, Padilla v. Hanft, C/A No. 02–04–2221–26AJ (D. S.C. 2004).

170. Id. at 5.

No sources are provided for the following statements: "Padilla admits that the apartment building plan was resurrected when he first met senior al Qaeda operational planner and 11 September 2001 mastermind Khalid Sheikh Mohammad. . . ." "Padilla admits that he accepted the mission." Padilla "admits to meeting with numerous key al-Qaeda leadership figures and senior operational planners, and to planning plots against the United States with them."[171] What is the basis for these "admissions"? A transcript or tape recording on a particular day? Was the admission made under coercion, possibly torture, or induced by drugs? The Declaration does not say.

The Quirin *Model*

In papers filed in South Carolina, the administration looked partly to the Nazi saboteur case to "confirm the military's long-settled authority—independent of and distinct from criminal process—to detain enemy combatants for the duration of an armed conflict."[172] It claimed that the "precise facts" of *Quirin* "were indistinguishable in every material respect from the instant facts."[173] With Padilla, President Bush "determined, in terms indistinguishable from those used by the Court in *Quirin*, that petitioner is 'closely associated with al Qaeda' and has 'engaged in . . . hostile and war-like acts, including conduct in preparation for acts of international terrorism . . . on the United States.' . . . Indeed, the factual parallels are striking."[174]

As for "striking parallels" between *Quirin* and Jose Padilla, there are five fundamental differences. First, the eight German saboteurs were charged with four offenses: violation of the "law of war," violation of Articles of War 81 and 82, and conspiracy. No formal charges were ever brought against Padilla during his three and a half years of military confinement. On November 17, 2005, the administration released him from military detention and indicted him in Florida on charges that had nothing to do with dirty bombs or plans to blow up apartment buildings.[175]

---

171. Id. at 6, 8.

172. Respondent's Answer to the Petition for Writ of Habeas Corpus, Padilla v. Hanft, C/A No. 02–04–2221–26AJ (D. S.C. August 30, 2004), at 9 (hereafter "Respondent's Answer").

173. Respondent's Opposition to the Motion for Summary Judgment, Padilla v. Hanft, c/A No. 02:04–2221–26AJ (D. S.C. November 22, 2004), at 15.

174. Respondent's Answer, at 14.

175. The four charges against the Nazi saboteurs: 39 Landmark Briefs 310–13 (1975); Fisher, Nazi Saboteurs on Trial, at 61–63; Fisher, Military Tribunals and Presidential Power, at 103–05. For Padilla's indictment in November 2005, see Indictment, United States v.

Second, President Roosevelt assigned counsel to the eight German sabo-teurs.[176] Three colonels, a major, and a captain were assigned to represent the men during the tribunal and before the Supreme Court.[177] Padilla received the counsel of public defender Donna Newman during his month of confine-ment as a material witness in New York City, but after his designation as an enemy combatant on June 9, 2002, the government barred her from meeting with him. It was not until shortly after the Supreme Court decided to hear his case—almost two years later—that Padilla was able to consult with counsel again and only under very restricted conditions.

Third, the government held a trial for the eight German saboteurs in 1942, stretching from July 8 to August 1. A military tribunal started its deliberations less than two weeks after the men were apprehended. Padilla was arrested on May 8, 2002, on a material witness warrant. On June 9, 2002, after his designa-tion as enemy combatant, he was transferred to the custody of the Defense Department and received no trial until November 17, 2005, with his indict-ment in Florida. His trial did not begin until April 2007, almost five years after his arrest.

Fourth, the evidence against the eight German saboteurs was clear and uncontested. It included recovered boxes of explosives and fuses, the defen-dants' own testimony, and the testimony of individuals in the United States who collaborated with them.[178] No evidence, worthy of the name, was pre-sented against Padilla other than third-hand hearsay in the Mobbs and Rapp Declarations. Claims and assertions by executive officials are not evidence. As explained later, a decision by the Fourth Circuit on September 9, 2005, gave the impression of stating facts and evidence against Padilla but only by seri-ously distorting the procedure followed (summary judgment).

Fifth, the military order and proclamation issued by President Roosevelt in 1942 applied to eight Germans who were "subjects, citizens or residents of any nation at war with the United States" and "who during time of war enter or attempt to enter the United States . . . to commit sabotage, espionage, hostile or warlike acts, or violations of the law of war."[179] The military order issued

Hassoun, No. 4–60001-CR-COOKE (S.D. Fla. November 17, 2005), at 4, and Eric Lichtblau, "Threats and Responses: The Padilla Case; in Legal Shift, U.S. Charges Detainee in Terror-ism Case," New York Times, November 23, 2005, at A1.

176. 7 Fed. Reg. 5103 (1942).

177. Fisher, *Nazi Saboteurs on Trial*, at 52, 56.

178. Id. at 29–32, 34–42, 80–84; Fisher, *Military Tribunals and Presidential Power*, at 92–93, 126.

179. 7 Fed. Reg. 5101, 5103 (1942).

by President Bush on November 13, 2001, applied to a general population of noncitizens in the United States who assisted with the 9/11 attacks, were members of al Qaeda, engaged in international terrorism, or harbored terrorists. Roosevelt's action applied to eight named individuals, with trial and personnel specified; the Bush order covered a population of approximately 18 million resident noncitizens. Those individuals were vulnerable to be taken into custody and designated as enemy combatants, with no assurance of a trial. Military tribunals have never before expressly discriminated against such a broad and open-ended class of persons. Even President Roosevelt's proclamation for the German saboteurs did not discriminate based on citizenship status. His proclamation applied to "all *persons* who are subjects, citizens or residents of any nation at war with the United States."[180]

Actions in the Fourth Circuit

On February 28, 2005, District Judge Henry F. Floyd held that Congress had not authorized Padilla's indefinite detention without trial and that the President possessed no inherent constitutional powers to subject Padilla to indefinite military detention.[181] Although the administration maintained that *Quirin* was "wholly on point," Judge Floyd was "unconvinced."[182] The treatment of the Nazi saboteurs followed express congressional authorization; no similar authority could be found to justify the handling of Padilla.[183] *Quirin* turned on whether the saboteurs should be tried by military tribunal or civilian court. The issue with Padilla: was whether he would be charged and tried at all. *Quirin* was decided before the Non-Detention Act. *Quirin* involved a war that had a definite ending date, but the war against terrorism does not.[184]

The Fourth Circuit reversed Judge Floyd. In holding for the administration on September 9, 2005, Judge Michael Luttig began his decision by stating—as fact—that Padilla was "associated with forces hostile to the United States in Afghanistan and took up arms against United States forces in that country in our war against al Qaeda."[185] Those are extraordinary words, condemning Padilla in the opening sentence. The paragraph continues: "Upon his escape to Pakistan from the battlefield in Afghanistan, Padilla was recruited, trained,

---

180. Id. at. 5101 (Proclamation 2561, emphasis added).
181. Padilla v. Hanft, 389 F.Supp.2d 678 (D. S.C. 2005).
182. Id. at 686.
183. Id. at 686–87.
184. Id. at 687 n.10.
185. Padilla v. Hanft, 423 F.3d 386, 388 (4th Cir. 2005).

funded, and equipped by al Qaeda leaders to continue prosecution of the war in the United States by blowing up apartment buildings in this country. Padilla flew to the United States on May 8, 2002, to begin carrying out his assignment, but was arrested by civilian law enforcement authorities upon his arrival at O'Hare International Airport in Chicago."[186]

Although presented as *fact*, the statements are actually unproven *allegations* by the administration based on sources not revealed to Padilla or his attorneys. Why didn't Judge Luttig make that clear at the beginning? Only later does he mention the procedure being followed: "For purposes of Padilla's summary judgment motion, the parties have stipulated to the facts as set forth by the government. J.A. [Joint Appendix] 30–31. It is only on these facts that we consider whether the President has the authority to detain Padilla."[187] Elsewhere in his opinion, Judge Luttig continues to talk about "facts." "Under the facts as presented here, Padilla unquestionably qualifies as an 'enemy combatant'. . . ."[188] Still later he begins a paragraph: "These facts unquestionably establish that Padilla poses the requisite threat. . . ."[189]

Under the summary judgment procedure, Padilla's attorneys were willing *to assume as fact* the allegations made by the administration in order to avoid a lengthy trial and move directly to the legal issue: Did President Bush have authority to detain him? As is obvious in all summary judgment cases, "assuming as fact" does not mean *agreeing as fact*. The reader of Luttig's opinion might assume that the cited passage (J.A. 30–31) contained a stipulation by both parties to the facts that appear in his opening paragraph and subsequent statements. That is false. J.A. 30–31 only cites a statement by an attorney in the Solicitor General's office, advising the court that Padilla's attorneys "have an argument that they would like to present to the Court initially, that would *assume* the Government's facts as set forth in our return and the attached declaration [the Rapp Declaration], and that would say even under those facts, the President lacked the authority to detain Mr. Padilla as an enemy combatant."[190]

At various points Padilla specifically *disputed* the allegations made about him by the administration. When he signed his habeas petition on June 30, 2004, he stated that he was not an "enemy combatant," had "never joined

186. Id.

187. Id. at 390 n.1.

188. Id. at 391.

189. Id. at 396.

190. Statement by David B. Salmons in Transcript of Status Conference, September 14, 2004, Joint Appendix, Padilla v. Hanft, No. 05–6396 (4th Cir. 2004), at 30 (emphasis added), available at http:www.wiggin.com/db30/cgi-bin/pubs/Joint%20Appendix%20Part%201 .pdf.

a foreign Army and was not arrested on a foreign battlefield," and "carried no weapons or explosives when he was arrested." He rejected "the factual allegations underlying the Government's designation of him as an 'enemy combatant.'"[191] To the extent that Judge Luttig relied on information supplied by the administration, there is good reason to be cautious about its claims. Nowhere does Luttig acknowledge that an earlier administration claim in the Mobbs Declaration (about Padilla's plans for a "dirty bomb") had been jettisoned by the administration as either unreliable or impossible to justify. Judge Luttig should have explained at the outset of his opinion that he was deciding a summary judgment motion, under which Padilla's attorneys *assumed without agreeing to* allegations set forth by the government. Instead, he used uncorroborated "facts" offered by the administration to decide the law.

It would have been instructive for the Fourth Circuit to take judicial notice of other areas where the Bush administration claimed to be operating on facts, not assertions, but failed utterly to substantiate its allegations. Administration claims about Iraqi weapons of mass destruction, Iraqi attempts to seek uranium from a country in Africa, the availability of mobile vans to disperse biological agents, the purchase of aluminum tubes to pursue nuclear weapons, drones to spread chemical and biological agents, and other WMD capabilities were found to have no factual basis.[192]

On August 16, 2007, a jury in Florida convicted Padilla of terrorism conspiracy charges, along with two co-defendants. The case had nothing to do with allegations about a "dirty bomb" or blowing up apartment buildings. A key piece of physical evidence introduced at trial was a "mujahideen data form" that Padilla supposedly filled out to attend a terrorist training camp in Afghanistan. Padilla's fingerprints were on the form but it was impossible to determine if they were placed there in Afghanistan or after being detained by the United States and held at the naval brig.[193] On January 22, 2008, Padilla was sentenced to seventeen years in prison. The government had urged the court to sentence him to life in prison. In announcing the decision, the trial judge said that

191. Petition for Writ of Habeas Corpus, June 30, 2004, Joint Appendix, Padilla v. Hanft, No. 05–6396 (4th Cir. 2004), at 7, available at http://www.wiggin.com/db30/cgi-bin/pubs/Joint%20Appendix%20Part%201.pdf.

192. Louis Fisher, "Justifying War Against Iraq," in Rivals for Power: Presidential-Congressional Relations 289–313 (James A. Thurber ed., 3d ed. 2006).

193. Peter Whoriskey, "Jury Convicts Jose Padilla of Terror Charges," Washington Post, August 17, 2007, at A1; Abby Goodnough and Scott Shane, "Padilla Is Guilty on all Charges in Terror Trial," New York Times, August 17, 2007, at A1.

the government had offered no evidence linking Padilla to specific terrorism acts or engaging in any plot to overthrow the U.S. government.[194] When Padilla was arrested in May 2002, Attorney General John Ashcroft had said Padilla was part of an "unfolding terrorist plot to attack the United States."[195]

ALI AL-MARRI

Another significant enemy combatant case involved a resident alien, Ali al-Marri, a citizen from Qatar who studied computer science at Bradley University in Peoria, Illinois. He was first arrested by the FBI on December 12, 2001, as a material witness in the investigation of the 9/11 attacks. He was transferred to New York City and on January 28, 2002, formally arrested on a charge of credit card fraud. He was indicted on February 6, 2002. He pled not guilty. Other charges came on January 22, 2003: making a false statement to the FBI, making a false statement in a bank application, and using a means of identification of another person to influence the action of a federally insured financial institution. He pled not guilty to those charges also. A pre-trial conference was scheduled for July 2, 2003, with a jury trial to begin on July 21, 2003.[196]

Before the trial could begin, President Bush designated al-Marri an enemy combatant on June 23, 2003. At that point he was transferred to a naval brig in Charleston, South Carolina. Efforts by his attorney to file a habeas petition in Illinois failed. Relief, if any, would have to come in the judicial district where he was confined.[197] He continued to be held at the brig without charges brought against him. On July 8, 2005, a district judge in Charleston held that the AUMF authorized his detention, relying on the plurality ruling of four Justices of the Supreme Court in *Hamdi* v. *Rumsfeld* (2004).[198] Al-Marri remained at the naval brig throughout 2005 and 2006, the only noncitizen on the American mainland held as an enemy combatant, spending his time in a small cell in solitary confinement. He last saw his wife, two sons, and three daughters in 2001, just before his arrest in Peoria. The legal question crystallized in this

194. Kirk Semple, "Padilla Gets 17-Year Term for Role in Conspiracy," New York Times, January 23, 2008, at A14.

195. Id.

196. Al-Marri v. Bush, 274 F.Supp.2d 1003, 1004 (C.D. Ill. 2003).

197. Id. at 1009–10, aff'd, Al-Marri v. Rumsfeld, 360 F.3d 707 (7th Cir. 2004), cert. denied, 543 U.S. 809 (2004).

198. Al-Marri v. Hanft, 378 F.Supp.2d 673 (D. S.C. 2005).

manner: "May the government indefinitely detain a foreigner living legally in the United States, without charges and without access to the courts?"[199]

In his appeal to the Fourth Circuit, the administration claimed that al-Marri was an al Qaeda sleeper agent sent to the United States for a second wave of terrorist attacks, trained in Afghanistan in the use of poisons.[200] On June 11, 2007, the Fourth Circuit ruled that the President may not declare an individual in the country an "enemy combatant" and hold that person indefinitely. The court said the administration may charge al-Marri with a crime, initiate deportation proceedings, hold him as a material witness in connection with a grand jury investigation, or detain him for a limited time pursuant to the Patriot Act. "But military detention of al-Marri must cease."[201] On August 23, the Fourth Circuit agreed with the Bush administration's request to have the full ten-member court review the ruling of the three-judge panel.[202] On March 13, 2008, al-Marri's attorneys requested a district court to grant interim relief to permit regular and frequent (monitored) telephone calls with family members, faster access to mail sent to him, unrestricted access to news (in newspapers, magazines, and television), and full access to religious materials—all for the purpose of reversing the virtual isolation.[203]

This chapter focused on the history of military tribunals, the Nazi saboteur case, the Non-Detention Act, and the enemy combatant cases of Hamdi, Padilla, and al-Marri. The next chapter looks at a much larger population of enemy combatants: those detained at the U.S. naval base in Guantánamo Bay, Cuba. Similar issues arise concerning indefinite detention without charges, confidential evidence presented by the administration, and lack of access by the detainees and their attorneys to that evidence.

199. Adam Liptak, "In a War with Vague Boundaries, a Terror Detainee Longs for Court," New York Times, January 5, 2007, at A1.

200. Sari Horwitz, "Detainee Rights at Center of Fight," Washington Post, February 2, 2007, at A6; Adam Liptak, "Judges Pose Questions on Bush Detainee Policy," New York Times, February 2, 2007, at A14.

201. Al-Marri v. Wright, 487 F.3d 160, 195 (4th Cir. 2007). See Adam Liptak, "Judges Say U.S. Can't Hold Man as 'Combatant,'" New York Times, June 12, 2007, at A1; Carol D. Leonnig, "Judges Rule Against U.S. on Detained 'Combatant,'" Washington Post, June 12, 2007, at A1.

202. "Court Will Reconsider Ruling in Terrorism Case," Washington Post, August 24, 2007, at A5.

203. Memorandum of Law in Support of Motion for Interim Relief from Prolonged Isolation and Other Unlawful Conditions of Confinement, Ali Saleh Kahlah Almarri v. Gates, C/A 2:05–2259–HFF-FSC (D. S.C. March 13, 2008).

CHAPTER 7

Guantánamo

During military operations in Afghanistan in late 2001, U.S. forces captured several thousand individuals thought to be associated with the Taliban or al Qaeda. Many were brought to the U.S. naval base at Guantánamo Bay, Cuba. What system did the administration have to separate individuals associated with terrorism from those mistakenly apprehended? Were detainees protected by federal statutes and international treaties prohibiting torture, or could U.S interrogators inflict pain to extract intelligence? Did federal courts have jurisdiction to hear claims brought by detainees? Could the executive branch withhold confidential documents from detainees and their attorneys? Those and other issues reached the courts.

INTERROGATION METHODS

U.S. forces captured thousands of suspects in Afghanistan and other countries without knowing whether they were actually linked to terrorist operations against the United States. American soldiers relied on judgments from members of the Northern Alliance (Tajiks, Uzbeks, etc.) who had been fighting the Taliban in a civil war. Newspaper stories reported a bounty-hunter system, with members of the Northern Alliance given $5,000 if they identified a Taliban and $20,000 if they linked someone to al Qaeda.[1] There were reports of Pakistani officials being paid as much as $10,000 to turn over suspects.[2] Hundreds of those apprehended were brought to Guantánamo, where U.S. officials over time acknowledged that the population represented a mix of terrorist fighters and innocent people erroneously swept up. Over the years, hundreds would be released. Moazzam Begg, seized in Pakistan in January 2002, was imprisoned for three years in Bagram, Kandahar, and Guantánamo.

---

1. Petition for Writ of Certiorari, Hamdi v. Rumsfeld, No. 03–7338, U.S. Supreme Court, at 9 n.8.

2. John White and Julie Tate, "In Guantanamo Bay Documents, Prisoners Plead for Release," Washington Post, March 5, 2006, at A8.

Initially labeled an "enemy combatant," he was later released without explanation, apology, or any type of reparation.[3] Murat Kurnaz, a German man of Turkish origin, was apprehended in Pakistan for a reported $3,000 bounty payment. After being tortured in a prison camp in Kandahar, he was taken to Guantánamo and held there for more than four years as an "enemy combatant." He was finally released in July 2006. The record showed no evidence of terrorist activity.[4]

At the naval base, detainees were first housed in steel mesh outdoor cages, exposed to the elements. The United States might have been ill-prepared to receive such large numbers, but photos of prisoners kept in cages sent a message to the world that America regarded them as animals, not humans. The men were moved from those temporary quarters (Camp X-Ray) to a new facility (Camp Delta), modeled after maximum-security prisons in the United States. There was one key difference. The facilities at Guantánamo were used to interrogate and abuse detainees.[5] Many of the harsh methods developed at the naval base were transported to Afghanistan and Iraq and applied there, including the prison at Abu Ghraib.

There is no persuasive evidence that inhumane and painful interrogation yields better intelligence than techniques that comply with statutory and treaty standards. "Aggressive" methods may generate information not obtained with legal methods, but the information is likely to be inaccurate and false, motivated not to provide truth but to stop pain: "under sufficient coercion nearly anyone can be made to confess to anything."[6] News reports, relying on current and former U.S. government officials, explained that the alleged (false) link between Iraq and al Qaeda—used to justify war in 2003—came from a prisoner interrogated in Egypt who said he fabricated the story to escape painful

---

3. Moazzam Begg, Enemy Combatant: My Imprisonment at Guantánamo, Bagram, and Kandahar (2006).

4. Craig Whitlock, "U.S. Free Longtime Detainee," Washington Post, April 25, 2006, at A9; Mark Landner and Souad Mekhennet, "Freed German Detainee Questions His Country's Role," New York Times, November 11, 2006, at A5; Cem Özdemir, "A Visit with a Man Wrongly Detained at Guantanamo," Der Spiegel, September 14, 2006, at http://www.spiegel.de/international/0,1518,druck–437087,00.html.

5. See Joseph Margulies, Guantánamo and the Abuse of Presidential Power (2006); Michael Ratner and Ellen Ray, Guantánamo: What the World Should Know (2004).

6. John H. Langbein, Torture and the Law of Proof 5 (2006 ed.). See Josh White, "Interrogation Research Is Lacking, Report Says," Washington Post, January 16, 2007, at A15. See also a 374-page report from the Intelligence Science Board published by the National Defense Intelligence College, December 2006, available at http://www.fas.org/irp/dni/educing.pdf.

questioning.[7] Military interrogators have long understood that persons being questioned were protected by the Geneva Conventions and that force was prohibited.[8] The Army manual of 1992 stated that the Conventions and U.S. policy "expressly prohibit acts of violence or intimidation, including physical or mental torture, threats, insults, or exposure to inhumane treatment as a means of or aid to interrogation." Acts in violation of those prohibitions "are criminal acts punishable under the UCMJ" (Uniform Code of Military Justice).[9]

As noted in the Army manual, experience "indicates that the use of prohibited techniques is not necessary to gain the cooperation of interrogation sources." Torture is "a poor technique that yields unreliable results, may damage subsequent collection efforts, and can induce the source to say what he thinks the interrogator wants to hear." Once the use of torture by U.S. personnel becomes public or is known by enemies and allies, the result "will bring discredit upon the US and its armed forces while undermining domestic and international support for the war effort." Torture and inhumane methods may place Americans and allied troops in enemy hands "at a greater risk of abuse by their captors." Knowing that the enemy abuses Americans and allied prisoners of war "does not justify using methods of interrogation specifically prohibited" by the Geneva Conventions and U.S. policy.[10]

Examples of physical torture are identified in the Army manual: electric shock; infliction of pain through chemicals or bondage; forcing an individual to stand, sit, or kneel in abnormal positions for prolonged periods of time; food deprivation; and any form of beating. Examples of mental torture: mock executions, abnormal sleep deprivation, and chemically induced psychosis. Prohibited forms of coercion include threats to torture the subject, his family, or others to whom he owes loyalty; intentionally denying medical assistance in exchange for information sought; and threatening or implying that rights guaranteed by the Geneva Conventions will not be provided unless the individual cooperates.[11]

Those passages appeared in the 1992 manual. They were updated in September 2006 to reflect the disclosure of conditions at Abu Ghraib and con-

7. Douglas Jehl, "Qaeda-Iraq Link U.S. Cited Tied to Coercion Claim," New York Times, December 9, 2005, at A1.

8. U.S. Department of the Army, FM 34–52 Intelligence Interrogation, September 28, 1992, at 1–7.

9. Id. at 1–8.

10. Id.

11. Id.

gressional passage of the Detainee Treatment Act of 2005. Among the new prohibited actions: forcing the detainee to be naked, perform sexual acts, or pose in a sexual manner; placing hoods or sacks over the head of a detainee; using duct tape over the eyes; "waterboarding" (simulated drowning); and using "military working dogs."[12] In determining whether a method is permissible, the interrogator should ask: "If the proposed approach technique were used by the enemy against one of your fellow soldiers, would you believe the soldier had been abused?"[13]

The United States has developed humane standards to minimize the brutality and cruelty of war. Codes written by Francis Lieber during the Civil War helped influence the Hague and Geneva Conventions.[14] Long before those comprehensive efforts, American military and political leaders understood the reasons for avoiding inhumane treatment of prisoners. One is the principle of reciprocity. Abuse of enemy forces invites (and justifies) abuse of friendly troops. In guerrilla wars, misconduct can imperil a successful military campaign. During the War of Independence, when reports of British cruelty toward American prisoners reached General George Washington, he did not react in kind. He prohibited his troops from "plundering any person whatsoever, whether Tories or others," and expected that "humanity and tenderness to women and children will distinguish brave Americans, contending for liberty, from infamous mercenary ravagers, whether British or Hessians."[15] Urged to retaliate against British abuses, he concluded that "Humanity and Policy forbid the measure. Experience proves, that their wanton Cruelty injures rather than benefits their cause."[16]

General Winfield Scott held to those principles during the Mexican War, realizing that abuses or atrocities committed by his men would incite insurgent and guerrilla uprisings.[17] In May 2007, when Army Gen. David H. Petraeus learned that many U.S. troops in Iraq supported torture of suspects and were unwilling to report abuses by their colleagues, he posted an open letter on a military Web site, telling soldiers: "This fight depends on securing the population, which must understand that we—not our enemies—occupy the

12. U.S. Department of the Army, FM 2–22–3 (FM 34–52), Human Intelligence Collector Operations, September 2006, at 5–21 (para. 5–75), available at http://fl1.findlaw.com/news.findlaw.com/hdocs/dod/armyfm2223humanintel.pdf.

13. Id. at 5–22 (para. 5–76).

14. Louis Fisher, Military Tribunals and Presidential Power 71–90 (2005).

15. 6 The Writings of George Washington 466 (Fitzpatrick, John C., ed.).

16. Fisher, Military Tribunals and Presidential Power, at 7–8.

17. Id. at 32–33.

moral high ground." For those who believed that torture is sometimes needed to quickly obtain crucial information, he counseled: "Beyond the basic fact that such actions are illegal, history shows that they also are frequently neither useful nor necessary."[18]

A popular justification for torture is the "ticking-bomb" scenario. If a suspect has information about a pending nuclear attack, isn't it better to torture one individual than lose hundreds of thousands of innocent persons? The fallacy of the argument lies in the first word. No one knows if the suspect has the information. Torture will make him talk but the information may not be useful or accurate. What if the question is changed, replacing a thirty-year-old, dark-skinned Muslim male with a four-year old white Christian girl? If the logic is compelling for him, why not her?

If the ticking-bomb scenario justifies torture against a terrorist, why not allow torture for domestic law-enforcement efforts? Drug smuggling, criminal syndicates, and other illegal operations do great damage to U.S. national security interests. The costs far exceed al Qaeda terrorism. Why not let FBI agents and local police use "aggressive" interrogation methods? Granted, the evidence could not be used in court, but one could plausibly argue that the information obtained may help deter future crimes. Using torture against suspected terrorists helps justify it elsewhere.

After 9/11 there were widespread reports, often confirmed by U.S. agencies, of detainees being kicked, punched, slammed into walls, and subjected to cruel, inhuman, and degrading treatment.[19] Some detainees died from beatings.[20] American officers admitted to improperly using dogs in interrogation to terrify detainees.[21] Private contractors were involved in abusive interrogations.[22] Maj. Gen. Geoffrey D. Miller, a central figure in the abuse of detainees

18. Thomas E. Ricks, "Gen. Petraeus Warns against Using Torture," Washington Post, May 11, 2007, at A3.

19. R. Jeffrey Smith, "General Cites Problems at U.S. Jails in Afghanistan," Washington Post, December 3, 2004, at A1; Douglas Jehl, "Report Warned C.I.A. on Tactics in Interrogation," New York Times, November 9, 2005, at A1.

20. Josh White, "2 Died After '02 Beatings by U.S. Soldiers," Washington Post, March 12, 2005, at A14; Tim Golden, "In U.S. Report, Brutal Details Of 2 Afghan Inmates' Deaths," New York Times, May 20, 2005, at A1.

21. John White, "Officer Says He Wrongly Approved Use of Dogs," Washington Post, March 16, 2006, at A1.

22. Griff Witte and Renae Merle, "Contractors Are Cited in Abuses at Guantanamo," Washington Post, January 4, 2007, at D1; R. Jeffrey Smith, "Interrogator Says U.S. Approved Handling of Detainee Who Died," Washington Post, April 13, 2005, at A7. See also Eric Fair, "An Iraq Interrogator's Nightmare," Washington Post, February 9, 2007, at A19.

against who brought to Iraq and Afghanistan the interrogation methods he used at Guantánamo, invoked his right of self-incrimination during court-martial proceedings.[23] A few enlisted men were convicted in courts-martial and some sanctions were handed out to military officers, but the civilian officials who helped shape, justify, and authorize the abusive practices were never held accountable.

SHAPING DETAINEE POLICY

In the early months of 2002, executive officials in the Bush administration debated how to treat detainees at Guantánamo. The Defense Department and the Central Intelligence Agency wanted broad latitude when interrogating prisoners. The State Department insisted that the men were entitled to the protections of the four Geneva Conventions, completed in 1949 and agreed to by the United States in 1955. The treaties established standards for handling prisoners of war and civilians.

In a memo to President Bush on January 25, 2002, White House Counsel Alberto Gonzales summarized the competing positions. He told Bush that the Office of Legal Counsel (OLC) in the Justice Department had issued a formal legal opinion, concluding that the Third Geneva Convention on the treatment of prisoners of war (GPW) did not apply to al Qaeda because the group did not sign the treaty. In addition, OLC found "reasonable grounds" why the Geneva Conventions did not apply to the Taliban. It was Gonzales's understanding that Bush had decided that Geneva did not apply "and, accordingly, that al Qaeda and Taliban detainees are not prisoners of war under the GPW." Gonzales called the OLC analysis "definitive."[24]

Gonzales advised Bush that Secretary of State Colin Powell urged reconsideration of the decision on detainee treatment. Powell decided that GPW applied to both al Qaeda and the Taliban. He made four points: (1) the United States had never denied the applicability of the Geneva Conventions to either U.S. or opposing forces engaged in armed conflict; (2) if the administration now decided against compliance with Geneva, the United States could not

---

23. Josh White, "General Asserts Right on Self-Incrimination in Iraq Abuse Cases," *Washington Post*, January 12, 2006, at A1.

24. Memorandum from Gonzales to Bush, "Decision re Application of the Geneva Convention on Prisoners of War to the Conflict with Al Qaeda and the Taliban," January 25, 2002, at 1. Reprinted in Mark Danner, *Torture and Truth: America, Abu Ghraib, and the War on Terror* 83–87 (2004).

invoke the GPW if enemy forces threatened to mistreat U.S. or coalition forces captured during operations in Afghanistan; (3) noncompliance with Geneva invited condemnation from allies; and (4) other countries would be less inclined to turn over terrorists if the United States did not recognize a legal obligation to comply with GPW.[25]

To Gonzales, Powell's arguments were, on balance, "unpersuasive."[26] Terrorist actions in recent years amounted to a "new type of warfare—one not contemplated in 1949 when the GPW was framed—and requires a new approach in our actions toward captured terrorists."[27] Although the administration would not feel bound by GPW in the treatment of detainees, "the U.S. will continue to be constrained by (i) its commitment to treat the detainees humanely and, to the extent appropriate and consistent with military necessity, in a manner consistent with the principles of GPW, (ii) its applicable treaty obligations, (iii) minimum standards of treatment universally recognized by the nations of the world, and (iv) applicable military regulations regarding the treatment of detainees."[28]

This approach rejected binding legal obligations, pursuant to treaty commitments, and replaced them with a unilateral administration policy that could be altered, modified, or rescinded whenever executive officials chose to. In this formulation and reformulation of policy, Congress was excluded. The memo substituted executive fiat for the rule of law. The attitude in the Gonzales memo would be reflected in administration decisions in many other areas, including NSA surveillance and "extraordinary detention," to be discussed in subsequent chapters.

The choice of administration policy over binding law appears in a memo President Bush signed on February 7, 2002. He embraced the Justice Department position that none of the Geneva provisions should apply to al Qaeda. He also accepted that he had authority under the Constitution "to suspend Geneva as between the United States and Afghanistan, but I decline to exercise that authority at this time. Accordingly, I determine that the provisions of Geneva will apply to our present conflict with the Taliban."[29] The conditional

25. Id. at 3.

26. Id.

27. Id.

28. Id. at 4.

29. "Humane Treatment of al Qaeda and Taliban Detainees," memorandum of February 7, 2002, from President Bush to the Vice President, the Secretary of State, the Secretary of Defense, the Attorney General, Chief of Staff to the President, Director of Central Intelligence, Assistant to the President for National Security Affairs, and Chairman of the Joint Chiefs of Staff, at 1–2. Reprinted in Danner, Torture and Truth, at 105–106.

"at this time" allowed Bush to suspend Geneva protections to the Taliban whenever he wanted to. In this same memo, he determined that the Taliban detainees "are unlawful combatants and, therefore, do not qualify as prisoners of war under Article 4 of Geneva."[30] He added: "Of course, our values as a Nation, values that we share with many nations in the world, call for us to treat detainees humanely, including those who are not legally entitled to such treatment. Our Nation has been and will continue to be a strong supporter of Geneva and its principles. As a matter of policy, the United States Armed Forces shall continue to treat detainees humanely and, to the extent appropriate and consistent with military necessity, in a manner consistent with the principles of Geneva."[31]

There are several positions here. President Bush expressed his support of Geneva and its principles without being legally bound by them. He was limited only by the policy he set, not by the treaties the United States had signed with other nations. Even with those qualifications, had this memo not been classified but instead posted at prison sites in Guantánamo, Afghanistan, and Iraq, it might have given salutary instruction to U.S. soldiers to treat detainees humanely. It was not declassified until June 17, 2004, after the worldwide revelations of prisoner abuse at the Iraqi prison camp of Abu Ghraib.

STEPS TOWARD TORTURE

The administration prepared legal analyses to allow U.S. interrogators to abuse detainees. Drafting defective legal advice required several steps. The first was to exclude those within the administration who knew the most about military law: the Judge Advocate General corps. Second: place the detainees in a location supposedly beyond the reach of federal judges. Third: conclude that existing treaties and federal statutes do not apply to the detainees. Fourth: justify interrogation methods that would be impermissible if used by the U.S. military on prisoners of war (or by federal or state law-enforcement officers on those arrested of crimes). Legal analyses were highly classified and shared with a small circle of executive officials. In June 2004, many of the documents became public.

30. Id. at 2.
31. Id.

JAG Officers

Administration experts most knowledgeable and experienced about military law, especially those in the Judge Advocate General offices, were largely circumvented in the early stages of deciding how domestic and international law applied to detainees. Not until June 2004, after public disclosures of Abu Ghraib, did the defective and misguided legal analyses generated by the Justice Department begin to leak to the public.In July 2005, a group of former JAG officers representing all of the military services signed a joint letter denouncing the administration's policy that invited and encouraged the torture and mistreatment of detainees. The abuse of prisoners, they said, "hurts America's cause in the war on terror, endangers U.S. service members who might be captured by the enemy, and is anathema to the values Americans have held dear for generations." The Army manual "authorizes techniques that have proven effective in extracting life-saving information from the most hardened enemy prisoners."[32] During formulation of administration policy, a number of JAG officers had been highly critical of OLC legal analysis.[33]

A Law-Free Zone?

A second step toward torture occurred on December 28, 2002, when two attorneys in the Justice Department concluded that the "great weight" of legal authority indicated that a federal district court "could not probably exercise habeas jurisdiction" over noncitizens detained at Guantánamo.[34] The underlying message: little reason to worry about judicial scrutiny if U.S. interrogators decided to treat detainees inhumanely.

The Justice Department attorneys did not invent a new strategy. Over the centuries, other countries chose to place "enemies" at locations where courts supposedly could not reach them. That technique led to the Habeas Corpus Act of 1679. Parliament impeached the Earl of Clarendon, Lord High Chancellor of England, for imprisoning the king's subjects "in remote islands, garrisons, and other places, thereby to prevent them from the benefit of the law, and to produce precedents for the imprisoning any other of his majesty's subjects

---

32. 151 Cong. Rec. S8791 (daily ed. July 25, 2005).

33. Id. at S8794–96. See also Josh White, "Military Lawyers Fought Policy on Interrogations," Washington Post, July 15, 2005, at A1.

34. Memorandum for William J. Haynes II, General Counsel, Department of Defense, from Patrick F. Philbin, Deputy Assistant Attorney General, and John C. Yoo, Deputy Assistant Attorney General, December 28, 2001, at 1.

in like manner."[35] A bill to prevent the transportation of English subjects "beyond the sea" (outside judicial reach) was reported from committee and given a hearing before the Commons. Lawmakers who feared the legislation would undermine the Crown's power were rebutted by this warning: "He that is sent to Jersey or Guernsey, may be sent to Tangier, and so never know what his crimes are, and no *Habeas Corpus* can reach him. All convictions must be by a Plebian Jury, which now they cannot have. . . . [I]t does not take away the King's power at all, but secures the subject."[36]

The bill, barely clearing the House in 1670 by a vote of 100 to 99, did not survive the Lords. The Commons continued to debate and pass legislation to protect subjects held outside the country. Each time the Lords blocked final action. Finally, in 1679, the bill cleared Parliament with this name: "An Act for the better secureing the Liberty of the Subject and for Prevention of Imprisonments beyond the Seas."[37] Several sections of the statute provide habeas rights to individuals held on the islands of Jersey and Guernsey, in Scotland and Ireland, "or Places beyond the Seas . . . within or without the Dominions of His Majestie."[38] The statute covered the King's "Subjects." Sections relating to "illegall Imprisonments in Prisons beyond the Seas" applied to "Subject of this Realme" or to any persons who resided "in this Realme."

Do Treaties and Statutes Bind the President?

Step three toward torture appeared in another OLC memo, offering forty-two pages of analysis to conclude that international treaties and federal laws do not apply to al Qaeda and Taliban detainees.[39] It was this OLC analysis that Gonzales, in his letter to Bush, regarded as "definitive." And it was on the basis of this OLC opinion that Attorney General John Ashcroft wrote to Bush on February 1, 2002, describing different ways of shielding U.S. interrogators from possible criminal prosecutions. If Bush determined that Afghanistan was a "failed state" and therefore unable to be a party to the Geneva Conventions, the treaty's protections would not apply and "various legal risks of liability,

35. 6 Howell's State Trials 330 (1816). See William F. Duker, A Constitutional History of Habeas Corpus 53 (1980).

36. Duker, A Constitutional History of Habeas Corpus, at 53.

37. Habeas Corpus Act of 1679, 31 Car. 2, c. 2.

38. Id., sec. 11. See also sections 10 and 15.

39. Memorandum for William J. Haynes II, General Counsel, Department of Defense, from John Yoo, Deputy Assistant Attorney General, and Robert J. Delahunty, Special Counsel, January 9, 2002.

litigation, and criminal prosecutions are minimized."[40] A President's determination of a treaty "would provide the highest assurance" that no court would hear charges that American military and civilian officials violated Geneva Convention rules relating to the conduct and interrogation of detainees." Ashcroft advised Bush that the War Crimes Act of 1996 "makes violation of parts of the Geneva Convention a crime in the United States."[41]

If the Bush administration intended to treat detainees "humanely," why this effort by top administration officials to demonstrate that federal courts would have no jurisdiction to hear grievances from detainees? Why Ashcroft's concern that interrogation officials might face criminal prosecution and suggestions about how to minimize that possibility? What kinds of interrogation techniques did the administration have in mind?

The Bybee Memo

The final step in justifying torture was a fifty-page memo sent from OLC head Jay Bybee to Gonzales. As with many legal memos, it is not written with overwhelming grace or clarity, but the purpose was never in doubt. The administration decided to invite the abuse and torture of detainees and wanted to supply full legal protection for those involved.

Dated August 1, 2002, Bybee first addressed the meaning of the U.S. statute that implements the Convention Against Torture and Other Cruel, Inhuman, and Degrading Treatment or Punishment (CAT). The statute defines torture as an act committed by a person "acting under the color of law specifically intended to inflict severe physical and mental pain or suffering (other than pain or suffering incidental to lawful sanctions) upon another person within his custody or physical control." The phrase "severe mental pain or suffering" meant the prolonged mental harm caused by or resulting from

(A) the intentional infliction or threatened infliction of severe physical pain or suffering, (B) the administration or application, or threatened administration or application, of mind-altering substances or other procedures calculated to disrupt profoundly the senses or the personality, (C) the threat of imminent death, and (D) the threat that another person will imminently be subject to death, severe

40. Letter from Ashcroft to Bush, February 1, 2002, at 1. In this letter, Ashcroft refers to a Supreme Court decision in Clark v. Allen, 331 U.S. 503 (1947), to conclude that when the President makes a determination about a treaty, it becomes a political question, which a court will not decide. Yoo and Delahunty had cited that case in their memo to Haynes.

41. Id. at 1.

physical pain or suffering, or the administration or application of mind-altering substances or other procedures calculated to disrupt profoundly the sense or personality.[42]

The statute applies to actions by U.S. individuals "outside the United States" and includes fines and imprisonment for not more than twenty years, unless death results from conduct prohibited by the statute. In that case, punishment can be death or imprisonment for any term of years or for life.[43]

Those penalties prompted the Justice Department to develop legal doctrines to shield abusive U.S. interrogators. Bybee advised Gonzales that for an act to constitute torture as defined by the statute "it must inflict pain that is difficult to endure." Bybee offered this understanding of physical pain: "Physical pain amounting to torture must be equivalent in intensity to the pain accompanying serious physical injury, such as organ failure, impairment of bodily function, or even death."[44] Those definitions of extreme pain are not drawn from the torture statute. Bybee borrowed them from statutes that have nothing to do with torture or interrogation. He relied on statutes that define an emergency medical condition for the purpose of providing health benefits.[45] Through this analysis he concluded that American interrogators may inflict physical pain provided it does not result in organ failure, impairment of bodily function, or death.

To protect interrogators from prosecution, Bybee looked at the statutory meaning of "specifically intended." For an interrogator to act with specific intent, "he must expressly intend to achieve the forbidden act." The infliction of pain "must be the defendant's precise objective." If an interrogator acted knowing that severe pain or suffering was "reasonably likely to result from his action, but no more, he would have acted only with general intent" rather than specific intent.[46] Through this reasoning, even if an interrogator knew that severe pain would result from his actions, "if causing such harm is not his objective, he lacks the requisite specific intent even though the defendant did not act in good faith. Instead, a defendant is guilty of torture only if he acts with the express purpose of inflicting severe pain or suffering on a person within his custody or physical control."[47]

---

42. 18 U.S.C. § 2340 (2000).

43. Id. at § 2340A.

44. Memorandum from Bybee to Gonzales, "Re: Standards of Conduct for Interrogation under 18 U.S.C. §§ 2340–2340A," August 1, 2002, at 1 (hereafter "Bybee Memo").

45. Id. at 5–6.

46. Id. at 3–4.

47. Id. at 4.

Bybee offered other interpretations to shield U.S. interrogators engaged in abusive techniques. In trying to eliminate the fear of prosecution, he also removed legal limits, personal accountability, and previous standards of official conduct. Under Bybee's reading, if the objective of an American interrogator was to pry loose intelligence from a detainee and the questioning inflicted severe pain or suffering, the interrogator had not violated the torture statute or any treaty. The severe pain or suffering was merely incidental, not the principal or intended purpose.

Bybee applied the same analysis to mental pain or suffering. To commit torture, an interrogator "must specifically intend to cause prolonged mental harm." The interrogator "could negate a showing of specific intent to cause severe mental pain or suffering by showing that he had acted in good faith that his conduct would not amount to the acts prohibited by the statute." If the interrogator "has a good faith belief that his actions will not result in prolonged mental harm, he lacks the mental state necessary for his actions to constitute torture," even if in fact the detainee suffers from prolonged mental harm.[48] Bybee's legal reasoning drained anti-torture statutes and treaties of meaning and enforcement value.

Another method of diluting the meaning of the torture statute was to look at the ratification history of the Convention Against Torture (CAT). Bybee said that the Reagan administration took the position that CAT "reached only the most heinous act." What was the source of the word "heinous"? The Reagan administration had adopted this interpretation: "The United States understands that, in order to constitute torture, an act must be a deliberate and calculated act of an extremely cruel and inhuman nature, specifically intended to inflict excruciating and agonizing physical or mental pain or suffering."[49] The Reagan administration distinguished torture from "lesser forms of cruel, inhuman, or degrading treatment or punishment, which are to be deplored and prevented, but are not so universally and categorically condemned as to warrant the severe legal consequences that the Convention provides in cases of torture."[50] Bybee concluded that CAT "was intended to proscribe only the most egregious conduct" and that its text, ratification history, and negotiating history "all confirm that Section 2340A reaches only the most heinous acts."[51]

Bybee suggested other ways of limiting anti-torture statutes and treaties. One was his interpretation of the President's authority under Article II as

48. Id. at 8.
49. Id. at 16.
50. Id. at 17.
51. Id. at 22.

Commander in Chief. Even if an interrogator arguably violated the torture statute, the statute would be unconstitutional "if it impermissibly encroached on the President's constitutional power to conduct a military campaign." As Commander in Chief, the President "has the constitutional authority to order interrogations of enemy combatants to gain intelligence information concerning the military plans of the enemy."[52] Because this power, as interpreted by Bybee, comes from the Constitution, no statute or treaty could limit it.

Following this reasoning, if an American interrogator flatly violated the torture statute by committing "heinous" acts, the Justice Department could decide not to prosecute the person because the abuse was justified by the President's constitutional power as Commander in Chief. It is quite true that codes of modern warfare, designed to make war less brutal, always recognized that military commanders needed flexibility to win wars. But there were limits even to the principle of military necessity.[53] Bybee recognized no limits with his expansive interpretation of the Commander in Chief Clause.

One last card remained to be played: a list of defenses Bybee thought might be useful to U.S. interrogators who faced prosecution and punishment. Probably no other Justice Department document attempts to advise the accused how best to defend themselves in court. Bybee, however, suggested that certain "justification defenses might be available that would potentially eliminate criminal liability." Standard criminal law defenses, ranging from necessity to self-defense, "could justify interrogation methods needed to elicit information to prevent a direct and imminent threat to the United States and its citizens."[54] Bybee understood that the administration wanted to allow abusive methods of interrogation, and it was his assignment to remove prosecution as a likely or successful threat.

Working Groups

OLC supplied a legal framework for the Defense Department "working groups": officials from different agencies called together to hammer out final administration policy. A Defense Department memo of October 11, 2002, discussed "more aggressive interrogation techniques than the ones presently used" at Guantánamo. Those techniques "may be required in order to obtain information from detainees that are resisting interrogation efforts and

52. Id. at 31.
53. Fisher, *Military Tribunals and Presidential Power*, at 75–77.
54. Bybee Memo, at 39.

are suspected of having significant information essential to national security." The memo states that the detainees at Guantánamo "are not protected by the Geneva Conventions (GC),"[55] even though the Bush memo of February 7, 2002, concluded that the Taliban would be covered by Geneva, at least "at this time."

On January 15, 2003, Defense Secretary Rumsfeld directed his general counsel to establish a Working Group within the department "to assess the legal, policy, and operational issues relating to the interrogation of detainees held by the U.S. Armed Forces in the war on terrorism."[56] His memo was issued before the March 2003 military operations against Iraq, but its scope was broad enough to cover all detainees in Guantánamo, Afghanistan, Iraq, or other locations.

When the report of the Working Group was released, first as a draft on March 6, 2003, and later as a final report completed on April 4, 2003, the impact of Bybee's memo was evident. The reports of the Working Group were organized to cover the Geneva Conventions, CAT, interpretations about "specifically intended," the Commander in Chief Clause, and access by a U.S. interrogator to the doctrines of necessity and self-defense.[57] Both reports stated that the torture statute "does not apply to the conduct of U.S. personnel" at Guantámamo. Both interpret the torture statute as not applying "to the President's detention and interrogation of enemy combatants pursuant to his Commander-in-Chief authority."[58] The April 4 report describes a number of authorized interrogation techniques that would later appear in photos from Abu Ghraib, including hooding and nudity. Clothing could be removed, "to be done by military police if not agreed to by the subject." Nudity creates "a feeling of helplessness and dependence." Anxiety could be increased in various ways, including the "simple presence of [a] dog without directly threatening action."[59]

55. Department of Defense, "Legal Brief on Proposed Counter-Resistance Strategies," Memorandum for Commander, Joint Task Force 170, JTF 170-SJA, October 11, 2002, at 1 (paragraphs 1 and 2), declassified June 21, 2004.

56. Office of the Secretary of Defense, "Detainee Interrogations," Memorandum for the General Counsel of the Department of Defense, January 15, 2003, declassified June 21, 2004.

57. "Working Group Report on Detainee Interrogations in the Global War on Terrorism: Assessment of Legal, Historical, Policy, and Operational Considerations," March 6, 2003 (Draft); "Working Group Report on Detainee Interrogations in the Global War on Terrorism: Assessment of Legal, Historical, Policy, and Operational Considerations," April 4, 2003 (Final Report).

58. Page 7 of March 6 draft; page 8 of April 4 report.

59. Pages 64–65 of April 4 report.

The April 4 report anticipated political damage if abusive treatment became public: "Should information regarding the use of more aggressive interrogation techniques than have been used traditionally by U.S. forces become public, it is likely to be exaggerated or distorted in the U.S. and international media accounts, and may produce an adverse effect on support for the war on terrorism."[60] Participation by U.S. military personnel in aggressive interrogations "would constitute a significant departure from traditional U.S. military norms and could have an adverse impact on the cultural self-image of U.S. military forces."[61]

ABU GHRAIB

In April 2004, three national security cases reached the Supreme Court for oral argument: the Hamdi and Padilla cases (involving U.S. citizens) and the issue of holding detainees at Guantánamo. During the Hamdi argument, Justice Stevens asked Deputy Solicitor General Paul Clement whether he thought there was "anything in the law that curtails the method of interrogation that may be employed." Clement assured the Court that safeguards existed. The United States was "signatory to conventions that prohibit torture and that sort of thing. And the United States is going to honor its treaty obligations."[62] To Clement, drawing on the experience of those who actually conduct interrogations, "the last thing you want to do is torture somebody or try to do something along those lines."[63] Using coercion to get information leaves one wondering "about the reliability of the information you were getting." The lessons drawn from interrogators is that the way to "get the best information from individuals is that you interrogate them, you try to develop a relationship of trust."[64]

During the Padilla oral argument, Justices continued to ask about the torture of detainees. Clement said that the President should be free to use "traditional authority to make discretionary judgments" in deciding what is the necessary appropriate force for military actions, as in Afghanistan. He coun-

---

60. Id. at 69.

61. Id. For a review of the drafting of the OLC and Working Group memos, see Jane Mayer, "The Memo," New Yorker, February 27, 2006, at 32–41.

62. U.S. Supreme Court, Hamdi v. Rumsfeld, oral argument, April 28, 2004, at 48–49.

63. Id. at 50.

64. Id.

seled against "judicial management of the executive's war-making power."[65] One of the Justices said that "if the law is what the executive says it is, whatever is necessary and appropriate in the executive's judgment," the result would be an "executive, unchecked by the judiciary." Under those circumstances, "what is it that would be a check against torture?" Clement replied: "Well, first of all, there are treaty obligations." Moreover, if a U.S. military person committed a war crime "on a harmless, you know, detained enemy combatant or a prisoner of war," the government would put the soldier or officer on trial in a court-martial.[66]

The Court wanted to know from Clement what would happen if the President or executive officials said that mild torture would be helpful in extracting information. What would constrain such conduct? "Is it just up to the good will of the executive? Is there a judicial check?" Having earlier referred to treaty constraints and the understanding of interrogators that torture is ineffective in getting reliable information, Clement now discouraged any judicial interference with presidential decisions. The fact that executive discretion during war "can be abused is not a good and sufficient reason for judicial micromanagement and overseeing of that authority." In time of war "you have to trust the executive to make the kind of quintessential military judgments that are involved in things like that."[67]

Knowing what was in the Bybee Memo and in the draft and final report of the Working Group, it is extraordinary to hear Clement at oral argument talk about treaty obligations as binding, that experienced interrogators know that torture is unnecessary and self-defeating, and that any interrogator who violated the torture statute or committed war crimes would stand trial before a court-martial. One wing of the Justice Department (OLC) seemed wholly disconnected with another (the SG's office). After Clement concluded his oral argument, that evening photos of U.S. abuse of detainees held at the Abu Ghraib prison in Iraq began to be broadcast on the CBS News program "60 Minutes."[68]

The U.S. military had already begun an inquiry into these abuses. An investigation initiated on January 19, 2004, led to the appointment of Maj. Gen.

65. U.S. Supreme Court, Rumsfeld v. Padilla, oral argument, April 28, 2004, at 17.

66. Id. at 22.

67. Id. at 23.

68. "Photos Show U.S. Troops Abusing Iraqi Prisoners," Los Angeles Times, April 29, 2004, at A4; James Risen, "G.I.'s Are Accused of Abusing Iraqi Captives," New York Times, April 29, 2004, at A13; "Photographs Reveal Atrocities by U.S. Soldiers," Washington Times, April 29, 2004, at A5.

Antonio M. Taguba, whose report began circulating on Web sites in early May. He described "numerous incidents of sadistic, blatant, and wanton criminal abuses" inflicted on detainees, referring to the abuses as "systemic and illegal."[69] Several American soldiers had committed "egregious acts and grave breaches of international law."[70] His report detailed such actions as keeping detainees naked for several days at a time, a male military police guard having sex with a female detainee, using unmuzzled dogs to intimidate and terrify detainees, and sodomizing a detainee with a chemical light and perhaps a broomstick.[71]

Taguba's report, although rich in detail and professional analysis, was limited to the 800th Military Police Brigade and the Abu Ghraib prison. He did not cover abuses in other prisons in Iraq and Afghanistan. Nor was there an effort to examine criminal conduct outside the MP brigade, particularly commanders at a high level and civilian officials in the executive branch who might have known about the incidents, condoned them, and approved the political and legal theories that justified abusive interrogations. Most criminal charges after Abu Ghraib were filed against enlisted men and women from a reserve unit. Although evidence suggested that military intelligence officers played a key role in the abuses, the initial round of criminal charges did not target them.

General Taguba paid a price for his probity and integrity, forced into retirement in January 2007 because he had been "overzealous."[72] He said that some evidence of abuse toward prisoners at Abu Ghraib had not been made public, including a videotape of a male soldier in uniform sodomizing a female detainee.[73] Taguba found evidence of abuse by other units, including military intelligence and the CIA.[74] He became convinced that the American guards at Abu Ghraib had not abused prisoners on their own initiative. "Somebody was giving them guidance, but I was legally prevented from further investigation into higher authority. I was limited to a box."[75] He said that abusive interrogation methods used in Guantánamo had been transported to Iraq by Maj. Gen.

69. Article 15–6 Investigation of the 800th Military Police Brigade, at 16.

70. Id. at 50.

71. Id. at 16–17. The Taguba Report is reprinted in Danner, Torture and Truth: America, Abu Ghraib, and the War on Terror.

72. David S. Cloud, "General Says Prison Inquiry Led to His Forced Retirement," New York Times, June 17, 2007, at 10.

73. Id. See also Josh White and Amy Goldstein, "Abu Ghraib Investigator Points to Pentagon," Washington Post, June 17, 2007, at A7.

74. Seymour M. Hersh, "The General's Report," New Yorker, June 25, 2007, at 63.

75. Id. at 61.

Geoffrey Miller, previously commander at the naval base.[76] Documentary re-cords are now available to demonstrate the deliberate planning of torture by Bush administration officials.[77]

Following Taguba's report, several other investigations of Abu Ghraib and other prisons were conducted, including those by former Secretary of Defense James R. Schlesinger and Maj. Gen. George R. Fay. Their reports, written at a high level of generality, stayed largely clear of assigning blame or account-ability to military officers or civilian leaders.[78] The Schlesinger panel said it "did not have full access to information involving the role of the Central Intel-ligence Agency in detention operations."[79] It concluded that Lt. Gen. Ricardo Sanchez, the overall commander in Iraq, "should have taken stronger action in November when he realized the extent of the leadership problems at Abu Ghraib."[80]

In his February 2002 memo, President Bush decided that the Geneva Conventions applied to the Taliban but not to al Qaeda. Nevertheless, White House Counsel Gonzales in a May 15, 2004, op-ed piece stated that Iraq was a party to the Geneva Conventions and that the United States "recognizes that these treaties are binding in the war for the liberation of Iraq." He said there "has never been any suggestion by our government that the conventions do not apply in that conflict." Responding to news reports that questioned the U.S. commitment to the treaties, he wrote: "make no mistake that the United States is bound to observe the rules of war in the Geneva Conventions."[81] If the treaties are binding, why did top officials in the administration prepare legal memos and policy papers repeatedly insisting that the Commander in Chief Clause trumps statutes and treaties?

The shoddy quality of administration legal analysis, combined with world condemnation of U.S. conduct at Abu Ghraib and other prisons, forced the White House to revisit Bybee's memo. At a press briefing on June 22, 2004, Gonzales and three other executive officials met with reporters to clarify ad-ministration policy. He said that to the extent that some of the documents "in the context of interrogations, explored broad legal theories, including legal

76. Id. at 63–65.

77. Jameel Jaffer and Amrit Singh, Administration of Torture: A Documentary Record from Washington to Abu Ghraib and Beyond (2007).

78. Danner, Torture and Truth, at 329–79.

79. Id. at 331.

80. Id. at 338.

81. Albert R. Gonzales, "The Rule of Law and the Rules of War," New York Times, May 15, 2004, at A27.

theories about the scope of the President's power as Commander-in-Chief, some of their discussion, quite frankly, is irrelevant and unnecessary to support any action taken by the President." If "over-broad discussions" and "abstract legal theories" invited misinterpretation, they could be replaced "with more concrete guidance addressing only those issues necessary for the legal analysis of actual practices."[82]

Two points. Gonzales did not repudiate the Bybee Memo, including the Commander in Chief argument. Some passages were simply not necessary, too easy to misread, and possibly too abstract and broad. In that sense, the Bybee Memo was put on the shelf, not nullified. Second, Gonzales did not rule out abusive interrogations. He expressly said that his briefing "does not include CIA activities."[83] One of the reporters asked: "Are we wrong to assume then, that the CIA is not subject to these categories of interrogation technique?" Gonzales decided not "to get into questions related to the CIA."[84] His response implied that the administration agreed to new restrictions on military interrogations but adopted a different—and more generous—standard for the CIA. Later developments underscored that the CIA could do what the military could not.

At the end of 2004, the OLC issued a new memo to replace what Bybee had written. Signed by Daniel Levin, the first two sentences are straightforward: "Torture is abhorrent both to American law and values and to international norms. This universal repudiation of torture is reflected in our criminal law, for example, 18 U.S.C. §§ 2340–2340A; international agreements, exemplified by the United Nations Convention Against Torture (the 'CAT'); customary international law; centuries of Anglo-American law; and the long-standing policy of the United States, repeatedly and recently reaffirmed by the President."[85] Levin's memo "supersedes the August 2002 Memorandum in its entirety."[86] Withdrawing and replacing the Bybee Memo was not the same as repudiating it and its interpretations of presidential power. Levin, unlike Bybee, did indicate his respect for statutory policy on torture: "We must, of course, give effect to the statute as enacted by Congress."[87] As explained later

---

82. Id.

83. Id. at 4.

84. Id.

85. Office of Legal Counsel, U.S. Department of Justice, Memorandum for James B. Comey, Deputy Attorney General, "Re: Legal Standards Applicable Under 18 U.S.C. §§ 2340–2340A, December 30, 2004," at 1 (citations omitted).

86. Id. at 2.

87. Id. at 4. For background on the rewriting of OLC memos, see Jack Goldsmith, The Terror Presidency: Law and Judgment Inside the Bush Administration (2007).

in this chapter, many of Bybee's constitutional theories resurfaced a year later when Congress decided to pass new legislation on torture.

ROUND ONE: *RASUL*

In OLC memos, the administration argued that the U.S. naval base in Guantánamo was outside the United States and therefore beyond the jurisdiction of federal judges to hear cases brought by detainees. That legal theory prevailed on July 30, 2002, when District Judge Colleen Kollar-Kotelly ruled that the detainees held at the naval base were outside the sovereign territory of the United States and they could not use federal courts to pursue petitions for habeas relief.[88] She relied heavily on a 1950 decision by the Supreme Court that was not on all fours with the facts at Guantánamo. The Court in *Johnson* v. *Eisentrager* (1950) noted that aliens within the country have a number of rights, including access to federal courts, and those rights expand as they declare an intent to become a U.S. citizen. Judge Kollar-Kotelly said it was "undisputed that the individuals held at Guantanamo Bay do not seek to become citizens."[89] To her, the essential point was not that the detainees at the naval base were enemy aliens, but they were aliens held outside the territory over which the United States was sovereign.[90] However, unlike the detainees at the naval base, the individuals in *Eisentrager* had been charged, tried, and found guilty.

The United States occupies the naval base under a lease entered into with the Cuban government in 1903. The lease provides: "While on the one hand the United States recognizes the continuance of the ultimate sovereignty of the Republic of Cuba over [the military base at Guantanamo Bay], on the other hand the Republic of Cuba consents that during the period of occupancy by the United States of said areas under the terms of this agreement the United States shall exercise complete jurisdiction and control over and within said areas. . . ."[91] The United States therefore possessed jurisdiction but not sovereignty.

The D.C. Circuit agreed with Judge Kollar-Kotelly that *Eisentrager* had been correctly cited for the principle that the detainees at Guantánamo could not seek habeas relief in federal court.[92] Several cases in the Ninth Circuit

---

88. Rasul v. Bush, 215 F.Supp.2d 55 (D.D.C. 2002).
89. Id. at 66.
90. Id. at 69.
91. Id. at 69 n.14.
92. Al Odah v. United States, 321 F.3d 1134 (D.C. Cir. 2003).

explored the right of the detainees to file a habeas petition.[93] In one of those cases, the Ninth Circuit rejected the legal doctrine that the government could put detainees in a black hole in Cuba outside the reach of courts. It denied that the executive branch possessed "unchecked authority" to imprison persons indefinitely (foreign citizens included) on territory under the sole jurisdiction and control of the United States, without giving them access to some kind of judicial forum and legal counsel.[94] The Ninth Circuit decided that *Eisentrager* did not control the case of the detainees held at Guantánamo. The important factor was not "sovereignty" but rather "territorial jurisdiction."[95]

The Supreme Court did not take the Ninth Circuit case but did agree to hear the consolidated cases out of the D.C. Circuit (*Rasul* and *Al Odah*). When the case was argued on April 20, 2004, matters did not go well for the administration. John J. Gibbons, for the detainees, told the Justices that officials from the executive branch "assert that their actions are absolutely immune from judicial examination whenever they elected to detain foreign nationals outside our borders."[96] Did it make a difference if the administration detained foreign nationals versus U.S. citizens? The habeas statute is not limited to U.S. citizens. With certain exceptions, the writ of habeas corpus extends to a "prisoner."[97]

Several Justices were uncomfortable about the scope of power sought by the administration. Justice Breyer flagged two problems. The first: "It seems rather contrary to an idea of a Constitution with three branches that the executive would be free to do whatever they want, whatever they want without a check." The second: "several hundred years of British history" interpreting habeas corpus ran contrary to the administration's claim of power.[98] For Justices who believed that relief to the detainees was barred by the 1950 decision, Gibbons disagreed. He pointed to several distinctions. *Eisentrager* covered admitted enemy aliens who had received a hearing before a military tribunal. The detainees at Guantánamo did not admit to being enemy aliens and had never received a hearing.[99] When *Eisentrager* came up during oral argument, Justices said they found it "a hard opinion to fathom," a "very

---

93. Coalition of Clergy v. Bush, 189 F.Supp.2d 1036 (C.D. Cal. 2002); Coalition of Clergy, Lawyers, & Professors v. Bush, 310 F.3d 1153 (9th Cir. 2002); Gherebi v. Bush, 262 F.Supp.2d 1064 (C.D. Cal. 2003); Gheribi v. Bush, 352 F.3d 1278 (9th Cir. 2003).

94. Gheribi v. Bush, 352 F.3d at 1283.

95. Id. at 1287–88, 1289–90.

96. U.S. Supreme Court, Rasul v. Bush, oral argument, April 20, 2004, at 3.

97. 28 U.S.C. § 2241(c) (2000).

98. U.S. Supreme Court, Rasul v. Bush, oral argument, April 20, 2004, at 42.

99. Id. at 9.

difficult decision to understand," and "ambiguous and not clearly determinative."[100]

Toward the end of oral argument, Solicitor General Ted Olson offered a position the Court rejected. On the issue of whether the naval base was outside the jurisdiction of U.S. federal courts, he said that the "question of sovereignty is a political decision. It would be remarkable for the judiciary to start deciding where the United States is sovereign and where the United States has control."[101] It would be even more remarkable for the administration to exclusively decide that question, allowing alien detainees in the continental United States (and Hawaii) to have some rights while keeping others offshore in a law-free zone. Olson compared the situation of the naval base to detainees "in a field of combat where there are prisons in Afghanistan where we have complete control with respect to the circumstances." Justices found the analogy strained and unconvincing, noting that Afghanistan "is not a place where American law is, and for a century, has customarily been applied to all aspects of life," as was the case with the naval base.[102]

On June 28, 2004, in a 6 to 3 decision, the Court rejected *Eisentrager* as an automatic bar on detainee access to a habeas petition. It ruled that federal courts have jurisdiction to consider challenges to the legality of detaining foreign nationals captured abroad, in connection with hostilities, and held at Guantánamo. Writing for the majority, Justice Stevens summarized six key facts about *Eisentrager*. The prisoners were (1) enemy aliens, (2) had never been or resided in the United States, (3) were captured outside U.S. territory and held there in military custody as a POW, (4) were tried and convicted by a military tribunal sitting outside the United States, (5) were tried and convicted for offenses against laws of war committed outside the United States, and (6) were at all times imprisoned outside the United States. By contrast, the detainees at Guantánamo were not nationals of countries at war with the United States, had denied being engaged in or plotting acts of aggression against the United States, were never afforded access to any tribunal or even charged with or convicted of wrongdoing, and for two years had been detained in a territory over which the United States exercised exclusive jurisdiction and control.[103]

Relying on a 1973 Court decision, Stevens observed that a prisoner's presence within the territorial jurisdiction of a federal district court is not "an invariable prerequisite" to the exercise of district court jurisdiction under

100. Id. at 30–31, 44.
101. Id. at 51.
102. Id. at 52.
103. Rasul v. Bush, 542 U.S. 466, 475–76 (2004).

the habeas statute, and that a district court properly acts within its jurisdiction as long as "the custodian [of the detainee] can be reached by service of process."[104] Nothing in *Eisentrager* or any other case, Stevens said, "categorically excludes aliens detained in military custody outside the United States from the 'privilege of litigation' in U.S. courts." Federal courts, he maintained, "have traditionally been open to nonresident aliens."[105] In a concurrence, Kennedy agreed that Guantánamo was "in every practical respect a United States territory" and expressed concern that the detainees at the naval base were "being held indefinitely, and without benefit of any legal proceeding to determine their status."[106]

Scalia's dissent, joined by Rehnquist and Thomas, claimed that the majority "overrules *Eisentrager*" even though Stevens had taken pains to show how several elements of *Eisentrager* differed from the detainees held at the naval base.[107] For Scalia, the fact that the detainees "are not located within the territorial jurisdiction of any federal district court" should be "the end of these cases."[108] He believed that the President as Commander in Chief "and his subordinates had every reason to expect that the internment of combatants at Guantanamo Bay would not have the consequence of bringing the cumbersome machinery of our domestic courts into military affairs."[109]

ROUND TWO: *HAMDAN*

The administration responded to *Rasul* by establishing a Combatant Status Review Tribunal (CSRT). A panel of three military officers, who had nothing to do with the capture of a detainee or with interrogation procedures, would provide a hearing for each detainee. For the first time, detainees at the naval base were given notice to explain the grounds for their detention and had an opportunity to challenge their designation as enemy combatant. Each detainee would have a "personal representative"—a military officer, not a lawyer—with access to information in DOD files on the detainee's background. The detainee could appear before the panel to present evidence and call witnesses if

104. Id. at 478–79.
105. Id. at 484.
106. Id. at 487–88.
107. Id. at 497.
108. Id. at 490.
109. Id. at 506.

"reasonably available."[110] The administration had no obligation to share with the detainee classified evidence used to designate him an enemy combatant.

It should not have taken a Supreme Court ruling to initiate these elementary procedures. The administration knew it had picked up detainees from Afghanistan and other countries under suspect conditions, often relying on informants who could have made mistakes or might have had financial incentives to falsely label someone Taliban or al Qaeda. Not being told who made the accusation against them, detainees were in no position to know whether information about them flowed from malice, vengeance, or ignorance. The administration acknowledged that many of the detainees at the naval base should never have been apprehended and began releasing large numbers.

While the status review panels did their work, the administration began hearings for those who had already been designated as enemy combatants and therefore eligible to be tried by military tribunal. One of the tribunals involved Salim Ahmed Hamdan, whose case would wind through the federal judiciary and eventually reach the Supreme Court in 2006. Rules adopted for the proceedings allowed witnesses to testify anonymously for the prosecution. It was unclear how the tribunal would judge whether evidence or testimony could have been obtained by coercion.[111]

Detainee Treatment Act

Photos from Abu Ghraib and reports of torture at Guantánamo and other U.S. facilities pressured Congress to pass legislation to prohibit (once again) cruel and inhumane treatment of detainees held by the United States. Beyond humanitarian concerns, some administration officials understood that bringing detention policies into conformity with international law standards would strengthen the fight against terrorism. Islamic extremists used reports of detainee abuse to recruit new members. Others in the administration, including Vice President Dick Cheney, strongly opposed any softening of interrogation methods.[112]

Senator John McCain, subjected to years of torture during his imprisonment in North Vietnam, took the lead in drafting remedial legislation. His

110. Department of Defense, News Transcript, "Defense Department Background Briefing on the Combatant Status Review Tribunal," July 7, 2004, at 1–2.

111. Neil A. Lewis, "U.S. Terrorism Tribunals Set to Begin Work," New York Times, August 22, 2004, at 17.

112. Tim Golden and Eric Schmitt, "Detainee Policy Sharply Divides Bush Officials," New York Times, November 2, 2005, at A1.

amendment, to bar all U.S. government agencies from "cruel, inhuman, or degrading" treatment of detainees, passed the Senate by a vote of 90 to 9.[113] The size of that margin convinced the administration to drop its threat of a presidential veto and begin negotiations.[114] President Bush endorsed the amendment after McCain agreed to add language giving civilian interrogators legal protections already afforded to military interrogators.[115]

McCain's efforts produced the Detainee Treatment Act (DTA) of 2005. No individual in the custody of the U.S. government, "regardless of nationality or physical location, shall be subject to cruel, inhuman, or degrading treatment or punishment."[116] The statute sent a mixed signal by specifying certain defenses for U.S. personnel prosecuted for their interrogations and providing counsel to represent them.[117] The statute placed some limits on detainee access to federal courts through habeas action.[118] The law appeared to allow U.S. agencies to transfer persons to other countries for "cruel, inhuman, or degrading treatment or punishment" if such persons are not technically in U.S. custody. (The practice of "extraordinary rendition" is covered in Chapter 10.)

In signing the bill, President Bush created considerable doubt about his willingness to carry out the law. In one statement, he said he would construe the DTA "in a manner consistent with the constitutional authority of the President to supervise the unitary executive branch and as Commander in Chief and consistent with the constitutional limitations on the judicial power."[119] With most signing statements, one can determine whether the President carried out the law as written. With interrogations, no one knows unless they are present in the room.

A second statement by Bush seemed to embrace the purpose of the legislation. On closer inspection, he insisted on adopting his own meaning. He said his administration "is committed to treating all detainees held by the United States in a manner consistent with our Constitution, laws, and treaty obliga-

---

113. Charles Babington and Shailagh Murray, "Senate Supports Interrogation Limits," Washington Post, October 6, 2005, at A1.

114. "White House Eases Hard-Line Stance," Los Angeles Times, December 4, 2005, at A9.

115. Josh White, "President Relents, Backs Torture Ban," Washington Post, December 16, 2005, at A1.

116. 119 Stat. 2739, sec. 1003(a) (2005).

117. Id. at 2740, sec. 1004.

118. Id. at 2741–42, sec. 1005(e).

119. 41 Weekly Comp. of Pres. Doc. 1919 (2005).

tions, which reflect the values we hold dear."[120] Notice the choice of "consistent with" rather than "in compliance with." The first is policy; the second is law. The next two sentences: "Our policy has also been not to use cruel, inhuman, or degrading treatment, at home or abroad. This legislation now makes that a matter of statute for practices abroad." The statement concludes: "I will continue to work with the Congress to ensure that the United States can effectively fight the war on terror while upholding its commitment to the rule of law."[121] The rule of law means that the President will carry out the law as enacted by Congress and not—through a signing statement—convert statutory law into discretionary administration policy.

The Court's Decision

On June 29, 2006, the Supreme Court in *Hamdan* v. *Rumsfeld* clarified a number of legal issues about military tribunals. The Bush administration had argued that "inherent" powers available to the President under Article II included full authority to create military commissions. For the Justice Department, presidential power under Article II "includes the inherent authority to create military commissions even in the absence of any statutory authorization, because that authority is a necessary and longstanding component of his war powers. . . . Throughout our Nation's history, Presidents have exercised their inherent commander-in-chief authority to establish military commissions without any specific authorization from Congress."[122] The administration cited earlier cases for the proposition that the President may determine that the Geneva Conventions do not apply to al Qaeda in Afghanistan or elsewhere, and that al Qaeda detainees do not qualify as prisoners of war.[123]

In *Hamdan*, the Court held that the type of military commission fashioned by the administration was not authorized by Congress. Existing law, including Article 21 of the Uniform Code of Military Justice (UCMJ), did not provide a mandate to the President to authorize any type of commission he decided to create, nor did the Court find anything in the text or legislative history of the Authorization for Use of Military Force (AUMF) that intended to expand or alter the authorization set forth in Article 21.[124] The Court found nothing

120. Id. at 1920.

121. Id.

122. Brief for Respondents, Hamdan v. Rumsfeld, No. 05–184, Supreme Court of the United States, February 23, 2006, at 21–22.

123. Id. at 38.

124. Hamdan v. Rumsfeld, 126 S.Ct. 2749, 2775 (2006).

in the Detainee Treatment Act to authorize the commission.[125] Through this reasoning the court determined that the administration had transgressed fundamental principles of separation of powers. The type of commission established by the administration "risk[ed] concentrating in military hands a degree of adjudicative and punitive power in excess of that contemplated either by statute or by the Constitution."[126]

The Court ruled that the military commission established under the Bush military order, in terms of its structure and procedures, violated both the UCMJ and the Geneva Conventions.[127] President Bush failed to comply with UCMJ Article 36 because he had made an insufficient determination "to justify variances from the procedures governing courts-martial."[128] Article 36 places two restrictions on the President. No procedural rule he adopts may be "contrary to or inconsistent with" the UCMJ—"however practical it may seem." Second, the rules prescribed by the President must be "uniform insofar as practicable." Any rule adopted for a military commission must be the same as those applied to a court-martial unless the President can show that such uniformity is impracticable. The Court expressed concern that the accused and his civilian counsel "may be excluded from, and precluded from ever learning what evidence was presented during, any part of the proceeding that either the Appointing Authority or the presiding offices decides to close."[129] Moreover, neither "live testimony nor witnesses' written statements need be sworn."[130]

It was not necessary for the administration to follow every procedure established in the UCMJ, but "any departure must be tailored to the exigency that necessitates it."[131] The rules set forth in the Manual for Courts-Martial "must apply to military commission unless impracticable."[132] Nothing in the record before the Court "demonstrate[d] that it would be impracticable to apply court-martial rules in this case."[133] The unwillingness or inability of the administration to demonstrate impracticability "is particularly disturbing when considered in light of the clear and admitted failure to apply one of the most

125. Id.
126. Id. at 2780.
127. Id. at 2791–98.
128. Id. at 2791.
129. Id. at 2786.
130. Id. at 2786–87.
131. Id. at 2790.
132. Id. at 2791.
133. Id. at 2792.

fundamental protections afforded not just by the Manual for Courts-Martial but also by the UCMJ itself: the right to be present."[134]

THE MILITARY COMMISSIONS ACT

The Court's decision forced the administration to seek statutory authority from Congress. *Hamdan* marked a clear and pointed rebuff to the administration's legal and constitutional reasoning, and yet executive officials responded as though no serious deficiencies existed in the structure and procedures they had adopted for military commissions. At congressional hearings, witnesses from the executive branch advised Congress that it need only pass legislation to endorse what the administration had previously stitched together.

The Administration's Bill

At a hearing on July 11, 2006, before the Senate Judiciary Committee, Acting OLC head Steven Bradbury claimed that the Court "did not address the President's constitutional authority and did not reach any constitutional question."[135] In fact, the Court reached (and decided) two constitutional issues. It rejected the administration's argument that the President possessed sufficient authority under Article II and did not need statutory authority from Congress. Second, it decided that Congress had the constitutional authority under Article I to impose on the President the procedural constraints of the UCMJ.

Congressional hearings revealed a major divide between civilian and military lawyers in the administration. Attorneys from the military services objected to the use of evidence derived from hearsay or coercion, the exclusion of defendants from their trials, and allowing classified evidence to be provided to a defense lawyer but not to the defendant.[136] The civilian officials who drafted the new procedures saw no problems with denying defendants the right to confront accusers or even be present at their own trials.[137] To John D. Hutson,

134. Id.

135. "The Supreme Court's Decision in *Hamdan* v. *Rumsfeld*," hearing before the Senate Committee on the Judiciary, 109th Cong. (2006), available at http://judiciary.senate.gov/print_testimony.cfm?id=1986&wit_id=5505.

136. R. Jeffrey Smith, "Top Military Lawyers Oppose Plan for Special Courts," Washington Post, August 3, 2006, at A11.

137. R. Jeffrey Smith, "White House Proposal Would Expand Authority of Military Courts," Washington Post, August 2, 2006, at A4.

the Navy's top uniformed lawyer from 1997 to 2000, the administration's proposed rules allowed the government to tell a detainee: "We know you're guilty. We can't tell you why, but there's a guy, we can't tell you who, who told us something. We can't tell you what, but you're guilty."[138] If evidence is classified and cannot be shown to the defendant, or if an informer cannot be revealed to the accused without sacrificing national interests, one option is for the government to drop the charges based on that information.[139]

At hearings before the Senate Armed Services Committee on August 2, 2006, Senator Lindsey Graham emphasized the importance of reciprocity, which "is the key guiding light for me. Do not do something in this committee that you would not want to happen to our troops." He asked if an American service member were tried in a foreign land, "would we want to have that trial conducted in a fashion that the jury would receive information about the accused's guilt not shared with the accused, and that person be subject to penalty of death?" Providing classified information only to the defense counsel didn't satisfy Graham either, "because I think most lawyers feel an ethical obligation to have information shared with their client."[140]

The Court's ruling in *Hamdan* removed from the backrooms of the administration a military commission process that was supposed to assure "swift justice" but that had been strikingly unsuccessful over a period of five years in ever prosecuting or convicting a single alleged terrorist. One of the prosecutors assigned to the commission charged with trying Salim Ahmed Hamdan called the system "a half hearted and disorganized effort by a skeleton group of inexperienced attorneys to prosecute fairly low-level accused in a process that appears to be rigged."[141] A virtue of a democratic republic is the capacity to deliberate on public policy in the open, forcing executive officials to justify their programs and obtain authority from the legislature. Success is never guaranteed by that process, but it offers more hope and constitutional legitimacy than the unilateral and secretive model pursued by the Bush administration.

138. Id.

139. For comparable options of dropping charges when the administration does not want "state secrets" disclosed, see Louis Fisher, In the Name of National Security: Unchecked Presidential Power and the *Reynolds* Case 230–40 (2006).

140. "The Future of Military Commissions," hearing before the Senate Armed Services Committee, August 2, 2006.

141. "The Supreme Court's Decision in Hamdan v. Rumsfeld," hearings before the Senate Committee on the Judiciary, 109th Cong. (2006), statement by Lt. Com. Charles D. Swift, JAGC, U.S. Navy, available at http://judiciary.senate.gov/print_testimony.cfm?id=1986&wit_id=5510 (the prosecutor was Air Force Capt. John Carr).

Senators tried to understand what types of interrogation techniques would be permitted by the McCain Amendment. Senator Carl Levin asked Attorney General Gonzales whether he believed that the use of testimony obtained through such techniques as "waterboarding, stress positions, intimidating use of military dogs, sleep deprivation, sensory deprivation, [and] forced nudity" would be consistent with Common Article 3. Gonzales said he could not "imagine that such testimony would be reliable, and therefore, I find it unlikely that any military judge would allow such testimony in his evidence."[142] His reply discouraged those techniques only if the administration intended to prosecute a detainee before a military commission.

When the administration's bill (S. 3861) was introduced in the Senate on September 7, it included this language: "The President's authority to convene military commissions arises from the Constitution's vesting in the President of the executive power and the power of the Commander in Chief of the Armed Forces."[143] The administration had presented that position to the Supreme Court in its legal briefs and arguments—a position the Court squarely repudiated. The language on inherent Article II presidential authority was stripped from the bill that became law.

As negotiations continued, it appeared that several Republican Senators would block the bill the administration favored. President Bush "warned defiant Republican Senators" that he would close down a CIA interrogation program if they succeeded in passing their version of a bill regulating detention of enemy combatants.[144] His threat implied that the agency was conducting interrogations in a manner that went beyond established military practices and constituted cruel, inhuman, and degrading treatment. Newspaper stories described a rebellion within Republican ranks.[145] During this period, the administration barely had enough votes to gain the support of the House Judiciary Committee in passing a bill that the White House wanted.[146]

142. "The Future of Military Commissions," hearing before the Senate Armed Services Committee, August 2, 2006.

143. S. 3861, 109th Cong., sec. 2(3) (2006).

144. Peter Baker, "GOP Infighting on Detainees Intensifies," Washington Post, September 16, 2006, at A1.

145. Carl Hulse, Kate Zernike, and Sheryl Gay Stolberg, "How 3 G.O.P. Veterans Stalled Bush Detainee Bill," New York Times, September 17, 2006, at 1; John M. Donnelly, "Detainee Treatment Fractures GOP: Influential Senators' Challenge to Bush Proposal on Terrorist Suspects Keeps Issue at Cutting Edge of Security Debate," Cong. Q. Weekly Report, September 18, 2006, at 2458.

146. Charles Babington, "House Panel Supports Tribunal Plan, 20 to 19," Washington Post, September 21, 2006, at A6.

In the days that followed, opposition from the Republican Senators melted and the White House gained the upper hand. The Senate Armed Services Committee had acted in bipartisan fashion by reporting, 15 to 9, a bill that rejected the draft submitted by the administration.[147] However, the committee bill was never brought to the Senate floor. Republican Senators worked with executive officials to produce a substitute bill more to the liking of the administration. An amendment by Senator Levin, Democrat of Michigan, to call up the committee bill failed by a vote of 43 to 54.[148]

The enacted bill became the Military Commissions Act (MCA) of 2006. The statute defines "unlawful enemy combatant" to include a person "who has engaged in hostilities or who has purposefully and materially supported hostilities against the United States or its co-belligerents," and a person "who, before, on, or after the date" of the enactment of the Military Commissions Act "has been determined to be an unlawful enemy combatant by a Combatant Status Review Tribunal or another competent tribunal established under the authority of the President or the Secretary of Defense."[149] The statute also defines a *lawful* enemy combatant: a person who is "a member of the regular forces of a state party engaged in hostilities against the United States" and "a member of a militia, volunteer corps, or organized resistance movement [who wears] a fixed distinctive sign recognizable at a distance, carr[ies] their arms openly, and abide[s] by the law of war."[150] Those definitions apply to all *persons*, both U.S. citizens and aliens.

Procedural Protections

The MCA placed restrictions on habeas petitions. No person may invoke the Geneva Conventions or any of its protocols in any habeas action to which the United States "or a current or former officer, employee, member of the Armed Forces, or other agent of the United States is a party as a source of rights in any court of the United States or its States or territories."[151] Any "alien unlawful enemy combatant is subject to trial by military commission."[152]

---

147. 152 Cong. Rec. S10243 (2006) (statement by Senator Levin).
148. Id. at S10263.
149. 120 Stat. 2601, sec. 3(a)(1) (2006).
150. Id.
151. Id. at 2631, sec. 5(a).
152. Id. at 2602, sec. 3(a)(1) (§948c).

The statute supposedly prohibits compulsory self-incrimination.[153] Yet it permits statements gained by coercion to be admitted at trial. A statement obtained before December 30, 2005 (the date of the DTA), where the degree of coercion is disputed, may be admitted as evidence if the military judge finds that (1) "the totality of the circumstances renders the statement reliable and possessing sufficient probative values" and (2) "the interests of justice would best be served by admission of the statements into evidence."[154] How can evidence obtained by coercion be considered "reliable" and have "probative" value? As for evidence obtained after enactment of the DTA, if the degree of coercion is disputed the statements may be admitted only if the military judge finds (1) and (2) above and finds that "the interrogation methods used to obtain the statements do not amount to cruel, inhuman, or degrading treatment" prohibited by section 1003 of the DTA.[155]

Other procedures cover access to witnesses and evidence. The accused is permitted to present evidence in his defense, cross-examine witnesses who testify against him, and examine evidence admitted against him on the issue of guilt or innocence and for sentencing.[156] Those guarantees are undermined by the use of classified information. To protect that information from disclosure the military judge, upon motion by the government, shall delete specified items from documents, offer substitutes or summaries of the information, or provide a substitution of relevant facts that the classified information would tend to prove.[157] Suppose the government deletes the name of the informer. The accused has no right of confrontation and no right to meaningfully examine evidence presented against him.

It is not clear from the statute whether the accused's attorney would have access to classified information. The defense counsel "shall have a reasonable opportunity to obtain witnesses and other evidence as provided in regulations prescribed by the Secretary of Defense."[158] When the accused and his attorney seek documents from the government, the military judge (upon motion of government counsel) shall authorize deletions, provide a substitute or summary, or offer a substitute of facts the classified information would tend to prove.[159]

---

153. Id. at 2607, sec. 3(a)(1) (§948r).
154. Id. (§948r(c)).
155. Id. (§948r(d)).
156. Id. at 2608, sec. 3 (a)(1) (§949a(b)(A)).
157. Id. at 2612, sec. 3(a)(1) (§949d(f)(2)(A)).
158. Id. at 2614 (§949j(a)).
159. Id. at 2614–15 (§948j(c)(1)).

One section covers the President's obligation to comply with treaties. The statute authorizes the President to "interpret the meaning and application of the Geneva Conventions and to promulgate higher standards and administrative regulations for violations of treaty obligations which are not grave breaches of the Geneva Conventions."[160] The President issues those interpretations by executive order and publishes them in the *Federal Register*. The order "shall be authoritative (except as to grave breaches of common Article 3) as a matter of United States law, in the same manner as other administrative regulations." Although those orders are "authoritative," they are not necessarily permanently binding or exclusive. The statute further provides: "Nothing in this section shall be construed to affect the constitutional functions and responsibilities of Congress and the judicial branch of the United States."[161]

Several provisions bear on torture and interrogations, attempting to define the liability of U.S. officers who interrogate detainees. When are they subject to prosecution under the War Crimes Act? The term "grave breaches of Common Article 3" means any of nine specified acts, usually accompanied by intent.[162] For example, the bill defines torture: "The act of a person who commits, or conspires or attempts to commit, an act *specifically intended* to inflict severe physical or mental pain or suffering (other than pain or suffering incidental to lawful sanctions) upon another person within his custody or physical control for the purpose of obtaining information or a confession, punishment, intimidation, coercion, or any reason based on discrimination of any kind."[163] What happens if the "specific intent" is to obtain information and the physical or mental is only incidental and not intended?

The CIA Exception

Throughout the controversy over interrogation methods, the administration consistently argued that whatever limitations apply to questioning by the military, CIA interrogators are less restricted. Unlike the public Army manual, the CIA in 1963 drafted the KUBARK manual as a secret document to justify aggressive interrogations that did not comply with Geneva.[164] In his press briefing on June 22, 2004, discussing the Bybee Memo and the adoption of new

---

160. Id. at 2632.
161. Id.
162. Id. at 2633–35.
163. Id. at 2633 (emphasis added).
164. Margulies, Guantánamo and the Abuse of Presidential Power, at 33–34.

standards for interrogations by the military, White House Counsel Gonzales refused to "get into questions related to the CIA." The Detainee Treatment Act of 2005 prohibited cruel, inhuman, or degrading treatment of persons "in the custody" of the Defense Department or "in the custody" of the U.S. government. What of persons transferred by the CIA to other countries and placed in their custody (extraordinary rendition)? What types of interrogation methods would be allowed? Did the signing statements by President Bush open the door to more "aggressive" techniques of interrogation by the CIA? Those issues are examined more closely in Chapter 10.

On February 11, 2008, the Bush administration announced that it intended to bring capital murder charges against six men held at Guantánamo, including Khalid Sheikh Mohammed. The trials would be conducted on the basis of information the men disclosed to FBI and military questioners without the use of coercive methods. According to the government, the men made admissions after being given food whenever they were hungry as well as Starbucks coffee.[165] That explanation contradicts the administration's previous position that coercive interrogations were required to obtain essential intelligence.

ROUND THREE: *BOUMEDIENE*

The Court's decision in *Hamdan* sparked new litigation about the rights of detainees held at Guantánamo. Their attorneys argued that the ruling supported the position that the DTA "does not apply to pending cases and does not affect the federal courts' jurisdiction over Petitioners' habeas actions." In their view, the Court "decisively rejected the Government's attempt to invoke the DTA to insulate its activities at Guantanamo Bay from habeas review."[166] Challenges were also brought against the legitimacy of the Combatant Status Review Tribunals (CSRTs) used by the government to justify the detentions.[167]

165. Josh White, Dan Eggen, and Joby Warrick, "U.S. to Try 6 on Capital Charges over 9/11 Attacks," Washington Post, February 12, 2008, at A1.

166. Supplemental Brief of Petitioners Boumediene, et al., and Khalid Regarding the Supreme Court's Decision in *Hamdan* v. *Rumsfeld*, Boumediene v. Bush, No. 05–5062; Khalid v. Bush, No. 05–5063 (D.C. Cir. August 8, 2006), at 1.

167. The Guantanamo Detainees Supplemental Brief Addressing the Effect of the Supreme Court's Opinion in *Hamdan* v. *Rumsfeld*, 126 S.Ct. 2749 (2006), on the Pending Appeals, Al Odah v. United States of America, Nos. 05–5064, 05–5095 through 05–5116 (D.C. Cir. August 8, 2006).

On February 20, 2007, the D.C. Circuit held that the Military Commissions Act denied jurisdiction to federal courts to consider the habeas petitions filed by detainees at Guantánamo previous to the date of the statute. The court further ruled that the statute deprived courts of jurisdiction to hear the habeas appeals and did not violate the Suspension Clause of the Constitution (prohibiting suspension of the writ of habeas corpus unless required by public safety in cases of rebellion or invasion). The court found no cases allowing aliens outside the territory of the sovereign to seek relief by habeas petitions.[168] By concluding that certain constitutional protections available to persons inside the United States are not available to aliens "outside of our geographic borders,"[169] the court revived the issue whether Guantánamo was "sovereign" U.S. territory or merely under the "jurisdiction" of the United States. The court denied that a "*de facto* sovereignty" existed at the naval base.[170]

In a lengthy dissent, Judge Judith W. Rogers agreed that it was the intent of Congress in passing the MCA to withdraw jurisdiction from federal courts, but held that the statute offended the Suspension Clause. For that reason, the statute was void and did not deprive federal courts of jurisdiction.[171] She rejected the majority's reasoning that Congress may suspend habeas corpus for the detainees because they have no individual rights under the Constitution. The Suspension Clause, she noted, "makes no reference to citizens or even persons."[172] Moreover, unlike the majority, she regarded the placement of the Suspension Clause in Article I "as a conscious determination of a limit on Congress's powers."[173]

Judge Rogers pointed to three examples in the past where Congress provided an adequate replacement for habeas petitions.[174] In contrast, she found the CSRTs established by the DTA to be deficient, in part because (1) the burden is on detainees to produce evidence explaining why they should *not* be detained, (2) they might not have access to classified information used to detain them, (3) they must proceed without benefit of counsel, and (4) the board of military judges lacks the independence of federal judges because they are "subject to command influence."[175] Also, the DTA limited judicial review to

---

168. Boumediene v. Bush, 476 F.3d 981, 989 (D.C. Cir. 2007).
169. Id. at 991 (citing Zadvydas v. Davis, 533 U.S. 678, 693 [2001]).
170. Id. at 992.
171. Id. at 994–95 (Rogers, J., dissenting).
172. Id. at 995.
173. Id. at 998 (for majority's position see id. at 993–94).
174. Id. at 1004.
175. Id. at 1005.

the record developed by the CSRT to assess whether it complied with its own standards. Continued detention could be justified by a CSRT on the basis of evidence obtained by torture.[176] Congress has the power under Article I to suspend the writ, but it had not done so.[177] Judge Rogers pointed out that the framers "could have granted plenary power to the President to confront emergency situations, but they did not; they could have authorized the suspension of habeas corpus during any state of war, but they limited suspension to cases of 'Rebellion or Invasion.'"[178]

Initially, the Supreme Court on April 2, 2007, refused to hear the case. Three Justices (Breyer, Souter, and Ginsburg) said they would grant the petitions for appeal and two more (Stevens and Kennedy) indicated they would take the case if the administration failed to provide adequate remedies to the detainees.[179] On June 29, the Court reversed course and agreed to take the case.[180] At oral argument on December 5, 2007, Seth P. Waxman presented the case for Guantánamo detainees. He said they had been confined at the naval base "for almost six years, yet not one has ever had meaningful notice of the factual grounds of detention or a fair opportunity to dispute those grounds before a neutral decision-maker."[181]

In periods of national crisis, the legislative and judicial branches have forfeited their independence and offered their support to presidential initiatives, no matter how ruinous to the nation and its citizens. It is the obligation of scholars, citizens, and the media to constantly press upon Congress and the courts the need to safeguard individual rights, constitutional values, and structural checks. Those values are far more important than a show of national unity behind a particular President. Patriotism worth its name grants the highest priority to the nation—not to the Chief Executive—and knows the difference between the two.

176. Id. at 1006.

177. Id. at 1007.

178. Id. at 1009. See also Josh White, "Guantanamo Detainees Lose Appeal," Washington Post, February 21, 2007, at A1; Stephen Labaton, "Court Endorses Curbs on Appeal by U.S. Detainees," New York Times, February 21, 2007, at A1.

179. Boumediene v. Bush, 127 S.Ct. 1478 (2007).

180. Robert Barnes, "Justices To Weigh Detainee Rights," Washington Post, June 30, 2007, at A1; William Glaberson, "In Shift, Justices Agree to Review Detainees' Case," New York Times, June 30, 2007, at A1.

181. U.S. Supreme Court, Boumediene v. Bush, oral argument, December 5, 2007, at 4.

CHAPTER 8

State Secrets Privilege

After newspapers in December 2005 revealed secret eavesdropping by the National Security Agency (NSA), dozens of lawsuits challenged the legality of the program. The Bush administration invoked the "state secrets privilege" to block the disclosure of agency documents (see chapter 9). In cases involving the government's "extraordinary rendition" program, used to transfer individuals to countries for abusive interrogations, the Bush administration also asserted the state secrets privilege (see chapter 10). In these cases, the Justice Department relies primarily on *United States* v. *Reynolds* (1953), the first time the Supreme Court recognized the privilege (and was misled by the government in doing so). Two earlier precedents are also cited to justify state secrets: the Aaron Burr trial of 1807 and a Civil War spy case. Neither one applies to contemporary disputes.

AARON BURR'S TRIAL

In its brief in *Reynolds*, the Justice Department cited the Burr trial for support.[1] Later the department produced a list of what it called successful assertions of the evidentiary privilege, with the second example dating from 1807: "Confidential information and letters relating to Burr's conspiracy."[2] A district court in 1977 claimed that the state secrets privilege "can be traced as far back as Aaron Burr's trial in 1807."[3] In 1989, the D.C. Circuit conceded that "the exact origins" of the privilege "are not certain," but found its "initial roots" in Burr's trial and its "modern roots" in *Reynolds*.[4] According to a district court in 2004, the origins of the state secrets privilege "can be traced back to the treason trial of Aaron Burr."[5] However, these references

1. Brief for the United States, United States v. Reynolds, No. 21, U.S. Supreme Court, October Term, 1952, at 10–11.
2. Id. at 24.
3. Jabara v. Kelley, 75 F.R.D. 475, 483 (D. Mich. 1977).
4. In re U.S., 872 F.2d 472, 474–75 (D.C. Cir. 1989).
5. Edmonds v. U.S. Dept. of Justice, 323 F.Supp.2d 65, 70 (D.D.C. 2004).

to the Burr trial are highly misleading justifications for the state secrets privilege.

The decision in 2004 correctly noted that former Vice President Burr had sought access to a letter that General James Wilkinson—the primary government witness against him—had sent to President Thomas Jefferson. The letter "purportedly contained information" about Burr "of whose guilt," Wilkinson said, "there can be no doubt." The government objected to producing the letter, asserting that it was "improper to call upon the president to produce the letter of Gen. Wilkinson, because it was a private letter, and probably contained confidential communications, which the president ought not and could not be compelled to disclose. It might contain state secrets, which could not be divulged without endangering the national safety."[6]

While it is accurate to say that the Burr trial involved what might have been "confidential communications" and "state secrets," it is not true that the Jefferson administration told the court it could not see the letter. Chief Justice John Marshall concluded that the letter did not contain "any matter the disclosure of which would endanger the public safety." He did not take at face value the word of the administration. He made an independent assessment. He was willing to consider suppressing the letter upon learning "it is not the wish of the executive to disclose," but immediately said: "*if it be not immediately and essentially applicable to the point.*"[7] In a criminal trial, with the death penalty looming, Burr was entitled to see the documents.

Jefferson's Indictment

With extraordinary carelessness, President Jefferson publicly condemned Burr as guilty before he ever had a trial. In his Sixth Annual Message, delivered December 2, 1806, Jefferson alerted Congress to the plans of several private individuals who had armed themselves to carry out a military expedition "against the territories of Spain."[8] In response to a House resolution adopted on January 16, 1807, requesting additional information on the situation,[9] Jefferson submitted a message on January 22. He said that much of the information was in the form of letters "containing such a mixture of rumors, conjectures,

6. Id., citing United States v. Burr, 25 Fed. Cas. 30, 31 (C.C.D. Va. 1807) (No. 14,692d).

7. 25 Fed. Cas. at 37 (emphasis added).

8. 1 A Compilation of the Messages and Papers of the Presidents 394 (James D. Richardson ed. 1925) (hereafter "Richardson").

9. Annals of Cong., 9th Cong., 2d Sess. 334–59 (1807).

and suspicions" that it would be inappropriate and unjust to identify particular individuals involved in the conspiracy "except that of the principal actor, whose guilt is placed beyond question."[10] He identified Aaron Burr as "the prime mover." Jefferson referred to three letters he had received from General Wilkinson concerning Burr's activities: letters of October 21, December 14, and December 18, 1806. Having watched Jefferson function as both Executive and Supreme Judge, if not executioner, Burr had every right to see the letters.

Chief Justice Marshall recognized that if he issued a subpoena to Jefferson for the letters, it might be interpreted as a sign of disrespect to the office of the presidency. However, Marshall was more concerned that his own branch would lose respect if it failed to give an accused access to information needed for his defense. He declined to say whether that result would "tarnish the reputation of the government; but I will say, that it would justly tarnish the reputation of the court which had given its sanction to its being withheld." If Marshall were a party to the withholding of documents needed by a defendant, "it would be to deplore, most earnestly, the occasion which should compel me to look back on any part of my official conduct with so much self-reproach as I should feel, could I declare, on the information now possessed, that the accused is not entitled to the letter in question, if it should be really important to him."[11]

Jefferson's letter of June 12, 1807, to George Hay, one of the government attorneys handling the prosecution, referred to the President's right to independently decide "what papers coming to him as president the public interest permits to be communicated, and to whom." He then assured the court of his "readiness under that restriction voluntarily to furnish on all occasions whatever the purposes of justice may require." As to the October 21 letter from General Wilkinson, Jefferson said he had given it to Attorney General Caesar Rodney to be taken to Richmond for the trial. He closed by expressing "a perfect willingness to do what is right."[12] Nothing in this record indicates a decision by Jefferson to prevent Burr from gaining access to documents needed for his defense.

Writing again on June 17, Jefferson was satisfied that the correspondence he had released to Attorney General Rodney "will have substantially fulfilled the object of a subpoena from the district court of Richmond."[13] If Burr believed

10. 1 Richardson at 400.
11. United States v. Burr, 25 Fed. Cas. 30, 37 (C.C.D. Va. 1807) (No. 14,692d).
12. Id. at 65.
13. Id. at 69.

"there are any facts within the knowledge of the heads of department or of myself, which can be useful for his defense, from a desire of doing anything our situation will permit in furtherance of justice," those officials would be available for deposition in Washington, D.C.[14] Jefferson drew the line only at having to personally attend the trial at Richmond, pointing to the impracticality of traveling from one court to another throughout the country.[15]

Jefferson's willingness to give Burr access to requested documents is plain. He reminded Hay that he had written to Rodney "to send on the letter of General Wilkinson of October 21st, referred to in my message of January 22d." When Jefferson received the letter he "immediately saw that it was not the one desired, because it had no relation to the facts stated under that reference." Rodney searched through the papers and could not locate the one that Jefferson (and Burr) wanted. Jefferson told Hay that "[n]o researches shall be spared to recover this letter, and if recovered, it shall immediately be sent on to you." Jefferson offered Hay an option: "General Wilkinson probably has copies of all the letters he wrote me, and having expressed a willingness to furnish the one desired by the Court, the defendant can still have the benefit of it."[16] Jefferson told Hay on August 7: "With respect to the paper in question it was delivered to the Attorney Genl with all the other papers relating to Burr."[17]

Burr Defends Himself

Aaron Burr faced two charges: one on treason, the second a misdemeanor for "setting on foot" a military expedition against the territory of Spain. On September 1, 1807, the jury found him not guilty of treason.[18] The court then moved to consider seven counts of the misdemeanor charge. Two days later Burr asked whether a Wilkinson letter he had requested was in court. Hay said he had searched for the letter but could not find it. He had a copy, "which was ready to be produced." Burr replied that he "was not disposed to admit a copy." Chief Justice Marshall announced that "unless the loss of the original be proved, a copy cannot be admitted."[19] Burr insisted that the letter written

14. Id.

15. Id.

16. Id. at 253–54.

17. 9 The Writings of Thomas Jefferson 61n (Ford ed. 1898). This volume, edited by Paul Leicester Ford, reproduces many of the letters from Jefferson to Hay regarding the Burr trial. See 52n–64n.

18. United States v. Burr, 25 Fed. Cas. 180–81 (C.C.D. Va. 1807) (No. 14,693).

19. Id. at 189.

by Wilkinson on November 12, 1806, to Jefferson "was material to his defense." Hay responded that he "had that letter, and would produce it."[20] Indicating that there were some matters in the Wilkinson letters "which ought not to be made public," he was willing to put them "in the hands of the clerk confidentially, and he could copy all those parts which had relation to the cause." There then followed this discussion:

> The counsel for Colonel Burr were not satisfied with this proposal. They demanded the whole letters.
>
> Mr. Hay said he was willing that Mr. Botts, Mr. Wickham, and Mr. Randolph [Burr's attorneys] should examine them. He would depend on their candor and integrity to make no improper disclosures; and if there should be any difference of opinion as to what were confidential passages, the court should decide.
>
> Mr. Martin [representing Burr] objected to this as a secret tribunal. The counsel had a right to hear the letters publicly, without their consent.
>
> Mr. Burr's counsel united in refusing to inspect anything that was not submitted to the inspection of their client.
>
> The CHIEF JUSTICE saw no real difficulty in the case. If there were any parts of the letters confidential, then a public examination would be very wrong; otherwise they ought to be read.
>
> Mr. Hay said the president wrote to him when he understood the process had been awarded, that he had reserved to himself the province of deciding what parts of the letters ought to be published and what parts required to be kept secret; that they wished everything to be as public as possible except those parts which were really confidential. The discussion continued till the court adjourned.[21]

On the following day, Burr requested two letters from Wilkinson to Jefferson, one of which had been subpoenaed. Regarding Jefferson as in contempt of court, Burr said he had a right to demand process of contempt but the procedure would be "unpleasant" and "produce delay." Of the October 21 letter, he now said a copy would be sufficient "if duly authenticated." As to the November 12 letter, Burr said he had reason to believe that the whole letter had been shown to others to cause him injury, and that the whole letter ought therefore be produced.[22] Hay told the court he would produce the November 12 letter, except for two passages "which he could not submit to public inspection." The key word here is *public*, because Hay was willing to show the entire letter to

20. Id. at 190.
21. Id.
22. Id.

the court. He agreed to turn over the letter, with certain parts removed because they were "not material for the purposes of justice, for the defense of the accused, or pertinent to the issue now about to be joined." As a check on the accuracy of the proposed substitute, he was "willing to refer to the judgment of the court, by submitting the original letter to its inspection."[23] That single admission distinguishes the Burr trial from the state secrets privilege established in *Reynolds*, where the government refused to release a document to the court.

Chief Justice Marshall said that in criminal cases, courts will always apply the rules of evidence "so as to treat the defence with as much liberality and tenderness as the case will admit."[24] He recognized that the President "might receive a letter which it would be improper to exhibit in public, because of the manifest inconvenience of its exposure." Notice again the word *public*. Withholding a document from the public does not mean withholding it from a court or a litigant. Marshall advised Burr: "The occasion for demanding it ought, in such a case, to be very strong, and to be fully shown to the court before its production could be insisted on." He admitted that "much reliance must be placed on the declaration of the president."

Having given some ground here, Marshall proceeded to reject the conventional distinction between a President's "private" and "public" (or official) papers. As he explained: "Letters to the president in his private character, are often written to him in consequence of his public character, and may relate to public concerns. Such a letter, though it be a private one, seems to partake of the character of an official paper, and to be such as ought not on light ground to be forced into public view."[25] Forcing a letter into "public view" is not the same as sharing it with a judge.

Marshall summed up his dilemma. Jefferson had not personally objected "to the production of any part of this letter." He had left it in the hands of Hay. Marshall assumed that Jefferson "has no objections to the production of the whole, if the attorney has not." If Jefferson had transmitted the letter and stated that "in his judgment the public interest required certain parts of it to be kept secret," Marshall would have paid "all proper respect."[26] All proper respect is not the same as blind acquiescence to executive assertions, which is what the Supreme Court did in *Reynolds*. Marshall said he was inclined to let

23. Id.
24. Id. at 191.
25. Id. at 192.
26. Id.

Burr see the letter. After he looked at it "it will yet be a question whether it shall go to the jury or not." On September 5, Hay asked the court for time to seek guidance from Jefferson.

Verdict: Not Guilty

On September 9, Hay presented a certificate from Jefferson, indicating the parts of Wilkinson's letter that should not be made public. Jefferson, describing certain passages as "entirely confidential," provided a "correct copy of all those parts which I ought to permit to be made public." The parts "not communicated are in nowise material for the purposes of justice on the charges of treason or misdemeanor depending against Aaron Burr; they are on subjects irrelevant to any issues which can arise out of those charges, & could contribute nothing towards his acquittal or conviction."[27]

Marshall's decision on September 9 explored a number of legal issues. Could hearsay or the declarations of third persons be received in evidence? What are the elements of a conspiracy? What is the statutory meaning of "setting on foot" a military expedition? Can a military expedition be set on foot when a single soldier has been enlisted for that purpose? What is an expedition? An enterprise? Suppose that Burr originated the enterprise (which Marshall said "is very probably the case")? Others might have provided the means. Marshall pointed out that Burr was not indicted for being "connected with the enterprize, but for providing certain specific means."[28] As these questions from Marshall multiplied and he revealed his own answers, the government's case grew bleak.

At one point Marshall observed that the testimony produced by the government's attorney "disproves his own charge."[29] He inquired of the government: "gentlemen will consider whether they are not wasting the time and money of the United States, and of all those persons who are forced to attend here, whilst they are producing such a mass of testimony which does not bear upon the cause."[30] When the government moved to discharge the jury, Burr objected and insisted on a verdict. The jury retired and returned with a judgment of "Not guilty."[31] Further discussion about access to government documents was no longer necessary.

27. 9 The Writings of Thomas Jefferson 64n (Ford ed. 1898).
28. United States v. Burr, 25 Fed. Cas. 193–98 (C.C.D. Va. 1807) (No. 14,694).
29. Id. at 200.
30. Id. at 201.
31. Id.

There are many reasons why the Aaron Burr trial has no application to the current state secrets case. The principal reason is that he was tried in a criminal case for treason. Lawsuits over state secrets are civil cases. Also, the Jefferson administration understood that Burr had a right to gain access to evidence used against him, and if the administration refused to surrender the evidence it had to drop the charges. That choice would resurface in future state secrets cases: Either the government releases requested documents or it loses the case.

SPY CASES

In *Reynolds*, the Supreme Court described the government's attempt to invoke the state secrets privilege as a privilege "well established in the law of evidence." Among the cases the Court cited for that proposition, and standing first in line, is the Civil War government spy case, *Totten* v. *United States* (1875).[32] President Abraham Lincoln had entered into a contract with William A. Lloyd to proceed to the South and collect data on the number of Confederate troops stationed at different points, plans of forts and fortifications, and other information that might be useful to the federal government. For his services Lloyd was to be paid $200 a month, but he received funds only to cover his expenses. After he died his family sought to recover compensation for his services. Here are the reasons the Court rejected the lawsuit:

> It may be stated as a general principle, that public policy forbids the maintenance of any suit in a court of justice, the trial of which would inevitably lead to the disclosure of matters which the law itself regards as confidential, and respecting which it will not allow the confidence to be violated. On this principle, suits cannot be maintained which would require a disclosure of the confidences of the confessional, or those between husband and wife, or of communications by a client to his counsel for professional advice, or of a patient to his physician for a similar purpose. Much greater reason exists for the application of the principle to cases of contract for secret services with the government, as the existence of a contract of that kind is itself a fact not to be disclosed.[33]

Obviously this decision is far afield from the state secrets privilege. The Court was merely addressing the confidentiality that exists in certain types of communications: between confessor and priest, husband and wife, client

---

32. United States v. Reynolds, 345 U.S. at 6–7, n.11.
33. Totten v. United States, 92 U.S. 105, 107 (1875).

and attorney, patient and doctor. To those privileged communications the Court added the confidentiality that exists between a President and someone he hires as a spy. Lincoln paid Lloyd from a contingent fund that Congress had placed under presidential control.[34] By its very nature, a secret contract could not be taken into court at some later date to be enforced. At issue was not a broad class of secrets the government had a right to keep privileged. Rather, it was a matter of ordinary contracts (enforceable in court) and secret contracts (which are not). Whoever enters into a secret agreement with the government cannot expect relief in the courts. If there is a dispute, the branch of government that can provide an immediate remedy is the executive agency that entered into the agreement. Congress could also enact a private bill to offer relief. That is the basic difference between *Totten* and the state secret privilege. The case in *Totten* was not justiciable. A state secrets case *is* justiciable, but the private litigant may not be able to gain access to certain agency documents.

The Supreme Court in *Totten* described the service stipulated in Lloyd's contract as "a secret service; the information sought was to be obtained clandestinely, and was to be communicated privately; the employment and the service were to be equally concealed." Both Lincoln and Lloyd, said the Court, "must have understood that the lips of the other were to be for ever sealed respecting the relation of either to the matter."[35] Any effort in court to publicize the agreement "would itself be a breach of a contract of that kind."[36] Nothing can be drawn from this unique and narrow case to justify withholding state secrets over the broad domains of national security and foreign affairs.

Other Espionage Lawsuits

The *Totten* principle has been applied to a number of other lawsuits involving spies. Charles de Arnaud served as a spy for General John C. Frémont during the Civil War and was paid for his services. Twenty-four years later he tried to obtain additional compensation from the government. Relying on *Totten*, the Supreme Court in 1894 rejected his request. Aside from being barred by the statute of limitations (requiring claims to be presented within six years), the Court found unpersuasive Arnaud's argument that he was not really a spy, covered by *Totten*, but rather a "military expert."[37] Two years earlier the Court

34. Id. at 106.
35. Id.
36. Id. at 107.
37. De Arnaud v. United States, 151 U.S. 483, 493 (1894).

of Claims had rejected a petition by another spy for General Frémont who sought compensation for his services.[38]

In 1954, the Court of Claims dismissed a petition seeking expenses and compensation for secret services allegedly performed for the Psychological Warfare Branch of the Military Intelligence Department and other federal agencies, partly behind enemy lines. The necessity for secrecy prevented any effort to recover funds in court.[39] In disallowing recovery, the court said it was governed by *Totten*.[40] In two rulings in 1980 and 1981, the Court of Claims rejected efforts by two individuals to be compensated for work they did for the CIA, one in performing undercover intelligence activities and the other for espionage.[41] A separate case involved a Vietnamese who claimed that he did covert work for the CIA from 1962 to 1964 and said he deserved back pay for his services and additional compensation. The Federal Circuit, in 1988, relied on *Totten* to deny him relief.[42] In 2001, a district court applied *Totten* against an individual who tried to recover damages for breach of an alleged contract with the CIA.[43]

In another case, John Patrick Savage presented himself as a CIA agent to a British company. He wanted to borrow $8 million with the promise to pay $35 million within a matter of weeks. The promissory note did not mention the CIA, the United States, or any other third party. Receiving nothing on the due date, the company sued Savage's agent in the English courts and won a $35 million judgment. Receiving nothing, the company filed suit against the United States in federal court. The government cited *Totten* and the state secrets privilege as a defense, but the case turned on two questions. Was Savage actually a CIA agent? If he was, did the agency authorize him to enter into the contract? The evidence was mixed on the first, nonexistent on the second. As noted by the Court of Federal Claims, Savage's promise to pay the company $35 million on an $8 million note amounted to 330 percent interest, a rate "that would make a loan shark blush."[44] Individuals are ill-advised to

---

38. Allen v. United States, 27 Ct. Cl. 89 (1892).

39. Tucker v. United States, 118 F.Supp. 371 (Ct. Cl. 1954).

40. Id. at 372–73.

41. Simrick v. United States, 224 Ct. Cl. 724 (1980); Mackowski v. United States, 228 Ct. Cl. 717 (1981), cert. denied, 454 U.S. 1123 (1981).

42. Guong v. United States, 860 F.2d 1063 (Fed. Cir. 1988).

43. Kielczynski v. U.S. C.I.A., 128 F.Supp.2d 151 (E.D.N.Y. 2001).

44. Monarch Assur. P.L.C. v. United States, 42 Fed.Cl. 258, 264 (1998). See also Monarch Assur. P.L.C. v. United States, 36 Fed.Cl. 324 (1996).

enter into a "contract" with someone who purports to be a CIA agent but lacks proper credentials.[45]

Totten has become a popular cite for the government and for courts. An article in 2001 reported that although the *Totten* doctrine had been invoked only six times between 1875 and 1951, after 1951 it was cited more than sixty-five times. Many of those cases had nothing to do with contracts for secret services.[46] A good example is a 1981 decision by the Supreme Court. The issue was whether the Navy had to prepare and release to the public an environmental impact statement for the construction in Hawaii of a facility for storing nuclear weapons. The Court held that the statement was not required. It closed with a passage from *Totten* ("public policy forbids the maintenance of any suit in a court of justice, the trial of which would inevitably lead to the disclosure of matters which the law itself regards as confidential").[47] However, the Hawaiian case was unrelated to an espionage contract.

"Mr. and Mrs. Doe"

Totten was tested most recently in a case decided by the Supreme Court in 2005. A husband and wife team ("John and Jane Doe") sued the United States and the CIA Director, alleging that the agency had failed to provide them with the financial assistance it had promised for their espionage services during the Cold War. As citizens of a foreign country, they wanted to defect to the United States. It was their understanding that if they agreed to conduct espionage for a certain period of time, the CIA would arrange for their travel to and resettlement in the United States and would provide financial security for the remainder of their lives. After carrying out espionage they were brought to the United States, given false identities, and provided with education, medical benefits, and a living stipend. When Mr. Doe's salary from professional employment reached a certain level, the stipend was discontinued with the understanding that if he lost his job the CIA would resume making payments. After he was laid off, he and his wife contacted the agency and learned that

45. Monarch Assur. P.L.C. v. United States, 244 F.3d 1356 (Fed. Cir. 2001).

46. Sean C. Flynn, "The *Totten* Doctrine and Its Poisoned Progeny," 25 Vt. L. Rev. 793, 793–94 (2001). See also Daniel L. Pines, "The Continuing Viability of the 1875 Supreme Court Case of *Totten* v. *United States*," 53 Adm. L. Rev. 1273 (2001); Major Kelly D. Wheaton, "Spycraft and Government Contracts: A Defense of *Totten* v. *United States*," The Army Lawyer, August 1997, at 9–17.

47. Weinberger v. Catholic Action of Hawaii, 454 U.S. 139, 146–47 (1981).

the stipend would not be restored because of budget constraints. They were told that the agency had various types of appeal processes, which they tried without success.[48]

A district court found that their claims were not barred by *Totten*.[49] The record indicated that the CIA had told the couple that a process existed through which they could appeal their request. Thus, even if *Totten* foreclosed any court from judging their contractual benefits, it appeared that the agency had offered certain procedural rights that could be litigated.[50] The court concluded that having the judiciary look at the CIA's procedures for reviewing complaints would not jeopardize a national security secret.[51]

The Ninth Circuit, affirming in part, agreed that issues of fact existed as to whether the couple had been deprived of due process under CIA regulations.[52] The essence of the case was not about breaching a secret agreement. The Does went to court "not to reveal secret information: They filed suit under fictitious names and revealed only minimal, non-identifying details in their complaint."[53] The Ninth Circuit pointed out that the government "has not thus far asserted the state secrets privilege in this case and has therefore not complied with the required procedures."[54] The next year, the Ninth Circuit denied a petition for rehearing and another petition for rehearing en banc.[55]

The Justice Department, in a brief requesting the Supreme Court to take the case, argued that the Ninth Circuit's decision was "inconsistent with this Court's decision in *Totten*."[56] The Civil War case barred the suit "because respondents' claims cannot proceed without disclosing facts that would damage national security: whether respondents actually had an espionage relationship with the CIA and, if so, the details of that relationship."[57] The government disagreed that *Totten* was somehow "subsumed" under the state secrets privilege announced in *Reynolds*. To the government, *Reynolds* confirmed that *Totten* posed a jurisdictional bar "where the very subject matter of the

48. Doe v. Tenet, 99 F.Supp.2d 1284, 1285–88 (W.D. Wash. 2000).
49. Id. at 1293–94.
50. Id. at 1289–90.
51. Id. at 1290.
52. Doe v. Tenet, 329 F.3d 1135 (9th Cir. 2003).
53. Id. at 1148.
54. Id. at 1151.
55. Doe v. Tenet, 353 F.3d 1141 (9th Cir. 2004).
56. Petition for a Writ of Certiorari, Tenet v. Doe (U.S. Supreme Court 2004), at 7.
57. Id. at 9.

action [is] a contract to perform espionage."[58] *Totten's* rule of dismissing contractual spy cases "does not require formal invocation of the state secrets privilege."[59]

The lawyers representing the Does treated *Totten* as part of the state secrets privilege and not a jurisdictional bar. They viewed *Totten* "as an early kernel of the state secrets privilege (or of its broader family, Executive privilege)."[60] The government denied that *Reynolds* overruled *Totten*.[61] The Civil War case retained an "independent force after *Reynolds*" by erecting a "jurisdictional bar" to prohibit any litigation about espionage agreements. Those disputes are not justiciable.[62] Other briefs were filed to elaborate on this issue.[63]

In a unanimous opinion, the Supreme Court decided that the suit was barred by *Totten*. It denied that *Reynolds* replaced or altered *Totten's* categorical bar to lawsuits that involve espionage agreements. It also rejected the plaintiffs' argument that conditions had changed since *Totten*, with federal courts given greater access to classified documents. Said the Court: "The state secrets privilege and the more frequent use of *in camera* judicial proceedings simply cannot provide the absolute protection we found necessary in enunciating the *Totten* rule."[64] The decision underscores the point that *Totten* applies to a unique category of government spy cases that are unenforceable in court. In contrast, state secrets cases can be litigated and require certain procedural steps by the government to withhold documents from plaintiffs. The government may find that by invoking the state secrets privilege it loses the case.

In the NSA surveillance cases, discussed in chapter 9, private telecom companies argued in court that they had entered into a secret espionage agreement with the government and could not adequately defend themselves because of the presence of state secrets. That type of case is unique. In the *Totten/Tenet* cases the private parties were plaintiffs; the telecoms are defendants.

58. United States v. Reynolds, 345 U.S. 1, 11 n.26 (1953).

59. Petition for a Writ of Certiorari, at 17.

60. Response to Petition for Writ of Certiorari, Tenet v. Doe, No. 03-1395 (U.S. Supreme Court 2004), at 12.

61. Reply Brief for the Petitioners, Tenet v. Doe, No. 03-1395 (U.S. Supreme Court 2004), at 3.

62. Id. at 4–5.

63. Brief for the Petitioners, Tenet v. Doe, No. 03-1395 (U.S. Supreme Court 2004); Brief for the Respondents, Tenet v. Doe, No. 03-1395 (U.S. Supreme Court 2004); Reply Brief for the Petitioners, Tenet v. Doe, No. 03-1395 (U.S. Supreme Court 2004).

64. Tenet v. Doe, 544 U.S. 1, 11 (2005).

REYNOLDS: THREE WIDOWS IN COURT

In *United States* v. *Reynolds* (1953), the Supreme Court for the first time recognized and upheld the state secrets privilege. The government argued in court that disclosure of an accident report about the crash of a B-29 would do grave damage to national security. A half-century later, after the government had declassified and released the accident report, it was obvious that it contained no state secrets. Instead, it showed that the government had acted negligently by not installing proper equipment. The Court, misled by the government about the presence of national security secrets, never looked at the document.

The case began when three widows brought an action under the Federal Tort Claims Act, suing the government for negligence in the midair explosion of a B-29 bomber on October 6, 1948, over Waycross, Georgia. Five of eight crew members perished, as did four of the five civilian engineers on board, who had served as technical advisers to an Air Force project. They provided assistance to the secret equipment tested on the flight, all of which was known to newspaper readers who learned of the crash the next day.[65] The widows of three engineers requested several key documents, including the accident report and depositions of the surviving crew members.

The Federal Tort Claims Act of 1946 authorizes federal agencies to settle claims against the United States caused by negligent or wrongful acts of federal employees acting within the scope of their official duties.[66] Congress directed federal courts to treat the government in the same manner as a private individual, deciding the dispute on the basis of facts and with no partiality in favor of the government. The United States "shall be liable in respect of such claims . . . in the same manner, and to the same extent as a private individual under like circumstances, except that the United States shall not be liable for interest prior to judgment, or for punitive damages."[67] If there was any "balancing test" to be applied by federal courts in these cases, Congress had supplied the standard. The government was to be treated the same as any other litigant.

Other than the exceptions listed in the statute, Congress authorized courts to adjudicate claims against the government and decide them fairly in light of available facts. Congress empowered the courts to exercise independent judgment. There was no reason for judges to accept at face value a government's

65. Louis Fisher, In the Name of National Security: Unchecked Presidential Power and the *Reynolds* Case 1–2 (2006).

66. 60 Stat. 843, sec. 403(1) (1946).

67. Id. at 843–44, sec. 410(a).

claim that an agency document requested by plaintiffs was somehow privileged, without the court itself examining the document to verify the government's assertion. To uncritically accept the government's word would be to abdicate the court's duty to protect the ability of each party to present its case fairly in court. It would leave control in the hands of self-interested executive claims. To allow executive officials to withhold documents that revealed government negligence would make a nullity of the tort claims statute.

Action in District Court

The lawsuit, filed on June 21, 1949, was assigned to Judge William H. Kirkpatrick in the Eastern District in Pennsylvania. Representing the women were Charles J. Biddle and Francis Hopkinson of Drinker, Biddle & Reath, a prominent law firm in Philadelphia. Biddle submitted thirty questions to the government, requesting that it provide answers and submit copies of identified records and documents. The government responded to the interrogatories on January 5, 1950.[68] The first question asked whether the government had directed an investigation into the crash. If so, the government was to attach to its answer a copy of the reports and findings of the investigation.[69] The government acknowledged that there had been an investigation but refused to produce the accident report.[70] No claim of state secrets was invoked at that time.

Question 7 in the interrogatories: "Was any engine trouble experienced with the said B-29 type aircraft on October 6, 1947, prior to the crash?"[71] The government's unhelpful reply: "Yes, almost immediately before the crash." The last two questions sought information about possible mechanical or engineering defects on the B-29 for the three months immediately preceding the crash. Was it necessary at any time to postpone a scheduled flight of the plane because of those defects? The government said "No."[72] The last question asked whether the government had prescribed modifications for the B-29 engines to prevent overheating and to reduce fire hazards. If so, when were the modifications prescribed? If any modifications had been carried out, the interrogatory asked for details. The government's answer to this crucial question was a blunt

68. Fisher, In the Name of National Security, at 31–35.
69. Transcript of Record, Supreme Court of the United States, October Term, 1952, No. 21, United States v. Reynolds (hereafter "Transcript of Record"), at 8.
70. Id. at 12.
71. Id. at 9.
72. Id. at 14.

"No."[73] When the declassified accident report was discovered on the Internet in 2000, the falsity of that answer was obvious.

The government offered five reasons for withholding the accident report and the statements of the three surviving crew members. The first: "Report and findings of official investigation of air crash near Waycross, Georgia, are privileged documents, part of the executive files and declared confidential, pursuant to regulation promulgated under authority of Revised Statute 161 (5 U.S. Code 22)."[74] The citation was to the Housekeeping Statute, which dates back to 1789 and merely directed agency heads to keep custody of official documents. It did not in any way authorize the withholding of documents from litigants or the courts.[75] The other four reasons relied on hearsay rules.[76]

*Pre-*Reynolds *Guidance*

Before the district court's decision, several courts had issued important rulings on access to government documents considered too sensitive, privileged, or secret to be shared with a private plaintiff. Judges concluded that the documents should be given to the court to independently determine and verify whether the government had accurately characterized the contents.[77] A district court decision in 1944 involved the federal government's prosecution of a private company. An issue was whether the company was a government contractor in the secret defense program at Hanford, Washington, a project designed to create fission of uranium derivatives for an atomic bomb. To show that the company was indeed a federal agency, the government needed to produce the contract, but the original was with the General Accounting Office in Washington, D.C. As a substitute, the government offered oral testimony from a major. The district judge found that acceptable: "The right of the Army to refuse to disclose confidential information, the secrecy of which it deems necessary to national defense, is indisputable."[78]

Could the government prosecute someone on the basis of a document it refused to release? The court asked whether "secondary evidence" (not the contract but the major's oral testimony) was admissible in a courtroom.[79]

73. Id.
74. Fisher, In the Name of National Security, at 36.
75. Id. at 36, 44–48.
76. Id. at 36.
77. Id. at 37–42.
78. United States v. Haugen, 58 F.Supp. 436, 438 (E.D. Wash. 1944).
79. Id. at 439.

It now found it unsatisfactory to rely on "a copy of the copy."[80] Because the government failed to present the "best evidence" available to it, the judge decided he should have sustained the initial objection to the major's testimony.[81] The court therefore dismissed the government's case. The government learned that withholding a document came at a cost.

In its appeal to the Ninth Circuit, the government decided to share the disputed document with the trial court. The government moved to reopen the case by submitting the evidence to the court.[82] The trial proceeded. The government gave the contract to the court "for its consideration."[83] After examining the contract and concluding that the company was an agency of the United States, the Ninth Circuit affirmed the conviction.[84]

Struggles over access to government documents appear in several other early cases. In a 1946 lawsuit, plaintiffs requested a copy of the record prepared by the U.S. Naval Board of Investigation regarding collisions between inbound and outbound vessels of a convoy. The government withheld the record, arguing that disclosure would seriously hamper the administration of the Navy Department. A district court decided that plaintiffs were entitled to the record. No reasons of national security had been presented to justify the claim of privilege.[85] In the government's appeal, letters were received from the Judge Advocate of the Navy and the Acting Secretary of the Navy, both urging the appellate court to refuse access to the Navy Board's record, because it would interfere with the Navy's investigatory and fact-finding procedure and would be prejudicial to the department's best interests.[86] After the Second Circuit rejected the government's position, the district court gave the plaintiffs access to the documents.[87] In referring to the sovereign's command *Soit droit fait al partie* (Let right be done to the party), it added: "But right cannot be done if the government is allowed to suppress the facts in its possession."[88]

A 1948 case involved a collision between a private automobile and an Army jeep. The government gave the plaintiff copies of statements made by the driver and his immediate superior but refused to furnish a copy of the

80. Id. at 440.

81. Id.

82. Haugen v. United States, 153 F.2d 850, 851 (9th Cir. 1946).

83. Id. at 852.

84. Id. at 853.

85. Bank Line Limited v. United States, 68 F.Supp. 587, 588 (D. N.Y. 1946).

86. Bank Line v. United States, 163 F.2d 133, 135–36 (2d Cir. 1947).

87. Bank Line v. United States, 76 F.Supp. 801 (D. N.Y. 1948).

88. Id. at 804.

statement of a major. A district court pointed out that the Federal Tort Claims Act placed the United States, with respect to claims covered by the statute, on a par with private litigants.[89] It denied that the major's statement was privileged. No claim had been made "that any military secrets, possibly protected by the scope of common law privilege, are involved."[90] It relied in part on a district court decision handed down a few months earlier involving a tanker. The author of that decision was Judge Kirkpatrick. A tort action under the Admiralty Act put the government in all respects on a par with private individuals in litigation. Judge Kirkpatrick held that the seaman was entitled to receive written statements, taken by the Federal Bureau of Investigation, made by witnesses who had personal knowledge of the damage done to the tanker.[91]

An appellate court vacated Kirkpatrick's order because of confusion about which documents the government would be compelled to hand over.[92] Kirkpatrick issued a new order to clarify what he meant by witnesses to the accident.[93] The appellate court was now in a position to decide whether there was good cause to obtain the FBI statements, and it reversed Kirkpatrick. Access to the statements might be unnecessary because the plaintiffs had the names and addresses of the persons who had made statements to the FBI and could therefore interview them directly.[94]

In a 1949 case, a plaintiff directed the government to produce a report of an investigation conducted by the Navy of an air crash in Bayside, Long Island, resulting in the death of a private citizen.[95] The plaintiff claimed that government negligence contributed to the accident. The government argued that the person operating the plane, although an employee of the government, was acting unlawfully and not within the scope of his official duties. The government also opposed the motion for production of documents on the ground that the report was privileged.[96]

To determine whether the report contained military secrets that would be detrimental to the interest of U.S. armed forces or national security if disclosed, the district judge directed the government to produce the report for his examination. He received the report, read it, and saw "nothing in it which

89. Wunderly v. United States, 8 F.R.D. 356, 357 (D. Pa. 1948).
90. Id.
91. O'Neill v. United States, 79 F.Supp. 827 (D. Pa. 1948).
92. Alltmont v. United States, 174 F.2d 931 (3d Cir. 1949).
93. Alltmont v. United States, 87 F.Supp. 214 (D. Pa. 1949).
94. Alltmont v. United States, 177 F.2d 971, 978–79 (3d Cir. 1949).
95. Cresmer v. United States, 9 F.R.D. 203 (D. N.Y. 1949).
96. Id. at 204.

would in any way reveal a military secret or subject the United States and its armed forces to any peril by reason of complete revelation."[97] In the absence of a showing of a war secret or a threat to national security, the judge ruled that "it would appear to be unseemly for the Government to thwart the efforts of a plaintiff in a case such as this to learn as much as possible concerning the cause of the disaster."[98] The court gave the plaintiff access to the report.

Two other important decisions were handed down before Judge Kirkpatrick ruled on the B-29 case. A district court warned the United States what would happen if it failed to comply with a court order to produce documents requested by a private party. The government could first submit the documents to the court for independent scrutiny to test the government's claim of privilege. Failure to follow that procedure meant that the court would dismiss the government's effort to file an antitrust action against the company.[99] The Supreme Court affirmed that judgment on April 24, 1950.[100]

The other lawsuit was decided by a district court on May 12, 1950. A private party brought a tort claims action against the government after the crash of an Air Force plane. The government refused to permit the private parties to see public documents, including the official investigative report of the accident.[101] The government also withheld the names of any witnesses and their statements. The case was on all fours with the B-29 litigation. The court underscored its duty under the Federal Tort Claims Act to adjudicate disputes in an independent manner and assure that plaintiffs have adequate access to documents to prepare their case:

> It is not the exclusive right of any such agency of the Government to decide for itself the privileged nature of any such documents, but the Court is the one to judge of this when contention is made. This can be done by presenting to the Judge, without disclosure in the first instance to the other side, whatever is claimed to have that status. The Court then decides whether it is privileged or not. This would seem to be the inevitable consequence of the Government submitting itself either as plaintiff or defendant to litigation with private persons.[102]

The court ruled that the plaintiffs had shown good cause to have the requested materials submitted to them by the government.[103]

97. Id.
98. Id.
99. United States v. Cotton Valley Operators Committee, 9 F.R.D. 719 (D. La. 1949).
100. United States v. Cotton Valley Operators Committee, 339 U.S. 940 (1950).
101. Evans v. United States, 10 F.R.D. 255, 257 (D. La. 1950).
102. Id. at 257–58.
103. Id. at 258.

The District Court Decides

Guided by these lower court precedents, Judge Kirkpatrick decided on June 30, 1950, that the report of the B-29 accident and the findings of the Air Force's investigation "are not privileged."[104] The interrogatories had flushed out some basic facts, but the government's answers "are far short of the full and complete disclosure of facts which the spirit of the rules requires."[105] In response to the question, "Describe in detail the trouble experienced," the government answered: "At between 18,500 or 19,000 feet manifold pressure dropped to 23 inches on No. one engine."[106] To Kirkpatrick, it was "obvious" that the government "knows more about the accident than this."[107]

On July 20, Judge Kirkpatrick issued an order permitting the plaintiffs to inspect the requested documents and set a deadline of August 7 for the government to produce the material.[108] On July 24, the Justice Department presented to Judge Kirkpatrick a number of letters, affidavits, and statements, explaining why the documents should not be released to the plaintiffs.[109] On August 9, Kirkpatrick met in court to hear from Francis Hopkinson for the plaintiffs, two attorneys from the Justice Department, and two colonels from the Judge Advocate General's Office of the Air Force. Thomas J. Curtin, Assistant U.S. Attorney, brought with him an affidavit signed by Maj. Gen. Reginald C. Harmon, Judge Advocate General of the U.S. Air Force, who stated that information and findings of the accident report and survivor statements "cannot be furnished without seriously hampering national security, flying safety and the development of highly technical and secret military equipment."[110]

At the August 9 hearing, Curtin also produced an undated claim of privilege by the Secretary of the Air Force, Thomas K. Finletter. This turned out to be the pivotal document, spawning great confusion in the case decided by

104. Brauner v. United States, 10 F.R.D. 468, 472 (D. Pa. 1950).

105. Id. at 471.

106. Id.

107. Id.

108. Fisher, In the Name of National Security, at 51.

109. Id. at 51–56.

110. Affidavit of the Judge Advocate General, United States Air Force, Reynolds v. United States, Civil Action No. 10142, U.S. District Court for the Eastern District of Pennsylvania, 7 August 1950, signed by Maj. Gen. Reginald C. Harmon (hereafter "Harmon affidavit"). The affidavit was not filed with the court until October 10, 1950. However, Thomas J. Curtin of the Justice Department brought this affidavit with him to the August 9 hearing; Transcript of Proceedings, 9 August 1950, Brauner and Palya v. United States, Civil Action No. 9793, and Reynolds v. United States, Civil Action No. 10142 (E.D. Pa. 1950), 4 (hereafter "Proceedings for 9 August 1950").

the Supreme Court in 1953 and subsequent litigation in the 2003–2006 period when the three families went back to court to charge that the government had deceived the judiciary. Finletter said that the B-29 carried "confidential equipment on board and any disclosure of its mission or information concerning its operation or performance would be prejudicial to this Department and would not be in the public interest."[111] However, a day after the crash, newspaper readers knew about the confidential equipment. Why did Finletter warn about disclosing the plane's mission or information concerning its operation or performance? Was that type of information in the accident report or the survivor statements sought by the widows? It would be discovered, a half century later, that those documents disclosed nothing about the plane's secret mission or the confidential equipment. Intentionally or not, Finletter's statement was a red herring.

Finletter regarded the compulsory production of the investigative report as "prejudicial to the efficient operation of the Department of the Air Force, is not in the public interest, and is inconsistent with national security." He invoked the privileged status of the requested reports "and must respectfully decline to permit their production."[112] Three points need to be made. First, Finletter was not relying primarily on common law or the state secrets privilege. He relied on statutory authority granted by Congress in the Housekeeping Statute. Second: nothing in that statute implied any authority on the part of federal agencies to withhold documents sought in litigation.[113] Third: Finletter's last line might imply the state secrets privilege, in the sense that no matter what a federal judge ordered the executive branch could refuse. As the government learned in district court and the Third Circuit, refusal meant losing the case.

At the August 9 hearing, Judge Kirkpatrick said it was his impression that the government was not arguing that the case involved "the well recognized common law privilege in regard to secrets or facts which might seriously harm the Government in its diplomatic relations, military operations or the national security." Curtin of the Justice Department asked him to "pass that for a minute, because that does come into this case in the second document" (the

---

111. Claim of Privilege by the Secretary of the Air Force, Reynolds v. United States, Civil Action No. 10142 (E.D. Pa. 1950), 2, filed with the court on 10 October 1950 (hereafter "Finletter statement"). The five-page Finletter statement is not paginated. Although not filed until October 10, Curtin brought it with him to the August 9 hearing.

112. Finletter statement, at 5.

113. Fisher, In the Name of National Security, at 44–48.

Finletter statement).[114] Curtin insisted that "the findings of the head of the Department are binding, and the judiciary cannot waive it."[115] When it came to statutory interpretation of agency authority over access to documents, he said the department's judgment "is final."[116]

Kirkpatrick pursued that point. Putting statutory questions to the side, he wanted to know if the government did claim a common law privilege over military secrets, would the government's decision be final and unreviewable by a court? Curtin: "There is no other interpretation. In other words, I say that the Executive is the person who must make that determination, not the Judiciary."[117] The state secrets privilege had made its appearance, even if the Justice Department never expressly claimed that privilege in its briefs submitted to the district court.

On September 21, Judge Kirkpatrick directed the government to produce for his examination several documents "so that this court may determine whether or not all or any parts of such documents contain matters of a confidential nature, discovery of which would violate the Government's privilege against disclosure of matters involving the national or public interest." The documents included the accident report and statements of the three surviving crew members.[118] When the government failed to produce the documents, he ruled in favor of the three widows.[119] As earlier cases had signaled, the government's refusal to produce documents—either to plaintiffs or to a trial court—always ran a risk. The court could simply decide for the plaintiff.

The Third Circuit Affirms

The government gave notice on April 20, 1951, that it would appeal Judge Kirkpatrick's decision.[120] To the government, the ultimate issue was whether the Housekeeping Statute "and the Constitutional doctrine of separation of powers creates in the head of an executive department a discretion, to be exercised

114. Proceedings for 9 August 1950, at 6.

115. Id. at 9.

116. Id. at 10.

117. Id.

118. Amended Order, 21 September 1950, Brauner and Palya v. United States, Civil Action No. 9793, and Reynolds v. United States, Civil Action No. 10142 (E.D. Pa. 1950), at 2.

119. Fisher, In the Name of National Security, at 56–57.

120. Notice of Appeal to the United States Court of Appeals for the Third Circuit, Brauner and Palya v. United States, Civil Action No. 9793; Reynolds v. United States, Civil Action No. 10142 (E.D. Pa. 1951).

by him, to determine whether the public interest permits disclosure of official records."[121] No one argued that state secrets should be "disclosed" to the public. Delivering documents to a district judge, to be read in chambers, could not be called disclosure. The government essentially argued that access to evidence in a trial would be decided not by the judiciary, but by one of the parties to the case: the executive branch.

The government looked to British precedents for guidance: "We believe that all controlling governmental and judicial material, here and in England, clearly supports the view that, in this type of case at least, disclosure by the head of an executive department cannot be coerced."[122] Why speak about "disclosure" when the procedure contemplated was always *in camera* inspection by a judge? The analogy to Great Britain was strained, because the U.S. Constitution recognizes values and principles that broke decisively with British history and practice, including an independent judiciary capable of deciding against the executive branch, even in cases of national security. The American framers were well aware of the British legal model, which placed all of external affairs, foreign policy, and the war power in the executive, and firmly rejected it.[123]

On December 11, 1951, the Third Circuit upheld the district court's decision: "considerations of justice may well demand that the plaintiffs should have access to the facts, thus within the exclusive control of their opponent, upon which they were required to rely to establish their right of recovery."[124] In tort claims cases, where the government had consented to be sued as a private person, whatever claims of public interest might exist in withholding accident reports "must yield to what Congress evidently regarded as the greater public interest involved in seeing that justice is done to persons injured by governmental operations whom it has authorized to enforce their claims by suit against the United States."[125]

Beyond matters of public law, the Third Circuit concluded that granting the government its "sweeping privilege" would be "contrary to a sound public policy."[126] It would be a small step, the court said, "to assert a privilege against any disclosure of records merely because they might prove embarrassing to

121. Brief for the United States, Reynolds v. United States, No. 10483 (3d Cir. 1951), 1 (hereafter "Government's Brief"), at 6.

122. Id.

123. Fisher, Presidential War Power, at 1–16.

124. Reynolds v. United States, 192 F.2d 987, 992 (3d Cir. 1951).

125. Id. at 994.

126. Id. at 995.

government officers."[127] The court rejected the government's position that it was within "the sole province of the Secretary of the Air Force to determine whether any privileged material is contained in the documents and . . . his determination of this question must be accepted by the district court without any independent consideration of the matter by it. We cannot accede to this proposition."[128] To allow the government a a party to "conclusively determine the Government's claim of privilege is to abdicate the judicial function and permit the executive branch of the Government to infringe the independent province of the judiciary as laid down by the Constitution."[129]

Final Step: Supreme Court

Having lost in district court and the Third Circuit, the government petitioned the Supreme Court for a writ of certiorari. After looking to history, practices in the states, and British rulings, the government for the first time began to press the state secrets privilege: "There are well settled privileges for state secrets and for communications of informers, both of which are applicable here, the first because the airplane which crashed was alleged by the Secretary [of the Air Force] to be carrying secret equipment, and the second because the secrecy necessary to encourage full disclosure by informants is also necessary in order to encourage the freest possible discussion by survivors before Accident Investigation Boards."[130]

The fact that the plane was carrying secret equipment was known to newspaper readers the day after the crash.[131] The fundamental issue, which the government repeatedly muddled, was whether the accident report and the survivor statements contained secret information. As it turns out, they did not.[132] In its brief, the government invoked "the so-called 'state secrets' privilege," asserting that the claim of privilege by Secretary of the Air Force Finletter "falls squarely" under that privilege for various reasons. Nothing in the government's argument had anything to do with the *contents* of the accident report or the survivors' statements. Had those documents been made available to the district court it would have seen nothing that related to military

127. Id.

128. Id. at 996–97.

129. Id. at 997.

130. Brief for the United States, United States v. Reynolds, No. 21, U.S. Supreme Court, October Term, 1952, at 11.

131. Fisher, In the Name of National Security, at 1–2.

132. Id. at 166–69.

secrets or confidential equipment. At various places the government's brief misled the Supreme Court on the contents of the accident report. It asserted: "to the extent that the report reveals military secrets concerning the structure or performance of the plane that crashed or deals with these factors in relation to projected or suggested secret improvements it falls within the judicially recognized 'state secrets' privilege."[133] "To the extent"? In the case of the accident report and the survivor statements, the extent was zero.[134]

On March 9, 1953, the Supreme Court ruled that the government had presented a valid claim of privilege. It did so without looking at the documents. Divided 6 to 3, the Court offered confused principles of judicial supervision: "The court itself must determine whether the circumstances are appropriate for the claim of privilege, and yet do so without forcing a disclosure of the very thing the privilege is designed to protect."[135] If the government can keep the actual documents from the judge, even for *in camera* inspection, there is no basis for a judge to "determine whether the circumstances are appropriate for the claim of privilege." The court merely accepts at face value an assertion by the government, an assertion that in this case proved to be false. Nor is there any reason to regard *in camera* inspection as "disclosure." The Court reasoned that in the case of the privilege against disclosing documents, the Court "must be satisfied from all the evidence and circumstances" before it decides to accept the claim of privilege.[136] Without actual documents, a court has no "evidence" other than self-serving assertions by executive officials.

The Supreme Court cautioned that judicial control "over the evidence of a case cannot be abdicated to the caprice of executive officers."[137] If an executive officer acted capriciously and arbitrarily, a court would have no way of spotting that behavior unless it personally examined the disputed documents. Denied access to evidence, federal courts necessarily rely on vapors and allusions. Through the process adopted by the Court, judicial control was clearly "abdicated to the caprice of executive officers." The Court surrendered to the executive branch fundamental judicial duties over questions of privileges and evidence. The Court served not justice but the executive branch. It signaled that in this type of national security case, the courtroom tilts away from the private litigant and becomes a safe haven for executive power.

133. Brief for the United States, United States v. Reynolds, No. 21, U.S. Supreme Court, October Term, 1942, at 45.

134. For access to the accident report, see pages 10a–68a of http://www.fas.org/sgp/othergov/reynoldspetapp.pdf.

135. United States v. Reynolds, 345 U.S. at 8.

136. Id. at 9.

137. Id. at 9–10.

The Supreme Court had two valid avenues before it. It could have followed the path taken by the district court and the Third Circuit, deciding in favor of the three widows because the government declined to release the accident report and the survivor statements. As an alternative, it could have asked the government to submit the disputed documents to the district court for *in camera* review. Instead, the Court selected a third option that was the least justified, assuming on the basis of ambiguous statements produced by the government that the claim of state secrets had merit. In so doing, it resorted to a jumbled reasoning process that invited future lower courts to injure the rights of private citizens and inflict damage on fair procedures and the rule of law. By failing to examine the documents, the Court took the risk of being fooled. As it turned out, it was, raising disturbing questions about the capacity of the judiciary to function as an independent, trusted branch in the field of national security.

FRAUD AGAINST THE COURT

Judith Loether was seven weeks old when her father, Albert Palya, died in the B-29 crash. As she grew up, she learned that he had been killed in an effort to develop secret equipment. After she had her first son in 1975, she began thinking more about her father's death. By the time she turned 41, she had a better appreciation of how young her father was at the time of the accident. She began to dig deeply into the B-29 aircraft and the special equipment it carried.

On February 10, 2000, she stayed overnight with friends and used their computer. For the first time she entered the combination "B-29" plus "accident" into a search engine. The first hit that came up was a Web site run by Michael Stowe, Accident-Report.com. Stowe had a hobby of collecting and selling military accident reports.[138] He told Loether he had the accident report she wanted. Within a couple of weeks she received the report and began reading it with great care, expecting to find passages on state secrets. To her surprise, there were none. The report contained a few references to "secret equipment," but she already knew that from newspaper stories about the crash. She began sending out postcards to find the other families involved in the *Reynolds* litigation: the Brauners and Patricia J. Herring.[139]

---

138. Fisher, In the Name of National Security, at 166.

139. E-mail to author from Patricia J. Herring. Patricia J. Reynolds remarried and changed her name after the death of her husband.

Loether, the Brauners, and Herring decided to sue the government for deceiving the federal courts. Eventually they turned to the law firm that had brought the original case, Drinker Biddle. The firm filed a motion for a writ of *coram nobis*, charging that the government had misled the Supreme Court and committed fraud against it. The writ is a motion to a court to review and correct its judgment because it was based on an error of fact. In 1827, Justice Joseph Story recognized the fundamental principle at play: "Every Court must be presumed to exercise those powers belonging to it, which are necessary for the promotion of public justice; and we do not doubt that this Court possesses the power to reinstate any cause, dismissed by mistake."[140]

Two principles of law compete. One is the general rule of judicial finality. As expressed by the Supreme Court in 1944, society is well served "by putting an end to litigation after a case has been tried and judgment entered."[141] Every case cannot be relitigated. Bringing finality to a legal dispute offers important benefits, but a second principle also demands respect. A court needs to revisit a judgment after discovering that fraud cast a shadow over the original ruling. Tolerating fraud in a particular case reduces respect for judges and lowers confidence in the courts. There are serious consequences in allowing fraud to infect a ruling: "Tampering with the administration of justice in the manner indisputably shown here involves far more than an injury to a single litigant. It is wrong against the institutions set up to protect and safeguard the public, institutions in which fraud cannot complacently be tolerated consistently with the good order of society. . . . The public welfare demands that the agencies of public justice be not so impotent that they must always be mute and helpless victims of deception and fraud."[142]

On March 4, 2003, Wilson M. Brown III, of Drinker, Biddle petitioned the Supreme Court for a "writ of error *coram nobis* to remedy fraud upon this Court." The petition asked the Court to vacate its decision in *Reynolds* and reinstate the original judgment by the district court; award the widows and their families damages to compensate them for their losses; and award them attorneys fees and single or double costs as a sanction against the government's misconduct.[143] With the benefit of the declassified accident report and survivor statements, the petition detailed specific negligence by the Air Force that

---

140. The Palmyra, 12 Wheat. 1, 10 (1827).

141. Hazel-Atlas Co. v. Hartford Co., 322 U.S. 238, 244 (1944).

142. Id. at 246. For examples of *coram nobis* cases, see Fisher, In the Name of National Security, at 170–76.

143. Petition for a Writ of Error *Coram Nobis* to Remedy Fraud upon This Court, In re Patricia J. Herring, No. 02M76, i.

led to the accident.[144] The government filed a brief opposing the petition.[145] Without explanation, the Court on June 23, 2003, denied the petition.[146] The three families had to begin again in the lower courts.

On October 1, 2003, the families filed an action in district court in Pennsylvania to remedy fraud on the court. They argued that the government's action "was intended to and did subvert the processes of this Court, the Court of Appeals, and the United States Supreme Court."[147] In an opposing brief, the government denied that the statements signed by Finletter and Harmon constituted lies: "neither Secretary Finletter's claim of privilege, nor General Harmon's affidavit, makes any specific representation concerning the contents of those documents [the accident report and witness statements]."[148] Yet it was because of the Finletter-Harmon statements that both the district court and the Third Circuit supported *in camera* review and the Supreme Court was convinced that the accident report contained secret information.

The government had a reason to withhold the accident report from Judge Kirkpatrick. The report revealed clear negligence on the part of the Air Force, which did not install heat shields and failed to brief the civilian engineers before the flight on the use of parachutes and emergency aircraft evacuation.[149] Had Kirkpatrick looked at the report, it would have been obvious that the government had lied on its response to Question 31 of the interrogatories, which asked whether any modifications had been prescribed for the B-29 engines to prevent overheating and reduce the risk of fire hazard. The government's answer: "No."[150] Reading the declassified accident report today, one can see other answers by the government that are either inaccurate or false.

Through its own doing, the government had invited problems. The first was negligence by the Air Force. Why not simply concede mistakes and pay the widows the sums that Judge Kirkpatrick had awarded: $80,000 each to

144. Fisher, In the Name of National Security, at 177–82.

145. Id. at 182–86.

146. In re Herring, 539 U.S. 940 (2003).

147. Independent Action for Relief from Judgment to Remedy Fraud on the Court, Herring v. United States (E.D. Pa. 2003), at 14.

148. Brief in Support of Defendant's Motion to Dismiss, Herring v. United States, Civil Action No. 03-5500 (LDD) (E.D. Pa. 2004), at 18 n.6.

149. Fisher, In the Name of National Security, at 192–93.

150. Plaintiffs' Memorandum in Opposition to Defendant's Motion to Dismiss, Herring v. United States, Civil Action No. 03-5500 (LDD) (E.D. Pa. 2004), at 11 (hereafter "Plaintiffs' Memorandum").

Phyllis Brauner and Elizabeth Palya, and $65,000 to Patricia Herring?[151] In their brief in 2003, the three families gave this answer: the desire of the government to "fabricat[e] a 'test case' for a favorable judicial ruling on claims of an executive or 'state secrets' privilege—a case built on the fraudulent premise that the documents in question contained 'secret' military or national security information."[152]

District Judge Legrome D. Davis held oral argument on May 11, 2004. Both sides spent considerable time trying to understand the meaning of the Finletter–Harmon statements. Wilson Brown said that the Finletter statement "could not have been clearer" in saying that the Air Force objected to releasing the documents because they were "concerned with this confidential mission and equipment of the Air Force," and that there was an intent on the part of the government to suggest to the courts that these documents "contained references to confidential missions and descriptions of confidential equipment that were secret."[153] The government denied that the Finletter statement made representations "regarding the contents of the report or . . . that the report actually contains any specific description of the equipment or the nature of the mission, although there actually is an allusion to the nature of the mission."[154]

In the original litigation, apparently the federal judges and attorneys for the widows never said to the government: "We have no idea what those statements mean. Do they say that the accident report and the survivor statements contain military secrets or state secrets?" Would the government have replied: "Why, no, Your Honor. Those documents, requested by the plaintiffs, do not contain any military secrets or state secrets"? It was to the government's advantage to allow the statements to remain ambiguous. It was the responsibility of the plaintiffs and the judiciary to remove the cloud. Instead, they left it there.

Judge Davis released his decision on September 10, 2004, granting the government's motion to dismiss and instructing the Clerk of Court to "statistically close this matter."[155] He deferred to the government with this reasoning: "In all likelihood, fifty years ago the government had a more accurate under-

151. Fisher, In the Name of National Security, at 58.

152. Plaintiffs' Memorandum, at 12.

153. Transcript of Hearing Before the Honorable Legrome D. Davis, Herring v. United States, CV-03–5500 LDD (E.D. May 11, 2004), at 18.

154. Id. at 41.

155. Memorandum and Order, Herring v. United States, Civil Action No. 03-CV-5500-LDD (E.D. Pa. Sept. 20, 2004), at 21.

standing 'on the prospect of danger to [national security] from the disclosure of secret and sensitive information' than lay persons could appreciate or that hindsight now allows."[156] That was an assumption on Davis's part. It also improperly implied that "disclosure" to Judge Kirkpatrick would have been disclosure to the public.[157]

The families appealed to the Third Circuit. On September 22, 2005, the appellate court decided for the government. The second paragraph made it clear where the court would end up: "Actions for fraud upon the court are so rare that this Court has not previously had the occasion to articulate legal definition of the concept. The concept of fraud upon the court challenges the very principle upon which our judicial system is based: the finality of a judgment."[158] What counted for the Third Circuit was not having to revisit and redo an earlier decision, even if the government had misled the judiciary.

What information in the accident report was so crucial and sensitive to national security that it could not be shared even with a judge in chambers? The Third Circuit pointed to three possibilities: "The accident report revealed, for example, that the project was being carried out by 'the 3150th Electronics Squadron,' that the mission required an 'aircraft capable of dropping bombs' and that the mission required an airplane capable of 'operating at altitudes of 20,000 feet and above.'"[159] The last two elements cannot be a state secret. It was public knowledge that the confidential equipment was on board a B-29 flying at 20,000 feet and that the aircraft was capable of dropping bombs. That's what bombers do. It is implausible to regard the first element as so sensitive in nature that it could not have been submitted for *in camera* review. If reference to the 3150th Electronics Squadron was indeed sensitive, the government could have blackened it out and released the accident report to the families. On May 1, 2006, the Supreme Court refused to take the case.[160]

The value given short shrift in this *coram nobis* case is the need to protect the integrity, independence, and reputation of the federal judiciary. The Supreme Court in *Reynolds* accepted at face value the government's assertion that the accident report and survivors' statements contained state secrets. That assertion was false. By accepting the government's claim and by not examining the documents, the Court appeared to function as an arm of the executive

---

156. Id. at 8 (citing Halperin v. NSC, 452 F.Supp. 47 [D.D.C. 1978]).

157. Fisher, In the Name of National Security, at 198–200.

158. Herring v. United States, 424 F.3d 384, 386 (3d Cir. 2005).

159. Id. at 391 n.3.

160. Herring v. United States, 547 U.S. 1123 (2006).

branch and failed to exercise independent judgment. When courts operate in that manner, litigants and citizens lose faith in the judiciary, the rule of law, and the system of checks and balances.

THE JUDGE RUNS THE COURTROOM

Deciding questions of privileges and access to evidence is central to the conduct of a trial by the judge. In his standard treatise on evidence, John Henry Wigmore recognized the existence of "state secrets" but also concluded that the scope of that privilege had to be decided by a judge, not executive officials. He agreed that there "must be a privilege for *secrets of State, i.e.,* matters whose disclosure would endager [*sic*] the Nation's governmental requirements or its relations of friendship and profit with other nations." Yet he cautioned that this privilege "has been so often improperly invoked and so loosely misapplied that a strict definition of its legitimate limits must be made."[161] On the duty to give evidence, Wigmore was unambiguous: "Let it be understood, then, that there is no exemption, for officials as such, or for the Executive as such, from the universal testimonial duty to give evidence in judicial investigations."[162] Wigmore posed the key question: Who should determine the necessity for secrecy? The executive or the judiciary? As with other privileges, it should be the court: "Both principle and policy demand that the determination of the privilege shall be for the Court."[163]

The issues explored by Wigmore resurfaced in the late 1960s and early 1970s, when expert committees attempted to define "state secrets" and determine which branch should decide the scope and application of privileges in court. An Advisory Committee on Rules of Evidence, appointed by Chief Justice Earl Warren in March 1965, held its initial meeting and began work three months later. In December 1968, the committee completed a preliminary draft of rules of evidence. Among the many proposals was Rule 5–09, covering "secrets of state," defined as "information not open or theretofore officially disclosed to the public concerning the national defense or the international relations of the United States."[164] Nothing in that definition prevented the ex-

---

161. 8 John Henry Wigmore, Evidence in Trials at Common Law § 2212a (3d ed. 1940) (emphasis in original).

162. Id. at § 2370.

163. Id. at § 2379.

164. 46 F.R.D. 161, 272 (1969).

ecutive branch from releasing state secrets to a judge to be read in chambers. It merely restricted the disclosure *to the public.*

The committee recognized that the government "has a privilege to refuse to give evidence and to prevent any person from giving evidence upon a showing of substantial danger that the evidence will disclose a secret of state."[165] Drawing language and ideas from *Reynolds,* the committee said that the privilege may be claimed only by the chief officer of the department administering the subject matter that the secret concerned. That officer would be required to make a showing to the judge, "in whole or in part in the form of a written statement." The trial judge "may hear the matter in chambers, but all counsel are entitled to inspect the claim and showing and to be heard thereon."[166] The judge "may take any protective measure which the interests of the government and the furtherance of justice may require."[167]

If the judge sustained a claim of privilege for a state secret involving the government as a party, the court would have several options. When the claim deprived a private party of "material evidence," the judge could make "any further orders which the interests of justice require, including striking the testimony of a witness, declaring a mistrial, finding against the government upon an issue as to which the evidence is relevant, or dismissing the action."[168] The draft report placed final control with the judge, not the agency head.

Because of that feature and others, the Justice Department vigorously opposed the draft. It wanted the proposed rule changed to recognize that the executive's classification of information as a state secret was final and binding on judges.[169] A revised draft, renumbering the rule from 5–09 to 509, was released in March 1971. It eliminated the definition of "a secret of state" and therefore had to strike "secret" from various places in the rule. The new draft rewrote the general rule of privilege to prevent any person from giving evidence upon a showing of "reasonable likelihood of danger that the disclosure of the evidence will be detrimental or injurious to the national defense or the international relations of the United States."[170] Final control remained with the judge.

---

165. Id. at 273.

166. Id.

167. Id.

168. Id. at 273–74.

169. 26 Federal Practice and Procedure 423 (Charles Alan Wright and Kenneth W. Graham, Jr., eds., St. Paul, Minn.: West Publishing Co., 1992).

170. 51 F.R.D. 315, 375 (1971).

In addition to opposition from the Justice Department, several prominent members of Congress voiced their objections.[171] The Supreme Court sent the proposed rules of evidence to Congress on February 5, 1973, to take effect July 1, 1973. New language for Rule 509 included a redrafted definition of secret of state: "A 'secret of state' is a governmental secret relating to the national defense or the international relations of the United States."[172] Congress concluded that it lacked time to thoroughly review all the proposed rules of evidence within ninety days and vote to disapprove particular ones. It passed legislation to provide that the proposed rules "shall have no force or effect" unless expressly approved by Congress.[173] Approval never came. Among the proposals rejected was Rule 509.

Two years later, Congress passed the rules of evidence, including Rule 501 on privileges. It comes down squarely on the side of authorizing courts to decide the scope of a privilege. The rule covers all parties to a case, including the government. It does not recognize any authority on the part of the executive branch to dictate the reach of a privilege. There is no acknowledgment of state secrets. The only exception in Rule 501 concerns civil actions at the state level. Rule 501 provides: "Except as otherwise required by the Constitution of the United States or provided by Act of Congress or in rules prescribed by the Supreme Court pursuant to statutory authority, the privilege of a witness, person, government, State, or political subdivision thereof shall be governed by the principles of the common law *as they may be interpreted by the courts* of the United States in the light of reason and experience. . . ."[174]

The legislative history of Rule 501 explains how and why the provisions on state secrets were deleted.[175] When the bill reached the House floor, it came with a closed rule that prohibited amendments. The privileges covered by the rule included government secrets, husband and wife, physician and patient, and reporters. Those who drafted the rule were so divided "that we would never get a bill if we got bogged down in that subject matter which really ought to be taken up separately in separate legislation."[176] The Senate Judiciary Committee described the fractious nature of the debate: "Critics attacked, and proponents defended, the secrets of state and official information privileges,"

171. 117 Cong. Rec. 29894–96 (1971). See also the objections by Deputy Attorney General Richard Kleindienst, id. at 33648, 33652–53.

172. 56 F.R.D. 183, 251 (1972).

173. 119 Cong. Rec. 3755, 7651–52 (1973); Pub. L. 93–12, 87 Stat. 9 (1973).

174. 88 Stat. 1934 (1975) (emphasis added).

175. H. Rept. No. 93-650, 93d Cong., 1st Sess. (1973), at 8.

176. 120 Cong. Rec. 1409 (1974) (statement by Rep. Dennis).

the husband–wife privilege "drew fire," the doctor–patient privilege "seemed to satisfy no one," the attorney–client privilege "came in for its share of criticism," and many objections were raised about the failure to include a reporter's privilege.[177] Under those cross-pressures, Congress abandoned efforts to produce a rule on state secrets.[178]

Executive officials who invoke the state secrets privilege often understand that the branch that decides questions of relevance, privileges, and evidence is the judiciary, not the executive. On February 10, 2000, CIA Director George J. Tenet signed a formal claim of state secrets in the case of Richard M. Barlow, adding: "I recognize it is the Court's decision rather than mine to determine whether requested material is relevant to matters being addressed in litigation."[179] That language stands as a model of executive subordination to the rule of law and undergirds the constitutional principle of judicial independence.

INVOKING PRIVILEGES AT A COST

If the government decides to invoke the state secrets privilege, courts have many effective methods to protect their integrity. They can tell the executive branch that if it wants to assert the privilege, even to the point of withholding requested documents from *in camera* inspection, it will lose the case. That was the position taken by the district court and the Third Circuit in *Reynolds*. It was the proper position, and the Supreme Court would have protected its dignity and independence by following the same course. It failed to do so and paid a price, as did the three widows. Telling the executive branch it will lose a case applies to three categories of cases: When the government brings a criminal case, when it brings a civil case, and when it is a defendant as it was in the tort claims case of *Reynolds*.

In criminal cases, it has long been recognized that if federal prosecutors want to charge someone with a crime, the defendant has a right to gain access to documents to establish innocence. In the decade before *Reynolds*, federal courts had reviewed procedures for allowing access to documents in a

177. S. Rept. No. 93-1277, 93d Cong., 2d Sess. (1974), at 6.

178. Louis Fisher, "State Your Secrets: When the Government Cloaks Itself in Privilege, Judges Must Rule," *Legal Times*, June 26, 2006, at 68–69.

179. Declaration of Formal Claim of State Secrets Privilege and Statutory Privilege by George J. Tenet, Director of Central Intelligence, Richard M. Barlow v. United States, Congressional Reference No. 98-887X, U.S. Court of Federal Claims, at 7.

criminal case. A 1944 decision disagreed that judicial deference to executive departments could allow the suppression of documents in a criminal proceeding that might "tend to exculpate."[180] If the government decides to prosecute someone, it must either release documents that may clear the person's name or drop the case. In 1946 the Second Circuit reminded the government that when it "institutes criminal proceedings in which evidence, otherwise privileged under a statute or regulation, becomes importantly relevant, it abandons the privilege."[181]

The Watergate Tapes case of 1974 involved executive privilege, not state secrets, but in ruling against President Nixon the Supreme Court recognized that in a criminal case, where defendants need information to protect their rights in court, the President's general authority over agency information could not override the specific need for evidence.[182] "The ends of criminal justice would be defeated if judgments were to be founded on a partial or speculative presentation of the facts. The very integrity of the judicial system and public confidence in the system depend on full disclosure of all the facts, within the framework of the rules of evidence."[183]

The Court drew a distinction: "We are not here concerned with the balance between the President's generalized interest in confidentiality and the need for relevant evidence in *civil litigation*."[184] Still, lower courts frequently tell the government that when it brings a civil case against a private party, it must be prepared to either surrender documents sought by the defendant or drop the charges. Once a government official seeks relief in a court of law, the official "must be held to have waived any privilege, which he otherwise might have had, to withhold testimony required by the rules of pleading or evidence as a basis for such relief."[185] The choice: Give up the privilege or abandon the case.

In 1958, the Eighth Circuit dismissed a lawsuit brought by the Secretary of Labor after he refused to obey court orders directing him to produce for the defendants four statements taken by the Secretary's investigators. The government argued that the statements were privileged. To the court, the issue of privilege was one for the judiciary.[186] In 1961, the government lost a

180. United States v. Andolschek, 142 F.2d 503, 505n (2d Cir. 1944).
181. United States v. Beekman, 155 F.2d 580, 584 (2d Cir. 1946).
182. United States v. Nixon, 418 U.S. 683 (1974).
183. Id. at 709.
184. Id. at 712 n.19 (emphasis added).
185. Id. See also United States v. Cotton Valley Operators Committee, 9 F.R.D. 719 (D. La. 1949), judgment aff'd, 339 U.S. 940 (1950).
186. Mitchell v. Bass, 252 F.2d 513, 517 (8th Cir. 1958).

case when the National Labor Relations Board refused to permit testimony sought by a company charged with unfair labor practices. The Fifth Circuit insisted that "fundamental fairness" required that the company "be allowed to introduce testimony that may impeach the evidence offered against it. The N.L.R.B. cannot hide behind a self-erected wall evidence adverse to its interest as a litigant."[187] Other decisions underscore the principle that when the government brings a civil suit, it waives any privilege.[188]

The third and last category is when a private party brings a case against the government, as in a tort claims action. The government may be put in the position of either releasing requested documents or losing the case. In *Reynolds*, both the district court and the Third Circuit told the government that if it insisted on withholding the accident report and the survivor statements, it would lose. Only at the level of the Supreme Court was the government allowed to both withhold documents and prevail on the merits. To prevent abuse of the judiciary, a trial court must at least conduct *in camera* review to examine the government's claim of privilege, including state secrets. As noted in a 1980 case: "Any other rule would permit the Government to classify documents just to avoid their production even though there is need for their production and no true need for secrecy."[189]

In 1977, private citizens sued the government after the arrest of over a thousand persons who demonstrated against the Vietnam War. The plaintiffs subpoenaed White House tapes. The D.C. Circuit rejected the position that a presidential privilege of confidentiality "was absolute in the context of civil litigation."[190] The court emphasized that there is "a strong constitutional value in the need for disclosure in order to provide the kind of enforcement of constitutional rights that is presented by a civil action for damages, at least where, as here, the action is tantamount to a charge of civil conspiracy among high officers of government to deny a class of citizens their constitutional rights and where there has been sufficient evidentiary substantiation to avoid the inference that the demand reflects mere harassment."[191]

---

187. NLRB v. Capitol Fish Co., 294 F.2d 868, 875 (5th Cir. 1961).

188. United States v. San Antonio Portland Cement Co., 33 F.R.D. 513, 515 (D. Texas 1963); United States v. Gates, 35 F.R.D. 524, 529 (D. Colo. 1964); General Engineering, Inc. v. NLRB, 341 F.2d 367, 376 (9th Cir. 1965).

189. American Civil Liberties U. v. Brown, 619 F.2d 1170, 1173 (7th Cir. 1980).

190. Dellums v. Powell, 561 F.2d 242, 244 (D.C. Cir. 1977).

191. Id. at 247. See Louis Fisher, "State Secrets Privilege: Invoke It at a Cost," *National Law Journal*, July 31, 2006, at 23.

Courts must take care to restore confidence in the judiciary, in the sanctity of the courtroom, and the system of checks and balances. The state secrets privilege is qualified, not absolute. Otherwise there is no adversary process in court, no exercise of judicial independence over the evidence needed, and no fairness accorded to private litigants who challenge the government. In 1971, the D.C. Circuit stated that an "essential ingredient of our rule of law is the authority of the courts to determine whether an executive official or agency has complied with the Constitution and with the mandates of Congress which define and limit the authority of the executive. Any claim to executive absolutism cannot override the duty of the court to assure that an official has not exceeded his charter or flouted the legislative will."[192] To grant an executive official absolute authority over agency documents would empower the government "to cover up all evidence of fraud and corruption when a federal court or grand jury was investigating malfeasance in office, and this is not the law."[193]

The scope of the state secrets privilege has been especially broad after the events of 9/11. On a range of issues, the executive branch has invoked the privilege in an effort to defeat challenges of illegality and unconstitutionality in court. The next two chapters examine the privilege in two areas: use of the National Security Agency to conduct surveillance without seeking a warrant from a court, and the practice of the executive branch to take suspects to another country for interrogation and torture (extraordinary rendition).

192. Committee for Nuclear Responsibility, Inc. v. Seaborg, 463 F.2d 788, 793 (D.C. Cir. 1971).

193. Id. at 794. See Robert M. Pallitto and William G. Weaver, Presidential Secrecy and the Law (2007), and William G. Weaver and Robert M. Pallitto, "State Secrets and Executive Power," 120 Pol. Sci. Q. 120 (2005).

CHAPTER 9

NSA Surveillance

Following the 9/11 attacks, the Bush administration secretly authorized the National Security Agency (NSA) to eavesdrop on telephone conversations and e-mails without first seeking warrants from a special court created by Congress. This program, in violation of federal law, became public in December 2005 as a result of leaks to the *New York Times*. When the NSA program was challenged in court, the administration invoked the state secrets privilege in an effort to block access to documents requested by private parties claiming injury. Federal judges varied in their responses, some acquiescing to executive power, others allowing the lawsuits to proceed. Congress debated whether to grant retroactive immunity to AT&T and other telecoms that provided assistance to the administration.

ESTABLISHING LIMITS ON WIRETAPS

For most of U.S. history, presidential authority to engage in warrantless eavesdropping for national security purposes was never clarified by statute or judicial rulings. In this legal vacuum, Presidents were able to expand their powers in time of emergency. On May 21, 1940, on the eve of World War II, President Franklin D. Roosevelt sent a confidential memo to his Attorney General, Robert H. Jackson, authorizing and directing him to obtain information "by listening devices" to monitor the conversations or other communications "of persons suspected of subversive activities against the Government of the United States, including suspected spies." Roosevelt told Jackson to keep these investigations "to a minimum and to limit them in so far as possible to aliens."[1]

In the landmark case of *Olmstead* v. *United States* (1928), the Supreme Court decided that the use of wiretaps by prohibition agents to monitor and intercept phone calls did not violate the Constitution. The Court reasoned that the taps—small wires inserted in telephone wires leading from residences—did

---

1. Louis Fisher and David Gray Adler, American Constitutional Law 736 (Durham: Carolina Academic Press, 7th ed., 2007).

not enter the premises of the home or office. Without physical entry there was neither "search" nor "seizure" under the Fourth Amendment.[2] This strained analysis drew a scathing dissent from Justice Louis Brandeis, who accurately predicted that technology would soon overwhelm the Fourth Amendment unless the Court met the challenge with open eyes.

Over the next few decades, federal courts wrestled with new forms of technological intrusion, ranging from "detectaphones" (an instrument placed against the wall of a room able to pick up sound waves on the other side) to placing concealed microphones within the home. Other variations of electronic eavesdropping blossomed. Police used "spike mikes," a small electronic listening device pushed through the wall of an adjoining house until it touched the heating duct of a suspect's dwelling. Law enforcement officers with earphones could listen to conversations taking place on both floors of the house.[3]

In 1967, the Supreme Court put a halt to these practices by returning to basic principles. By a 7 to 1 decision, it declared unconstitutional the placing of electronic listening and recording devices on the outside of public telephone booths to obtain incriminating evidence. Although there was no physical entrance into the area occupied by the suspect, the Court ruled that he had a legitimate expectation of privacy within the phone booth. In a decision broad enough to accommodate technological advances, the Court held that the Fourth Amendment "protects people, not places."[4] In response to this decision, Congress passed legislation in 1968 requiring law-enforcement officers to obtain a judicial warrant before placing taps on phones or installing bugs (concealed microphones). If an "emergency" existed, communications could be intercepted for up to forty-eight hours without a warrant in cases involving organized crime or national security. This legislation is often referred to as "Title III authority."

The 1968 statute established national policy on *domestic* wiretaps. The executive branch claimed that warrantless surveillances for national security purposes were lawful as a reasonable exercise of presidential power. A section of Title III stated that nothing in it limited the President's constitutional power to "take such measures as he deems necessary to protect the Nation against actual or potential attack or other hostile acts of a foreign power, to obtain foreign intelligence information deemed essential to the security of the United States, or to protect national security information against foreign intelligence

2. 277 U.S. 438 (1928).
3. Fisher and Adler, American Constitutional Law, at 735–37.
4. Katz v. United States, 389 U.S. 347, 351 (1967).

activities." Nor should anything in Title III "be deemed to limit the constitutional power of the President to take such measures as he deems necessary to protect the United States against the overthrow of the Government by force or other unlawful means, or against any other clear and present danger to the structure or existence of the Government."[5] Congress, feeling an obligation to say something, chose general language to largely duck the issue. It soon found it necessary to reenter the field and pass comprehensive legislation on national security surveillance.

ILLEGAL DOMESTIC SURVEILLANCE

Eavesdropping by the executive branch emerged as a powerful issue in the 1960s after it was publicly disclosed that U.S. intelligence agencies had been monitoring political activities of Americans. In 1967, when the U.S. Army wanted the NSA to eavesdrop on American citizens and domestic groups, the agency agreed to carry out the assignment.[6] A four-year investigation by a Senate committee, assisted by Captain Christopher Pyle, who had inside knowledge about military surveillance of civilian politics, brought the program fully into the open and shut it down.[7]

The NSA also began to put together a list of those who opposed the Vietnam War. Adding names to a domestic "watch list" led to the creation of MINARET: a tracking system that allowed the agency to follow individuals and organizations involved in the antiwar movement.[8] In this manner NSA agreed to use its surveillance powers to violate the First and Fourth Amendments. From mid-1969 to early 1970, the White House directed the FBI to install (without warrants) seventeen wiretaps to eavesdrop on government officials and reporters.[9] Newspaper stories in 1974 revealed that the CIA had been extensively involved in illegal domestic surveillance, infiltrating dissident groups in the country and collecting close to 10,000 files on American citizens. CIA Director William Colby later acknowledged the existence of this program while testifying before a Senate committee.[10]

5. 82 Stat. 214 (1968).

6. James Bamford, Body of Secrets 428 (2002 ed.).

7. Frank J. Donner, The Age of Surveillance: The Aims and Methods of America's Political Intelligence System 287–320 (1981).

8. Bamford, Body of Secrets, at 428–29; James Bamford, The Puzzle Palace 323–24 (1983 ed.).

9. Richard E. Morgan, Domestic Intelligence 6 (1980).

10. Kathryn S. Olmsted, Challenging the Secret Government 11–12, 35 (1996).

The Huston Plan

On June 5, 1970, President Richard Nixon met with the heads of several intelligence agencies to initiate a program to monitor what the administration considered to be radical individuals and groups in the United States. Attending the meeting was Tom Charles Huston, a young aide working in the White House. He drafted a forty-three-page, top secret memorandum that became known as the Huston Plan. He put the matter bluntly to Nixon: "Use of this technique is clearly illegal; it amounts to burglary."[11] His plan, which Nixon approved, directed the NSA to intercept, without judicial warrant, the domestic communications of U.S. citizens using international phone calls or telegrams.[12]

Under pressure from FBI Director J. Edgar Hoover and Attorney General John Mitchell, Nixon withdrew the Huston Plan.[13] Placed in a White House safe, Huston's blueprint became public in 1973 after Congress investigated the Watergate affair and uncovered documentary evidence that Nixon had ordered the NSA to illegally monitor American citizens.[14] To conduct its surveillance operations under such programs as SHAMROCK (in operation from August 1945 to May 1975), NSA entered into agreements with such U.S. companies as Western Union and RCA Global. U.S. citizens, expecting privacy, learned that American companies had been turning over the telegrams to the NSA.[15]

Judicial Response

A 1972 decision by the Supreme Court scrutinized the government's use of warrantless electronic surveillance to prevent what the Nixon administration feared was an attempt by domestic organizations to attack and subvert the existing structure of government. As the Court framed the issue, it needed to balance both "the Government's right to protect itself from unlawful subversion

---

11. Keith Olson, Watergate 16 (2003); Fred Emery, Watergate 25 (1995 ed.); Loch K. Johnson, America's Secret Power 133–56 (1989).

12. Bamford, Body of Secrets, at 430. For more details on the Huston plan, see Athan Theoharis, Spying on Americans: Political Surveillance from Hoover to the Huston Plan 13–39 (1978).

13. Emery, Watergate, at 26–27.

14. Bamford, Body of Secrets, at 431–32.

15. Id. at 438–39; Morgan, Domestic Intelligence, at 75–76. For further details on domestic surveillance during the 1960s and 1970s, see testimony by Frederick A. O. Schwarz, Jr., "Ensuring Executive Branch Accountability," before the Subcommittee on Commercial and Administrative Law of the House Committee on the Judiciary, March 29, 2007, at 4, 10–11.

and attack" and "the citizen's right to be secure in his privacy against unreasonable Government intrusion."[16]

In district court, individuals prosecuted by the government requested all records of warrantless surveillance directed at them. They asked for a hearing to determine whether any of the evidence used to indict them was tainted by illegal actions. The district court held that the warrantless electronic surveillance could not be justified on the ground that some domestic organizations were trying to subvert government. Warrants were needed. The court directed the government to fully disclose to the defendants any illegally monitored conversations and ordered an evidentiary hearing to determine the extent of the taint.[17] The court rejected the government's argument that the Attorney General, "as agent of the President, has the constitutional power to authorize electronic surveillance without a court warrant in the interest of national security."[18] The court expressly dismissed the claim of a broad "inherent" presidential power.[19] The President was "still subject to the constitutional limitations imposed upon him by the Fourth Amendment."[20]

The Sixth Circuit affirmed, unimpressed by the government's sweeping argument that the power at issue in the case "is the inherent power of the President to safeguard the security of the nation."[21] The court reminded the government that the Fourth Amendment "was adopted in the immediate aftermath of abusive searches and seizures directed against American colonists under the sovereign and inherent powers of King George III."[22] The framers drafted the Constitution "to provide a check upon 'sovereign' power," relying on three coordinate branches of government "to require sharing in the administration of that awesome power."[23] The Sixth Circuit paused to reflect on historical lessons: "It is strange, indeed, that in this case the traditional power of sovereigns like King George III should be invoked on behalf of an American President to defeat one of the fundamental freedoms for which the founders of this country overthrew King George's reign."[24]

16. United States v. United States District Court, 407 U.S. 297, 299 (1972).

17. United States v. Sinclair, 321 F.Supp. 1074 (E.D. Mich. 1971).

18. Id. at 1076.

19. Id. at 1077.

20. Id. at 1078 (citing District Judge Ferguson in United States v. Smith, 321 F.Supp. 424, 425 [C.D. Cal. 1971]).

21. United States v. United States Dist. Ct. for E.D. of Mich., 444 F.2d 651, 658 (6th Cir. 1971).

22. Id. at 665.

23. Id.

24. Id.

Unanimously, the Supreme Court affirmed the Sixth Circuit. The fundamental value in the concept of a warrant issued under the Fourth Amendment "is its issuance by a 'neutral and detached magistrate.'"[25] The Bush administration would dismiss that value after 9/11. Fourth Amendment freedoms, said the Court in 1972, "cannot properly be guaranteed if domestic security surveillances may be conducted solely within the discretion of the Executive Branch. The Fourth Amendment does not contemplate the executive officers of [the] Government as neutral and disinterested magistrates."[26] Executive officers charged with investigative and prosecutorial duties "should not be sole judges of when to utilize constitutionally sensitive means in pursuing their tasks."[27]

The government said that the domestic surveillances at issue in the case were directed primarily at collecting and maintaining intelligence about subversive forces—not to gather evidence for criminal prosecution. It further argued that courts lacked the knowledge and expertise to determine whether domestic surveillance was needed to protect national security.[28] Themes of that nature would be heard again after 9/11. In 1972, the Court concluded that those arguments did not justify departure from the Fourth Amendment.[29]

The Court looked to language inserted by Congress in Title III of the Omnibus Crime Control Act of 1968, which declined to specify the President's power to conduct warrantless national security surveillance. The Court held that the language merely disclaimed congressional intent to define presidential power in that statute and did not affirmatively grant any authority to the President.[30] In rejecting the government's broad argument in this particular case for domestic surveillance, the Court found no reason to define the boundaries of surveillance over foreign powers.

The FISA Statute

The Court's decision in 1972 pressured Congress to adopt statutory guidelines for the President's power to conduct surveillance over foreign powers. Congress created the Church and Pike Committees to study the scope of executive branch illegality and propose a system of legislative and judicial checks. From those hearings and congressional reports came the creation of new Intelligence

25. United States v. United States District Court, 407 U.S. at 316.
26. Id. at 316–17.
27. Id. at 317.
28. Id. at 318–19.
29. Id. at 320.
30. Id. at 302–08 (Section 2511(3) of the Omnibus Crime Control Act).

Committees in the House and the Senate to monitor the agencies of the intelligence community, including the NSA and the CIA. Shortly thereafter came the landmark Foreign Intelligence Surveillance Act (FISA) of 1978. In congressional hearings, Attorney General Edward H. Levi testified in support of legislation that would require "independent review at a critical point by a detached and neutral magistrate."[31] The theory of independent and inherent presidential power would be replaced by a judicial check. FISA established a special court, the Foreign Intelligence Surveillance Court (FISC), or FISA court, to assure outside supervision on the exercise of executive power. At the same time, Congress established a Court of Review to hear appeals by the government when the court denied applications to engage in electronic surveillance. FISA made clear that the statutory procedures for electronic surveillance within the United States for foreign intelligence purposes "shall be the exclusive means" of conducting such surveillance. The purpose was to drive one more nail in the claim of inherent presidential power.

WARRANTLESS SURVEILLANCE AFTER 9/11

On December 16, 2005, the *New York Times* reported that President George W. Bush, in the period immediately following the 9/11 attacks, had secretly authorized the NSA to listen to Americans and others inside the United States without a court-approved warrant. The administration decided that the exclusive framework of FISA was not legally binding and followed an executive-made process. As reported in the *Times*, the NSA had been monitoring the international telephone calls and international e-mails "of hundreds, perhaps thousands" of people over the intervening years in an effort to obtain evidence about terrorist activity.[32]

In a weekly radio address, President Bush conceded that he had authorized the NSA, "consistent with U.S. law and the Constitution, to intercept the international communications of people with known links to Al Qaeda and related terrorist organizations."[33] He and other executive officials referred

31. "Electronic Surveillance within the United States for Foreign Intelligence Purposes," hearings before the Subcommittee on Intelligence and the Rights of Americans of the Senate Committee on Intelligence, 94th Cong., 2d Sess. 76 (1976).

32. James Risen and Eric Lichtblau, "Bush Lets U.S. Spy on Callers Without Courts," New York Times, December 16, 2005, at A1.

33. "Bush on the Patriot Act and Eavesdropping," New York Times, December 18, 2005, at 30.

to NSA eavesdropping as the Terrorist Surveillance Program (TSP). As later acknowledged by the administration, the term Terrorist Surveillance Program was not used before the *New York Times* broke the story.[34] The term was selected not only to give the operation a name, but also to attract public and congressional support for its legitimacy. Opponents of the NSA activity, in their lawsuits challenging the administration, refer to it as the "warrantless surveillance program."[35]

In a news conference on December 19, Bush said that as President "and Commander in Chief, I have the constitutional responsibility and the constitutional authority to protect our country. Article II of the Constitution gives me that responsibility and the authority necessary to fulfill it." In addition to a constitutional source of authority, Bush identified a statutory source: the Authorization of Use of Military Force (AUMF) that Congress had passed immediately after 9/11 to use military force against Al Qaeda.[36] Also on December 19, Attorney General Alberto Gonzales held a press briefing on the TSP, claiming that "the President has the inherent authority under the Constitution, as Commander-in-Chief, to engage in this kind of activity."[37] When asked why the administration did not seek a warrant from the FISA court, Gonzales replied that the administration continued to seek warrants from the court but was not "legally required" to do that in every case if another statute (such as the AUMF) granted the President independent authority.[38] The administration would continue to cite both Article II and the AUMF, but over time the emphasis fell increasingly on the constitutional source. Under this argument, Congress could pass legislation such as FISA, but the administration was at liberty to ignore statutory law and rely solely on executive-made law.

Gonzales underscored the need for "the speed and the agility" that the FISA process lacked: "You have to remember that FISA was passed by the Congress in 1978. There have been tremendous advances in technology" since

34. Letter from J. M. McConnell, Director of National Intelligence, to Senator Arlen Specter, July 31, 2007, discussed also in a letter from Attorney General Alberto R. Gonzales to Senator Patrick J. Leahy, August 1, 2007.

35. Al-Haramain Islamic Foundation, Inc. v. Bush, 451 F.Supp.2d 1215, 1218 n.1 (D. Or. 2006).

36. 41 Weekly Comp. Pres. Doc. 1885 (2005).

37. Press briefing by Attorney General Alberto Gonzales and General Michael Hayden, Principal Deputy Director for National Intelligence, available from http://www.whitehouse. gov/news/releases/2005/12/print/20051219–1.html.

38. Id.

that time.[39] Why did the administration not ask Congress to amend FISA to grant the President greater flexibility, as was done several times after 1978 and even after 9/11? Gonzales said he was advised "that would be difficult, if not impossible."[40]

Formal Legal Defense

On January 19, 2006, OLC produced a forty-two-page "white paper" defending the legality of the TSP. It offered two arguments, one statutory (AUMF), the other constitutional (Article II). It claimed that Congress, in passing the AUMF, "by statute has confirmed and supplemented the President's recognized authority under Article II of the Constitution to conduct such warrantless surveillance to prevent further catastrophic attacks on the homeland."[41] The statute authorized the President to "use all necessary and appropriate force against those nations, organizations, or persons he determines planned, authorized, committed, or aided the terrorists attacks" of September 11 in order to prevent "any future acts of international terrorism against the United States."[42] OLC concluded that "warrantless communications intelligence targeted at the enemy in time of armed conflict is a traditional and fundamental incident of the use of military force authorized by the AUMF."[43]

The language "all necessary and appropriate force" in AUMF does not authorize a President to do whatever he wants to, particularly if it violates an existing law like FISA. If Congress after 9/11 wanted to modify the FISA procedures to grant the President wider authority without a judicial check, it knew how to do it. It would amend FISA by bringing up a bill to debate changes, with all members of Congress aware of what they are doing. Lawmakers might have considered this language: "notwithstanding the provision in Title II, Section 201(b), Subsection (f), of the Foreign Intelligence Surveillance Act, the President is hereafter authorized to engage in the following type of warrantless surveillance." In floor debate, lawmakers must know that the bill intends to waive the judicial check in FISA. That was never done.

39. Id. at 2.
40. Id. at 4.
41. "Legal Authorities Supporting the Activities of the National Security Agency Described by the President," Office of Legal Counsel, U.S. Department of Justice, January 19, 2006, at 2 (hereafter "OLC Study").
42. 115 Stat. 224 (2001).
43. OLC Study, at 2.

Amendments to statutory law are not made by implication, with members unaware of what they are voting on and what they might be changing. There is no basis for finding in the debate on the AUMF that members of Congress understood they were setting FISA aside to allow the President to conduct warrantless surveillance over domestic matters. It is quite true, as OLC said, that FISA "also contemplates that Congress may authorize such surveillance by a statute other than FISA."[44] Congress is always at liberty to adopt a future statute modifying an earlier one. But when it acts, it does so expressly and consciously, not by vague and unspoken implications.

What of the Article II argument? OLC said that NSA's activities under the TSP "are supported by the President's well-recognized inherent constitutional authority as Commander in Chief and sole organ for the Nation in foreign affairs to conduct warrantless surveillance of enemy forces for intelligence purposes to detect and disrupt armed attacks on the United States."[45] Four claims or concepts in this sentence deserve close attention: well-recognized, inherent, Commander in Chief, and sole organ.

Some attorneys in the executive branch may accept that the President's power to conduct warrantless surveillance is "well-recognized," but there is no such recognition by federal courts, members of Congress, or the academic community. The record is quite mixed. Some experts offer support for independent and inherent presidential power in foreign affairs; others flatly deny such sweeping and unchecked powers. In FISA, Congress left no room for inherent and independent authority to conduct warrantless surveillance.

Are there "inherent" powers for the President? This position requires extreme caution and wariness. First, it is a claim or assertion, not fact. Second, it has a self-serving motivation, for it comes from the branch claiming the authority. Third, the word "inherent" has an indefinite and indefinable quality that leaves the door open for illegal, unconstitutional, and extraconstitutional powers. Fourth, claims of "inherent" presidential authority have been used in recent years to justify military commissions (rejected by the Supreme Court in *Hamdan*), torture memos, indefinite detention of U.S. citizens designated as "enemy combatants," extraordinary rendition, and the TSP.

To appreciate the dangers of "inherent" power, compare three words used to decide the source of constitutional authority: *express, implied,* and *inherent.* The first two preserve and protect constitutional government. Express powers appear in black and white. They can be seen in print and analyzed, usually accompanied by extensive meaning from history and framers' intent. Implied also fulfills the Constitution, because an implied power must be reasonably drawn from an existing express power. For example, the President has an express power to see that the laws are faithfully executed. If a Cabinet or other executive official prevents the discharge of a law, the President has an implied power to remove the individual to assure compliance with the law. Express and implied powers are consistent with a constitutional system of limited government.

The same cannot be said of "inherent." The word is defined in some dictionaries as an "authority possessed without it being derived from another. . . . Powers over and beyond those explicitly granted in the Constitution or reasonably to be implied from express powers." Inherent can mean a power that "inheres" in an office or position, or something that is "intrinsic" or "belonging by nature." The purpose of a constitution is to specify and confine government powers to protect rights and liberties reserved to individuals. That objective is undermined by vague and open-ended sources of authority, including "inherent."[46]

What powers come from "Commander in Chief"? It is analytically meaningless to merely cite three words from Article II as though the case for presidential power is self-evident and needs no further argument. One has to explain what those words mean. Close scrutiny eliminates any notion of plenary power for the President as Commander in Chief. Those powers are constrained and checked by authorities given to Congress in Article I, by the framers' rejection of the broad prerogatives given to the King by William Blackstone and British writers, and the principle of civilian supremacy over the military. Congress is an essential part of that civil power.

Finally, what of "sole organ"? In the history of American constitutional doctrines, there is probably nothing as shallow, empty, and misleading as the OLC claim that the President as "sole organ" in foreign affairs is given some type of exclusive, plenary power. The phrase comes from a speech by Rep. John Marshall in 1800, when he said that the President "is the sole organ of the nation in its external relations, and its sole representative with foreign nations."[47] In his decades of distinguished federal service, as Secretary of State, member of the House, and Chief Justice of the Supreme Court, Marshall at no time advocated an independent, inherent, or exclusive power of the President over external affairs. The purpose of the speech in 1800 was merely to

46. Louis Fisher, "Invoking Inherent Powers: A Primer," 37 Pres. Stud. Q. 1, 2 (2007).
47. 10 Annals of Cong. 613 (1800).

state that President John Adams had a constitutional duty under the Take Care Clause to see that an extradition treaty with Britain was faithfully carried out. That was all. The context of his speech makes it clear that he was speaking of presidential power to execute *the policy of Congress*, whether expressed in statute or treaty. Marshall never implied any authority of the President to act independent of statutes or treaties, much less in opposition to them (as the Bush administration claimed it could with FISA). For example, Chief Justice Marshall ruled in 1804 that when a presidential proclamation in time of war conflicts with a statute passed by Congress, the statute prevails.[48]

What OLC does is to take Marshall's speech not as it was given, and not as it was intended, but as it was misinterpreted and distorted by Justice George Sutherland's dicta in *United States* v. *Curtiss-Wright* (1936).[49] Sutherland promoted misconceptions about Marshall's speech, the concept of sovereignty, inherent presidential power, extraconstitutional powers, the distinction between external and internal affairs, and the competing powers of Congress.[50]

Secret Briefings

After initiating the NSA surveillance, the Bush administration offered to brief eight members of Congress and the chief judge of the FISA court. The lawmakers (called the "Gang of Eight") included the chairman and ranking member of the two Intelligence Committees, the Speaker and Minority Leader of the House, and the Senate Majority and Minority Leaders. The lawmakers were directed by executive officials not to take notes or share what they heard with colleagues or their staff. Excluded from the Gang of Eight, the Judiciary Committees (with jurisdiction over federal courts) were not briefed.

It is usually constructive for the executive branch to brief and consult with members of Congress *provided the program is legal and constitutional.* Briefing members about an illegal program does not make it legal. Moreover, the Gang of Eight was not the proper model. It was established as a means of informing the congressional leadership and the top levels of the Intelligence Committees about a pending covert action.[51] The law defines covert action as an activity

48. Little v. Barreme, 2 Cr. (6 U.S.) 170, 179 (1804).

49. OLC Study, at 1, 6–7, 14, 30.

50. Louis Fisher, "Presidential Inherent Power: The 'Sole Organ' Doctrine," 37 Pres. Stud. Q. 139 (2007).

51. 50 U.S.C. § 413b(c)(2) (2000).

"to influence political, economic, or military conditions abroad."[52] The TSP had nothing to do with destabilizing or altering a foreign country.

What duty falls on a member of the Gang of Eight after being briefed that a program waives FISA and dispenses with an independent judicial check? They are not bound by some vow of secrecy demanded by the executive officials doing the briefing. Lawmakers belong to a separate branch with separate institutional responsibilities, including the duty to assure that the executive branch complies with the law. After being briefed, lawmakers may reach out to colleagues, staff cleared to deal with classified matters, and to the leadership of the Judiciary Committees to seek their legal and constitutional advice. Members of Congress take an oath to the Constitution, not to the President. They have a special obligation to protect the powers of their institution and the constituents they represent.

What duty falls on a chief judge of the FISA court after being briefed about a program that violated statutory policy by operating without a judicial warrant? The duty was not to remain silent and be co-opted by the executive branch. There was a need for the other ten judges on the court to be told about the NSA program. They should have then, collectively, decided what to do to remain within the law. The primary obligation was to honor the judicial check that Congress placed in FISA.

SECRET EXECUTIVE LAW

NSA's surveillance program directly challenged questions about the constitutional duty of Congress to make law. In the Steel Seizure Case of 1952, Justice Robert Jackson eloquently summarized the principles of the U.S. Constitution: "With all its defects, delays and inconveniences, men have discovered no technique for long preserving free government except that the Executive be under the law, and that the law be made by parliamentary deliberations."[53] Simple words but profound. The Executive is under the law, not above it or outside it. The law is made by Congress. Under the guise of "inherent" power, the executive branch claimed the right with the TSP to ignore statutory law and prefer executive-made law done in secret. Other countries have adopted that model at great cost to democratic institutions and individual rights.

52. Id. at § 413b(e).
53. Youngstown Co. v. Sawyer, 343 U.S. 579, 655 (1952).

After the *New York Times* revealed NSA's surveillance program in December 2005, President Bush in a radio address said that he had authorized the agency to conduct the activity "consistent with U.S. law and the Constitution."[54] In subsequent statements he continued to refer to "U.S. law" or "authority," but he meant law created solely and secretly within the executive branch, even when contrary to statutory law. His administration repeatedly referred to independent authority derived from Article II. President Bush announced that he "reauthorized this program more than 30 times since the Sept. 11 attacks."[55] The words legal, lawful, authorized, and reauthorized all referred to decisions made wholly within the executive branch.

A Hospital Visit

After initiating the TSP, the administration reviewed the program periodically to judge its legality. In March 2004, OLC concluded that the program had a number of legal deficiencies and recommended that it not be reauthorized until changed. The presidential order to reauthorize the program contained a line for the Attorney General to sign. Attorney General John Ashcroft and Deputy Attorney General James Comey agreed with the OLC analysis and recommendation. Ashcroft was hospitalized with a serious illness and transferred his powers to Comey.

On the evening of March 10, 2004, in his capacity as Acting Attorney General, Comey was heading home with his security detail about 8 o'clock. He received a call from Ashcroft's chief of staff that he had heard from Mrs. Ashcroft, who understood that White House Counsel Gonzales and White House Chief of Staff Andrew Card were on their way to the hospital. Comey thought that Gonzales and Card, knowing of the legal objections raised by the Justice Department to the TSP, might try to convince Ashcroft to reverse Justice's position and agree to sign the reauthorization form.

Comey called his chief of staff and told him to get as many of Comey's people as possible to the hospital immediately. He called FBI Director Robert Mueller and asked that he come to the hospital. Comey's car reached the hospital, and he raced up the stairs to Ashcroft's room and found Mrs. Ashcroft standing by the bed. As Comey explained to the Senate Judiciary Committee

54. "Bush on the Patriot Act and Eavesdropping," New York Times, December 18, 2005, at 30.

55. David E. Sanger, "In Address, Bush Says He Ordered Domestic Spying," New York Times, December 18, 2005, at 30.

on May 15, 2007, he was concerned there might be a White House effort to have Ashcroft sign the form and he was in no condition to be subjected to this pressure.[56] He tried to get Ashcroft oriented to the issue before Gonzales and Card arrived. He then went out in the hallway to call Mueller, who was on his way. Aware of the circumstances, Mueller directed FBI agents not to have Comey removed from Ashcroft's room if Gonzales and Card tried to do that. Within a few minutes, OLC head Jack Goldsmith and a senior Justice official, Patrick Philbin, arrived and entered Ashcroft's room. Comey sat down in a chair at the head of Ashcroft's bed, Goldsmith and Philbin stood behind him, and Mrs. Ashcroft stood by the bed holding her husband's arm.

When Gonzales and Card entered the room, Gonzales carried an envelope and explained to Ashcroft why they were there and why they wanted him to approve the reauthorization of the TSP. Lifting his head from the pillow, Ashcroft defended the position that Justice had taken and said his opinion did not matter because he was not Attorney General. Pointing to Comey, he said he was the Attorney General. Gonzales and Card left. When Mueller arrived, Comey briefed him on what had happened.[57]

Card called Comey and told him to come to the White House immediately. Comey said that after the conduct he had just witnessed, he would not come without a witness. Card responded: "What conduct? We were just there to wish him well."[58] Comey called Solicitor General Ted Olson, explained what had happened, and asked him to join him at the White House as a witness. They reached the White House that evening at about 11 o'clock.[59] Card asked Olson to sit outside while he talked to Comey alone. Gonzales arrived and brought Olson into the room, and the four discussed the situation. Card said he had heard there might be a number of resignations at the Justice Department over the incident. Comey concluded that he could not stay if the administration decided to engage in conduct that the Justice Department said had no legal basis.[60] Others prepared to resign included FBI Director Mueller, Comey's chief of staff, Ashcroft's chief of staff, and quite likely Ashcroft.[61]

---

56. Transcript of May 15, 2007, hearings on U.S. attorney firings by the Senate Committee on the Judiciary, CQ Transcriptions. The transcript is not numbered but the remark by Comey appears on page 13.

57. Id. at 14–15.

58. Id. at 16.

59. Id. at 17.

60. Id. at 19.

61. Id. at 20–21.

The mass resignations were averted when President Bush met with Comey and Mueller in the Oval Office two days later. As Comey was leaving, Bush asked to see him privately in a separate room for about fifteen minutes; Bush did the same with Mueller. From those two meetings Comey understood that he was to do "the right thing" as he saw it.[62] To Comey, that meant that Justice would not sign the reauthorization form until the program satisfied legal standards. During this review by Justice, the White House proceeded with the TSP without the approval of Comey or the Justice Department.[63] After two or three weeks and the acceptance of changes urged by Justice, the reauthorization form received the signature of the Attorney General.[64]

Hayden's Testimony

Michael V. Hayden appeared before the Senate Intelligence Committee on May 18, 2006, to testify on his nomination to be CIA Director. Previously he had served as NSA Director at the time the surveillance plan was initiated. At the hearing, he defended the legality of the NSA program on constitutional—not statutory—grounds. He did not refer to the AUMF for legal justification. In recalling his service at NSA after 9/11, he told the committee that when he talked to NSA lawyers "they were very comfortable with the Article II arguments and the President's inherent authorities."[65] When they came to him and discussed the lawfulness of the NSA program, "our discussion anchored itself on Article II."[66] The attorneys "came back with a real comfort level that this was within the President's authorities [i.e., Article II]."[67]

This legal advice was not put in writing and Hayden "did not ask for it." Instead, "they talked to me about Article II."[68] What could they have talked about? The President as Commander in Chief? What other words in Article II could have clarified the legal issue and produced a comfort level? Apparently the NSA General Counsel was not asked to prepare a formal legal memo defending the TSP. No paper trail or accountability. Just informal talks.

62. Id. at 21.

63. Id. at 32.

64. Id. at 43.

65. "Nomination of General Michael V. Hayden, USAF, to be Director of the Central Intelligence Agency," hearing before the Senate Select Committee on Intelligence, 109th Cong., 2d Sess. 30 (May 18, 2006).

66. Id. at 31.

67. Id. at 54.

68. Id.

Hallway discussions about legal and constitutional issues are not likely to look as persuasive or as sound when put on paper and submitted to experts for their independent assessment.

At the Senate hearing, Hayden repeatedly claimed that the NSA program was legal and that the CIA "will obey the laws of the United States and will respond to our treaty obligations."[69] Given what he said throughout the hearing, what did he mean by "law"? National policy decided by statute and by treaty? Or a policy purely executive-made, based on someone's interpretation of Article II? During the hearing, he treated "law" as the latter. After 9/11, while head of the NSA, he told the committee he "had two lawful programs in front of me, one authorized by the President [the TSP], the other one would have been conducted under FISA as currently crafted and implemented."[70] In other words, he had two choices: one authorized by statutory law, the other in violation of it. He told one Senator: "I did not believe—still don't believe—that I was acting unlawfully. I was acting under a lawful authorization."[71] He meant a presidential directive issued under Article II, even if in violation of the exclusive policy set forth in FISA.

Hearing him insist that he had acted legally in implementing the NSA program, a Senator said: "I assume that the basis for that was the Article II powers, the inherent powers of the President to protect the country in time of danger and war." Hayden replied: "Yes, sir, commander in chief powers."[72] Immediately after 9/11, CIA Director George Tenet asked Hayden whether as NSA Director he could "do more" to combat terrorism with surveillance. Hayden answered: "Not within current law."[73] In short, the administration knowingly and consciously decided to act against statutory policy and do so secretly. It knew that the NSA eavesdropping program it wanted to conduct was illegal under FISA but decided to go ahead, banking on Article II powers.

At one point in the hearing, Hayden referred to the legal and political embarrassments of NSA during the Nixon administration, when it conducted warrantless eavesdropping against domestic groups. In discussing what should be done after 9/11, he told one group: "Look, I've got a workforce out there that remembers the mid-1970s." He asked the Senate committee to forgive him for using "a poor sports metaphor," but he had advised the group in this manner:

69. Id. at 57.
70. Id. at 66.
71. Id. at 104.
72. Id. at 107.
73. Id. at 54.

"Since about 1975, this agency has had a permanent one ball, two strike count against it, and we don't take many close pitches."[74] TSP was a close pitch. As Congress learns more about the program, the public can decide whether NSA swung and missed a third time.

CHALLENGES IN COURT

A number of private parties challenged the legality and constitutionality of NSA's eavesdropping. To show the injury necessary to have a case litigated, plaintiffs argued that the contacts they previously had with clients over the telephone were now impossible because of NSA monitoring. To maintain contact they had to travel to see clients personally, including in countries outside the United States. The government intervened in these cases, asking that the lawsuits be dismissed on the ground that litigation would inevitably disclose "state secrets" injurious to the nation. That argument was weakened when the Bush administration decided to publicly acknowledge the existence of the TSP and publicly defend its legality. As explained later, more "secret" details about the program would become public.

California Case

On July 20, 2006, a federal district judge held that the state secrets privilege did not block action on the lawsuit. The judge denied the government's motion to have the case dismissed or go to summary judgment on the issue of the state secrets privilege. Under summary judgment, a court does not begin the time-consuming process of depositions and trial but goes immediately to the legal issue. As a result of the judge's ruling, the lawsuit was allowed to proceed—a significant defeat for the Bush administration.[75]

In this case, plaintiffs alleged that AT&T and its holding company had collaborated with the NSA in conducting a massive warrantless surveillance program that illegally tracked the domestic and foreign communications of millions of Americans. The plaintiffs charged violations of the First and Fourth Amendment of the Constitution, FISA, different sections of other federal laws, and California's Unfair Competition Law. In attempting to have the case dismissed, the government advanced three arguments: "(1) the very

74. Id. at 49.
75. Hepting v. AT&T Corp., 439 F.Supp.2d 974 (N.D. Cal. 2006).

subject matter of this case is a state secret; (2) plaintiffs cannot make a *prima facie* case for their claims without classified evidence and (3) the [state secrets] privilege effectively deprives AT&T of information necessary to raise valid defenses."[76]

To the court, the first step in analyzing the state secrets privilege is to decide whether the information is actually a "secret."[77] The court pointed to public reports about the TSP in the *New York Times* on December 16, 2005. It noted that President Bush, the following day, confirmed the existence of the program. Bush publicly described the mechanism by which the program was authorized and reviewed. Attorney General Gonzales talked about the program in public briefings and public hearings. The Justice Department publicly defended the legality and constitutionality of the TSP. Based on this public record, the court said "it might appear that none of the subject matter in this litigation could be considered a secret given that the alleged surveillance programs have been so widely reported in the media."[78]

The court recognized that just because a factual statement has been made public does not guarantee that the facts are true or that the activity was not a genuine secret. Even if a previously secret program has been leaked, verification of the program by the government could be harmful.[79] Also, media reports may be unreliable.[80] In this case, the administration had "publicly admitted the existence of a 'terrorist surveillance program,' which the government insists is completely legal." Moreover, given the scope of the TSP, the court found it "inconceivable" that it could exist without the acquiescence and cooperation of a telecommunications provider. The size of AT&T, its public acknowledgment that it performs classified contracts, and the fact that it employees thousands of people with government security clearances provided enough verifiable public information to reject the state secrets privilege as an absolute bar on litigation.[81] Following this reasoning, the court concluded that the plaintiffs were entitled "to at least some discovery."[82]

As to whether plaintiffs had shown injury to establish standing and the right to sue AT&T, the court concluded that the plaintiffs "have sufficiently alleged that they suffered an actual, concrete injury traceable to AT&T and

76. Id. at 985.
77. Id. at 986.
78. Id. at 989.
79. Id. at 990.
80. Id. at 991.
81. Id. at 992.
82. Id. at 994.

redressable by this court."[83] On those grounds, the court allowed the case to proceed, with each side at liberty to request additional documents to support their position.

A week later, the government prevailed in an NSA case decided in Illinois. A federal district court dismissed a class-action lawsuit against a Bush administration program that involved the collection and monitoring of phone numbers. Actual conversations were not listened to (the program revealed by the *New York Times* in December 2005). As to the phone-number program, the administration neither confirmed nor denied its existence.[84] By invoking the state secrets privilege, the government sought to prevent the plaintiffs from seeking additional facts or documents to establish that they had been harmed or would suffer harm in the future. The judge ruled that the plaintiffs were unable to find relief in the courts and had to seek redress from the political branches.

Detroit/Sixth Circuit

In the California case, the federal court let the case continue without deciding the merits. On August 17, 2006, District Judge Anna Diggs Taylor in Detroit ruled that the TSP violated the Constitution and federal statutes. Like the judge in California, Taylor noted that the administration had admitted the existence of a warrantless program that listened to communications with one party in the United States.[85] Contrary to the arguments of NSA, Taylor was persuaded that the plaintiffs were able to establish "a *prima facie* case" based solely on the government's public admissions about the TSP.[86] As to injury, plaintiffs provided documentation that "they are stifled in their ability to vigorously conduct research, interact with sources, talk with clients and, in the case of the attorney Plaintiffs, uphold their oath of providing effective and

83. Id. at 1001. For newspaper stories on this decision, see Arshad Mohammed, "Judge Declines to Dismiss Lawsuit Against AT&T," Washington Post, July 21, 2006, at A9; John Markoff, "Judge Declines to Dismiss Privacy Suit Against AT&T," New York Times, July 21, 2006, at A13.

84. Terkel v. AT&T, 441 F.Supp.2d 899, 912 (N.D. Ill. 2006); Adam Liptak, "Judge Rejects Customer Suit Over Records from AT&T," New York Times, July 26, 2006, at A13; Mike Robinson, "Judge Dismisses Lawsuit on AT&T Data Handover," Washington Post, July 26, 2006, at A6.

85. American Civil Liberties v. National Sec. Agency, 438 F.Supp.2d 754, 765 (E.D. Mich. 2006).

86. Id.

ethical representation of their clients."[87] Plaintiffs cited additional injury by having to travel to meet with clients and other individuals.

The NSA argued that it could not defend itself in court "without the exposure of state secrets." Judge Taylor disagreed, pointing out that the Bush administration "has repeatedly told the general public that there is a valid basis in law for the TSP." Moreover, the NSA contended that the President has statutory authority under the AUMF and the Constitution to authorize continued use of the TSP, and presented that case "without revealing or relying on any classified information."[88] Taylor found the agency's argument that it could not defend itself "without the use of classified information to be disingenuous and without merit."[89]

Judge Taylor examined constitutional and statutory arguments presented by the plaintiffs, starting with the language of the Fourth Amendment: "The right of the people to be secure in their persons, houses, papers, and effects, against unreasonable searches and seizures, shall not be violated, and no Warrants shall issue, but upon probable cause, supported by Oath or affirmance, and particularly describing the place to be searched, and the persons or things to be seized." She said the Fourth Amendment was adopted "to assure that Executive abuses of the power to search would not continue in our new nation."[90] Judicial rulings emphasized that executive officials could not be trusted to be neutral and disinterested magistrates or the sole judges on the extent of their prosecutorial powers. In enacting FISA, Congress insisted on a body outside the executive branch—the FISA court—to provide independent review. However, the TSP "has undisputedly been continued for at least five years, it has been undisputedly been implemented without regard to FISA . . . and obviously in violation of the Fourth Amendment."[91]

Judge Taylor further concluded that unchecked use of search and seizure has damaged First Amendment rights of speech, press, and the ability of citizens to function effectively through organizations. FISA, she pointed out, explicitly admonished that "no United States person may be considered . . . an agent of a foreign power solely upon the basis of activities protected by the First Amendment."[92] President Bush, she said, "has undisputedly violated the

---

87. Id.
88. Id.
89. Id. at 766.
90. Id. at 774.
91. Id. at 775.
92. Id. at 776.

Fourth in failing to procure judicial orders as required by FISA, and accordingly has violated the First Amendment rights of these Plaintiffs as well."[93]

The next constitutional issue: separation of powers. Judge Taylor recalled the framers' resentment of the General Warrants authorized by King George III, helping precipitate the break with England. She cited language from Justice Robert Jackson that "emergency powers are consistent with free government only when their control is lodged elsewhere than in the Executive who exercises them."[94] President Bush, by acting in a manner forbidden by FISA, functioned outside the law decided by legislative deliberations and attempted to combine the powers of government into one branch.

The Bush administration defended the TSP by relying on the AUMF. Judge Taylor observed that the AUMF "says nothing whatsoever of intelligence or surveillance."[95] Could authority for the TSP be *implied* in the AUMF? She said that by passing FISA and Title III on wiretaps, Congress had provided "the exclusive means by which electronic surveillance of foreign intelligence communications may be conducted."[96] Prior warrants must be obtained from judges. Whereas FISA offered a fifteen-day exception in time of a declaration of war, the executive branch allowed TSP to function for more than five years without congressional authorization. The administration's argument that the AUMF somehow modified FISA, without direct and explicit amendment, "cannot be made by this court."[97]

Did President Bush have some inherent power to authorize the TSP? The government, said Judge Taylor, "appears to argue here that, pursuant to the penumbra of Constitutional language in Article II, and particularly because the President is designated Commander in Chief of the Army and Navy, he has been granted the inherent power to violate not only the laws of the Congress but the First and Fourth Amendments of the Constitution, itself."[98] She continued: "We must first note that the Office of the Chief Executive has itself been created, with its powers, by the Constitution. There are no hereditary Kings in America and no powers not created by the Constitution. So all 'inherent powers' must derive from that Constitution."[99] The argument that "inherent powers justify the program here in litigation must fail."[100]

---

93. Id.
94. Id. at 778 (citing Youngstown v. Sawyer, 343 U.S. 579, 652 [1952]).
95. Id. at 779.
96. Id. at 772.
97. Id. at 779.
98. Id. at 780.
99. Id. at 781.
100. Id.

Finally, Judge Taylor addressed the government's argument that practical considerations justified the TSP, including the difficulty of obtaining judicial warrants in a timely manner. She pointed to previous decisions that rejected "practical arguments" used to justify emergency actions by executive officers, including the supposed lack of judicial competence, the danger of security leaks, and unacceptable delay.[101] She observed that the government never proposed amendments to FISA to alleviate these practical problems.[102] She found the government's plea for "speed and agility," as reasons to bypass statutory and constitutional requirements, to be "weightless."[103]

The government appealed. On July 6, 2007, the Sixth Circuit reversed Judge Taylor on the ground that the plaintiffs lacked standing to bring the suit. Writing for a 2 to 1 panel, Judge Alice M. Batchelder concluded that if litigation in a state secrets case "would necessitate admission or disclosure of even the existence of the secret, then the case is non-justiciable and must be dismissed on the pleadings," i.e., without proceeding to trial and the merits.[104] What was meant by "admission or disclosure"? The administration had already admitted the existence of the program. Did "disclosure" mean showing a judge confidential documents in chambers? If that were true, the executive branch would win every time it asserted state secrets, even if the intention was to conceal misconduct or illegality. In such cases there would be no judicial check. The government gave the district court an opportunity to review secret documents *in camera* to support the state secrets privilege. Each judge of the Sixth Circuit panel received the same documents, *in camera* and under seal. Judge Batchelder reviewed those documents.[105] It is not clear if the judges looked at partial and selective documents.

On the question of standing, Judge Batchelder said that the plaintiffs "do not—and because of the State Secrets Doctrine cannot—produce any evidence that any of their own communications have ever been intercepted by the NSA, under the TSP, or without warrants."[106] They could only assert "a mere belief," which the court found too "amorphous" and "speculative" to justify standing.[107] The NSA might be listening to their communications, but "the

---

101. Id.

102. Id. at 782.

103. Id.; Adam Liptak and Eric Lichtblau, "U.S. Judge Finds Wiretap Actions Violate the Law," New York Times, August 18, 2006, at A1; Dan Eggen and Dafna Linzer, "Judge Rules against Wiretaps," Washington Post, August 18, 2006, at A1.

104. ACLU v. National Sec. Agency, 493 F.3d 644, 650 n.2 (6th Cir. 2007).

105. Id. at 650, n.3.

106. Id. at 653.

107. Id. at 653–56.

alternative possibility remains that the NSA might *not* be intercepting, and might *never* actually intercept, any communication by any of the plaintiffs named in this lawsuit."[108] By deciding against any contacts with their clients, "the plaintiffs have negated any possibility that the NSA will ever actually intercept their communications and thereby avoided the anticipated harm."[109]

Judge Batchelder discussed other scenarios that would defeat the plaintiffs' ability to sue. If they attempted telephone and e-mail communications with their overseas contacts and the communications were not intercepted by the NSA, "there would be no injury to these plaintiffs due to the NSA's conduct." If the NSA did intercept a communication, "there would be no tangible injury until the NSA disclosed the information (presumably in a manner demonstrating a direct injury to the plaintiffs or their contacts)."[110] If NSA gave the information to law-enforcement officers, how would the plaintiffs know unless the government prosecuted them? The prosecutors could always claim they were acting independently on the basis of their own intelligence.

The plaintiffs argued that if NSA were to conduct its surveillance in compliance with FISA, "they would no longer feel compelled to cease their international telephone and email communications." Judge Batchelder questioned that position. If NSA had obtained FISA warrants for the type of overseas contacts used by the plaintiffs, "the plaintiffs would still not have known their communications were being intercepted, still faced the same fear of harm to their contacts, still incurred the same self-imposed (or contact-imposed) burden on communications and, therefore, still suffered the same alleged injury."[111] Because wiretaps are secret, "neither the plaintiffs nor their overseas contacts would know—with or without warrants—whether their communications were being tapped."[112] That is true. However, NSA surveillance approved by the FISA court is subject to minimization procedures to protect privileged communications. Warrantless NSA surveillance lacks those court-monitored procedures.

Judge Bachelder concluded that plaintiffs could never establish standing if they had no knowledge of what NSA was doing (either going to the FISA court or bypassing it). The result: NSA was left free to violate statutes and the Constitution without fear of a challenge in court. The only limitation on

108. Id. at 656 (emphasis in original).
109. Id.
110. Id. at 656, n.14.
111. Id. at 668.
112. Id. at 671–72.

illegal activity would be self-policing within the executive branch to terminate the NSA operation or bring it within legal (statutory) limits. Relying on one branch to police itself is not the form of government the framers created.

Judge Julia Smith Gibbons concurred on the standing issue. She placed two requirements on the plaintiffs. They must demonstrate "that they (1) are in fact subject to the defendant's conduct, in the past or future, and (2) have at least a reasonable fear of harm from that conduct." She agreed they may have satisfied the second test but had not shown they are subject to the agency's conduct.[113] Given the government's position on the state secrets privilege and the decision of the Sixth Circuit to read classified documents *in camera, ex parte*, it would be impossible for plaintiffs to do that.

Judge Ronald Lee Gilman dissented. He found that the attorneys included among the plaintiffs had alleged "a concrete, imminent, and particularized harm flowing from the TSP."[114] The attorney-plaintiffs "contend that they have had to travel internationally for face-to-face meetings at a significant expense in terms of time and money."[115] He concluded that the TSP "violates FISA and Title III and that the President does not have the inherent authority to act in disregard of those statutes."[116] He denied that the AUMF somehow implicitly repealed the "exclusive means" provision of FISA.[117] On February 19, 2008, the Supreme Court declined to take this case.

Islamic Charity

An unusual case developed when the al-Haramain Islamic Foundation, based in Oregon, obtained a top-secret calling log that showed it was a target of warrantless surveillance. The Treasury Department inadvertently gave the document to the organization during a routine discovery request. Al-Haramain returned the document but the trial court ruled that it could rely on memories of the log in litigating their case.[118] On November 16, 2007, the Ninth Circuit ruled that the organization could not refer to the document because it was covered by the state secrets privilege. Yet it allowed the charity to go forward with the lawsuit on other grounds. The appellate court rejected

113. Id. at 689–90.
114. Id. at 695.
115. Id. at 696.
116. Id. at 713.
117. Id. at 715.
118. Al-Haramain Islamic Foundation, Inc. v. Bush, 451 F.Supp.2d 1215, 1229 (D. Or. 2006).

the administration's argument that the lawsuit should be dismissed because it concerned a secret program. "In light of extensive government disclosures about the TSP, the government is hard-pressed to sustain its claim that the very subject matter of the litigation is a state secret. . . . [T]here has been a cascade of acknowledgments and information coming from the government. . . ."[119] Left to be argued was whether a statute passed by Congress (FISA) trumped a program created by the administration (TSP).

The Ninth Circuit's decision illustrates the incoherent standards followed by federal courts on state secrets cases. Having reviewed materials *in camera*, the court maintained that it took "very seriously our obligation to review the documents with a very careful, indeed a skeptical, eye, and not to accept at face value the government's claim or justification of privilege. Simply saying 'military secret,' 'national security,' or 'terrorist threat' or invoking an ethereal fear that disclosure will threaten our nation is insufficient to support the privilege." Yet a mere eleven lines down the court remarks: "That said, we acknowledge the need to defer to the Executive on matters of foreign policy and national security and surely cannot legitimately find ourselves second guessing the Executive in this arena."[120] That position undermines the reputation of the courts as an independent branch and announces in advance that fair consideration will not be shown to private litigants. Executive claims are entitled to respect, not deference, and that respect should be extended to both parties to a lawsuit.

El Paso Interview

The administration repeatedly argued in every court that it could not allow any additional information to be released about the TSP other than its very existence. Disclosure of any other facts or details, it said, would jeopardize national security. However, new facts emerged during an interview with National Intelligence Director Mike McConnell in El Paso, Texas, released on August 22, 2007. He discussed a decision by a FISA judge on a matter that had previously been held confidential. He said the FISA court approved the TSP but one of the eleven judges "looked at the same data and said well wait a minute[,] I interpret the law, which is the FISA law, differently. And it came down to, if it's on a wire and it's foreign in a foreign country, you have to have a warrant and so we found ourselves in a position of actually losing ground because it was

---

119. Al-Haramain Islamic Foundation, Inc. v. Bush, 507 F.3d 1190, 1193 (9th Cir. 2007).
120. Id. at 1203.

the first review [that gave us] less capability, we got a stay and that took us to the 31st of May."[121] There had been scattered press reports about this FISA judge, but McConnell was the first confirmation by an executive official.

Based on these media reports, ACLU filed a motion requesting certain orders issued by the FISA court on January 10, 2007, and any subsequent orders, plus any legal briefs submitted by the government in connection with those orders. ACLU acted in part on the basis of an August 1 television interview with House Minority Leader John Boehner, who gave new information about a FISA court order.[122] The government argued that the FISA court had no authority to unseal its own orders (or other sealed materials), but ACLU responded that every court had authority over its own docket and authority to unseal materials. After learning of the McConnell interview in El Paso, ACLU said it was evident that some portion of the sealed materials could be disclosed. If administration officials "can publicly discuss the sealed materials, the public should have firsthand access to them."[123]

McConnell was the first administration official to publicly discuss the assistance received from telecoms: "under the president's program, the terrorist surveillance program, the private sector had assisted us. Because if you're going to get access you've got to have a partner and they were being sued. Now if you play out the suits at the value they've claimed, it would bankrupt these companies. So my position was we have to provide liability protection to these private sector entities."[124] He explained that legislation passed in early August 2007 gave the private carriers prospective, but not retroactive, protection: "We've got a retroactive problem."[125] To the extent that private carriers like AT&T and other companies violated the law by giving the administration assistance, he wanted those illegalities washed away by law. Quite an irony. The administration had claimed full authority to enter into these agreements with private companies; it now said it needed authority from Congress to remedy the legal problems.

121. Chris Roberts, "Transcript: Debate on the Foreign Intelligence Surveillance Act," El Paso Times, August 22, 2007, at http://www.elpasotimes.com/news/ci_6685679, at 1 (hereafter "McConnell interview").

122. In re Certain Orders Issued by This Court on January 10th, 2007, and Subsequently Extended, Modified and/or Vacated, motion of the ACLU, at 2, n.1 (FISA Court, August 8, 2007).

123. In re Motion for Release of Court Records, reply by the ACLU in support of motion for release of court records, at 2 (FISA Court, September 14, 2007).

124. McConnell interview, at 2.

125. Id.

Toward the end of the interview, McConnell said that public discussion of the TSP program "means that some Americans are going to die, because we do this mission unknown to the bad guys because they're using a process that we can exploit and the more we talk about it, the more they will go with an alternative means and when they go to an alternative means, remember what I said, a significant portion of what we do, this is not just threats against the United States, this is war in Afghanistan and Iraq." The journalist from the *El Paso Times* asked: "So you're saying that the reporting and the debate in Congress means that some Americans are going to die?" McConnell responded: "That's what I mean. Because we have made it so public."[126] Steven Aftergood, director of the Project on Government Secrecy for the Federation of American Scientists, described the interview as "quite striking because he was disclosing more detail than has appeared anywhere in the public domain." Aftergood added: "If we're going to believe that Americans will die from discussing these things, then he is complicit in that. It's an unseemly argument. He's basically saying that democracy is going to kill Americans."[127]

Plaintiffs suing AT&T in the NSA case read the McConnell interview as damaging to the administration. Cindy Cohn, legal director for the Electronic Frontier Foundation, taking the lead in the AT&T case, remarked: "They've really undermined their own case."[128] The plaintiffs filed a motion asking the Ninth Circuit to consider as evidence the information released by McConnell in his interview.[129]

LEGISLATIVE REMEDIES

After the *New York Times* disclosed NSA's eavesdropping program, Congress drafted legislation to put the policy on firm legal footing. Better legislative oversight was needed to replace the skimpy "Gang of Eight" procedure exploited by the administration.[130] Executive officials testified that it was impractical in the post-9/11 period to expect the administration to obtain individual

126. Id. at 4.

127. Eric Lichtblau, "Role of Telecom Firms in Wiretaps Is Confirmed," New York Times, August 24, 2007, at A13.

128. Id.

129. Ellen Nakashima, "AT&T Plaintiffs Cite McConnell Remarks," Washington Post, September 1, 2007, at D3.

130. David D. Kirkpatrick, "Republicans Seek to Bridge Differences on Surveillance," New York Times, March 1, 2006, at A13.

warrants every time they needed to listen to a conversation of someone suspected of being connected with al Qaeda. They wanted Congress to recognize the President's inherent authority to conduct warrantless eavesdropping to collect foreign intelligence. Opponents said it would be better to have no legislation than to grant the President such sweeping, unchecked power.[131]

By early 2006, Republican leaders saw an advantage in passing legislation just before the November 2006 elections, allowing voters to compare the national security credentials of the two parties. But there were too many bills and too many contradictions.[132] Strong objections were voiced to legislation allowing the FISA court to decide the constitutionality of the NSA program.[133] How would that be done? Secret briefs submitted to the FISA court by the administration? Secret oral argument and eventually the release of a declassified, sanitized ruling? Constitutional issues should not be decided in that manner.

With Congress about to recess for the elections, the differences among the various bills were too large to bridge.[134] The House passed its bill, 232 to 191, but it was too unlike the Senate bill to assure quick resolution in conference committee.[135] Democratic victories in the November elections put an end not only to Republican control of Congress but to the Republican-drafted bills on national security surveillance.

Executive Self-Investigation

The executive branch had an opportunity to investigate the legality of NSA's program. One agency prepared to conduct a probe would have been the Office of Professional Responsibility (OPR), located within the Justice Department. OPR examines professional misconduct by government employees. Questions were raised whether DOJ attorneys had played inappropriate roles in authorizing and overseeing warrantless electronic surveillance. In the past, OPR had access to information at the highest levels. No one could recall OPR having to

131. Eric Lichtblau, "Administration and Critics, in Senate Testimony, Clash over Eavesdropping Compromise," New York Times, July 27, 2006, at A19.

132. Jonathan Weisman, "Republican Rift over Wiretapping Widens: Party at Odds on Surveillance Legislation," Washington Post, September 6, 2006, at A3.

133. Jonathan Weisman, "House GOP Leaders Fight Wiretapping Limits," Washington Post, September 13, 2006, at A7.

134. Keith Perine and Tim Starks, "House Panels Approve Surveillance Bill," C.Q. Weekly Report, September 25, 2006, at 2556.

135. Eric Lichtblau, "House Approves Powers for Wiretaps without Warrants," New York Times, September 29, 2006, at A18.

shut down an investigation because of lack of clearance. This time, however, the administration denied the security clearances to those within the office to investigate the matter.[136]

Appearing before the Senate Judiciary Committee hearing on July 16, 2006, Attorney General Gonzales testified that President Bush had personally intervened to prevent OPR from conducting an inquiry. Senator Specter asked why OPR wasn't given clearance. Gonzales replied that President Bush had restricted access "because this is such an important program."[137] A Justice Department official said that while some questioned the legality of the TSP, there was never an issue of legal ethics within the jurisdiction of OPR. Rep. Maurice Hinchey (D-N.Y.) disagreed, saying that OPR was the appropriate agency to investigate the performance of lawyers who evaluated surveillance programs and whether they were manipulated.[138]

After the November 2006 elections shifted congressional control to the Democrats, the administration partly reversed its position about DOJ reviewing NSA's program. Justice's Inspector General, Glenn Fine, said he would investigate whether Justice lawyers had complied with legal requirements. No effort would be made, however, to decide if NSA violated the Constitution or federal statutes. Other legal issues would be explored. Fine said that the White House had promised the necessary security clearances for his staff.[139] In November 2007, after Gonzales had been driven from government, the new Attorney General, Michael Mukasey, reopened the OPR investigation of the NSA program. The attorneys in that office now had the clearances to conduct an inquiry.[140]

136. Scott Shane, "With Access Denied, Justice Dept. Drops Spying Investigation," New York Times, May 11, 2006, A24; "Justice on a Short Leash: Why Did the President Cut Off Investigation of the NSA's Domestic Surveillance Program?" (editorial), Washington Post, July 22, 2006, at A16.

137. Neil A. Lewis, "Bush Blocked Ethics Inquiry, Official Says," New York Times, July 19, 2006, at A14.

138. Id.

139. Dan Eggen, "Justice Dept. to Examine Its Use of NSA Wiretaps," Washington Post, November 28, 2006, at A10; Eric Lichtblau, "Justice Official Opens Spying Inquiry," New York Times, November 28, 2006, at A19.

140. Dan Eggen, "Justice Dept. Reopens Surveillance Probe," Washington Post, November 14, 2007, at A4; Scott Shane, "Bush Approves Clearances for N.S.A. Inquiry," New York Times, November 14, 2007, at A15.

A Mid-Course Correction

Facing possible setbacks in court, the administration announced in January 2007 that it would no longer skirt the FISA court but would instead seek warrants from it, as required by statute. In a letter of January 17, Attorney General Gonzales informed the Senate Judiciary Committee that on January 10 a judge of the FISA court had issued orders authorizing the government "to target for collection international communications into or out of the United States where there is probable cause to believe that one of the communicants is a member or agent of al Qaeda or an associated terrorist organization." As a result of those orders, "any electronic surveillance that was occurring as part of the Terrorist Surveillance Program will now be conducted subject to the approval of the Foreign Intelligence Surveillance Court."[141] This statement seemed to comply with FISA, but did it contemplate a one-time, blanket judicial approval for all future national security wiretaps within this category?[142] Gonzales said that under these circumstances President Bush "has determined not to reauthorize the Terrorist Surveillance Program when the current reauthorization expires."[143]

The Gonzales position left unclear whether the administration agreed to comply with statutory authority or whether it kept in reserve its Article II, inherent power argument. If the latter, his response offered merely a temporary accommodation before reasserting inherent powers. Gonzales said that President Bush "is committed to using all lawful tools to protect our Nation from the terrorist threat, including maximum use of the authorities provided by FISA. . . ."[144] What was "lawful"? The administration had defended the President's asserted inherent authority as a "lawful tool" and insisted that the TSP "fully complies with the law."[145]

Press accounts interpreted the Gonzales letter as a repudiation of the TSP. In the *Washington Post*, Dan Eggen wrote that the Bush administration "has agreed to disband a controversial warrantless surveillance program run by the National Security Agency, replacing it with a new effort that will be overseen

141. Attorney General Alberto Gonzales to Senators Patrick Leahy and Arlen Specter, Chairman and Ranking Member of the Senate Committee on the Judiciary, January 17, 2007, at 1.

142. Id.

143. Id. at 2.

144. Id. at 1.

145. Id.

by the secret court that governs clandestine spying in the United States."[146] The title of his article, "Court Will Oversee Wiretap Program," suggested an ongoing, close judicial monitoring of warrants submitted to it, rather than what Gonzales appeared to describe: an advance, blanket authority for national security wiretaps. Eggen referred to "an abrupt reversal" by the administration rather than a partial and possibly temporary correction.[147]

Eggen correctly captured the ambiguity of the Gonzales letter. Executive officials would not say whether the administration intended to seek a warrant for each person to be monitored or whether the FISA court orders covered multiple cases. Officials told Eggen that the January 10 orders were scheduled to expire in ninety days, leaving doubt both about their extension and possible modifications.[148] Other news analyses reported dramatic shifts in administration policy. The headline in a *New York Times* story: "White House Retreats Under Pressure."[149] A *Washington Post* article carried a similar message: "Bush Retreats on Use of Executive Power."[150] The articles overstated the administration's position, claiming that Bush officials "implicitly abandoned their argument that the president's inherent power under Article II of the Constitution was all the authority he needed."[151] The letter by Gonzales could be read just as easily to support the Article II/inherent argument, to be invoked whenever the administration wanted to.

Appearing before the Senate Judiciary Committee, Gonzales did not agree to provide more documents to explain the decision.[152] He appeared to concede that the administration not only broke the law but knew it had done so: "The truth of the matter is we looked at FISA and we all concluded there's no way we can do what we have to do to protect this country under the strict reading of FISA."[153] There were reports that the FISA court orders would be shown

146. Dan Eggen, "Court Will Oversee Wiretap Program," Washington Post, January 18, 2007, at A1.

147. Id.

148. Id. Coverage by the *New York Times* also described the altered legal and political climate. Eric Lichtblau and David Johnston, "Court to Oversee U.S. Wiretapping in Terror Cases," New York Times, January 18, 2007, at A1.

149. Scott Shane, "White House Retreats Under Pressure," New York Times, January 18, 2007, at A16.

150. Peter Baker, "Bush Retreats on Use of Executive Power," Washington Post, January 18, 2007, at A4.

151. Id.

152. David Johnston and Scott Shane, "Senators Demand Details on New Eavesdropping Rules," New York Times, January 18, 2007, at A18.

153. Id. See also Dan Eggen, "Spy Court's Orders Stir Debate on Hill," Washington Post, January 19, 2007, at A6.

to House and Senate leaders and selected committees, including Intelligence and Judiciary, although access by the latter seemed restricted to chairmen and ranking members.[154]

The tentative and possibly temporary accommodation by the administration undermined its position in court that the NSA cases should be considered moot and dismissed. Had the Gonzales letter adopted a permanent policy or one that could be revisited and reversed? At a hearing on January 31, 2007, before the Sixth Circuit, one of the judges asked: "You could opt out at any time, couldn't you?" The Deputy Solicitor General acknowledged that possibility.[155]

Swerving Again: McConnell's Testimony

On May 1, 2007, Mike McConnell testified before the Senate Intelligence Committee and signaled that the administration might not be able to keep its pledge to seek warrants through the FISA court. He had served as NSA Director from 1992 to 1996. His written statement appeared to endorse FISA as the legal foundation for conducting national security wiretaps. The pending bill, he said, "seeks to restore FISA to its original focus on protecting the privacy interests of persons in the United States."[156] He could not "overstate how instrumental FISA has been in helping the IC [intelligence community] protect the nation from terrorist attacks since September 11, 2001."[157] Yet he also stated that FISA's requirement to obtain a court order, "based on a showing of probable cause, slows, and in some cases prevents altogether, the Government's efforts to conduct surveillance of communications it believes are significant to the national security."[158] How could a revised FISA take care of those difficulties?

In testimony before the Senate Intelligence Committee, Kenneth Wainstein of the Justice Department discussed what he considered to be the impractical requirement of obtaining a warrant from the FISA court for each national

154. Tim Starks, "Oversight Committees to Review Documents on NSA Wiretapping," C.Q. Weekly Report, February 5, 2007, at 402; Mark Mazzetti, "Key Lawmakers Getting Files about Surveillance Program," New York Times, February 1, 2007, at A11; Dan Eggen, "Records on Spy Program Turned Over to Lawmakers," Washington Post, February 1, 2007, at A2.

155. Adam Liptak, "Judges Weigh Arguments in U.S. Eavesdropping Case," New York Times, February 1, 2007, at A11.

156. "Modernizing the Foreign Intelligence Surveillance Act," statement by J. Michael McConnell, Director of National Intelligence, before the Senate Select Committee on Intelligence, May 1, 2007, at 1.

157. Id. at 2.

158. Id. at 5.

security surveillance operation. Critics of the administration "argue that the Intelligence Community should be required to seek FISA court approval each time a foreign target overseas happens to communicate with a person inside the United States." He regarded that as "an infeasible approach that would impose intolerable burdens on our intelligence efforts."[159] Was this another signal that the administration's pledge in January 2007 to adhere to FISA court review would not be followed in each instance?

Senior officials in the Bush administration told the committee they could no longer pledge to seek warrants from the FISA court for each domestic surveillance. They argued that the President had independent authority under the Constitution to order this type of surveillance without warrants and without complying with statutory procedures. McConnell referred several times to Article II as a source of inherent presidential authority. When asked by Senator Russ Feingold (D-Wisc.) whether the administration would no longer side-step the FISA court, McConnell replied: "Sir, the president's authority under Article II is in the Constitution. So if the president chose to exercise Article II authority, that would be the president's choice." He repeated that "Article II is Article II, so in a different circumstance, I can't speak for the president what he might decide."[160]

Why would an administration witness tell a congressional committee that Article II is in the Constitution, and that Article II is Article II? Those points are too obvious. The apparent message: Congress can legislate as it likes, but the President is not obliged to comply. McConnell's testimony was similar to Hayden's when nominated as CIA Director. Both men seemed coached to repeat the words "Article II, Article II, inherent, inherent." An executive assertion remains an assertion unless a witness offers a reasoned and informed argument, which neither McConnell nor Hayden attempted to do. McConnell's testimony, or at least his oral remarks, seemed to contradict the administration's efforts to convince federal courts that pending challenges to the TSP were moot.

On August 5, 2007, just before a one-month recess, Congress passed an amendment to FISA that gave the administration the discretion it had sought, although only for a period of 180 days.[161] Democrats provided the necessary

159. "The Need to Bring the Foreign Intelligence Surveillance Act into the Modern Era," Statement of Kenneth L. Wainstein, Assistant Attorney General, National Security Division, Department of Justice, before the Senate Select Committee on Intelligence, May 1, 2007, at 8.

160. James Risen, "Administration Pulls Back on Surveillance Agreement," New York Times, May 3, 2007, at A16.

161. Protect America Act of 2007, P.L. 110–55, 121 Stat. 552 (2007).

votes under the threat that a failure to do so would leave the country open to another terrorist attack. House Speaker Nancy Pelosi immediately called the law "unacceptable" and said it would be substantially revised when Congress returned after the break.[162] A key issue in drafting a permanent bill was whether to grant retroactive liability for the telecom firms that cooperated with the administration.[163]

Retroactive Immunity

In October 2007, the Senate Intelligence Committee agreed to give the telecoms legal immunity because they "acted in good faith" and believed TSP was legal and presidentially authorized.[164] Companies the size of AT&T have large and sophisticated offices of general counsel charged with independently determining that they comply with the law. They forfeit that duty if they merely accept executive branch assurances. The rule of law for national security would be nonexistent if an administration could go to private companies and secretly ask them to break the law to satisfy executive needs.

An editorial in the *Washington Post* said it did "not believe that these companies should be held hostage to costly litigation in what is essentially a complaint about administration activities."[165] The issue was not merely administration activities. NSA could not have conducted TSP without the telecoms. Wainstein stated that the letters that went to the companies from the administration "said very forcefully" the surveillance program was "being directed by the president, and this has been deemed lawful at the very highest levels of the government."[166] The companies had a choice: follow a public law passed by Congress or a classified policy created by the executive branch.

The Senate voted to give the telecoms retroactive immunity, and President Bush urged the House to adopt that language. On February 21, 2008, he argued that "[if] we do not give liability protection to those who are helping us,

162. Jim Rutenberg, "Wielding the Threat of Terrorism, Bush Outmaneuvers the Democrats," New York Times, August 7, 2007, at A14.

163. Helen Fessenden, "Senate Democrats Seek to Regroup Quickly on Surveillance Law Rewrite," The Hill, September 11, 2007, at 8.

164. Eric Lichtblau, "Senate Deal on Immunity for Telephone Companies," New York Times, October 18, 2007, at A22; Ellen Nakashima and Shailagh Murray, "Senate Panel Approves New Surveillance Bill," Washington Post, October 19, 2007, at A2.

165. "Progress on Surveillance" (editorial), Washington Post, October 27, 2007, at A14.

166. Eric Lichtblau, "Key Senators Raise Doubts on Eavesdropping Immunity," New York Times, November 1, 2007, at A16.

they won't help us. And if they don't help us, there will be no program. And if there's no program, America is more vulnerable."[167] A week later he said, "You cannot expect phone companies to participate if they feel like they're going to be sued."[168] The companies would have had immunity had they followed FISA procedures; they took a chance by agreeing to the administration's plan to depart from that law. On March 14 the House rejected the Senate's support for retroactive immunity. Instead, the House chose to submit the issue of telecom liability to a federal court, giving the telecoms an opportunity to use information the administration had regarded as state secrets.[169] The House–Senate differences went to conference committee in search of an acceptable compromise.

In times of emergency, government officials push boundaries to do what they think is necessary. Instead of pursuing a legislative strategy and working jointly with Congress, the Bush administration decided to act unilaterally and invoke inherent presidential power, a field of constitutional law filled with doubts, ambiguities, and open invitations to abuse. Exercising inherent power always comes at the cost of checks and balances, separation of powers, and the structural safeguards the framers adopted to assure that a concentration of power does not endanger individual liberties. Those issues also emerge in the next chapter.

167.   44 Weekly Comp. Pres. Doc. 259 (2008).

168.   Id. at 291.

169.   Eric Lichtblau, "House Votes to Reject Immunity for Phone Companies Involved in Wiretaps," New York Times, March 15, 2008, at A13; Jonathan Weisman, "House Passes a Surveillance Bill Not to Bush's Liking," Washington Post, March 15, 2008, at A2.

CHAPTER 10

Extraordinary Rendition

Sweeping interpretations of presidential power after 9/11 bore fruit in another area: "extraordinary rendition." Under this doctrine, the President claims to possess inherent authority to seize individuals and transfer them to other countries for interrogation and torture. In the past, Attorneys General and other legal commentators understood that Presidents (1) needed congressional authority for these transfers and (2) the purpose was to bring the person *to trial*. As recently as 1979, the Justice Department held that the President could not order someone extradited or rendered without authority granted by a treaty or statute. That view of the law changed radically after 9/11. The administration sent persons to other countries not to try them in open court but to interrogate and abuse them in secret. In lawsuits challenging this practice, the Bush administration regularly invoked the state secrets privilege.

LEGAL PRINCIPLES

Rendition, used as a substitute for an extradition treaty, means surrendering someone to another jurisdiction for trial. The verb *render* is used in the sense of giving up or delivering up. *Black's Law Dictionary* offers this definition: "The return of a fugitive from one state to the state where the fugitive is accused or convicted of a crime."[1] Rendition therefore applies to a judicial process: someone accused of a crime or someone already convicted. It has no application to detainees or enemy combatants held indefinitely by executive officials, with no plan to bring them before a federal judge for trial. Rendition often seems indistinguishable from the definition of extradition: "The official surrender of an alleged criminal by one state or nation to another having jurisdiction over the crime charged; the return of a fugitive from justice, regardless of consent, by the authorities where the fugitive is found."[2] Over time, rendition became associated with kidnappings and forcible abductions, but still for the purpose of bringing someone to trial.

1. Black's Law Dictionary 1322 (8th ed. 2004).
2. Id. at 623.

Requiring a Statute or Treaty

For most of U.S. history, Presidents had no independent or exclusive authority over extraditions and renditions. Congressional action was needed. In a letter to President Washington in 1791, Secretary of State Thomas Jefferson discussed the legal principles that guided the delivery of fugitives from one country to another. Nations found it necessary to enter into treaties or conventions to define "precisely the cases wherein such deliveries shall take place." The laws of the United States received every fugitive, "and no authority has been given to our Executives to deliver them up." Congress had to act, either by statute or treaty, to assure that fugitives were not surrendered to "tyrannical laws."[3] Jefferson explained the risks of giving up fugitives.[4] Even in relatively free governments, punishments could be so disproportionate to the crime that the thought of rendition or extradition was repugnant. In a draft prepared in 1792, he noted that in England "to steal a hare is death, the first offence." In his view, all excess punishments were a crime. It followed that "to remit a fugitive to excessive punishment is to be *accessary* to the crime."[5] In deciding to return someone to another country, the legislative branch had to decide the seriousness of the crime. Also, some type of judicial process was necessary by Justices of the Supreme Court or district judges.[6]

In 1793, Jefferson responded to the request by the French minister to the United States to have certain individuals handed over because they had committed crimes against France. Jefferson explained that the laws of the United States "take no notice of crimes committed out of their jurisdiction." The "most atrocious offender" is received "as an innocent man, and they have authorized no one to seize or deliver him." The consular convention with France included a provision for delivering up captains and crew members, but such actions required the review of the district judge of each state. Alleged criminals "cannot be given up, and if they be the crew of vessel, the act of Congress has not given authority to any one officer to send his process through all the States of the Union."[7]

Attorneys General repeatedly held that extradition and rendition require congressional action by statutes or treaties. In 1797, Attorney General Charles

3. 22 The Papers of Thomas Jefferson 266–67 (Charles T. Cullen, ed., 1986).

4. 23 The Papers of Thomas Jefferson 360 (1990) (letter to Charles Pinckney, April 1, 1792).

5. 1 American State Papers: Foreign Relations 258 (1833) (emphasis in original).

6. Id. See also his draft at 257–58.

7. 1 American State Papers: Foreign Relations 177 (1833).

Lee advised the State Department about a dispute that had arisen with Spain. The minister of Spain reported that the territorial rights of Spain had been violated by the actions of a Spanish subject who had taken refuge in Florida. Lee conceded that it would be an offense against the law of nations for any person within the United States "to go into the territory of Spain with intent to recover their property by their own strength, or in any other manner than its laws authorize and permit."[8] But the Constitution gave to the legislative branch, "in express words, the power of passing a law for punishing a violation of territorial rights."[9] No law covered the particular dispute with Spain. To resolve the matter, Congress had to act. The President had no independent or unilateral powers to transfer the offenders to Spain.

In 1821, Attorney General William Wirt prepared a lengthy analysis on the President's authority to deliver to another country subjects of that nation charged with offenses. Could the President act under his interpretation of the law of nations? After exploring the major treatises on international law, Wirt concluded that the duty to deliver up criminals "is so vague and uncertain as to the offences on which it rests" that nations decided to enter into treaties to identify the particular crimes that would trigger extradition.[10] Without specific authority granted by the legislative branch, either by treaty or by statute, "the President has no power to make the delivery."[11]

Attorney General Roger Taney followed similar reasoning in 1833. Portugal wanted two seamen, confined in Boston, turned over to face charges of piracy. Taney said that no law of Congress authorized the President to deliver up anyone found in the United States, charged with having committed a crime against a foreign nation, nor were there any treaty stipulations with Portugal for the delivery of offenders. Congress had decided, by an act of March 3, 1819, that it was the duty of government to bring such individuals to trial in the circuit court for the district into which they were brought or where they were found.[12] It was not "in the power of the President to send them to any other tribunal, domestic or foreign, upon the ground that evidence to convict them can more conveniently be obtained there."[13]

In 1841, Attorney General Hugh Legare examined whether states could enter into an agreement or compact, express or implied, to deliver up from

8. 1 Ops. Att'y Gen. 68, 68–69 (1797).
9. Id. at 69.
10. 1 Ops. Att'y Gen. 509, 519–20 (1821).
11. Id. at 521.
12. 2 Ops. Att'y Gen. 559 (1833).
13. Id.

their jurisdiction fugitives from justice to a foreign state. They could not do so, he said, without the consent of Congress. Moreover, in accordance with the practice of the executive department, "the President is not considered as authorized, in the absence of any express provision by treaty, to order the delivering up of fugitives from justice."[14] It was therefore necessary "to refer the whole matter to Congress."[15] He considered the rules laid down by Jefferson, "and sanctioned after the lapse of upwards of thirty years by another administration, as too solemnly settled to be now departed from."[16] In 1853, Attorney General Caleb Cushing endorsed Legare's opinion.[17]

Few administrations departed from those principles. Those that did paid a political price. During the Civil War, President Abraham Lincoln ordered the seizure of a Spanish subject (Jose Arguelles) and his return to Cuba for trial. No extradition treaty existed. Lincoln was rebuked in some quarters for exercising an "absolute despotism."[18] The Senate and the House requested documents from the administration to explain "under what authority of law or of treaty" the President delivered Arguelles to Spain.[19] Secretary of State William H. Seward defended Lincoln's action under the "law of nations," but Article I of the Constitution clearly gives that power to Congress.[20] New York proceeded to indict for kidnapping the U.S. marshal and the four deputies who had seized Arguelles. Although the prosecution went no farther, the damage done to Lincoln and presidential power was substantial.[21] Arguelles was convicted, fined, and sentenced to nineteen years "at the chain."[22]

14. 3 Ops. Att'y Gen. 661 (1841).

15. Id. at 662.

16. Id. For another example of an Attorney General opinion deciding, on the basis of a treaty and congressional statutes, that the President is authorized to send a fugitive from the United States to England *for trial*, see 4 Ops. Att'y Gen. 201 (1841).

17. 6 Ops. Att'y Gen. 85 (1853). In other opinions, Attorney General Cushing recognized that the President was restricted by treaty language and judicial decisions in cases of extradition; id. at 91 (1853); id. at 217 (1853); id. at 431 (1854). See also Attorney General Taney at 2 Ops. Att'y Gen. 452 (1831).

18. William G. Weaver and Robert M. Pallitto, "'Extraordinary Rendition' and Presidential Fiat," 36 Pres. Stud. Q. 102, 106 (2006).

19. Cong. Globe, 38th Cong., 1st Sess. 2484, 2545 (1864); H. Ex. Doc. No. 1, 38th Cong., 2d Sess. 35–36 (1865).

20. S. Ex. Doc. No. 48, 38th Cong., 1st Sess. 2 (1864). For a more thorough analysis by Secretary Sumner, see his June 24, 1864, letter to Rep. James F. Wilson, H. Ex. Doc. 1, 38th Cong., 2d Sess. 35–36 (1865).

21. Weaver and Pallitto, "'Extraordinary Rendition' and Presidential Fiat," at 107–08. See also Christopher H. Pyle, Extradition, Politics, and Human Rights 102–03 (2001).

22. H. Ex. Doc. No. 1, 3rd Cong., 2d Sess. 86 (1865).

The President's dependence on treaties and statutes to transfer someone to another country was well established throughout most of America's history. The Supreme Court in 1936 spoke unanimously about the President's lack of authority to act independently and unilaterally in such matters:

> It rests upon the fundamental consideration that the Constitution creates no executive prerogative to dispose of the liberty of the individual. Proceedings against him must be authorized by law. There is no executive discretion to surrender him to a foreign government, unless that discretion is granted by law. It necessarily follows that as the legal authority does not exist save as it is given by act of Congress or by the terms of a treaty, it is not enough that statute or treaty does not deny the power to surrender. It must be found that statute or treaty confers the power.[23]

In 1979, the Office of Legal Counsel (OLC) reviewed the President's power to transfer someone in U.S. custody to another country. The legal analysis was prompted by the revolution in Iran, the presence of the deposed Shah in the United States, and the call for his return. The Justice Department looked to statutory authority that allowed the transfer of the Shah to another country, but not to Iran. The statute prevented the return of someone to a country where he would be subject to political persecution, as would have been the case with the Shah. The legal rule was plain: "The President cannot order any person extradited unless a treaty or statute authorizes him to do so."[24]

Prisoners of War

In an article published in 2004, John Yoo broadly defended the President's authority to transfer suspected terrorists to other countries. He said the authority is derived from the President's powers under Article II, especially the Commander in Chief Clause.[25] In his search for historical examples, however, he could cite only a number of statutes that granted the President authority to detain vessels and crews and to decide prisoner-of-war policy.[26] Transfers of POWs to other countries sometimes put them to work on construction projects, but did not subject them to interrogation and torture.[27]

23. Valentine v. U.S. ex rel. Neidecker, 299 U.S. 5, 9 (1936).
24. 4A Ops. O.L.C. 149, 149 (1979).
25. John Yoo, "Transferring Terrorists," 79 Notre Dame L. Rev. 1183, 1184–85, 1192–1205 (2004).
26. Id. at 1206–22.
27. Id. at 1218–19.

According to Yoo, the President may "dispose of the liberty of captured enemy personnel as he sees fit,"[28] relying on Article II powers. At the same time, he says the President is subject "to certain constraints," including treaties and international law.[29] Those constraints may not exist, however, because Yoo argues that "statutes and treaties must be interpreted so as to protect the President's constitutional powers from impermissible encroachment and thereby to avoid any potential constitutional problems."[30] In short, presidential power can trump conflicting statutes and treaties. Although presidential power is "significantly constrained" by domestic law that applies criminal penalties to torture,[31] the President may decide not to prosecute offenders.

For Yoo, the "rule of law" has two meanings. Once the threshold of war is crossed, the new condition "changes the law's form and substance." Matters are then "governed by the laws of war."[32] In other words, law before the war (treaties and statutes) becomes subordinate to executive-made "laws of war." Yoo concludes: "This is not to say that these transfers [of suspects] are wholly ungoverned by law. It is only to make clear that these transfers are governed by a different set of rules—the laws of war—than those that apply in domestic, peacetime affairs."[33] However, this new set of rules depends on limitations developed wholly within the executive branch.

Kidnappings

Both before and after the 1979 OLC opinion, governments kidnapped and forcibly abducted individuals without treaty or statutory authority.[34] One scholar remarked on the strangeness of this practice. It is "a crime for private persons to receive stolen goods, but it is lawful for American courts to receive stolen people."[35] Courts did not officially sanction kidnapping or illegal abductions, but they tolerated them under what is gently called the "rule of noninquiry."[36] How someone was brought to court did not matter. Forcible abduction was

28. Id. at 1222.
29. Id. at 1185, 1223.
30. Id. at 1230.
31. Id. at 1232.
32. Id. at 1235.
33. Id.
34. Michael H. Cardozo, "When Extradition Fails, Is Abduction the Solution?" 55 Am. J. Int'l L. 127 (1961).
35. Pyle, Extradition, Politics, and Human Rights, at 263.
36. Id. at 263–99.

first sanctioned by the Supreme Court in 1886, allowing the transfer of someone from Peru to the United States.[37] It was reaffirmed in 1952 for bringing a defendant from Illinois to Michigan.[38]

Known as the Ker-Frisbie Doctrine, those two cases announce that the government's power to prosecute someone "is not impaired by the illegality of the method by which it acquires control over him."[39] Jurisdiction gained through "an indisputably illegal act" could be exercised by courts even though it rewarded "police brutality and lawlessness."[40] The continued vitality of Ker-Frisbie seemed undercut by the due process cases in the 1950s and 1960s, with the Supreme Court objecting to government practices that "shock the conscience."[41] Some courts looked to guidance from Justice Louis Brandeis's dissenting opinion in 1928, when he warned that crime is contagious: "If the government becomes a lawbreaker, it breeds contempt for the law."[42]

In 1974, the Second Circuit concluded that Ker-Frisbie could not be reconciled with the Supreme Court's expansion of the concept of due process, and that a court must divest itself of jurisdiction when a defendant is brought before it as the result of the government's "deliberate, unnecessary and unreasonable invasion of the accused's constitutional rights."[43] The circumstances of the case before the Second Circuit included allegations that the defendant was kidnapped in Uruguay, beaten, brought to Brazil for interrogation and torture, drugged by Brazilian-American agents, and placed on a Pan American Airways flight to the United States, where he was taken into custody by an Assistant U.S. Attorney.[44] Upon remand, a district court (without an evidentiary hearing) decided that the defendant had failed to show that U.S. officials participated in the abduction or torture.[45]

This type of abduction, however repugnant, was for the purpose of *bringing someone to trial.* Similar cases could be cited, such as Israeli agents kidnapping Adolf Eichmann from Argentina in 1960 and bringing him to Israel to be tried. Because there was no extradition treaty between Israel and Argentina, the UN Security Council asked Israel to pay reparations to Argentina, and it

37. Ker v. Illinois, 119 U.S. 436 (1886).
38. Frisbie v. Collins, 342 U.S. 519 (1952).
39. United States v. Toscanino, 500 F.2d 267, 271 (2d Cir. 1974).
40. Id. at 272.
41. Id. at 273 (citing Rochin v. California, 342 U.S. 165 [1952]).
42. Id. at 274 (citing Olmstead v. United States, 277 U.S. 438 [1928]).
43. Id. at 275.
44. Id. at 269–70.
45. United States v. Toscanino, 398 F.Supp. 916 (E.D. N.Y. 1975).

did.[46] Throughout the 1980s, the United States began to forcibly abduct alleged terrorists and drug lords in other countries and bring them to trial. In 1986, President Ronald Reagan authorized the CIA to kidnap criminal suspects.[47] As part of the U.S. intervention in Panama in December 1989, U.S. troops captured Antonio Noriega and brought him to trial in the United States. President George H. W. Bush directed that he be "turned over to civil law enforcement officials of the United States."[48] In 1992, the Supreme Court held that the government may kidnap people from foreign countries to *try them* in the United States.[49] Critics objected that U.S. Presidents could act in defiance of international law, an impression the Bush I and Clinton administrations attempted to dispel with several initiatives.[50]

ADDING AN ADJECTIVE

Putting "extraordinary" in front of rendition changes the meaning fundamentally. A process formerly bound by statutory and treaty law—reinforced by procedural safeguards in court—now entered the realm of independent and arbitrary executive law. Checks and balances disappeared. Presidents claimed the right not only to act in the absence of statutory or treaty authority but even in violation of them. After 9/11, officials in the Bush II administration defended the need to detain and interrogate suspected terrorists outside the country. In that sense, extraordinary rendition has parallels to putting detainees in Guantánamo: an effort to place them beyond the reach of judicial supervision and review. Rendition operates within the rule of law; extraordinary rendition falls outside. Rendition brings suspects to federal or state court; extraordinary rendition does not. The harsh and aggressive methods used in extraordinary rendition would undermine potential prosecutions because a court would exclude confessions or evidence that had been illegally coerced.

Prohibitions on Torture

In a series of statutes, the United States condemned torture and specifically prohibited the transfer of anyone to a country that practiced torture. In 1992,

46. Pyle, Extradition, Politics, and Human Rights, at 272–73.
47. Id. at 275.
48. 25 Weekly Comp. Pres. Doc. 1976 (1989).
49. United States v. Alvarez-Machain, 504 U.S. 655 (1992).
50. Louis Fisher and David Gray Adler, American Constitutional Law 711 (7th ed. 2007).

Congress passed the Torture Victim Protection Act. It establishes a civil action to recover damages from an individual who engages in torture or extrajudicial killing. Anyone who, "under actual or apparent authority, or color of law, of any foreign nation," subjects someone to torture shall be liable for damages to that individual.[51] The statute applied to torture committed by someone from a foreign nation.

In 1998, as part of the Foreign Affairs Reform and Restructuring Act (FARRA), Congress stated: "It shall be the policy of the United States not to expel, extradite, or otherwise effect the involuntary return of any person to a country in which there are substantial grounds for believing the person would be in danger of being subjected to torture, regardless of whether the person is physically present in the United States."[52] The statute directed federal agencies to implement the obligations of the United States under Article 3 of the UN Convention Against Torture (CAT). Regulations provide that if there is a decision to remove an alien to another country where torture is possible, an immigration judge must make that determination.[53]

In 1998, Congress passed the Torture Victims Relief Act. The first finding states: "The American people abhor torture by any government or person. The existence of torture creates a climate of fear and international insecurity that affects all people." The second finding: "Torture is the deliberate mental and physical damage caused by governments to individuals to destroy individual personality and terrorize society. The effects of torture are long term. Those effects can last a lifetime for the survivors and affect future generations." The third finding explains that torture is often used "as a weapon against democracy."[54] Part of the statute authorizes funds to use "the voice and vote of the United States" to support the work of the Special Rapporteur on Torture and the Committee Against Torture established under the CAT.[55] Article 3 of the CAT provides: "No State Party shall expel, return ("refouler") or extradite a person to another State where there are substantial grounds for believing that he would be in danger of being subjected to torture."[56] The Reagan administration and the Senate added this qualification: "the United States understands the phrase, 'where there are substantial grounds for believing that he would be in danger of being subjected to torture,' as used in article 3 of the

51. 106 Stat. 73 (1992); 28 U.S.C. § 1350 (2000).
52. 112 Stat. 2681–822, sec. 2242(a) (1998).
53. 8 C.F.R. § 208.16(c)(4) (1–1–07 ed.).
54. 112 Stat. 3016 (1998).
55. Id. at 3018, sec. 6(c)(2).
56. http://www/ohchr.org/english/law.cat.htm, accessed on August 18, 2007, at 2.

Convention, to mean 'if it is more likely than not that he would be tortured.'"[57] Even that looser definition would cover renditions to such countries as Egypt and Syria.

Renditions under Clinton

On June 21, 1995, President Bill Clinton signed Presidential Decision Directive (PDD) 39, setting forth the U.S. policy on counterterrorism. It authorized the Secretary of State and the Attorney General to "use all legal means available to exclude from the United States persons who pose a terrorist threat and deport or otherwise remove from the United States any such aliens."[58]

On September 3, 1998, FBI Director Louis J. Freeh advised the Senate Judiciary Committee about the use of force to abduct suspects *to bring them to trial.* The rendition process was governed by PDD 77, "which sets explicit requirements for initiating this method for returning terrorists to stand trial in the United States." Over the past decade the United States had returned 13 suspected international terrorists to stand trial in the United States.[59] Under this procedure, whatever force was used in making the arrests should not have compromised evidence needed for trial.

During hearings on February 2, 2000, before the Senate Intelligence Committee, CIA Director George Tenet described the rendition program: "Since July 1998, working with foreign governments worldwide, we have helped to render more than two dozen terrorists to justice. More than half were associates of Usama Bin Ladin's Al-Qa'ida organization."[60] Bringing suspects "to justice" implies delivering them for trial, but the phrase is somewhat vague, and Tenet did not say that all the suspects were brought to the United States. Paul Pillar, deputy chief of the CIA's Counterterrorist Center, interpreted Tenet's testimony to mean that some of the two dozen suspects were brought to the United States to stand trial, but "most were delivered to other countries where

57. http://www.ohchr.org/english/countries/ratification/9.htm, accessed on August 18, 2007, at 12.

58. http://www.fas.org/irp/offdocs/pdd39.htm, accessed on November 1, 2007, at 2. The PDD included procedures for apprehending and returning indicted terrorists to the United States for prosecution. Id. at 4.

59. http://www.fas.org/irp/congress/1998_hr/98090302_npo.html, accessed on August 11, 2007 (at 5).

60. https://www.cia.gov/news-information/speeches-testimony/2000/dci_speech_020200 .html, accessed on August 14, 2007 (at 3).

they were wanted for their crimes."[61] Does "wanted for crimes" mean being turned over to the judicial system or, instead, for interrogation and torture? If the latter, it is the first step toward extraordinary rendition. Turning suspects over to another country, like Egypt, means losing control over how the person is treated.

At a congressional hearing on April 17, 2007, Michael Scheuer described his duties during the Clinton administration in supervising the abduction of suspected terrorists. He testified that the CIA's rendition program began in late summer 1995: "I authored it and then ran and managed it against al-Qaeda leaders and other Sunni Islamists from August, 1995, until June 1999."[62] The purpose was "to take men off the street who were planning or had been involved in attacks on the United States or its allies" and "seize hard copy or electronic documents in their possession when arrested." However, "interrogation was never a goal under President Clinton." The men captured were not to be brought to the United States or held in U.S. custody. The CIA was to take "each captured al-Qaeda leader to the country which had an outstanding legal process for him."[63] If the country had not filed charges against the individual, abduction was not authorized.[64]

Scheuer testified that "no rendered al-Qaeda leader has ever been kidnapped by the United States. They have always first been either arrested or seized by a local security or intelligence service."[65] The purpose of the Bush II administration was quite different: abduct suspected terrorists (with or without local help), interrogate them under CIA custody, and transfer them to another country for additional interrogation and, most likely, torture.

Changes after 9/11

Abu Ghraib put the spotlight on the CIA. Agency officers conducted harsh, unsupervised interrogations at that prison and others. Newspaper reports in September 2004 disclosed that the agency had hidden at least two dozen detainees from Red Cross inspectors. The CIA moved these men called "ghost

---

61. Paul R. Pillar, Terrorism and U.S. Foreign Policy 118 (2003 ed.).

62. "Extraordinary Rendition in U.S. Counterterrorism Policy: The Impact on Transatlantic Relations," joint hearing before the Subcommittee on International Organizations, Human Rights, and Oversight and the Subcommittee on Europe of the House Committee on Foreign Affairs, 110th Cong., 1st Sess. 12 (2007).

63. Id.

64. Id.

65. Id. at 18.

detainees," out of Iraqi prisons for interrogation at other undisclosed locations made inaccessible to the Red Cross.[66] Permission for these transfers came from a confidential OLC draft opinion that specialists in international law condemned as sanctioning violations of the Geneva Conventions.[67] There should never have been any doubt about the prospects of torture. The State Department for years had condemned a number of countries for torturing and abusing detainees. Here is the department's description of the practices followed by Egypt in 2003. Victims were

> stripped and blind folded; suspended from a ceiling or doorframe with feet
> just touching the floor; beaten with fists, whips, metal rods, or other objects;
> subjected to electrical shocks; and doused with cold water. Victims frequently
> reported being subjected to threats and forced to sign blank papers for use against
> the victim or the victim's family in the future should the victim complain of
> abuse. Some victims, including male and female detainees and children reported
> that they were sexually assaulted or threatened with rape themselves or family
> members.[68]

Beginning in December 2004, Dana Priest of the *Washington Post* wrote a series of articles describing how the CIA transported suspected terrorists to undisclosed locations for abusive interrogations, beyond the reach of federal courts. The agency used a Gulfstream V turbojet, often seen at military airports from Pakistan to Indonesia to Jordan. At times the suspects could be seen hooded and handcuffed before being boarded. The CIA called the activity "rendition," but it was not an operation to bring suspects to trial.[69] Human rights organizations objected that the CIA's purpose was to transfer captives to countries that used brutal interrogation methods outlawed in the United States and in violation of the Convention Against Torture.[70]

66. Douglas Jehl, "C.I.A. Cites Order on Supervised Interrogations," New York Times, September 11, 2004, at A5.

67. Dana Priest, "Memo Lets CIA Take Detainees Out of Iraq," Washington Post, October 24, 2004, at A1; Douglas Jehl, "U.S. Action Bars Rights of Some Captured in Iraq," New York Times, October 26, 2004, at A1. For the text of this March 19, 2004 OLC draft memo, see http://www.washingtonpost.com/wp-srv/nation/documents/doj_memo031904.pdf, accessed August 13, 2007.

68. U.S. Department of State, Country Reports on Human Rights Practices, Egypt, 2003, at 3; http://www.state.gov/g/drl/rls/hrrpt/2003/27926.htm.

69. Dana Priest, "Jet Is an Open Secret in Terror War," Washington Post, December 27, 2004, at A1.

70. Id. See Trevor Paglen and A. C. Thompson, Torture Taxi: On The Trail of the CIA's Rendition Flights (2006); Stephen Grey, Ghost Plane: The True Story of the CIA Torture

Other news reports claimed that the CIA conducted its program under a classified directive signed by President Bush shortly after 9/11, allowing the agency to transport suspects without receiving case-by-case approval from the White House, the State Department, or the Justice Department.[71] Former detainees, subjected to these transfers, described what they called brutal interrogation techniques.[72] The Bush administration, declining to confirm or deny the CIA program, insisted that it did not hand over people to face torture. Former government officials estimated that the agency had flown from 100 to 150 suspected terrorists to interrogation sites.[73] The countries receiving suspects—Egypt, Syria, Saudi Arabia, Jordan, and Pakistan—were long identified by the State Department as habitually using torture. According to an administration spokesman, the CIA followed guidelines that required the receiving country to assure that prisoners would be treated humanely and that U.S. personnel would monitor compliance.[74] CIA Director Porter Goss acknowledged that the United States had a limited capacity to enforce these promises: "once they're out of our control, there's only so much we can do."[75] Former prisoners subjected to CIA transfers said they had been beaten, shackled, humiliated, subjected to electric shocks, and survived other abusive treatments.[76] Those eventually released include Maher Arar and Khaled El-Masri, discussed later in this chapter.

ADMINISTRATION DEFENSES

James L. Pavitt, after retiring from the CIA in August 2004, claimed that the policy of extraordinary rendition had been done in consultation with the National Security Council and disclosed to the appropriate congressional oversight committees. Briefings and consultation with lawmakers do not make an illegal program legal. Pavitt spoke after the Justice Department, at the CIA's request, drafted a confidential memo in March 2004 authorizing the agency

Program (2006); Jane Mayer, "Outsourcing Torture: The Secret History of America's 'Extraordinary Rendition' Program," New Yorker, February 14 and 21, 2005, at 106–23.

71. Douglas Jehl and David Johnston, "Rule Change Lets C.I.A. Freely Send Suspects Abroad," New York Times, March 6, 2005, at 1.

72. Id.

73. Id. at 1, 11.

74. Id. at 11.

75. Id.

76. Id.

to transfer detainees out of Iraq for interrogation. The memo concluded that the Geneva Conventions allowed the CIA to take Iraqis and non-Iraqis out of the country for questioning. Experts in international law rejected that reading of Geneva.[77]

On March 7, 2005, Attorney General Alberto Gonzales defended the practice of what was now called "extraordinary rendition." Although U.S. officials, meeting in private with reporters, referred to the threat of CIA transfers as an effective method of obtaining intelligence from suspected terrorists, Gonzales said that U.S. policy was not to send detainees "to countries where we believe or we know that they're going to be tortured."[78] For countries with a history of torture, the administration would seek assurances that torture would not be used. He conceded that the administration "can't fully control" what other nations do.[79] One CIA officer involved with renditions called the assurances given by other countries "a farce."[80]

European Investigations

In February 2003, an Egyptian cleric (Abu Omar, or Hassan Mustafa Osama Nasr) was seized by the United States on a sidewalk in Milan and taken out of the country.[81] Italian investigators, searching for his kidnappers, visited the Aviano Air Base in northern Italy and insisted on seeing records of any American planes that had flown into or out of the joint U.S.-Italian military facility around the time of the abduction. They also sought the logs of vehicles that had entered the base. Italian authorities suspected that Abu Omar was abducted as part of the CIA extraordinary rendition program. Law-enforcement authorities in other countries, including Germany and Sweden,

77. Dana Priest, "Ex-CIA Official Defends Detention Policies," Washington Post, October 27, 2004, at A21.

78. R. Jeffrey Smith, "Gonzales Defends Transfer of Detainees," Washington Post, March 8, 2005, at A3.

79. Id.

80. Dana Priest, "CIA's Assurances on Transferred Suspects Doubted," Washington Post, March 17, 2005, at A1, A22.

81. For further details on Abu Omar, see Margaret L. Satterthwaite, "Rendered Meaningless: Extraordinary Rendition and the Rule of Law," 75 G.W. L. Rev. 1333, 1340–42 (2007). See also the writings of Leila Nadya Sadat: "Ghost Prisoners and Black Sites: Extraordinary Rendition Under International Law," 37 Case W. Res. L. Rev. 309 (2006), and "Extraordinary Rendition, Torture, and Other Nightmares from the War on Terrorism," 75 G.W. L. Rev. 1200 (2007).

also investigated whether U.S. agents had violated their sovereignty by seizing suspects and transferring them to other locations for abusive interrogations.[82]

German prosecutors tried to determine who apprehended Khaled El-Masri, a German citizen vacationing in Macedonia. He was later taken to an American prison in Afghanistan in January 2004. A parliamentary investigation in Sweden found that CIA agents wearing hoods had orchestrated the December 2001 abduction of two Egyptian nationals, transferring them to Egypt for interrogation and torture.[83] Swedish authorities admitted they had invited the CIA to assist in the operation but vowed never again to let the agency take charge of such operations. One police chief told reporters: "In the future we will use Swedish laws, Swedish measures of force and Swedish military aviation when deporting terrorists."[84]

News reports disclosed that the CIA had been interrogating suspects at secret facilities ("black sites") in Eastern Europe. Although the *Washington Post* knew the identities of two countries in Eastern Europe (later identified as Poland and Romania), it decided not to publish the names at the request of officials in the Bush administration. There was also a black site in Thailand. Two al Qaeda operatives (Abu Zubaydah and Ramsi Binalshibh) were kept there until Thai officials insisted that the facility be closed.[85] Without affirming the existence of the secret prisons in Eastern Europe, the CIA asked the Justice Department to open a criminal investigation to determine who leaked the highly classified information to the *Washington Post*.[86]

In November 2005, several European governments authorized investigations into the CIA planes that flew regularly over the continent to carry suspects to interrogation facilities. Officials in Spain, Sweden, Norway, and the European Parliament began formal inquiries and sought information from the United States about the CIA flights. Prosecutors in Italy filed a formal extradition request for twenty-two U.S. citizens alleged to be CIA operatives, charged with abducting Abu Omar. A German prosecutor opened a criminal

82. Craig Whitlock, "Europeans Investigate CIA Role in Abductions," Washington Post, March 13, 2005, at A1.

83. Id. at A18.

84. Id. See also Craig Whitlock, "New Swedish Documents Illuminate CIA Action," Washington Post, May 21, 2005, at A1, A15.

85. Dana Priest, "CIA Holds Terror Suspects in Secret Prisons," Washington Post, November 2, 2005, at A1, A12.

86. David Johnston and Carl Hulse, "C.I.A. Asks Criminal Inquiry over Secret-Prison Article," Washington Post, November 9, 2005, at A17.

investigation into that same abduction to determine whether the CIA broke German law by bringing him first to Ramstein Air Base before flying him to Cairo. Another German prosecutor began a criminal investigation involving the seizure of El-Masri in Macedonia. Ireland and Denmark objected to the presence of CIA-operated aircraft in their countries.[87]

Rice Offers an Explanation

On behalf of the European Union, British Foreign Secretary Jack Straw wrote to Secretary of State Condoleezza Rice in late November 2005, asking her to clarify the issue of CIA detention camps in Europe. The top judicial figure in the Union warned that any EU country that hosted CIA prisons risked losing its EU voting rights.[88] Poland was already an EU member and Romania had applied to join. On the eve of Rice's five-day trip to Europe, the *New York Times* reported that CIA-operated planes had made 307 flights in Europe since 9/11: 94 in Germany, 76 in England, 33 in Ireland, 16 in Portugal, 15 in Spain, 15 in the Czech Republic, 13 in Greece, 6 in Poland, 5 in Italy, 4 in Romania, and lesser amounts in a dozen other countries.[89]

In an effort to rebut criticism of extraordinary rendition, Secretary Rice issued a detailed statement on December 5, 2005. A number of federal agencies contributed to her statement.[90] The Rice statement reads very much like a committee product, with each agency contributing its agenda but no one in charge to provide accuracy, credibility, and coherence. Instead of a persuasive refutation, Rice confused the CIA operation with traditional rendition and offered assurances that seem crafted by attorneys to mask meaning, conceal illegality, and insert hidden messages. As explained in the next thirteen points, the statement was much too artfully worded.

Rice maintained that "[f]or decades, the United States and other countries have used 'renditions' to transport terrorist suspects from the country where they were captured to their home country or to other countries where they

87. Craig Whitlock, "Europeans Probe Secret CIA Flights," Washington Post, November 17, 2005, at A22.

88. Glenn Kessler, "U.S. Will Address E.U. Questions on CIA Prisons," Washington Post, November 30, 2005, at A1.

89. Ian Fisher, "Reports of Secret U.S. Prisons in Europe Draw Ire and Otherwise Red Faces," New York Times, December 1, 2005, at A14.

90. White House press briefing, December 2, 2005, at 7, accessed at http://www.white-house.gov/news/releases/2005/12/print/20051202–2.html.

can be questioned, held, or brought to justice."[91] In the past, in cases of forcible abductions of questionable legality, the purpose was to bring drug lords and suspected terrorists *to trial*, not for abusive interrogations. Point two: Rice claimed that rendition "is not unique to the United States, or to the current administration," giving two examples. Ramzi Yousef was brought to the United States after being charged with the 1993 bombing of the World Trade Center and plotting to blow up airlines over the Pacific Ocean. The terrorist known as "Carlos the Jackal," captured in Sudan, was brought to France.[92] Those examples have nothing to do with extraordinary rendition. The individuals were not taken to a secret interrogation center, outside the judicial process, and subjected to torture. They were brought to court to face public charges, trial, conviction, and sentencing.

Three: responding to charges of torture and inhumane treatment, Rice insisted that the United States "does not permit, tolerate, or condone torture under any circumstances."[93] Contradicting that claim is the Bybee Memo and reports from detainees held at Abu Ghraib, Kandahar, Bagram, Guantánamo, and other U.S. facilities. Four: "The United States does not transport, and has not transported, detainees from one country to another for the purpose of interrogation using torture."[94] The key word here is "purpose." The administration would argue that the primary purpose was not "interrogation using torture" but "interrogation to obtain intelligence," with torture an incidental and secondary result. Five: "The United States does not use the airspace or the airports of any country for the purpose of transporting a detainee to a country where he or she will be tortured."[95] Again, the administration could say that the overriding purpose was to gather intelligence.

Six: "The United States has not transported anyone, and will not transport anyone, to a country when we believe he will be tortured. Where appropriate, the United States seeks assurances that transferred persons will not be tortured."[96] Torture is not eliminated by "beliefs" and "assurances." Seven: "With respect to detainees, the United States Government complies with its Constitution, its laws, and its treaty obligations. Acts of physical or mental

91. U.S. Secretary of State Condoleezza Rice, Remarks Upon Her Departure for Europe, December 5, 2005, at 1–2, available from http://www/state.gov/secretary/rm/2005/57602.htm.

92. Id. at 2.

93. Id.

94. Id.

95. Id.

96. Id.

torture are expressly prohibited."[97] The Bybee Memo, as endorsed by White House Counsel Gonzales, did not accept restrictions imposed by statutes and treaties. Eight:

> Violations of these and other detention standards have been investigated and punished. There have been cases of unlawful treatment of detainees, such as the abuse of a detainee by an intelligence agency contractor in Afghanistan or the horrible mistreatment of some prisoners at Abu Ghraib that sickened us all and which arose under the different legal framework that applies to armed conflict in Iraq. In such cases the United States has vigorously investigated, and where appropriate, prosecuted and punished those responsible.

This last point raised several issues. Rice now stated, contrary to her earlier claim, that the United States did torture detainees. Was this merely an unfortunate result of prison guards being poorly trained and supervised? Reference to "the different legal framework" appeared to offer a green light or justification to what was done. As to vigorous investigations and punishments, no penalties were meted out to the civilian and military leaders who consciously crafted and approved a system of interrogation that waived treaty and statutory restrictions and would have been prohibited under the Army Field Manual and the Geneva Conventions.

Nine: "It is also U.S. policy that authorized interrogation will be consistent with U.S. obligations under the Convention Against Torture, which prohibit cruel, inhuman, or degrading treatment."[98] "Consistent with" is not the same as being in compliance. "Consistent with" invites administrative choice and discretion instead of being legally bound. It is a matter of public record that confidential memos prepared by OLC and the Working Group developed policies that deliberately skirted statutory and treaty obligations.

Ten: "The intelligence so gathered has stopped terrorist attacks and saved innocent lives—in Europe as well as in the United States and other countries. The United States has fully respected the sovereignty of other countries that cooperate in these matters." A very shrewd argument. It implies that abusive interrogations helped gather intelligence that thwarted terrorist plots, helped protect Europe, and reminded some countries that they cooperated in the CIA flights and were fully complicit in what was done.

Eleven: "Because this war on terrorism challenges traditional norms and precedents of previous conflicts, our citizens have been discussing and debating

97. Id.
98. Id. at 3.

the proper legal standards that should apply. President Bush is working with the U.S. Congress to come up with good solutions." The first sentence draws attention to a new and different standard of interrogating detainees, apparently justifying harsh methods that in the past had been forbidden. Whatever public discussions were under way were the result of leaks of secret memos and the Abu Ghraib scandal. Far from working with Congress, President Bush threatened to veto the McCain anti-torture amendment until congressional support reached the supermajorities needed to easily override a veto. Bush then issued a signing statement that left the meaning of the statutory prohibition subject to his interpretation of presidential authority under Article II.

Twelve: "The United States is a country of laws. My colleagues and I have sworn to support and defend the Constitution of the United States. We believe in the rule of law."[99] It is true that the United States is a country of laws and Rice and her colleagues took an oath to support and defend the Constitution. It is also true that key administration officials, in secret, regularly rejected the binding nature of statutes and treaties and accepted the President's "inherent" authority as superior to legislative and judicial constraints. They subordinated law and the Constitution to the policies adopted by the administration.

Thirteen: "It is up to those governments and their citizens to decide if they wish to work with us to prevent terrorist attacks against their own country or other countries, and decide how much sensitive information they can make public. They have a sovereign right to make that choice."[100] A rather gratuitous concession that allies are sovereign countries. Also, it appears to be a warning that it would not be in their interest to publicly release information about CIA flights and the scope of their cooperation. She cautioned: "Debate in and among democracies is natural and healthy. I hope that that debate also includes a healthy regard for the responsibilities of government to protect their citizens."[101] Translation: being too open has a downside; countries in Europe should understand the need to keep CIA operations secret.

How Allies Reacted

Press accounts clarified some points. When Rice said the United States always respects the sovereignty of foreign countries when conducting intelligence operations on their soil (or over it), executive officials translated that as

99. Id.
100. Id.
101. Id.

diplomatic code that the United States had received permission for the CIA activities.[102] As a member of the German Parliament's foreign policy committee noted: "She's trying to throw the ball back into the European field."[103] After public disclosure of the prison camps, ABC News reported that two of the facilities had been closed, and eleven top al Qaeda detainees were flown out of Europe before Rice's arrival.[104] They may have been moved to new CIA camps in the North African desert.[105]

Although Rice did not formally acknowledge the CIA program, she did so implicitly. A reporter explained: "Without the debate over the covert jails, there would have been no reason for her statement."[106] To a Conservative member of the British Parliament, her statement "was drafted by lawyers with the intention of misleading an audience."[107] A Labour member of the British Parliament found her assertions "wholly incredible."[108] A U.S. editorial dismissed Rice's statement as "the same legalistic jujitsu and morally obtuse double talk that led the Bush administration into a swamp of human rights abuses in the first place."[109]

Some European leaders were offended by what they found to be a patronizing tone in Rice's statement, with the United States claiming a superior capacity to deal with events after 9/11. The Conservative MP from England said he "resent[ed] the fact that my country is foolishly being led into a misguided approach into combating terrorism by this administration." European countries had far greater experience "over many decades dealing with terrorism, and many of us have learned the hard way that dealing in a muscular way can often inflame the very terrorism you're trying to suppress."[110]

Toward the end of Rice's trip, European leaders began to fall in line and express their satisfaction with her explanations. Bernard Bot of the Netherlands said she "has covered all of our concerns," dismissing talk about secret prisons

102. Glenn Kessler, "Rice Defends Tactics Used against Suspects," Washington Post, December 6, 2005, at A1.

103. Id. at A26.

104. Id.

105. Joel Brinkley, "U.S. Interrogations Are Saving European Lives, Rice Says," New York Times, December 6, 2005, at A3.

106. Id.

107. Richard Bernstein, "Skepticism Seems to Erode Europeans' Faith in Rice," New York Times, December 7, 2005, at A16 (quoting Andrew Tyrie).

108. Id. (quoting Andrew Mullin).

109. "A Weak Defense" (Editorial), Washington Post, December 6, 2005, at A28.

110. Bernstein, "Skepticism Seems to Erode Europeans' Faith in Rice," at A16 (quoting Andrew Tyrie).

as "pure speculation."[111] Rice had "made it quite clear" that the United States did not violate international law.[112] To German Foreign Minister Walter Steinmeier, Rice had "reiterated that in the United States international obligations are not interpreted differently than in Europe."[113] (That could mean that European countries and the United States jointly agreed to violate international law.) NATO Secretary General Jaap de Hoop Scheffer announced that Rice had "cleared the air."[114] What became clear was not Rice's explanations, but the inability of European leaders to exercise any level of independent thought.

At Last: Coming Clean

When Rice returned from her trip to Europe, the State Department reiterated that it would deny the International Committee of the Red Cross access to "a very small, limited number" of prisoners held in secret around the world.[115] An inadvertent confirmation of what she had just denied? A newspaper story described the survival of secret CIA prisons, with some closed down in Europe and detainees transferred to other locations: "virtually all the programs continue to operate largely as they were set up."[116] In April 2006, investigators in Europe reported that the CIA had flown 1,000 undeclared flights over European territory since 2001. At times the planes stopped to pick up suspects and take them to other countries for torture.[117]

Dick Marty, a Swiss lawyer working for the Council of Europe, released findings in June 2006, concluding that at least nine European nations had colluded with the CIA to capture and secretly transfer suspected terrorists. In addition to Poland and Romania, he listed Bosnia, Britain, Germany, Italy, Macedonia, Sweden, and Turkey. Five other nations—Cyprus, Greece, Ireland,

111. Glenn Kessler, "Europeans Search for Conciliation With U.S.," Washington Post, December 9, 2005, at A16.

112. Id.

113. Id. at A26.

114. Id. See also Joel Brinkley, "Rice Appears to Reassure Some Europeans on Treatment of Terror Detainees," New York Times, December 9, 2005, at A6; Glenn Kessler, "Rice Wins Over E.U. Counterparts, Capping Months of Groundwork," Washington Post, December 10, 2005, at A16.

115. Steven R. Weisman, "U.S. Rebuffs Red Cross Request for Access to Detainees Held in Secret," New York Times, December 10, 2005, at A6.

116. Dana Priest, "Covert CIA Program Withstands New Furor," Washington Post, December 30, 2005, at A1.

117. Dan Bilefsky, "European Inquiry Says C.I.A. Flew 1,000 Flights in Secret," New York Times, April 27, 2006, at A12.

Portugal, and Spain—allowed CIA-chartered flights to land at their airports and transfer detainees to other locations. The investigation, conducted without subpoena powers, could not provide hard facts to establish the existence of secret prisons. Instead, it relied on flight data and satellite photos to make the case. For example, a Boeing jet with tail number N313P departed Kabul, Afghanistan, on September 22, 2003, landed in Szymany, Poland, remained there for sixty-four minutes, and continued to Bucharest, Romania, and Rabat, Morocco. Eight locations frequently cited for the conduct of abusive interrogations were identified: Algiers; Amman, Jordan; Baghdad; Cairo; Islamabad, Pakistan; Kabul; Rabat; and Tashkent, Uzbekistan.[118]

The Bush administration had taken pains not to acknowledge extraordinary rendition. After publication of the detailed report by the Council of Europe, President Bush confirmed the existence of the CIA program during a news conference on June 9, 2006. He was asked point-blank: "This week, a report from the European Council talked about some CIA flights, illegal CIA flights with the prisoners in Europe, and illegal CIA presence also in some European countries. Have these flights taken place, and did you discuss this in your meeting today?" Evidently prepared for the question, Bush said that "in cases where we're not able to extradite somebody who is dangerous, sometimes renditions take place. It's been a part of our Government for quite a period of time—not just my Government, but previous administrations have done so in order to protect people."[119] Bush did not explain that previous renditions were for the purpose of bringing suspects to trial

The decision to close down (at least temporarily) the CIA prisons was triggered in part by the Supreme Court's June 2006 decision in *Hamdan*. The Court ruled that detainees must be protected by the Geneva Conventions, including the provisions of Common Article 3 and its prohibitions on torture and humiliating, degrading treatment.[120] The FBI and the CIA had clashed

118. Craig Whitlock, "European Probe Finds Signs of CIA-Run Secret Prisons," Washington Post, June 8, 2006, at A16. See also Craig Whitlock, "European Report Details Flights by CIA Aircraft," Washington Post, November 29, 2006, at A14; Molly Moore and Julie Tate, "European Report Addresses CIA Sites," Washington Post, June 8, 2007, at A16; Stephen Grey and Doreen Carvajal, "Secret Prisons in 2 Countries Held Qaeda Suspects, Report Says," New York Times, June 8, 2007, at A14; Molly Moore, "Report Gives Details on CIA Prisons," Washington Post, June 9, 2007, at A1.

119. 42 Weekly Comp. Pres. Doc. 1111 (2006).

120. Dafna Linzer and Glenn Kessler, "Decision to Move Detainees Resolved Two-Year Debate among Bush Advisers," Washington Post, September 8, 2006, at A1.

repeatedly over methods of interrogation. FBI agents insisted that persuasion was more effective in obtaining intelligence than coercive techniques. CIA agents insisted on tougher, more aggressive approaches. Over time, the CIA prevailed.[121]

On September 6, 2006, in a lengthy statement, President Bush provided details of the CIA rendition program. In addition to the suspects held at Guantánamo, "a small number of suspected terrorist leaders and operatives captured during the war have been held and questioned outside the United States, in a separate program operated by the Central Intelligence Agency."[122] He claimed that information obtained from these interrogations "saved innocent lives by helping us stop new attacks—here in the United States and across the world." He insisted that the CIA procedures were "designed to be safe, to comply with our laws, our Constitution, and our treaty obligations."[123] Fourteen men held in CIA custody would be transferred to Guantánamo, where questioning would comply with the new Army Field Manual.[124]

Bush's announcement put an end to Rice's efforts to dissemble and misrepresent the CIA program. Her counterparts in Europe were similarly discredited. Sarah Ludford, a British member of the European Parliament and vice chairman of a parliamentary inquiry into the secret prisons, concluded that Bush "has now left the Europeans high and dry." British Prime Minister Tony Blair, she noted, "can be as loyal as he likes to George Bush, but George Bush, when it suits him, will turn around and pull the rug out from under his feet."[125] Javier Solana, the European Union's foreign policy chief, announced that "no country in the E.U., or candidate country, as far as I know, has had secret prisons."[126] The issue was never *having* secret prisons. It was the willingness of E.U. countries to *assist* in transferring suspects to secret prisons for torture. A November 2006 report by the European Parliament confirmed that many governments cooperated "passively or actively" with the CIA and knew that individuals were being abducted and transported to places for illegal

121. David Johnston, "At a Secret Interrogation, Dispute Flared over Tactics," New York Times, September 10, 2006, at A1.

122. Id. at 1570.

123. Id. at 1571.

124. Id. at 1573–74.

125. Kevin Sullivan, "Detainee Decision Greeted Skeptically," Washington Post, September 7, 2006, at A17.

126. Brian Knowlton, "Europeans' Views Mixed on News of C.I.A. Camps," New York Times, September 8, 2006, at A19.

interrogation methods.[127] When released in February 2007, the report admonished fifteen European nations and Turkey for helping the CIA.[128]

In addition to the fourteen men transferred to Guantánamo, others had been held in CIA custody and subjected to interrogation methods that would have been prohibited for the U.S. military. Marwan Jabour, picked up in May 2004, endured more than two years of incarceration, including being beaten and burned in Pakistan. He was moved to other CIA facilities, including in Afghanistan. Released on June 30, 2006, at a border crossing between Israel and Gaza, he was never charged with anything or understood why he was now set free.[129] Following the transfer of the fourteen, the administration continued to have suspected terrorists seized and placed in CIA custody overseas, with some moved to Guantánamo.[130] In March 2008, the CIA transferred another one of its detainees to Guantánamo.[131]

Continuing Investigations

In October 2006, prosecutors in Italy sought the indictment of Nicolo Pollari, the head of military intelligence (Sismi) since 2001. He was charged with complicity in the abduction of Abu Omar by U.S. intelligence agents. The investigation targeted government officials who had cooperated with the United States to violate the laws of Italy. Twenty-five operatives of the CIA were named in the case.[132] A month later, Pollari lost his job. Also removed from their positions were Gen. Mario Mori, head of Italy's civilian intelligence agency, and

127. Brian Knowlton, "Report Rejects European Denial of C.I.A. Prisons," New York Times, November 29, 2006, at A15.

128. Molly Moore, "E.U. Report Faults 16 Nations in Probe of Secret CIA Flights," Washington Post, February 15, 2007, at A14.

129. Dafna Linzer and Julie Tate, "New Light Shed on CIA's 'Black Site' Prisons," Washington Post, February 28, 2007, at A1.

130. Dafna Linzer, "CIA Held Al-Qaeda Suspect Secretly," Washington Post, April 28, 2007, at A16; Mark Mazzetti and David S. Cloud, "C.I.A. Held Qaeda Leader in Secret Prison for Months," New York Times, April 28, 2007, at A7; Scott Shane, "Rights Groups Call for End to Secret Detention of Suspects," New York Times, July 7, 2007, at A18. See Jane Mayer, "The Black Sites: A Rare Look Inside the C.I.A.'s Secret Interrogation Program," New Yorker, August 13, 2007, at 46.

131. Mark Mazzetti, "Officials Say C.I.A. Kept Qaeda Suspect in Secret Detention," New York Times, March 15, 2008, at A7; Joby Warrick, "U.S. Transfers Bin Laden Aide," Washington Post, March 15, 2008, at A3.

132. Ian Fisher and Elisabetta Povoledo, "Italy's Top Spy Is Expected to Be Indicted in Abduction Case," New York Times, October 24, 2006, at A3.

Emilio Del Mese, a national intelligence coordinator.[133] Testimony in the trial disclosed details about who participated in the abductions and how they were carried out.[134] In February 2007, Italy indicted twenty-six Americans (most of them CIA officers) for the abduction of Abu Omar. At the same time, the Swiss government authorized an investigation into the flight that was said to have transported him from Italy to Germany through Swiss airspace, before going to Egypt.[135] On February 28, 2007, the State Department announced that the United States would refuse to extradite CIA officers to Italy on the kidnapping charges.[136]

In late January 2007, German prosecutors issued arrest warrants for thirteen CIA operatives involved in the kidnapping of Khaled El-Masri in Macedonia. According to hotel records and flight logs, the crew of the CIA plane that took El-Masri to Afghanistan stayed for a few days at the Spanish resort island of Majorca. Although most of them used aliases, the hotel records show their passport numbers, hotel bills, and aviation records.[137] News reports called attention to another German citizen, Mohammed Haydar Zammar, who was arrested in Morocco and secretly transferred to Syria with the help of the CIA, assisted by German federal police.[138] In September 2007, German authorities dropped their efforts to have the thirteen CIA agents extradited to Germany. U.S. officials made it clear they would not cooperate. However, the arrest warrants remained in effect if the CIA employees decided to travel to Germany or elsewhere in the European Union.[139]

133. Sarah Delaney and Craig Whitlock, "Italian Spy Chief Out; Investigated in Abduction," Washington Post, November 21, 2006, at A24.

134. Craig Whitlock, "Testimony Helps Detail CIA's Post-9/11 Reach," Washington Post, December 15, 2006, at A1.

135. Ian Fisher, "Italians Indict C.I.A. Operatives in '03 Abduction," New York Times, February 17, 2007, at A1; Sarah Delaney and Craig Whitlock, "Milan Court Indicts 26 Americans in Abduction," Washington Post, February 17, 2007, at A1.

136. Craig Whitlock, "U.S. Won't Send CIA Defendants to Italy," Washington Post, March 1, 2007, at A12. For more on the Italian investigation, see Stephen Grey, Ghost Plane: The True Story of the CIA Torture Program 190–213 (2006).

137. Craig Whitlock, "Germans Charge 13 CIA Operatives," Washington Post, February 1, 2007, at A1; Mark Landler, "German Court Challenges C.I.A. over Abduction," New York Times, February 1, 2007, at 1; Craig Whitlock, "Travel Logs Aid German's Kidnap Probe," Washington Post, February 2, 2007, at A11.

138. Craig Whitlock, "In Another CIA Abduction, Germany Has an Uneasy Role," Washington Post, February 5, 2007, at A11.

139. Craig Whitlock, "Germans Drop Bid for Extraditions in CIA Case," Washington Post, September 24, 2007, at A9.

The United States assured British officials that no rendition flights had landed on British territory or passed through British airspace. CIA Director Hayden, during a visit to London in February 2008, disclosed that agency records now confirmed that rendition flights had stopped and refueled at the British island of Diego Garcia in the Indian Ocean. British officials had long denied any involvement in America's rendition program.[140]

LITIGATION

In court, the Bush administration told federal judges that terrorism suspects held in secret CIA prisons should not be permitted to reveal the "alternative interrogation methods" used to obtain information. Revealing those techniques "could reasonably be expected to cause extremely grave damage" to the nation. One lawsuit involved Majid Khan, a 26-year-old Pakistani national who lived in the United States for seven years. He was seized in Pakistan, held in CIA prison camps, and eventually moved to Guantánamo as part of the group of fourteen.[141] The administration argued that allowing individuals subjected to extraordinary rendition to litigate would risk the disclosure of state secrets and encroach on independent presidential authority. A Justice Department brief insisted that the state secrets privilege "is based on the President's Article II power to conduct foreign affairs and to provide for the national defense, and therefore has constitutional underpinnings."[142] Of course that is an assertion, not a fact, and has constitutional validity only if the assertions find support in court or in Congress.

Maher Arar

Born in Syria, Maher Arar moved to Canada with his parents when he was 17, studied at McGill University and the University of Quebec, and obtained a

140. John F. Burns, "C.I.A. Used a British Island to Transport Terrorism Suspects," New York Times, February 22, 2008, at A8; Kevin Sullivan, "U.S. Fueled 'Rendition' Flights on British Soil," Washington Post, February 22, 2008, at A16.

141. Carol D. Leonnig and Eric Rich, "U.S. Seeks Silence on CIA Prisons," Washington Post, November 4, 2006, at A1; U.S. Department of Justice, Respondents' Memorandum in Opposition to Petitioners' Motion for Emergency Access to Counsel and Entry of Amended Protective Order, Khan v. Bush, Civil Action No. 06-CV–1690 (RBW) (D.D.C. October 26, 2006).

142. U.S. Justice Department, Memorandum in Support of the United States Assertion of State Secrets Privilege, Arar v. Ashcroft (E.D. N.Y. January 18, 2005), at 3–4.

Master's degree in telecommunications. He married in 1994, had a daughter in 1997, and worked in Ottawa and Boston. He returned to Ottawa in 2001 to start his own consulting firm. A second child came in 2002. He is a dual citizen of Syria and Canada.

In September 2002, he was with his wife and children vacationing in Tunis. In response to a request from his former employer, he returned alone to Ottawa to consult with a prospective client. On September 26, 2002, he boarded an American Airlines flight from Zurich to JFK airport in New York, arriving there at 2:00 P.M. en route to Montreal. After his name was entered into the computer, he was pulled aside at immigration, fingerprinted and photographed, and denied the opportunity to phone family or attorney. He was kept at the airport until midnight, questioned by the New York Police Department and FBI agents. Interrogation continued the next day, when he was transferred to the Metropolitan Detention Center. He learned that he was suspected of being a member of a foreign terrorist organization.

On October 2, allowed to make a two-minute phone-call, he told his mother-in-law in Ottawa of his fear of being deported to Syria. Over the next few days he met with his lawyer and a Canadian consul. He told U.S. officials that he wanted to continue to Canada and that if he were sent to Syria he would be tortured. He had every reason to fear torture. Country reports prepared by the State Department consistently referred to Syria as "a military regime with virtually absolute authority in the hands of the President," a weak Parliament, and a judiciary with no independent powers over issues of national security.[143] The security forces commit "serious human rights abuses."[144] Torture methods included "administering electrical shocks; pulling out fingernails; forcing objects into the rectum; beating, sometimes while the victim is suspended from the ceiling; hyperextending the spine; bending the detainees into the frame of a wheel and whipping exposed body parts; and using a chair that bends backwards to asphyxiate the victim or fracture the victim's spine."[145]

Despite this clear understanding of how Syria treats prisoners, the commissioner of the Immigration and Naturalization Service (INS) in Washington, D.C., certified that Arar's removal to Syria was consistent with Article 3 of

143. U.S. Department of State, Country Reports on Human Rights Practices, Syria, 2002, at 1; http://www.state.gov/g/drl/rls/hrrpt/2002/18289.htm.

144. Id.

145. Id. at 2.

CAT.[146] After about a week at the Metropolitan Detention Center, U.S. officials flew Arar to Washington, D.C., and from there to Amman, Jordan, where he was blindfolded, chained, and put in a van. Whenever he tried to move or talk he was beaten. On October 9 he was driven to Damascus, Syria, and imprisoned at the Palestine Branch of Syrian military intelligence. He was placed in a cell, called a "grave," where he would remain for months. It measured three feet wide, six feet deep, and seven feet high. It had a metal door that prevented light from entering. There was no light source in the cell. From October 11 to 16 he was taken for interrogation and beaten on his palms, wrists, lower back, and hips with a shredded black electrical cable about two inches in diameter. His interrogators threatened him with electric shocks and with a car tire into which prisoners are stuffed, immobilized, and beaten. Under those conditions he falsely confessed that he had received military training in Afghanistan. In the second week he was forced in the tire, immobilized, but not beaten.[147]

On October 23 he met with a Canadian consul after being warned not to say anything about the beatings. In early November he was told to sign and place his thumbprint on every page of a handwritten document about seven pages long. Not allowed to read it, he was forced to sign and place his thumbprint on other documents as well. From October 23, 2002, to February 8, 2003, he met six times with the Canadian consul. In early April he was placed in an outdoor courtyard, the first time in six months he had seen sunlight. A seventh visit with the Canadian consul took place on August 14, when for the first time he described his cell and the beatings. Five days later he was forced to sign and put his thumbprint on a page that said he went to a training camp in Afghanistan. Afterwards he was transferred to a cell, 12 feet by 20 feet, with about fifty other people. On August 20 he was transferred to Sednaya prison and placed in a collective cell.

In late September, Arar was returned to the Palestine Branch and kept there for seven days. At a court hearing, the prosecutor read from his confession. Arar objected that he was forced to say he went to Afghanistan, but the court ignored his remarks. He was forced to sign and put his fingerprint on yet another document. He was brought back to the Palestine Branch, driven to the Canadian embassy, and taken to the Canadian consul's house to shower before flying out of Syria and returning to Canada.[148]

146. Grey, Ghost Plane, at 68.

147. This description comes the chronology provided by Arar after his release; http://www/maherarar.ca/mahers%20story.php, at 1–4.

148. Id. at 5–7.

Arar was never formally charged with anything. Syria found no evidence linking him with terrorism. On what possible grounds could the United States justify sending him to a country it regards as a terrorist nation? Why entrust the questioning of a supposed terrorist to Syrian interrogators? Was Syria now a surrogate or ally of the United States in gaining intelligence? What was it promised in return? The United States regularly reminds other nations about the importance of safeguarding democracy, protecting the rule of law, and respecting human rights and human dignity. The extraordinary rendition of Maher Arar violated all of those principles. An expert who assisted in Canada's investigation of the Arar abduction concluded that his treatment at the Palestine Branch "constituted torture as understood in international law."[149]

Arar filed a civil suit seeking money damages and declaratory relief from a number of U.S. officials in their individual and official capacities. On January 18, 2005, the Justice Department filed a memorandum in support of the state secrets privilege, claiming that the documents sought by Arar were "properly classified" and that disclosure "would interfere with foreign relations, reveal intelligence-gathering sources or methods, and be detrimental to national security."[150] Did the Bush administration know about the methods used by Syria? U.S. officials were not present. The Bush administration asked the court to dismiss Arar's case and enter judgment in favor of all U.S. officials, both in their individual and official capacities.

On February 16, 2006, a federal district court held that Arar lacked standing to bring a claim against the U.S. officials who were responsible for holding him incommunicado at the U.S. border and removing him to Syria for detention and torture. The court ruled that he failed to meet the statutory requirements of the Torture Victim Protection Act of 1992; any access to remedies was foreclosed, the court said, because of national security and foreign considerations. The decision states that the INS Regional Director, J. Scott Blackman, determined from available information that Arar was "clearly and unequivocally" a member of al Qaeda and therefore "clearly and unequivocally inadmissible to the United States."[151] Although that determination was based on information

149. Commission of Inquiry into the Actions of Canadian Officials in Relation to Maher Arar, Report of Professor Stephen J. Toope, Fact Finder, October 14, 2005, at 17; http://www.ararcommission.ca/eng/index.htm (under "Fact Finder's Report"), accessed August 19, 2007.

150. U.S. Department of Justice, Memorandum in Support of the United States' Assertion of State Secrets Privilege, Arar v. Ashcroft, C.A. No. 04-CV–249-DGT-VVP (E. N.Y. 2005), at 2–3.

151. Arar v. Ashcroft, 414 F.Supp.2d 250, 254 (E.D. N.Y. 2006).

later shown to be false, Blackman ordered Arar sent to Syria without review by an immigration judge.[152] Part of the defense by the Bush administration is that "the alleged torture occurred while Arar was in Syrian custody." However, U.S. officials knew he would be subjected to torture in Syria and may have sent him there for that very reason.[153]

At the end of the decision, the court examined the administration's claim that Arar's lawsuit threatened national security and foreign policy considerations. Holding that courts "must proceed cautiously" in reviewing policy-making issues that are the prerogative of the legislative and executive branches, it noted that Congress had "yet to take any affirmative position on federal-court review of renditions," even though it had passed many statutes prohibiting torture.[154] The court emphasized the importance of secrecy in national security and foreign affairs: "One need not have much imagination to contemplate the negative effect on our relations with Canada if discovery were to proceed in this case and were it to turn out that certain high Canadian officials had, despite public denials, acquiesced in Arar's removal to Syria."[155] As it turned out, Canada reached that conclusion and publicly apologized to Arar.

The court warned that "an erroneous decision [by the judiciary] can have adverse consequences in the foreign realm not likely to occur in the domestic context."[156] In this case, the erroneous decision and adverse consequences had already occurred—by the executive branch. Having decided statutory and constitutional claims against Arar, the court ruled that "the issue involving state secrets is moot."[157] Arar's complaint about his thirteen-day detention within the United States, denial of counsel, and being subject to coercive and involuntary custodial interrogation was dismissed without prejudice, permitting Arar to reargue those claims and present additional evidence.[158]

Seven months after the district court's ruling, a three-volume, 822-page judicial report in Canada concluded that Canadian intelligence officials had passed false warnings and bad information about Arar to the United States. Agents of the Canadian intelligence services, under pressure after 9/11 to find terrorists, falsely labeled him as a dangerous radical. The report found that Arar had no involvement in Islamic extremism and "categorically that there is

152. Id.
153. Id. at 262.
154. Id. at 281.
155. Id.
156. Id. at 282.
157. Id. at 287.
158. Id. at 283–88.

no evidence" that he did anything wrong or was a security threat. The United States refused to cooperate in the inquiry.[159]

Cleared by Canada, Arar remained on America's "watch list" as a terrorist threat to the United States.[160] Invited to testify before a congressional committee, he could do so only from Ottawa.[161] One week after the hearing, Secretary Rice admitted that the United States did not handle his case "as it should have been."[162] Her statement stopped short of an apology.

On January 26, 2007, Prime Minister Stephen Harper of Canada released a letter of apology to Maher Arar and his family. The government accepted all twenty-three recommendations in the judicial report, sent letters to both the Syrian and U.S. governments formally objecting to the treatment of Arar, and provided $9.75 million in compensation.[163] In August 2007, newly released sections of Canada's judicial report indicate that Canadian intelligence officials anticipated that the United States would send Arar to a third country to be tortured and that neither the Syrian government nor the FBI were convinced he was a significant security threat. His treatment appeared to be triggered by the coerced confession of Ahmad Abou el-Maati, a Kuwaiti-born Canadian who was imprisoned and tortured in Syria.[164] Arar appealed his case to the Second Circuit.

159. Doug Struck, "Canadian Was Falsely Accused, Panel Says," Washington Post, September 19, 2006, at A1; Ian Austen, "Canadians Fault U.S. for Its Role in Torture Case," New York Times, September 19, 2006, at A1.

160. Doug Struck, "Tortured Canadian Still on U.S. 'Watch List,'" Washington Post, December 16, 2006, at A16; Scott Shane, "Canadian to Remain on U.S. Terrorist Watch List," New York Times, January 23, 2007, at A11.

161. "Rendition to Torture: The Case of Maher Arar," joint hearing before the Subcommittee on International Organizations, Human Rights, and Oversight of the House Committee on Foreign Affairs and the Subcommittee on the Constitution, Civil Rights, and Civil Liberties of the House Committee on the Judiciary, 110th Cong., 1st Sess. (2007).

162. "Rice Admits U.S. Erred in Deportation Case," New York Times, October 25, 2007, at A10.

163. "Prime Minister releases letter of apology to Maher Arar and his family and announces completion of mediation process," available at http://www.pm.gc.ca/eng/media. asp?id=1510, accessed on August 17, 2007; Doug Struck, "Tortured Man Gets Apology from Canada," Washington Post, January 27, 2007, at A14; Ian Austen, "Canada to Pay $9.75 Million to Man Tortured in Syria," New York Times, January 27, 2207, at A5.

164. Ian Austen, "Deported Canadian Was No Threat, Report Shows," New York Times, August 10, 2007, at A9.

Khaled El-Masri

Khaled El-Masri was born in Kuwait in 1963 of Lebanese parents. He grew up in Lebanon, moved to Germany in 1985, and became a German citizen in 1995. At the end of 2003 he traveled to Skopje, Macedonia, for vacation. He was detained by Macedonian border officials on December 31 because of confusion over his name. They thought he was Khalid al-Masri, a suspect from the al Qaeda Hamburg cell. There was suspicion (later shown to be false) that El-Masri's German passport was a forgery. The Macedonians detained him until January 23, 2004, when they transferred him to CIA agents. They flew him to a secret prison called the "Salt Pit" in Kabul, Afghanistan, where he was held for five months in squalid conditions. He was repeatedly refused counsel or access to a representative of the German government.

Months later, the CIA concluded that his passport was genuine and it had imprisoned the wrong man. A former senior intelligence officer remarked: "Whatever quality control mechanisms were in play on September 10th were eliminated on September 11th."[165] On May 28, U.S. officials flew him from Kabul to Albania and left him alone, at night, on a hill. Three uniformed men drove him to the Tirana airport where he boarded a plane to Frankfurt. Upon reaching home he learned that his family, after he failed to return, had moved to Lebanon. They returned to Germany and were reunited.

On December 6, 2005, El-Masri sued CIA Director George Tenet, the airlines used by the CIA, and current and former employees of the agency.[166] The Bush administration asserted the state secrets privilege to block the litigation from moving to discovery and access to government documents. The new CIA Director, Porter Goss, stated that clandestine intelligence activities, by "their very nature," are not acknowledged by the United States and that it was necessary to protect "classified intelligence sources and methods from unauthorized disclosure and thereby avoid damage to the national security and our nation's conduct of foreign affairs."[167] How much damage to the United States had been done by the rendition? To Goss, neither El-Masri nor his attorneys

165. Dana Priest, "Wrongful Imprisonment: Anatomy of a CIA Mistake," Washington Post, December 4, 2005, at A1, A25.

166. Complaint, Khaled El-Masri v. George J. Tenet, Civil Action No. 1:05-cv–01417-TSE-TRJ (E.D. Va. 2005); Scott Shane, "German Held in Afghan Jail Files Lawsuit," New York Times, December 7, 2005, at A16.

167. Formal Claim of State Secrets Privilege by Porter J. Goss, Director, Central Intelligence Agency, El-Masri v. Tenet, Civil Action No. 1:05-cv–01417-TSE-TRJ (E.D. Va. 2006), at 4.

"possess the need-to-know required to access the classified information described in this declaration."[168]

On May 12, 2006, a federal district court held that the state secrets privilege was validly asserted and dismissed El-Masri's case.[169] Judge Thomas S. Ellis presented a confused account of the constitutional role assigned to the courts. On the one hand, he said that courts "must not blindly accept the Executive Branch's assertion" of state secrets but "must instead independently and carefully determine whether, in the circumstances, the claimed secrets deserve the protection of the privilege."[170] The depth of the court's inquiry "increases relative to the adverse party's need for the information the government seeks to protect." Courts "must carefully scrutinize the assertion of the privilege lest it be used by the government to shield 'material not strictly necessary to prevent injury to national security.'"[171]

On the other hand, "courts must also bear in mind the Executive Branch's preeminent authority over military and diplomatic matters" and must accept the executive branch's assertion of the privilege "whenever its independent inquiry discloses a '*reasonable danger* that compulsion of the evidence will expose military matters which, in the interest of national security, should not be divulged.'"[172] Once a court is satisfied that the claim is validly asserted, "the privilege is not subject to a judicial balancing of the various interests at stake."[173]

Nonetheless, Judge Ellis introduced a balancing test: El-Masri's "private interests must give way to the national interest in preserving state secrets."[174] How could one individual's "private" interest ever outweigh the claimed interest of the entire government or the nation? It depends on how one defines national interest. There was no national interest in picking up the wrong person and keeping him in prison for five months, with no ability to seek damages and no opportunity to force the government to concede a mistake and make restitution. El-Masri was not merely defending his own interests. He represented every individual, U.S. citizen or alien, who wants to avoid a like fate. It is in the national interest to prevent government abuse, especially when covered up by

168. Id. at 7.

169. El-Masri v. Tenet, 437 F.Supp.2d 530, 539 (E.D. Va. 2006).

170. Id. at 536.

171. Id., citing Ellsberg v. Mitchell, 709 F.2d 51, 58 (D.C. Cir. 1983).

172. Id. at 536–37, citing United States v. Reynolds, 345 U.S. 1, 10 (1953) (emphasis added by the district court).

173. Id. at 536, 537.

174. Id. at 539.

the state secrets privilege. It is in the national interest to have other branches of government, in this case the judiciary, independently supervise and judge unilateral and illegal executive actions. It is in the national interest to have an effective system of checks and balances and a separation of powers instead of a concentration of power.

Toward the end of his decision, Judge Ellis cautioned that nothing in his ruling "should be taken as a sign of judicial approval or disapproval of rendition programs; it is not intended to do either."[175] However, by accepting the state secrets privilege as readily as he did, he removed any opportunity for judicial check, scrutiny, or constraint on the extraordinary rendition program. The "propriety and efficacy" of the program, he said, "are not proper grist for the judicial mill."[176] Why not? What prevents courts from independently scrutinizing and passing judgment on abusive, illegal, and unconstitutional actions by the executive branch?

Putting legal issues to the side, Judge Ellis said that if El-Masri's allegations were true, "or essentially true, then all fair-minded people, including those who believe that the state secrets must be protected, that this lawsuit cannot proceed, and that renditions are a necessary step to take in this war, must also agree that El-Masri has suffered injuries as a result of our country's mistake and deserves a remedy." The source of that remedy, he said, "must be the Executive Branch or the Legislative Branch, not the Judicial Branch."[177] There is no reason to expect a remedy from an executive branch that initiated the program and attempted to block any litigation questioning it. If there are legitimate questions of illegality and unconstitutionality, the courts are as qualified as Congress to render a judgment. To have courts look the other way does not promote the rule of law or respect for the courts.[178]

German investigators disclosed that they had obtained a list of about twenty CIA operatives suspected in the abduction of El-Masri, but the U.S. government refused to cooperate or give any assistance. Prosecutors in Germany received the list from Spanish judicial authorities, who put it together based on a flight manifest of the airplane that stopped in Palma, on the island of Majorca, before flying to Skopje to pick up El-Masri.[179]

175. Id. at 540.

176. Id.

177. Id. at 541.

178. For news reports on this case, see Dana Priest, "Secrecy Privilege Invoked in Fighting Ex-Detainee's Lawsuit," Washington Post, May 13, 2006, at A3; Jerry Markon, "Lawsuit against CIA Is Dismissed," Washington Post, May 19, 2006, at A13.

179. Craig Whitlock, "German Lawmakers Fault Abduction Probe," Washington Post, October 4, 2006, at A18. See also Souad Mekhennet and Craig S. Smith, "German Spy Agency

El-Masri appealed his case to the Fourth Circuit. Writing for a unanimous panel on March 2, 2007, Judge Robert B. King noted two developments that occurred after the district court's decision: a June 7, 2006, draft report by the Council of Europe substantially affirming El-Masri's account of his rendition, and the public admission by President Bush three months later that the CIA program existed.[180] Nevertheless, the Fourth Circuit affirmed the decision by Judge Ellis. In so doing, it offered three arguments.

The first: "This inquiry is a difficult one, for it pits the judiciary's search for truth against the Executive's duty to maintain the nation's security."[181] The judiciary cannot search for truth if it accepts the assertion of state secrets and blocks access to disputed documents and eliminates the adversary process that is designed for truth-seeking. Abusive, illegal, and unconstitutional actions by the executive branch do not maintain national security. They undermine it. To allow the executive branch to engage in extraordinary rendition and torture serves to recruit terrorists and spread hate against the United States.

Second: the Fourth Circuit claimed that the judiciary does not abdicate its powers on state secrets cases. In fact, it does. Consider this passage:

> The *Reynolds* Court recognized this tension, observing that "[j]udicial control over the evidence in a case cannot be abdicated to the caprice of executive officers"—no matter how great the interest in the national security—but the President's ability to preserve state secrets likewise cannot be placed entirely at the mercy of the courts. . . . Moreover, a court evaluating a claim of privilege must "do so without forcing a disclosure of the very thing the privilege is designed to protect."[182]

Evidence is not "disclosed" when a court insists that sensitive documents be given to the trial judge to be examined *in camera*. Accepting assertions by one side is abdication, which is what the Fourth Circuit did: "in certain circumstances a court may conclude that an explanation by the Executive of why a question cannot be answered would itself create an unacceptable danger of injurious disclosure. . . . In such a situation, a court is obliged to accept the executive branch's claim of privilege without further demand."[183]

Admits Mishandling Abduction Case," June 2, 2006, at A8. For more details on El-Masri, see Grey, Ghost Plane, at 79–102.

180. El-Masri v. United States, 479 F.3d 296, 302 (4th Cir. 2007).

181. Id. at 304.

182. Id.

183. Id. at 305–06.

The Fourth Circuit rejected El-Masri's argument that the state secrets privilege represents a surrender of judicial control over access to documents: "As we have explained, it is the court, not the Executive, that determines whether the state secrets privilege has been properly invoked."[184] It is indeed the court that makes that determination, but it cannot decide in an informed manner unless it asks for and examines executive branch documents. Deferring to executive branch declarations and statements (classified or unclassified) weakens judicial control. Both the district court and the Fourth Circuit depended on a "Classified Declaration" that summarized executive branch claims without allowing judges to read the underlying documents.[185] Under those conditions, courts operate largely in the dark.

Third: the Fourth Circuit concluded that El-Masri "suffers this reversal not through any fault of his own, but because his personal interest in pursuing his civil claim is subordinated to the collective interest in national security."[186] There is no collective interest in what the government did to El-Masri. National interest is not advanced by apprehending and detaining the wrong people and letting the executive officials who committed the mistake remain unaccountable, at liberty to repeat the error. There is no collective interest in having the United States abuse innocent people while the world passes judgment on the health and vitality of the U.S. political and legal system. Nor is the legal dispute between one person and the collective interest. No litigant could ever prevail with that test. The conflict is between the interests raised by El-Masri for all potential victims who may be flown to another country for interrogation and torture. He represents a collective interest in prohibiting abusive and illegal programs by executive officials. There is a collective interest in assuring that constitutional values prevail over political and partisan shortcuts.[187] Justice Hugo Black used to inveigh against artificial "balancing tests" that put an individual on one side of the scale and the government on the other.[188] Often an individual speaks for the interests of society and the rule of law, and those interests must be protected against claims and assertions by government, especially claims of state secrets.

184. Id. at 312.

185. Id.

186. Id. at 313.

187. For articles on the Fourth Circuit decision, see Adam Liptak, "U.S. Appeals Court Upholds Dismissal of Abuse Suit against C.I.A., Saying Secrets Are at Risk," New York Times, March 3, 2007, at A6.

188. Barenblatt v. United States, 360 U.S. 109, 144 (1959) (Black, J., dissenting).

CIA INTERROGATIONS

After President Bush in September 2006 confirmed the existence and operation of CIA prisons abroad and the transfer of fourteen suspects to Guantánamo, the administration and Congress drafted legislation to comply with *Hamdan*. The White House and Republican Senators insisted on language that "would provide for continued tough interrogations of terrorism suspects by the CIA at secret detention sites."[189] The White House clearly intended to maintain two standards: one for interrogations conducted by the Defense Department, subject to the rules set forth in the Army Field Manual, and a separate procedure for the CIA. That distinction was openly discussed during debate on the military commissions bill.[190]

The Supreme Court's decision in *Hamdan* required military commissions to satisfy Common Article 3 of Geneva. The Article is given that name because it appears in all four Geneva Conventions, prohibiting "violence to life and person, in particular murder of all kinds, mutilation, cruel treatment and torture," and "outrages upon personal dignity, in particular, humiliating and degrading treatment."[191] Section 6 of the Military Commissions Act, enacted in October 2006 in response to *Hamdan*, required President Bush to issue an executive order to implement treaty obligations, including Common Article 3. In signing the bill, President Bush said it would allow the CIA "to continue its program for questioning key terrorist leaders and operatives."[192] The legislation, according to Bush, provided the "clarity our intelligence professionals need to continue questioning terrorists and saving lives. This bill provides legal protections that ensure our military and intelligence professionals will not have to fear lawsuits filed by terrorists simply for doing their jobs."[193]

The administration did not seek "clarity." It sought statutory authority to protect CIA employees who engage in aggressive and abusive interrogations and who transfer suspects to locations where torture is likely. As noted by Frederick Schwarz and Aziz Huq, clarity "was never the Administration's goal. After all, this was the Administration that for four years had used a standard of 'humane treatment' that lacked any definition whatsoever. Rather than clarity,

189. R. Jeffrey Smith and Charles Babbington, "White House, Senators Near Pact on Interrogation Rules," Washington Post, September 7, 2006, at A1.

190. Peter Baker, "GOP Infighting on Detainees Intensifies: Bush Threatens to Halt CIA Program if Congress Passes Rival Proposal," Washington Post, September 15, 2006, at A1.

191. 6 UST 3320 (1949).

192. 42 Weekly Comp. Pres. Doc. 1832 (2006).

193. Id.

the Administration sought license to torture."[194] Whatever clarity the statute might provide, the procedures followed by CIA interrogators would remain secret. It was widely believed—for good reason—that the methods would be prohibited by military interrogators. Otherwise, there would be no reason for the administration to repeatedly insist on a different standard for the CIA. Also, the provision for legal protections against lawsuits underscored that the CIA techniques would be aggressive, harsh, and of questionable legality. Bush claimed that the bill "complies with both the spirit and the letter of our international obligations."[195] Unless the CIA methods were made public and neutral observers would be in the room during interrogations, the extent of compliance could never be known.

In late July 2007, the White House agreed on procedures to allow the CIA to resume its interrogation of terrorism suspects overseas. News reports indicated that the methods would allow techniques "more severe" than those used by military personnel. Several executive officials said that the techniques excluded "waterboarding." The Justice Department concluded that the procedures did not violate the Geneva Conventions. Human rights groups objected that the authorization of indefinite, incommunicado detention and interrogation violated international law.[196] Apparently the International Committee of the Red Cross would be prohibited from visiting detainees held by the CIA.[197] The only person at that time that the agency acknowledged holding was Abd al-Hadi al-Iraqi, an Iraqi Kurd said to be one of Osama bin Laden's closest advisers. CIA officials said that he had produced valuable intelligence even though CIA interrogators, at that time, had followed the techniques approved in the Army Field Manual.[198]

The executive order issued by President Bush on July 20, 2007, interprets and applies Common Article 3 to the CIA. Prohibited interrogation practices include (1) torture (as defined by 18 U.S.C. § 2340), (2) acts prohibited by 18 U.S.C. § 2441d (including murder, torture, cruel or inhuman treatment, mutilation or maiming, intentionally causing bodily injury, rape, sexual assault or abuse, taking of hostages, or performing biological experiments), and (3) acts of cruel, inhuman, or degrading treatment prohibited by the Military

194. Frederick A. O. Schwarz, Jr., and Aziz Z. Huq, Unchecked and Unbalanced 92 (2007).
195. 42 Weekly Comp. Pres. Doc. 1832. (2006).
196. Mark Mazzetti, "Rules Lay Out C.I.A.'s Tactics in Questioning," New York Times, July 21, 2007, at A1.
197. Id. at A6.
198. Id.

Commissions Act and the Detainee Treatment Act. Also prohibited: (4) "willful and outrageous acts of personal abuse *done for the purpose of* humiliating or degrading the individual" (including sexual or sexually indecent acts, forcing the individual to perform sexual acts or to pose sexually), (5) threatening the individual with sexual mutilation, or using the individual as a human shield, and (6) acts *intended to* denigrate the religion, religious practices, or religious objects of the individual. Detainees are to receive the basic necessities of life, including adequate food and water, shelter from the elements, necessary clothing, protection from extremes of heat and cold, and essential medical care.[199]

The words "done for the purpose of" and "intended to" seem a backdoor way to condone torture or violations of Geneva. Nothing in Common Law 3 speaks of purpose or intent. The prohibitions are not qualified. The administration could argue that if the intent or purpose of CIA interrogation is to gather intelligence or prevent future terrorist attacks, CIA employees may commit outrageous acts to humiliate or degrade the individual or denigrate Islam. If interpreted or administered in that manner, the executive order cannot be reconciled with Common Article 3.[200]

In October 2007, newspaper stories reported that secret legal opinions prepared in the Justice Department endorsed such interrogation tactics as head-slapping, simulated drowning (waterboarding), and frigid temperatures.[201] When it was learned that the CIA had destroyed videotapes of interrogations, Attorney General Michael Mukasey assigned a career federal prosecutor to begin a criminal inquiry.[202] Congress passed legislation to ban waterboarding and other harsh interrogation tactics, but on March 8 President Bush vetoed the bill and the House was unable to override.[203] The purpose of the legislation was

199. Executive Order: Interpretation of the Geneva Conventions Common Article 3 as Applied to Programs of Detention and Interrogation Operated by the Central Intelligence Agency, July 20, 2007, available at: http://www.whitehouse.gov/news/releases/2007/07/print/20070720–4.html (emphasis added).

200. P. X. Kelley and Robert F. Turner, "War Crimes and the White House: The Dishonor in a Tortured New 'Interpretation' of the Geneva Conventions," Washington Post, July 26, 2007, at A21.

201. Scott Shane, David Johnston, and James Risen, "Secret U.S. Endorsement of Severe Interrogations," New York Times, October 4, 2007, at A1; David Johnston and Scott Shane, "Debate Erupts on Techniques Used by C.I.A.," New York Times, October 5, 2007, at A1.

202. Mark Mazzetti and David Johnston, "U.S. Announces Criminal Inquiry into C.I.A. Tapes," New York Times, January 1, 2008, at A1.

203. Steven Lee Myers, "Bush Vetoes Bill on C.I.A. Tactics, Affirming Legacy," New York

to limit the CIA to the interrogation techniques approved in the Army Field Manual.

The Bush administration and the United States paid a heavy political price for sending suspects to other countries for interrogation and torture. On numerous occasions the administration decided to deceive the American public and the international community until studies conducted by the Council of Europe, independent analyses by private parties, and the Supreme Court's decision in *Hamdan* forced it to admit what was widely known. An effective national security policy requires an administration to build trust with the public and to work jointly with Congress. The policy of extraordinary rendition violated both objectives.

Times, March 9, 2008, at A1; "Effort to Prohibit Waterboarding Fails in House," New York Times, March 12, 2008, at A17.

Conclusions

A film by Rainer Werner Fassbinder carries the title *Angst essen Seele auf* (Fear Eats the Soul). At various points in America's history, fear, anger, prejudice, and ignorance have done more harm to the nation than an enemy ever could. The Alien and Sedition Acts, the Red Scare, the post-WWII campaign against Communism—including loyalty security boards—are prominent examples of policies that degraded political institutions and individuals. After 9/11, the important need to safeguard America was sidetracked by such ill-conceived initiatives as military tribunals, Guantánamo, torture memos, holding U.S. citizens indefinitely by designating them "enemy combatants," NSA surveillance, and extraordinary rendition, all of which alienated allies, mobilized enemies, and damaged national power and prestige.

The announced purpose of U.S. antiterrorist policies after 9/11 was to bring democracy and the rule of law to the Middle East. At home, those values were regularly threatened by illegal, unconstitutional, secret, and unaccountable programs. The Bush administration claimed that terrorists hate America for its freedoms, yet its actions jeopardized those freedoms and brought the reputation of the United States lower in the eyes of the world. Senior lawyers and policymakers in the administration showed no interest, understanding, or commitment to the rule of law, democratic values, or the Constitution. The single, overriding goal was to maximize presidential power at all costs, and there were many. As one insider in the Bush administration remarked, after 9/11 top officials "dealt with FISA the way they dealt with other laws they didn't like: they blew through them in secret based on flimsy legal opinions that they guarded closely so no one could question the legal basis for the operations."[1] Lost in this drive for power was the system of checks and balances, individual rights and liberties, and the long-term needs of national security.

It has been said that in the period after 9/11 fear "restored to us the clarifying knowledge that evil exists, making moral, deliberate action possible once again."[2] Fear has that potential. It can also generate a sense of moral arrogance and superiority in fighting what is called evil, replacing deliberation

---

1. Jack Goldsmith, The Terror Presidency: Law and Judgment inside the Bush Administration 181 (2007).

2. Corey Robin, Fear: The History of a Political Idea 2 (2004).

with precipitate and unreasoned action. If the enemy is truly evil, why grant them traditional protections of the Geneva Conventions? Why not torture? It is argued that fear "can turn us from isolated men and women into a united people" and "bind us together" as part of a larger community.[3] That may be so, as during the Great Depression. It was not so with the Alien and Sedition Acts, the Anti-Masonic movement, exclusion of Chinese and Japanese individuals, and various campaigns against so-called radicals, subversives, Communists, and post-9/11 terrorists. Instead of building community values and tolerance, irrational hatred of abstract groups split society into bitter factions and helped jettison individual rights. Fear easily breeds intimidation, repression, and manipulation.[4]

Every nation makes mistakes, but there is no obligation to repeat them. It took some time for the United States to learn that loyalty does not mean mechanically saluting whatever government does. The Sedition Act of 1798 did lasting damage to the Federalist Party and eventually put it out of business. Statutes during World War I made it a crime to willfully obstruct military recruitment efforts. The FDR administration prosecuted "seditionists." Yet from the Korean War to the present time we have managed to avoid statutes that make it a crime to think independently and critically about the merits of a military commitment. Attacks on government, including national security policy, are legitimate parts of the democratic process.

It was not always so. At the time of the Whiskey Rebellion in 1794, some members of Congress were willing to support in whole the objections that President Washington directed at "self-created societies." Failure to back him, they reasoned, amounted to "desertion."[5] What they really deserted was independent judgment, their duty to support the Constitution, and the right of citizens to meet and discuss public policy. Citizens may oppose government actions whenever they decide to. Thinking independently and critically about government is more than a right. It is a duty. Unflinching deference to the Executive is something found in other societies, including the former Soviet Union, where the individual was nothing and the State everything.

Sedition laws should be inconceivable. In a system of self-government, citizens elect representatives to protect their rights. Those representatives should not then pass laws to prohibit criticism of elected officials. Sedition laws flourish when criticism of government is equivalent to "disloyalty." Federal judge

3. Id. at 3.
4. Id. at 14, 16, 19, 20, 23, 162.
5. Annals of Cong., 3d Cong., 1–2 Sess. 901 (1794).

George M. Bourquin, who handled many of the sedition cases in Montana at the time of World War I, said about hyper-patriotism: "In every age it, too, furnishes its heresy hunters and its witch burners, and it, too, is a favorite mask for hypocrisy, assuming a virtue which it haveth not."[6] When critics of the Iraq War were attacked as unpatriotic in 2005 for failing to support President George W. Bush and U.S. troops, Senator Chuck Hagel advised: "[t]o question your government is not unpatriotic—to *not* question your government is unpatriotic."[7]

In the post-9/11 period, many brave librarians, jealous of their rights, opposed FBI efforts to demand information about who used library computers. Librarians went to court to block an FBI subpoena to obtain the names of those who checked out a biography of Osama bin Laden. The American Library Association put pressure on Congress to change a provision in the USA Patriot Act. In this way, step by step, informed citizens who valued their liberties challenged and checked heavy-handed actions by government officials.[8]

Under the U.S. Constitution, the President is a temporary elected official with a duty to govern in a manner that upholds the dignity and freedom of the individual. In Federalist No. 51, James Madison said that "[j]ustice is the end of government. It is the end of civil society. It ever has been and ever will be pursued until it be obtained, or until liberty be lost in the pursuit."[9] In Federalist No. 10 he spoke about the different opinions that naturally exist in a republic and praised the "diversity in the faculties of men, from which the rights of property originate."[10] Protecting those faculties "is the first object of government."[11] He wanted individuals to develop their reasoning and skills in a climate of liberty that allows talents to flourish.

Spinoza had earlier defended the individual's right to think independently. No man's mind, he said, "can possibly lie wholly at the disposition of another, for no one can willingly transfer his natural right of free reason and judgment, or be compelled so to do." Any government attempting to control minds was, by definition, tyrannical. It was an abuse of sovereignty to seek to prescribe

6. Clemens P. Work, Darkest before Dawn: Sedition and Free Speech in the American West 118 (2006).

7. Glenn Kessler, "Hagel Defends Criticism of Iraq Policy," Washington Post, November 16, 2005, at A6 (emphasis added).

8. Christopher M. Finan, From the Palmer Raids to the Patriot Act: A History of the Fight for Free Speech in America 282–99 (2007).

9. The Federalist 358 (Benjamin F. Wright, ed. 2002 ed.).

10. Id. at 130.

11. Id. at 131.

what was true or false, or what opinions should be held. "All these questions," said Spinoza, "fall within a man's natural right, which he cannot abdicate even with his own consent."[12]

Especially after World War II, Presidents have pushed the limits of executive power under the theory that an activist agenda inevitably promotes the nation's interest. Throughout the twentieth century, academics in the fields of law, political science, and history championed the same cause, equating an expansion of presidential power with the national good.[13] They consistently ignored the fundamental structural safeguards that make republican and constitutional government possible: separation of powers and checks and balances.

In Federalist No. 4, John Jay warned that Executives "will often make war when their nations are to get nothing by it, but for purposes and objects merely personal, such as a thirst for military glory, revenge for personal affronts, ambition, or private compacts to aggrandize or support their particular families or partisans." Executives, he said, engage in wars "not sanctified by justice or the voice and interests of his people."[14] Jay and other framers did not pin their hopes on benevolent and well-intentioned Presidents. It was in the nature of single executives, monarchical or not, to initiate military conflicts of great cost to the nation. That has been the pattern particularly after World War II, with the wars in Korea, Vietnam, and Iraq II.

Some academics after 9/11 continue to insist that the nation is safer when it entrusts decisions of national security solely to the President and expert advisers, with subordinate or nonexistent roles assigned to Congress and the courts.[15] Nowhere in their studies is there any recognition of costly presidential decisions in Korea, Vietnam, and Iraq II. Far from displaying technical mastery and sound judgment, the presidential record is one of miscalculation, deceit, and incompetence. Strong words, perhaps, but what else can one say about Harry Truman's belief that he could go north in Korea without bringing

---

12. Benedict de Spinoza, A Theologico-Political Treatise 257 (2004 ed).

13. Louis Fisher, "Scholarly Support for Presidential Wars," 35 Pres. Stud. Q. 590 (2005); Louis Fisher, "Invoking Inherent Power: A Primer," 37 Pres. Stud. Q. 1, 7–11 (2007).

14. The Federalist 101 (Wright ed., 2002 ed.).

15. Eric A. Posner and Adrian Vermeule, Terror in the Balance: Security, Liberty, and the Courts (2007) ("Our central claim is that government [the executive branch] is better than courts or legislators at striking the correct balance between security and liberty during emergencies" [at 6]). For similar analysis see Richard A. Posner, Not a Suicide Pact: The Constitution in a Time of National Emergency (2006), and John Yoo, War by Other Means: An Insider's Account of the War on Terror (2006).

in the Chinese, that Lyndon Johnson would escalate the war in Vietnam on the basis of a second attack in the Tonkin Gulf that never happened, or that George W. Bush would make six claims of Iraqi terrorism and weapons of mass destruction and have each claim later proven to be patently false (the Iraq–al Qaeda link, aluminum tubes, uranium ore, drones, mobile labs, and chemical and biological weapons).[16]

Members of Congress are expected to check the President, including those of their own party. Madison understood the importance of each branch of government having "a will of its own."[17] To prevent a concentration of power in one branch, he wanted each branch to exercise "the necessary constitutional means and personal motives to resist encroachments of the others. . . . The interest of the man must be connected with the constitutional rights of the place."[18] Few lawmakers today have respect or understanding of their institutional powers and duties. When Congress fails to fight off encroachments, it gives a free hand to executive officials who are often oriented less to the national interest than to short-term partisan objectives.[19] White House aides show little regard for statutory limits, the Constitution, or the prerogatives of Congress. They want to fulfill what they see as the President's "mandate."

The Supreme Court has at various times placed its weight behind national power over individual freedom. In 1940, Justice Felix Frankfurter argued for an 8 to 1 Court that national security requires national unity, and one way of fostering national unity is to compel students to salute the American flag, even when it violates their religious beliefs.[20] The shallowness of that reasoning was recognized almost from the start, leading the Court three years later to mount a 6 to 3 majority to reverse itself. Strong public disapproval of the 1940 decision forced the Court's hand.[21] In striking down the compulsory flag salute, Justice Robert Jackson said that "[t]o believe that patriotism will not flourish if patriotic ceremonies are voluntary and spontaneous instead of a compulsory routine is to make an unflattering estimate of the appeal of our institutions to free minds."[22] In Federalist No. 10, Madison opposed efforts to

16. Fisher, Presidential War Power, at 81–104, 128–33, 211–35; Louis Fisher, "Justifying War against Iraq," in James A. Thurber, ed., Rivals for Power: Presidential-Congressional Relations 289–313 (2006).

17. The Federalist 355 (Federalist No. 51).

18. Id. at 356.

19. Louis Fisher, Congressional Abdication on War and Spending (2000).

20. Minersville School District v. Gobitis, 310 U.S. 586 (1940).

21. Louis Fisher, Religious Liberty in America: Political Safeguards 105–14 (2002).

22. West Virginia State Board of Education v. Barnette, 319 U.S. 624, 641 (1943).

force or enforce a unanimity of opinion. Jackson agreed: "Those who begin coercive elimination of dissent soon find themselves exterminating dissenters. Compulsory unification of opinion achieves only the unanimity of the graveyard."[23]

Three months after 9/11, the Senate Judiciary held hearings on military tribunals. A prepared statement by Attorney General John Ashcroft accused opponents of the administration of offering aid and comfort to terrorists: "We need honest, reasoned debate, and not fear-mongering. To those who pit Americans against immigrants and citizens against noncitizens, to those who scare peace-loving people with phantoms of lost liberty my message is this: Your tactics only aid terrorists, for they erode our national unity and diminish our resolve. They give ammunition to America's enemies, and pause to America's friends."[24] This broadside raised many questions. Who decides what is "honest" and "reasoned"? The administration? How much does the quest for "national unity" eliminate individual opinions and make Congress a subordinate branch? U.S. history does not support a superior knowledge or understanding by the executive branch, including in the realm of national security.

Self-government requires individuals to independently judge the government and participate in the formation and review of public policy. They cannot do that in ignorance. Popular sovereignty relies on publicly available information.[25] Executive decisions reached in secret deny Congress, the courts, and the general public access to necessary documents. Administration officials often classify information not for reasons of national security but to maximize executive power. Congress and the judiciary cannot perform their constitutional functions under these conditions. Concentration of power in the Executive always puts at risk the Constitution and individual rights and liberties.

On state secrets cases, federal judges have deferred to executive branch claims by falsely balancing a litigant's interest against such abstractions as the national interest, government interest, or "collective interest." Private interests, we are told, "must give way to the national interest in preserving state secrets."[26] Personal interests must be "subordinated to the collective interest in national

---

23. Id.

24. "Excerpts from Attorney General's Testimony before Senate Judiciary Committee," New York Times, December 7, 2001, at B6. See also "Ashcroft Defends Anti-terror Plan; Says Criticism May Aid U.S. Foes," New York Times, December 7, 2001, at A1.

25. Daniel N. Hoffman, Governmental Secrecy and the Founding Fathers: A Study in Constitutional Controls (1981).

26. El-Masri v. Tenet, 437 F.Supp.2d 530, 539 (E.D. Va. 2006).

security."[27] No national interest or collective interest is served by taking at face value what the executive branch says in court. No national or collective interest is furthered by arresting the wrong person and sending him to a prison in Afghanistan, as was done to Khaled El-Masri. The judiciary and Congress have a duty to assure that the adversary process in court is not rendered meaningless by the state secrets privilege. Private parties and judges must have an opportunity to gain access to facts needed for an informed judgment.[28] The branch empowered by the Constitution to decide the national interest and the collective interest is Congress—not the judiciary or executive officials.

It is time to reexamine the doctrine of official immunity. Courts weigh two conflicting values: the right of a citizen to be protected from oppressive or malicious actions on the part of federal officials, and the interest of the general public in shielding federal officials from harassment by malicious or ill-founded damage suits. Courts have decided that the threat of damage suits might inhibit the "fearless, vigorous, and effective administration of policies of government." The protection is quite broad. Officials enjoy immunity when they perform "discretionary acts." Decisions are privileged whenever taken "within the outer perimeter" of an official's line of duty.[29]

Those principles should not allow public officials to violate the law, the Constitution, or individual rights. Otherwise, they are at liberty to draft and implement public policy without any accountability, as was the case with the interrogation methods generated by the Bush administration after 9/11. OLC lawyers "were simply giving cover to their clients in the White House at the expense of their true clients, the American people and the U.S. Constitution."[30] Those who originated and drafted administration policy remained in the clear, while a few subordinates who carried out their policy paid a price.

Courts and juries have a capacity to hold government accountable. In 2007, a federal jury in Seattle found the city liable for the unlawful arrest of about

27. El-Masri v. United States, 479 F.3d 296, 313 (4th Cir. 2007).

28. Meredith Fuchs, "Judging Secrets: The Role Courts Should Play in Preventing Unnecessary Secrecy," 58 Adm. L. Rev. 131 (2006).

29. Barr v. Matteo, 360 U.S. 564, 571, 575 (1959). This decision relied heavily on Judge Learned Hand's opinion in Gregoire v. Biddle, 177 F.2d 579 (2d Cir. 1949). For further elaboration on the doctrine of official immunity, see Bivens v. Six Unknown Named Agents of Fed. Bur. of Narc., 456 F.2d 1339 (2d Cir. 1972); Bivens v. Six Unknown Fed. Narcotics Agents, 403 U.S. 388 (1970); Imbler v. Pachtman, 424 U.S. 409 (1976); Butz v. Economou, 438 U.S. 478 (1978).

30. Frederick A. O. Schwarz, Jr., and Aziz Z. Huq, Unchecked and Unbalanced: Presidential Power in a Time of Terror 188 (2007).

175 protesters during a meeting of the World Trade Organization in 1999.[31] Also in 2007, a federal judge in Boston ordered the federal government to pay nearly $102 million for the FBI's role in the wrongful murder convictions of four men. The judge said the misconduct ran "all the way up to the FBI director."[32] The previous year, the government paid $2 million to settle a suit involving the wrongful arrest of an Oregon lawyer.[33] It paid $300,000 to an Egyptian swept up in the New York City area after 9/11 and subjected to abuse for almost a year at a federal detention center. Government officials argued that the lawsuit should be dismissed because extraordinary circumstances justify extraordinary measures. In response, a federal judge ruled that the 9/11 attacks "do not warrant the elimination of remedies for the constitutional violations alleged here."[34] Those lawsuits provide a measure of justice, but rarely do they penalize the officials who developed and participated in the abusive policy.

Short of compensating victims of government errors, apologies can be offered. In 2007, the Justice Department issued a written apology to an Iraqi refugee who had been improperly imprisoned and pushed toward deportation. The mistaken arrest appeared to be part of ethnic profiling, in this case someone from the Middle East. The individual, Abdulameer Habeeb, had been in the United States legally after being jailed and tortured in Iraq during the regime of Saddam Hussein. The written apology was accompanied by an undisclosed financial sum.[35] Canada apologized for its role with Maher Arar, as well as providing financial compensation. The United States, responsible for sending him to Syria for interrogation and torture, has provided neither apology nor restitution.

After 9/11, there have been proposals for the creation of a National Security Court. The stated purpose: to avoid holding foreigners indefinitely without ever being charged, given counsel, or tried (as in Guantánamo) and to relieve existing federal courts of those cases. One proposal recommends a system of

31. "Jury Decides against Seattle in 1999 Arrests," New York Times, January 31, 2007, at A13.

32. Robert Barnes and Paul Lewis, "FBI Must Pay $102 Million in Mob Case," Washington Post, July 27, 2007, at A3.

33. Dan Eggen, "U.S. Settles Suit Filed by Ore. Lawyer," Washington Post, November 30, 2006, at A3.

34. Nina Bernstein, "U.S. Is Settling Detainee's Suit in 9/11 Sweep," New York Times, February 28, 2006, at A1.

35. Neil MacFarquhar, "Detention Was Wrong, and U.S. Apologizes," New York Times, August 24, 2007, at A17.

preventive detention for whoever fits "a Congressionally approved definition of the enemy." Specialized judges, on the basis of classified evidence, would review the detention of individuals who have not committed an overt criminal act but are considered dangerous. Analogies are drawn to the preventive detention of other people who have committed no crime but "are dangerous to society—the insane, child molesters, people with infectious diseases, and the like."[36]

A National Security Court would "make sure that there is a continuing rationale to detain people years after their initial cases were heard."[37] If congressional definitions of "the enemy" or "terrorist" are vague, as is a certainty, innocent people will be held for years just as they were after 9/11. Advocates of this type of court explain that detainees "need not be given the full panoply of criminal protections," such as meeting their lawyers right away and thus interrupting interrogations. A National Security Court, "while it would operate in public, would not have the same public and press access as an ordinary criminal trial."[38] There is every reason to believe that this kind of court, no matter how well-intentioned, would operate as a second-class tribunal for second-class citizens and aliens. It is true that the United States has specialized courts that deal with bankruptcy, taxes, and patents.[39] Those courts, however, do not operate in the netherworld of interrogations, classified information, national security claims, and preventive detention.[40] The FISA court deals with classified information and national security issues, but it has no role in detentions or prosecutions.

In 1927, Justice Louis Brandeis identified the values that made America special. The framers who won independence from England believed that "the final end of the State was to make men free to develop their faculties; and that in its government the deliberative forces should prevail over the arbitrary."[41] The purpose of government was to inspire independent thought and encourage public participation. The framers valued

36. Jack L. Goldsmith and Neal Katyal, "The Terrorists' Court," New York Times, July 11, 2007, at A23.

37. Id.

38. Id.

39. Id.

40. For responses to the Goldsmith–Katyal article, see "A New Court for Terror Suspects?" New York Times, July 16, 2007, at A16 (letter to the editor). See also Stuart Taylor, Jr., "The Case for a National Security Court," National Journal, February 24, 2007, at 15, and Kelly Anne Moore, "Take Al Qaeda to Court," New York Times, August 21, 2007, at A23.

41. Whitney v. California, 274 U.S. 357, 375 (1927) (Brandeis, J., concurring).

liberty both as an end and as a means. They believed liberty to be the secret of happiness and courage to be the secret of liberty. They believed that freedom to think as you will and to speak as you think are indispensable to the discovery and spread of political truth; that without free speech and assembly discussion would be futile; that with them, discussion affords ordinarily adequate protection against the dissemination of noxious doctrine; that the greatest menace to freedom is an inert people; that public discussion is a political duty; and that this should be a fundamental principle of the American government.[42]

To Brandeis, the framers understood that political order could not be secured "merely through fear of punishment for its infraction; that it is hazardous to discourage thought, hope and imagination; that fear breeds repression; that repression breeds hate; that hate menaces stable government; that the path to safety lies in the opportunity to discuss supposed grievances and proposed remedies; and that the fitting remedy for evil counsels is good ones." The framers believed in the power of reason and public discussion and they "eschewed silence coerced by law—the argument of force in its worst form."[43]

Brandeis warned about what fear can bring, particularly unreasoned fear. "Fear of serious injury cannot alone justify suppression of free speech and assembly. Men feared witches and burnt women. It is the function of speech to free men from the bondage of irrational fears."[44] The framers "did not exalt order at the cost of liberty."[45] A democratic society may never surrender its duty and right to think independently.[46] Free citizens cannot automatically defer to assertions and claims by those in authority, including the President. Lawmakers must demonstrate a capacity to think independently and explain their views clearly. If members of Congress merely take direction from the White House and routinely support presidential policies, they cease being representatives, forsake duties to their institution, and make impossible the system of checks and balances that safeguards constitutional government.

42. Id.

43. Id. at 375–76.

44. Id. at 376.

45. Id. at 377.

46. Richard D. Brown, The Strength of a People: The Idea of an Informed Citizenry in America, 1650–1870 (1996).

Selected Bibliography

Abel, Elie. Leaking: Who Does It? Who Benefits? At What Cost? (New York: Priority Press Publications, 1987).

Abshire, David M. Saving the Reagan Presidency: Trust Is the Coin of the Realm (College Station: Texas A&M University Press, 2005).

Alschuler, Albert W. Law without Values: The Life, Work, and Legacy of Justice Holmes (Chicago: University of Chicago Press, 2000).

Alterman, Eric. When Presidents Lie: A History of Official Deception and Its Consequences (New York: Viking, 2004).

Ambrose, Stephen E. Eisenhower: Soldier, General of the Army, President-Elect, 1890–1952 (New York: Simon & Schuster, 1983).

Andrew, Christopher. For the President's Eyes Only: Secret Intelligence and the American Presidency from Washington to Bush (New York: HarperCollins, 1995).

Arendt, Hannah. "Lying in Politics: Reflections on the Pentagon Papers," in Hannah Arendt, Crises of the Republic (New York: Harcourt Brace Jovanovich, 1972).

Arnold, Eric A., ed. A Documentary Survey of Napoleonic France (Lanham, Md.: University Press of America, 1994).

Association of the Bar of the City of New York. Report of the Special Committee on the Federal Loyalty-Security Program (New York: Dodd, Mead & Co., 1956).

Association of the Bar of the City of New York & Center for Human Rights and Global Justice. Torture by Proxy: International and Domestic Law Applicable to "Extraordinary Renditions" (New York: ABCNY & NYU School of Law, 2004).

Ball, Howard. Bush, the Detainees, and the Constitution: The Battle over Presidential Power in the War on Terror (Lawrence: University Press of Kansas, 2007).

Bamford, James. Body of Secrets (New York: Anchor Books, 2002).

———. The Puzzle Palace (New York: Penguin Books, 1983).

Barth, Gunther. Bitter Strength: A History of the Chinese in the United States, 1850–1870 (Cambridge, Mass.: Harvard University Press, 1964).

Baxter, David. "The Great Sedition Trial of 1944: A Personal Memoir," Journal of Historical Review, available at http://www/ihr.org/jhr/vo6/vo6p–23_Baxter.html.

Beale, Howard K., ed. The Diary of Edward Bates, 1859–1866 (Washington, D.C.: Government Printing Office, 1933).

Begg, Moazzam. Enemy Combatant: My Imprisonment at Guantánamo, Bagram, and Kandahar (New York: New Press, 2006).

Belknap, Michal. "Frankfurter and the Nazi Saboteurs," Yearbook 1982: Supreme Court Historical Society, at 66–71.

———. "The Supreme Court Goes to War: The Meaning and Implications of the Nazi Saboteur Case," 89 Military Law Review 59 (1980).

Berger, Margaret A. "How the Privilege for Governmental Information Met Its Watergate," 25 Case Western Reserve Law Review 747 (1975).

Berns, Walter. "Buck v. Bell: Due Process of Law?" 6 Western Political Quarterly 762 (1953).

Beveridge, Albert J. The Life of John Marshall (3 vols., Boston: Houghton Mifflin Co, 1919).

Biddle, Francis. In Brief Authority (New York: Doubleday, 1962).

Billington, Ray Allen. The Protestant Crusade, 1800–1860: A Study of the Origins of American Nativism (Chicago: Quadrangle Books, 1964 ed.).

Birmingham, Stephen. "Our Crowd": The Great Jewish Families of New York (New York: Harper & Row, 1967).

Bissell, Richard M., Jr. Reflections of a Cold Warrior (New Haven, Conn.: Yale University Press, 1996).

Black, Edwin. War against the Weak: Eugenics and America's Campaign to Create a Master Race (New York: Thunder's Mouth Press, 2003).

Boies, Henry M. Prisoners and Paupers (New York: Putnam, 1893).

Bok, Sissela. Secrets: On the Ethics of Concealment and Revelation (New York: Pantheon Books, 1983).

———. Lying: Moral Choice in Public and Private Life (New York: Pantheon Books, 1978).

Bontecou, Eleanor. The Federal Loyalty-Security Program (Ithaca, N.Y.: Cornell University Press, 1953).

Brachtenbach, Robert F. "The Privilege against Revealing Military Secrets," 29 Washington Law Review 59 (1954).

Brown, Richard D. The Strength of a People: The Idea of an Informed Citizenry in America, 1650–1870 (Chapel Hill: University of North Carolina Press, 1996).

Burgdorf, Robert L., Jr., and Marcia Pearce Burgdorf. "The Wicked Witch Is Almost Dead: *Buck v. Bell* and the Sterilization of Handicapped Persons," 50 Temple Law Quarterly 995 (1977).

Calkins, Richard M. "Grand Jury Secrecy," 63 Michigan Law Review 455 (1965).

Cardozo, Michael H. "When Extradition Fails, Is Abduction the Solution?" 55 American Journal of International Law 127 (1961).

Carlson, John Roy. Under Cover (New York: E. P. Dutton & Co., 1943).

Carrow, Milton M. "Governmental Nondisclosure in Judicial Proceedings," 107 University of Pennsylvania Law Review 166 (1958).

Caute, David. The Great Fear: The Anti-Communist Purge under Truman and Eisenhower (New York: Touchstone Book, 1978).

Ceplair, Larry and Steven Englund. The Inquisition in Hollywood (Urbana: University of Illinois Press, 2003 ed.)

Chafee, Zechariah, Jr. "Freedom of Speech in War Time," 32 Harvard Law Review 932 (1919).

Chesney, Robert M. "State Secrets and the Limits of National Security Litigation," 75 George Washington Law Review 1249 (2007).

———. "Democratic-Republican Societies, Subversion, and the Limits of Legitimate Political Dissent in the Early Republic," 82 North Carolina Law Review 1525 (2004).

Christoph, James B. "A Comparative View: Administrative Secrecy in Britain," 35 Public Administration Review 23 (1975).

Clark, Jane Perry. Deportation of Aliens from the United States to Europe (New York: Columbia University Press, 1931).

Clubb, O. Edmund. The Witness and I (New York: Columbia University Press, 1974).

Cole, David. Enemy Aliens: Double Standards and Constitutional Freedoms in the War on Terrorism (New York: New Press, 2003).

———, and Jules Lobel. Less Safe, Less Free: Why America Is Losing the War on Terror (New York: New Press, 2007).

Commission on Wartime Relocation and Internment of Civilians. Personal Justice Denied (Washington, D.C.: December 1982).

Cramer, Myron C. "Military Commissions: Trial of the Eight Saboteurs," 17 Washington Law Review and State Bar Journal 247 (1942).

Cross, Harold L. The People's Right to Know: Legal Access to Public Records and Proceedings (New York: Columbia University Press, 1953).

Cummings, Homer, and Carl McFarland. Federal Justice (New York: Macmillan, 1937).

Currie, David P. The Constitution in Congress: The Federalist Period, 1789–1801 (Chicago: University of Chicago Press, 1997).

Danelski, David. "The Saboteurs' Case," 1 Journal of Supreme Court History 61 (1996).

Daniels, Roger. The Politics of Prejudice: The Anti-Japanese Movement in California and the Struggle for Japanese Exclusion (Berkeley: University of California Press, 1977 ed.).

Danner, Mark. Torture and Truth: America, Abu Ghraib, and the War on Terror (New York: New York Review of Books, 2004).

Dennis, Lawrence and Maximilian St. George. A Trial on Trial: The Great Sedition Trial of 1944 (Newport Beach, Calif.: Institute for Historical Review, 1984, originally published in 1945 by the National Civil Rights Committee).

Devins, Neal, and Louis Fisher. "The Steel Seizure Case: One of a Kind?" 19 Constitutional Commentary 63 (2002).

Donner, Frank J. The Age of Surveillance: The Aims and Methods of America's Political Intelligence System (New York: Vintage Books, 1981).

Douglas, William O. The Court Years, 1939–1975 (New York: Vintage Books, 1981).

Dudziak, Mary L. "Oliver Wendell Holmes as a Eugenic Reformer: Rhetoric in the Writing of Constitutional Law," 71 Iowa Law Review 833 (1986).

Duker, William F. A Constitutional History of Habeas Corpus (Westport, Conn.: Greenwood Press, 1980).

Durr, Clifford J. "The Loyalty Order's Challenge to the Constitution," 16 University of Chicago Law Review 298 (1949).

DuVal, Benjamin S., Jr. "The Occasions of Secrecy," 47 University of Pittsburgh Law Review 579 (1986).

Ellsberg, Daniel. Secrets: A Memoir of Vietnam and the Pentagon Papers (New York: Viking, 2002).

Emery, Fred. Watergate (New York: Touchstone, 1995).

Fein, Bruce E. "Access to Classified Information: Constitutional and Statutory Dimensions," 26 William and Mary Law Review 805 (1985).

Finan, Christopher M. From the Palmer Raids to the Patriot Act: A History of the Fight for Free Speech in America (Boston: Beacon Press, 2007).

Fisher, Louis. "The State Secrets Privilege: Relying on *Reynolds*," 122 Political Science Quarterly 385 (2007).

———. Constitutional Conflicts between Congress and the President (Lawrence: University Press of Kansas, 2007).

———. (with David Gray Adler). American Constitutional Law (7th ed., Durham: Carolina Academic Press, 2007).

———. "Invoking Inherent Powers: A Primer," 37 Presidential Studies Quarterly 1 (2007).

———. "Presidential Inherent Power: The 'Sole Organ' Doctrine," 37 Presidential Studies Quarterly 139 (2007).

———. "The Scope of Inherent Powers," in George C. Edwards III and Desmond S. King, eds., The Polarized Presidency of George W. Bush (New York: Oxford University Press, 2007), at 31–64.

———. "Detention and Military Trial of Suspected Terrorists: Stretching Presidential Power," 2 Journal of National Security Law & Policy 1 (2007).

———. In the Name of National Security: Unchecked Presidential Power and the *Reynolds* Case (Lawrence: University Press of Kansas, 2006).

———. "State Your Secrets: When the Government Cloaks Itself in Privilege, Judges Must Rule," Legal Times, June 26, 2006, at 68–69.

———. "Justifying War in Iraq," in James A. Thurber, ed., Rivals for Power: Presidential-Congressional Relations (Lanham, Md.: Rowman & Littlefield, 2006), at 289–313.

———. "State Secrets Privilege: Invoke It at a Cost," National Law Journal, July 31, 2006, at 23.

———. Military Tribunals and Presidential Power: American Revolution to the War on Terrorism (Lawrence: University Press of Kansas, 2005).

———. "Scholarly Support for Presidential Wars," 35 Presidential Studies Quarterly 590 (2005).

———. Presidential War Power (2d ed., Lawrence: University Press of Kansas, 2004).

———. The Politics of Executive Privilege (Durham: Carolina Academic Press, 2004).

———. "Talking about Secrets," Legal Times, April 19, 2004, at 66–67.

———. Nazi Saboteurs on Trial: A Military Tribunal and American Law (Lawrence: University Press of Kansas, 2003).

———. Religious Liberty in America: Political Safeguards (Lawrence: University Press of Kansas, 2002).

———. Congressional Abdication on War and Spending (College Station: Texas A&M University Press, 2000).

———. Presidential Spending Power (Princeton: Princeton University Press, 1975).

Fitzpatrick, John C., ed. The Writings of George Washington (39 vols., Washington, D.C.: Government Printing Office, 1931–1944).

Flynn, Sean C. "The *Totten* Doctrine and Its Poisoned Progeny," 25 Vermont Law Review 793 (2001).

Franck, Thomas M., and Edward Weisband, eds. Secrecy and Foreign Policy (New York: Columbia University Press, 1974).

Frankel, Max. "The 'State Secrets' Myth," Columbia Journalism Review, September/October 1971, at 22–26.

Freeland, Richard M., The Truman Doctrine and the Origins of McCarthyism: Foreign Policy, Domestic Politics, and Internal Security, 1946–1948 (New York: New York University Press, 1985 ed.).

Fried, Albert. McCarthyism: The Great American Red Scare (New York: Oxford University Press, 1997).

Fuchs, Meredith. "Judging Secrets: The Role Courts Should Play in Preventing Unnecessary Secrecy," 58 Administrative Law Review 131 (2006).

Gardner, J. Steven. "The State Secret Privilege Invoked in Civil Litigation: A Proposal for Statutory Relief," 29 Wake Forest Law Review 567 (1994).

Goldsmith, Jack. The Terror Presidency: Law and Judgment inside the Bush Administration (New York: W. W. Norton, 2007).

Goodman, Paul. Towards a Christian Republic: Antimasonry and the Great Transition in New England (New York: Oxford University Press, 1988).

Grey, Stephen. Ghost Plane: The True Story of the CIA Torture Program (New York: St. Martin's Press, 2006).

Griffith, Robert. The Politics of Fear: Joseph R. McCarthy and the Senate (2d ed., Amherst: University of Massachusetts Press, 1987).

———, and Athan Theoharis, eds. The Specter: Original Essays on the Cold War and the Origins of McCarthyism (New York: New Viewpoints, 1974).

Griswold, Erwin N. "Secrets Not Worth Keeping," Washington Post, February 15, 1989, at A25.

———. "The Pentagon Papers Case: A Personal Footnote," Yearbook 1984, Supreme Court Historical Society, at 115.

Gromley, Charles R. "Discovery against the Government of Military and Other Confidential Matters," 43 Kentucky Law Journal 343 (1955).

Guy, J. A. The Court of Star Chamber and Its Records to the Reign of Elizabeth I (London: H.M.S.O., 1985).

Harper, Alan D. The Politics of Loyalty: The White House and the Communist Issue, 1946–1952 (Westport, Conn.: Greenwood Press, 1969).

Hersh, Seymour M. "The General's Report," New Yorker, June 25, 2007, at 63.

Higham, John. Strangers in the Land: Patterns of American Nativism, 1860–1925 (New Brunswick, N.J.: Rutgers University Press, 2004 ed.).

Hoffman, Daniel N. Governmental Secrecy and the Founding Fathers: A Study in Constitutional Controls (Westport, Conn.: Greenwood Press, 1981).

Irons, Peter. Justice at War (New York: Oxford University Press, 1983).

Jaffer, Jameel, and Amrit Singh. Administration of Torture: A Documentary Record from Washington to Abu Ghraib and Beyond (New York: Columbia University Press, 2007).

James, Ralph C., and Estelle James. "The Purge of the Trotskyites from the Teamsters," 19 Western Political Quarterly 5 (1966).

Johnson, Loch K. America's Secret Power (New York: Oxford University Press, 1989).

Johnson, Timothy D. Winfield Scott: The Quest for Military Glory (Lawrence: University Press of Kansas, 1998).

Jost, Kenneth. "Government Secrecy," CQ Researcher 1005–28 (December 2, 2005).

Kenny, Gerard J. "The 'National Security Wiretap': Presidential Prerogative or Judicial Responsibility," 45 Southern California Law Review 888 (1972).

Koestler, Arthur. Darkness at Noon (New York: Time Inc. Book Division, 1962).

Konvitz, Milton R. Civil Rights in Immigration (Ithaca, N.Y.: Cornell University Press, 1953).

———. The Alien and the Asiatic in American Law (Ithaca, N.Y.: Cornell University Press, 1946).

Kurland, Philip B., and Gerhard Casper, eds. Landmark Briefs and Arguments of the Supreme Court of the United States: Constitutional Law (Arlington, Va.: University Publications of America).

Labovitz, John R. Presidential Impeachment (New Haven, Conn.: Yale University Press, 1978).

Ladd, Bruce. Crisis in Credibility (New York: New American Library, 1968).

Langbein, John H. Torture and the Law of Proof (Chicago: University of Chicago Press, 2006 ed.).

Landau, Henry. The Enemy Within (New York: G. P. Putnam's Sons, 1973).

Laughlin, Harry Hamilton. Eugenical Sterilization in the United States (Chicago: Psychopathic Laboratory of the Municipal Court of Chicago, 1922).

Lee, Wen Ho. My Country versus Me (New York: Hyperion, 2001).

Levy, Leonard W. The Origins of the Fifth Amendment (New York: Macmillan, 1986).

Link, Eugene Perry. Democratic-Republican Societies, 1790–1800 (New York: Columbia University Press, 1942).

Lombardo, Paul A. "Three Generations, No Imbeciles: New Light on *Buck* v. *Bell*," 60 New York University Law Review 30 (1985).

Luebke, Frederick C. Bonds of Loyalty: German Americans and World War I (DeKalb: Northern Illinois University Press, 1974).

Lundy, James P. "Executive Privilege and the Air Force," 1 JAG Bulletin 13 (1959).

Maher, Christopher M. "The Right to a Fair Trial in Criminal Cases Involving the Introduction of Classified Information," 120 Military Law Review 83 (1988).

Margulies, Joseph. Guantánamo and the Abuse of Presidential Power (New York: Simon and Schuster, 2006).

Mason, Alpheus Thomas. "*Inter Arma Silent Leges*: Chief Justice Stone's Views," 69 Harvard Law Review 806 (1956).

———. Harlan Fiske Stone: Pillar of the Law (New York: Viking Press, 1956).

Mayer, Jane. The Black Sites: A Rare Look Inside the C.I.A.'s Secret Interrogation Program," New Yorker, August 13, 2007, at 46–57.

———. "The Memo," New Yorker, February 27, 2006, at 32–41.

———. "Outsourcing Torture: The Secret History of America's 'Extraordinary Rendition' Program," New Yorker, February 14 and 21, 2005, at 106–23.

McCartney, James. "What Should Be Secret?" Columbia Journalism Review, September/October 1971, at 40–44.

McClain, Charles J. In Search of Equality: The Chinese Struggle against Discrimination in Nineteenth-Century America (Berkeley: University of California Press, 1994).

McCloskey, Paul N., Jr. Truth and Untruth: Political Deceit in America (New York: Simon & Schuster, 1975).

Melanson, Philip H. Secrecy Wars: National Security, Privacy, and the Public's Right to Know (Washington, D.C.: Brassey's, 2001).

Miller, John C. Crisis in Freedom: The Alien and Sedition Acts (Boston: Little, Brown & Co., 1951).

Millman, Chad. The Detonators: The Secret Plot to Destroy America and an Epic Hunt for Justice (New York: Little, Brown, 2006).

Mink, Patsy T. "The Cannikin Papers: A Case Study in Freedom of Information," in Thomas M. Franck and Edward Weisband, eds., Secrecy and Foreign Policy (New York: Oxford University Press, 1974).

Mitchell, John J. "Government Secrecy in Theory and Practice: 'Rules and Regulations' As an Autonomous Screen," 58 Columbia Law Review 199 (1958).

Moorman, William A. "Executive Privilege and the Freedom of Information Act: Sufficient Protection for Aircraft Mishap Reports?" 21 Air Force Law Review 581 (1979).

Morgan, Richard E. Domestic Intelligence (Austin: University of Texas Press, 1980).

Morris, S. Brent. The Complete Idiot's Guide to Freemasonry (New York: Alpha Books, 2006).

Mowry, George E., ed. The Twenties: Fords, Flappers and Fanatics (Englewood Cliffs, N.J.: Prentice-Hall, 1963).

Moynihan, Daniel Patrick. Secrecy: The American Experience (New Haven, Conn.: Yale University Press, 1998).

Murray, Robert K. Red Scare: A Study in National Hysteria, 1919–1920 (New York: McGraw-Hill, 1964).

Nather, David. "A Rise in 'State Secrets,'" CQ Weekly Report, July 18, 2005, at 1958–66.

National Commission on Law Observance and Enforcement. Report on the Enforcement of the Deportation Law of the United States (Washington, D.C.: Government Printing Office, 1931).

"National Security and the Public's Right to Know: A New Role for the Courts under the Freedom of Information Act," 123 University of Pennsylvania Law Review 1438 (1975).

Navasky, Victor S. Naming Names (New York: Hill and Wang, 2003 ed.; originally published in 1980).

Newman, James R. "Control of Information Relating to Atomic Energy," 56 Yale Law Journal 769 (1947).

Note. "Evidence—State Secrets Privilege—Discovery under Federal Tort Claims Act," 28 New York University Law Review 1188 (1953).

Note. "The Executive Evidential Privilege in Suits against the Government," 47 Northwestern University Law Review 259 (1952).

Note. "Federal Courts—Rules of Civil Procedure—Secretary of Air Force Subject to Discovery in Suit under Federal Tort Claims Act," 65 Harvard Law Review 1445 (1952).

Note. "*In Camera* Inspection of National Security Files under the Freedom of Information Act," 26 Kansas Law Review 617 (1978).

Note. "Judicial Control of Secret Agents," 76 Yale Law Journal 994 (1967).

Note. "Keeping Secrets: Congress, the Courts, and National Security Information," 103 Harvard Law Review 906 (1990).

Note. "The Military and State Secrets Privilege: Protection for the National Security or Immunity for the Executive?" 91 Yale Law Journal 570 (1982).

Note. "National Security and the Public's Right to Know: A New Role for the Courts under the Freedom of Information Act," 123 University of Pennsylvania Law Review 1438 (1975).

Note. "Procedure—Discovery against the Government—Privilege for State Secrets," 100 University of Pennsylvania Law Review 917 (1952).

Note. "The Sedition Trial: A Study in Delay and Obstruction," 15 University of Chicago Law Review 691 (1948).

O'Brian, John Lord. National Security and Individual Freedom (Cambridge, Mass.: Harvard University Press, 1955).

————. "Loyalty Tests and Guilt by Association," 61 Harvard Law Review 592 (1948).

O'Hara, James B., and T. Howland Sachs. "Eugenic Sterilization," 45 Georgetown Law Journal 20 (1956).

Olmsted, Kathryn. Challenging the Secret Government: The Post-Watergate Investigations of the CIA and FBI (Chapel Hill: University of North Carolina Press, 1996).

Olson, Keith W. Watergate: The Presidential Scandal That Shook America (Lawrence: University Press of Kansas, 2003).

Orman, John M. Presidential Secrecy and Deception (Westport, Conn.: Greenwood Press, 1980).

Oshinsky, David M. A Conspiracy So Immense: The World of Joe McCarthy (New York: Oxford University Press, 2005 ed.; originally published in 1983).

Paglen, Trevor, and A. C. Thompson. Torture Taxi: On the Trail of the CIA's Rendition Flights (Hoboken, N.J.: Melville House Publishing, 2006).

Pallitto, Robert M., and William G. Weaver. Presidential Secrecy and the Law (Baltimore, Md.: Johns Hopkins University Press, 2007).

Parks, Wallace. "Secrecy and the Public Interest in Military Affairs," 26 George Washington Law Review 23 (1957).

Perine, Keith, and Tim Starks. "House Panels Approve Surveillance Bill," C.Q. Weekly Report, September 25, 2006, at 2556.

Peterson, H. C., and Gilbert C. Fite. Opponents of War, 1917–1918 (Seattle: University of Washington Press, 1957).

Pfaelzer, Jean. Driven Out: The Forgotten War against Chinese Americans (New York: Random House, 2007).

Pillar, Paul R. Terrorism and U.S. Foreign Policy (Washington, D.C.: Brookings Institution Press, 2003 ed.).

Pines, Daniel L. "The Continuing Viability of the 1875 Supreme Court Case of *Totten* v. *United States*," 53 Administrative Law Review 1273 (2001).

Pious, Richard M. "Torture of Detainees and Presidential Prerogative Power," in George C. Edwards III and Desmond S. King, eds. The Polarized Presidency of George W. Bush (New York: Oxford University Press, 2007), at 65–95.

————. The War on Terrorism and the Rule of Law (Los Angeles: Roxbury Publishing, 2006).

Posner, Eric A., and Adrian Vermeule. Terror in the Balance: Security, Liberty, and the Courts (New York: Oxford University Press, 2007).

Posner, Richard A. Not a Suicide Pact: The Constitution in a Time of National Emergency (New York: Oxford University Press, 2006).

Post, Louis F. The Deportations Delirium of Nineteen-Twenty: A Personal Narrative of an Historic Official Experience (Honolulu: University Press of the Pacific, 2003; reprinted from 1923 edition).

Prados, John, and Margaret Pratt Porter, eds. Inside the Pentagon Papers (Lawrence: University Press of Kansas, 2004).

Prange, Gordon W. At Dawn We Slept: The Untold Story of Pearl Harbor (New York: McGraw–Hill, 1981).

Preston, William, Jr. Aliens and Dissenters: Federal Suppression of Radicals, 1903–1933 (2d ed. Urbana: University of Illinois Press, 1994).

Pyle, Christopher H. Extradition, Politics, and Human Rights (Philadelphia: Temple University Press, 2001).

Rabban, David M. Free Speech in Its Forgotten Years (New York: Cambridge University Press, 1997).

Ratner, Michael, and Ellen Ray. Guantánamo: What the World Should Know (White River Junction, Vt.: Chelsea Green Publishing, 2004).

Rauh, Joseph L., Jr., and James C. Turner. "Anatomy of a Public Interest Case against the CIA," 11 Hamline Journal of Public Law and Policy 307 (1990).

Read, James Morgan. Atrocity Propaganda, 1914–1919 (New Haven, Conn.: Yale University Press, 1941).

Relyea, Harold C. "Government Secrecy: Policy Depths and Dimensions," 20 Government Information Quarterly 395 (2003).

———. "The Coming of Secret Law," 5 Government Information Quarterly 97 (1988).

———. "Increased National Security Controls on Scientific Communication," 1 Government Information Quarterly 177 (1984).

Ribuffo, Leo P. The Old Christian Right: The Protestant Far Right from the Great Depression to the Cold War (Philadelphia: Temple University Press, 1983).

Robin, Corey. Fear: The History of a Political Idea (New York: Oxford University Press, 2004).

Rogge. O. John. The Official German Report (New York: Thomas Yoseloff, 1961).

Ross, William G. Forging New Freedoms: Nativism, Education, and the Constitution, 1917–1927 (Lincoln: University of Nebraska Press, 1994).

Rourke, Francis E. "A Symposium: Administrative Secrecy: A Comparative Perspective," 35 Public Administration Review 1 (1975).

———. Secrecy and Publicity: Dilemmas of Democracy (Baltimore, Md.: Johns Hopkins University Press (1966).

———, ed. "Secrecy in American Bureaucracy," 72 Political Science Quarterly 540 (1957).

Rudenstein, David. The Day the Presses Stopped: A History of the Pentagon Papers Case (Berkeley: University of California Press, 1996).

Rutman, Darrett B. "The Book in Retrospect," 19 Cardozo Law Review 1283 (1998).

———. "The War Crimes and Trial of Henry Wirz," 6 Civil War History 117 (1960).

Sadat, Leila Nadya. "Extraordinary Rendition, Torture, and Other Nightmares from the War on Terror," 75 George Washington Law Review 1200 (2007).

———. "Ghost Prisoners and Black Sites: Extraordinary Rendition under International Law," 37 Case Western Reserve Journal of International Law 309 (2006).

Satterthwaite, Margaret L. "Rendered Meaningless: Extraordinary Rendition and the Rule of Law," 75 George Washington Law Review 1333 (2007).

Schoenfelt, Gabriel. "Has the 'New York Times' Violated the Espionage Act?" Commentary, March 2006, at 23–31.

Schrag, Peter. Test of Loyalty: Daniel Ellsberg and the Rituals of Secret Government (New York: Simon and Schuster, 1974).

Schrecker, Ellen W. No Ivory Tower: McCarthyism and the Universities (New York: Oxford University Press, 1986).

Schuck, Peter. Suing Government: Citizen Remedies for Official Wrongs (New Haven, Conn.: Yale University Press, 1983).

Schwartz, Bernard, ed. The Roots of the Bill of Rights (5 vols., New York: Chelsea House, 1980).

Schwarz, Frederick A. O., Jr., and Aziz Z. Huq. Unchecked and Unbalanced: Presidential Power in a Time of Terror (New York: New Press, 2007).

Scott, Winfield. Memoirs of Lieut.-General Scott, L.L.D. (Freeport, N.Y.: Books for Libraries Press, 1864).

"Separation of Powers and Executive Privilege: The Watergate Briefs," 88 Political Science Quarterly 582 (1973).

Seymour, Whitney North, Jr. "At Last, the Truth Is Out," 19 Cardozo Law Review 1359 (1998).

Shils, Edward A. The Torment of Secrecy: The Background and Consequences of American Security Policies (Chicago: Elephant Paperbacks, 1996 ed.).

Sirica, John J. To Set the Record Straight (New York: Norton, 1979).

Slaughter, Thomas P. The Whiskey Rebellion (New York: Oxford University Press, 1986).

Smith, James Morton. Freedom's Fetters: The Alien and Sedition Laws and American Civil Liberties (Ithaca, N.Y.: Cornell University Press, 1956).

Smith, J. David, and K. Ray Nelson. The Sterilization of Carrie Buck: Was She Feebleminded or Society's Pawn (Far Hills, N.J.: New Horizon Press, 1989).

Spinoza, Benedict. Theologico-Political Treatise (Mineola, N.Y.: Dover Publications, 2004).

Steele, Richard W. Free Speech in the Good War (New York: St. Martin's Press, 1999).

Steinberg, Peter I. The Great "Red Menace": United States Prosecution of American Communists, 1947–1952 (Westport, Conn.: Greenwood Press, 1984).

Stone, Geoffrey R. Perilous Times: Free Speech in Wartime (New York: W. W. Norton, 2004).

Street, Harry. "State Secrets—A Comparative Study," 14 Modern Law Review 121 (1951).

Taubeneck, T. D., and John J. Sexton. "Executive Privilege and the Court's Right to Know—Discovery against the United States in Civil Actions in Federal District Courts," 48 Georgetown Law Journal 486 (1960).

Taylor, Stuart, Jr. "The Case for a National Security Court," National Law Journal, February 24, 2007, at 15.

Tell, Larry. "The Cloak-and-Dagger Court," National Law Journal, August 10, 1981, at 1.

Temple, Hollee S. "Raining on the Litigation Parade: Is It Time to Stop Litigant Abuse of the Fraud on the Court Doctrine?" 39 University of San Francisco Law Review 967 (2005).

Theoharis, Athan G., ed. A Culture of Secrecy: The Government Versus the People's Right to Know (Lawrence: University Press of Kansas, 1998).

———. Spying on Americans: Political Surveillance from Hoover to the Huston Plan (Philadelphia: Temple University Press, 1978).

The Tower Commission Report (New York: Random House, 1987).

Truman, Harry S. Memoirs by Harry Truman (2 vols., Garden City, N.Y.: Doubleday & Co., 1956).

Turner, Serrin, and Stephen J. Schulhofer. The Secrecy Problem in Terrorism Trials (New York: Brennan Center for Justice at NYU School of Law, 2005).

Van Vleck, William C. The Administrative Control of Aliens: A Study in Administrative Law and Procedure (New York: Commonwealth Fund, 1932).

Vladeck, Stephen I. "Emergency Power and the Militia Acts," 114 Yale Law Journal 149 (2004).

Vose, Clement E. Constitutional Change (Lexington, Mass.: Lexington Books, 1972).

Wahlke, John C., ed. Loyalty in a Democratic State (Boston: D. C. Heath and Co., 1952).

Wallace, Max. The American Axis: Henry Ford, Charles Lindbergh, and the Rise of the Third Reich (New York: St. Martin's Griffin, 2003).

Ward, Townsend. "The Insurrection of the Year 1794, in the Western Counties of Pennsylvania," 6 Pennsylvania Historical Society Memoirs 119 (1858).

Warren, John H. III. "Administrative Law—Judicial Review, State Secrets, and the Freedom of Information Act," 23 South Carolina Law Review 332 (1971).

Weaver, William G., and Robert M. Pallitto. "'Extraordinary Rendition' and Presidential Fiat," 36 Presidential Studies Quarterly 102 (2006).

————. "State Secrets and Executive Power," 120 Political Science Quarterly 85 (2005).

Weber, Max. Economy and Society: An Outline of Interpretive Sociology, edited by Guenther Roth and Claus Wittich (New York: Bedminster Press, 1968).

Welch, William J. "Evidence; Privilege against Revealing State Secrets," 10 Oklahoma Law Review 336 (1957).

Wetlaufer, Gerald. "Justifying Secrecy: An Objection to the General Deliberative Privilege," 65 Indiana Law Journal 845 (1990).

Wharton, Francis. State Trials of the United States during the Administrations of Washington and Adams (Philadelphia: Carey and Hart, 1849).

Wheaton, Major Kelly D. "Spycraft and Government Contracts: A Defense of *Totten* v. *United States*," Army Lawyer, August 1997, at 9–17.

White, Stephen D. Sir Edward Coke and "The Grievances of the Commonwealth," 1621–1628 (Chapel Hill, N.C.: University of North Carolina Press, 1979).

Wigmore, John Henry. Evidence in Trials at Common Law (10 vols., Boston: Little, Brown, 1940).

Wilmhurst, W. L. The Meaning of Masonry (New York: Gramercy Books, 1980).

Winthrop, William. Military Law and Precedents (Washington, D.C.: Government Printing Office, 2d ed. 1920).

Wise, David. The Politics of Lying: Government Deception, Secrecy, and Power (New York: Random House, 1973).

Witcover, Jules. Sabotage at Black Tom: Imperial Germany's Secret War in America, 1914–1917 (Chapel Hill, N.C.: Algonquin Books, 1989).

Wittke, Carl. German-Americans and the World War (Columbus: Ohio State Archaeological and Historical Society, 1936).

Wohlstetter, Roberta. Pearl Harbor: Warning and Decision (Stanford, Calif.: Stanford University Press, 1962).

Wolfram, Harold W. "John Lilburne: Democracy's Pillar of Fire," 3 Syracuse Law Review 213 (1952).

Wolkinson, Herman. "Demands of Congressional Committees for Executive Papers," 10 Federal Bar Journal 103, 223, 319 (1949).

Work, Clemens P. Darkest before Dawn: Sedition and Free Speech in the American West (Albuquerque: University of New Mexico Press, 2006 ed).

Wright, Benjamin Fletcher, ed. The Federalist (Cambridge, Mass.: Harvard University Press, 1961).

Wright, Charles Alan, and Kenneth W. Graham, Jr. Federal Practice and Procedure, vols. 26 and 27 (St. Paul: West Publishing Co., 1992).

Yoo, John. War by Other Means; An Insider's Account of the War on Terror (New York: Atlantic Monthly Press, 2006).

————. The Powers of War and Peace: The Constitution and Foreign Affairs after 9/11 (Chicago: University of Chicago Press, 2005).

————. "Transferring Terrorists," 79 Notre Dame Law Review 1183 (2004).

Zagel, James. "The State Secrets Privilege," 50 Minnesota Law Review 875 (1966).

Zedalis, Rex J. "Resurrection of Reynolds: 1974 Amendment to National Defense and Foreign Policy Exemption," 4 Pepperdine Law Review 81 (1976).

Index of Cases

Index of Subjects